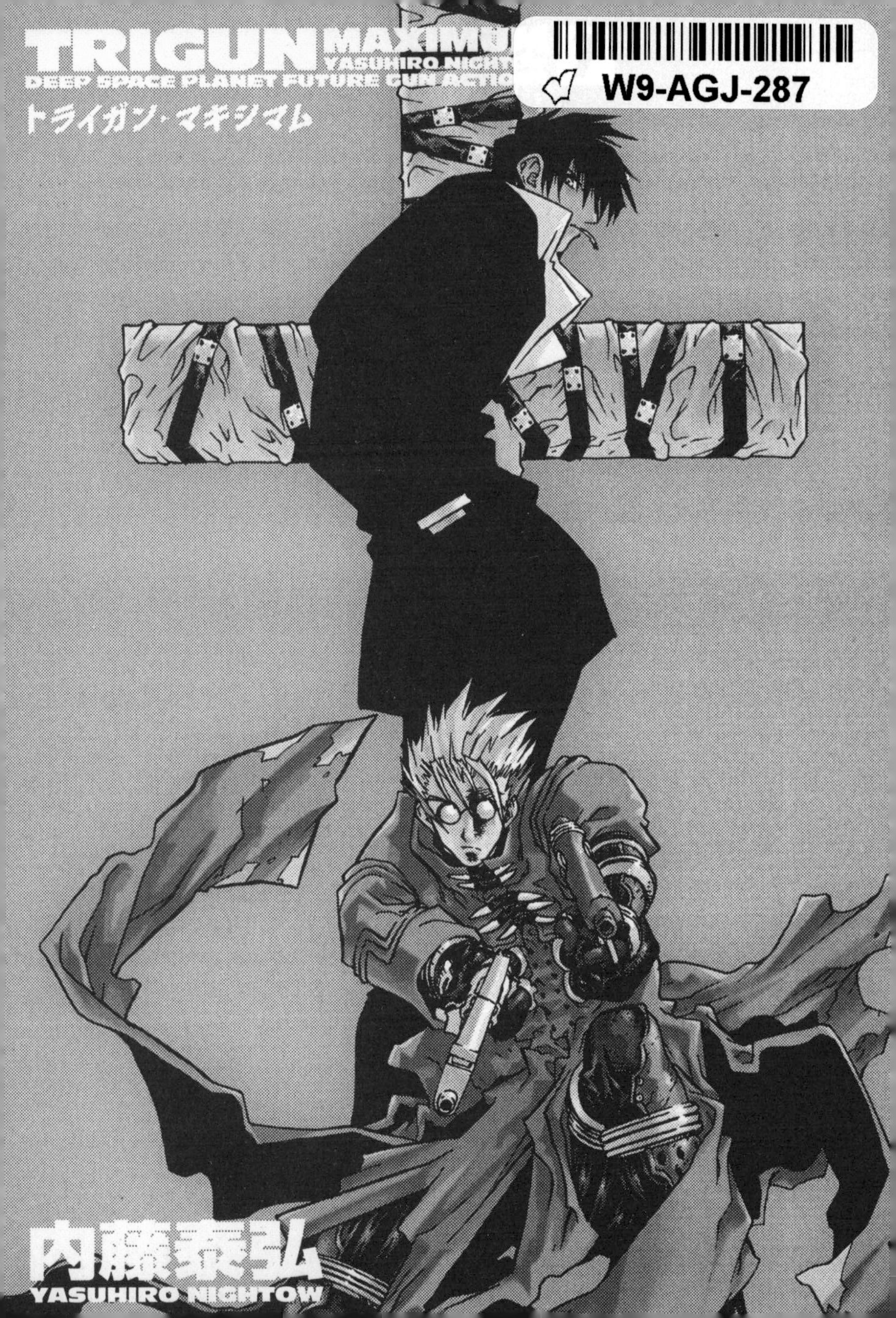
TRIGUN MAXIMU
YASUHIRO NIGHT
DEEP SPACE PLANET FUTURE GUN ACTIO
トライガン・マキシマム
内藤泰弘
YASUHIRO NIGHTOW

TRIGUN MAXIMUM
YASUHIRO NIGHTOW
DEEP SPACE PLANET FUTURE GUN ACTION!!
CONTENTS

TRIGUN MAXIMUM 7
HAPPY DAYS.

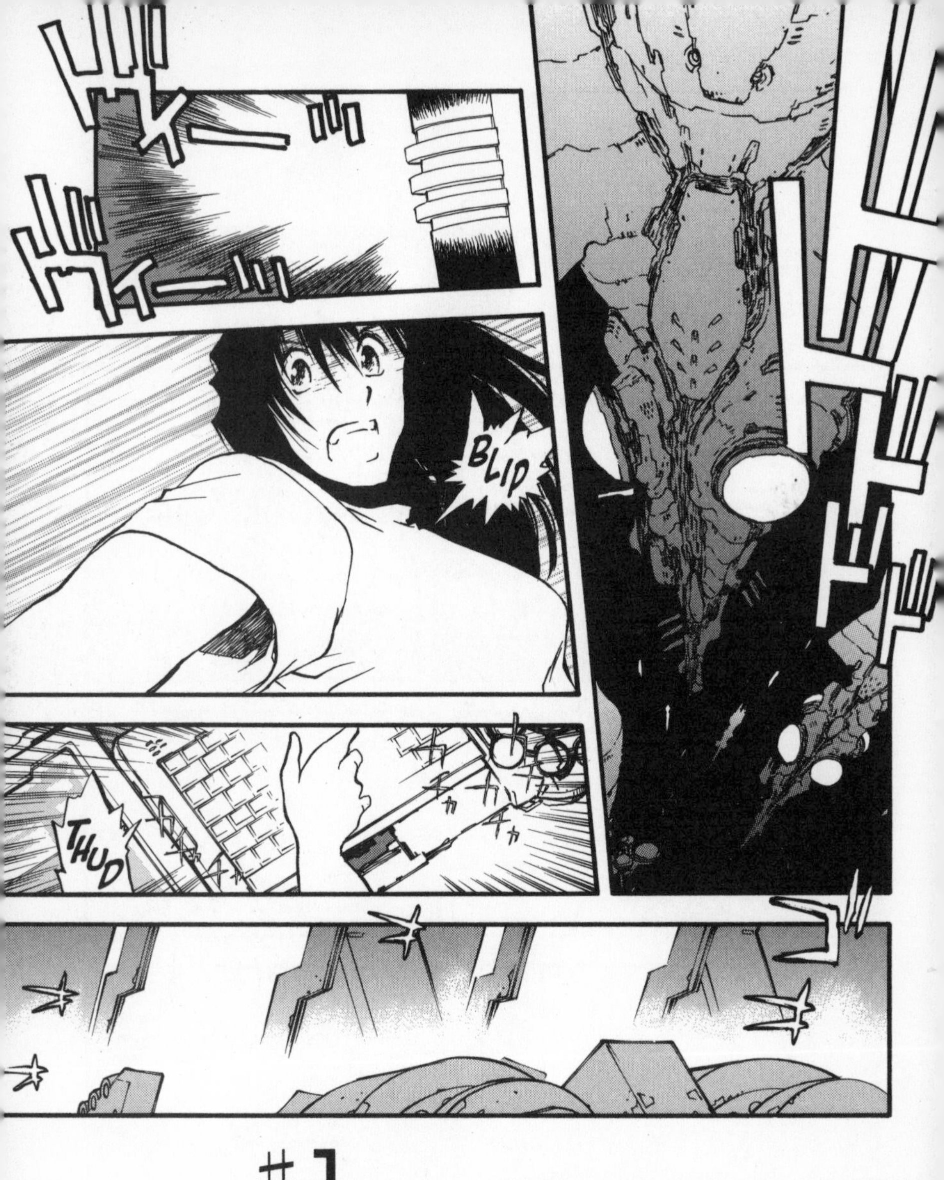
BLIP
THUD

#1. happy days.

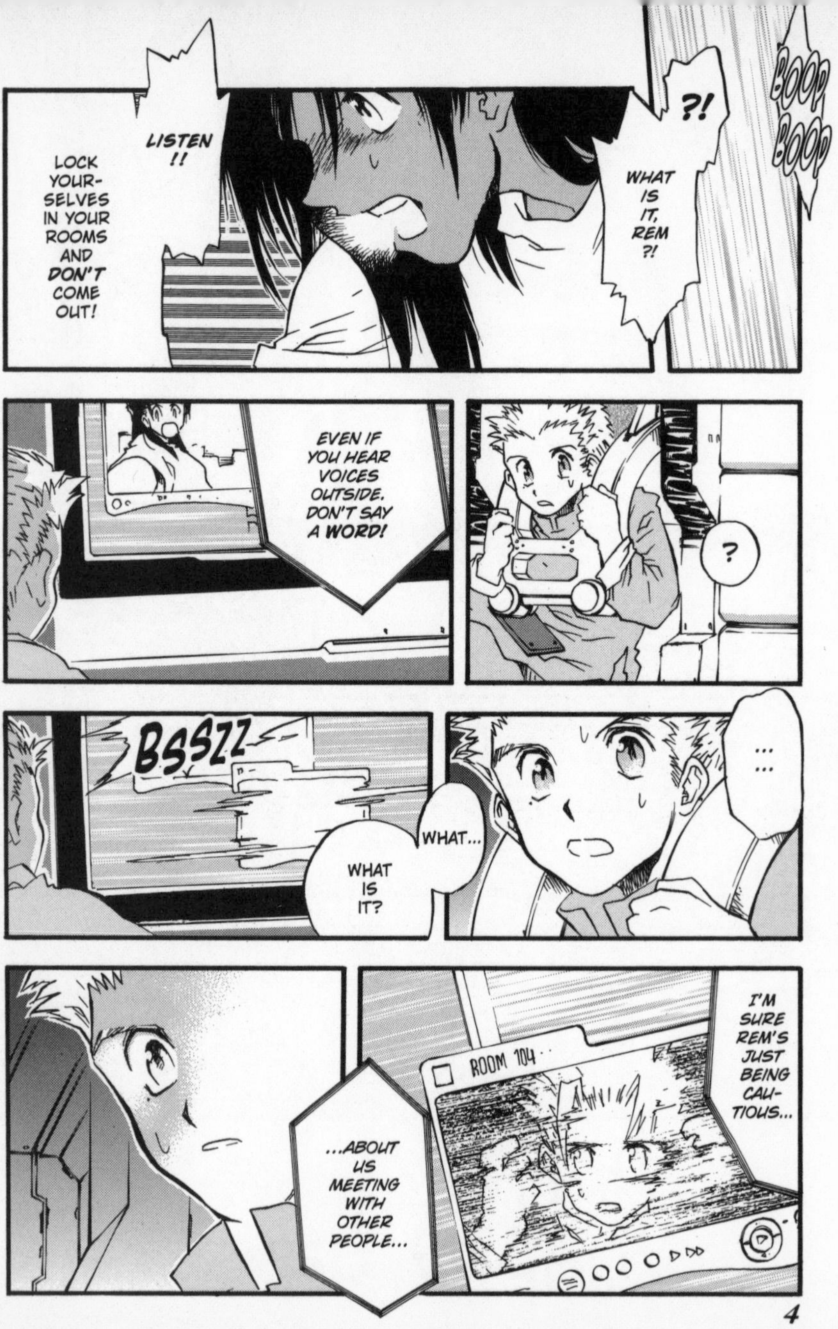
BOOP BOOP
?!
WHAT IS IT, REM ?!
LISTEN !!
LOCK YOUR-SELVES IN YOUR ROOMS AND DON'T COME OUT!
?
EVEN IF YOU HEAR VOICES OUTSIDE. DON'T SAY A WORD!
……
WHAT...
WHAT IS IT?
BSSZZ
I'M SURE REM'S JUST BEING CAU-TIOUS...
...ABOUT US MEETING WITH OTHER PEOPLE...
ROOM 104

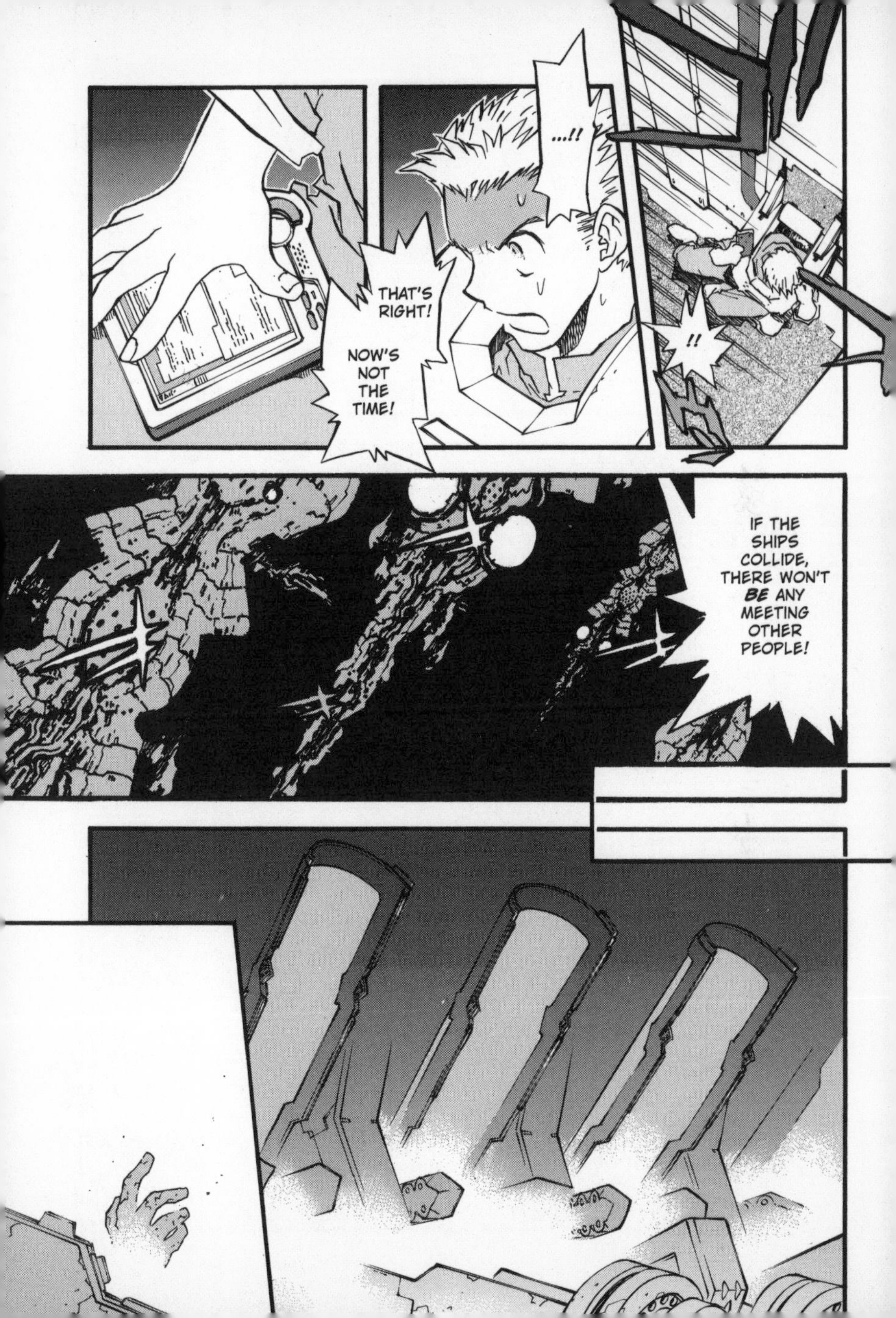
!!
...!!
THAT'S RIGHT!
NOW'S NOT THE TIME!
IF THE SHIPS COLLIDE, THERE WON'T *BE* ANY MEETING OTHER PEOPLE!

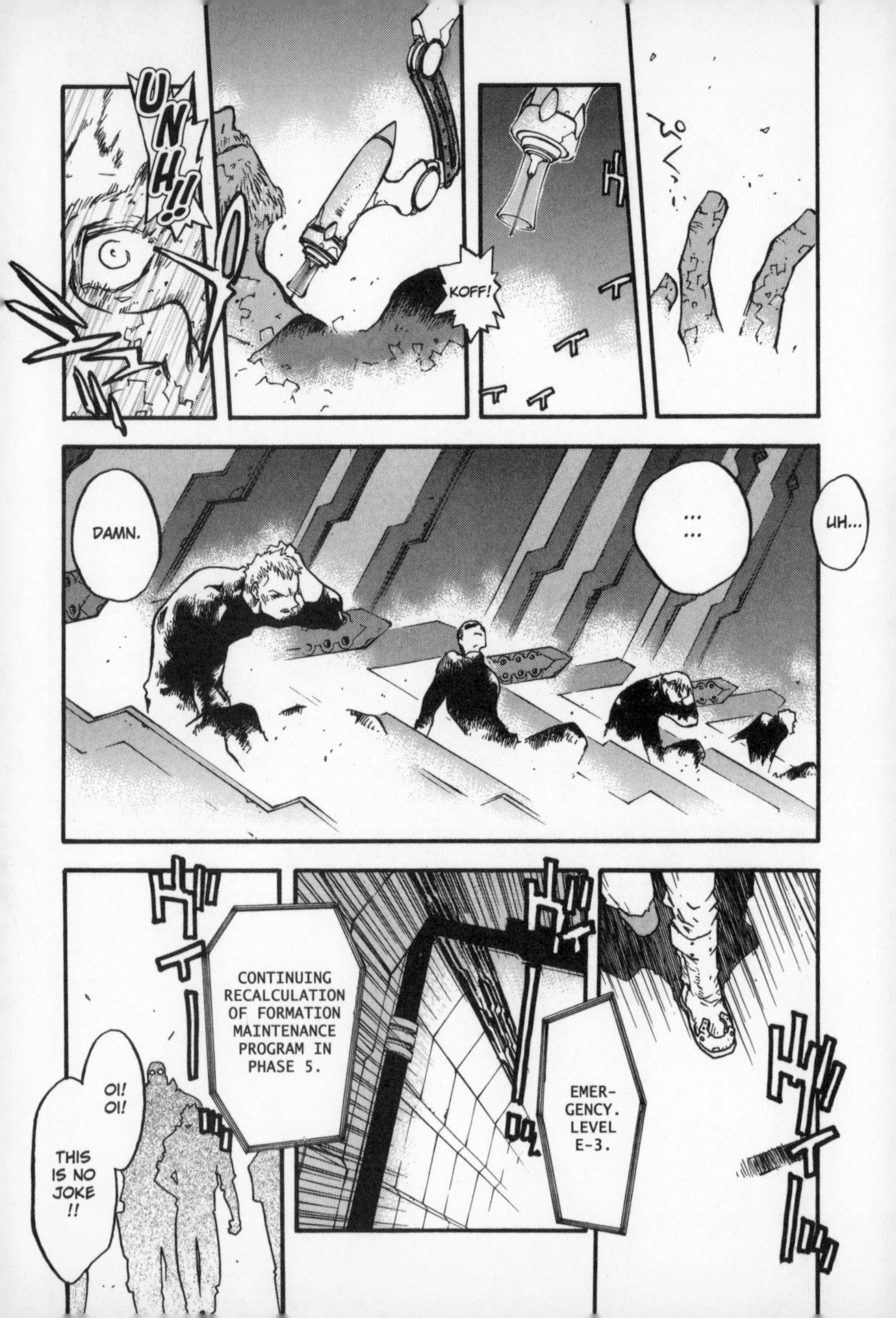
KOFF!
UNH!!
UH...
...
...
DAMN.
EMER-
GENCY.
LEVEL
E-3.
CONTINUING
RECALCULATION
OF FORMATION
MAINTENANCE
PROGRAM IN
PHASE 5.
OI!
OI!
THIS
IS NO
JOKE
!!

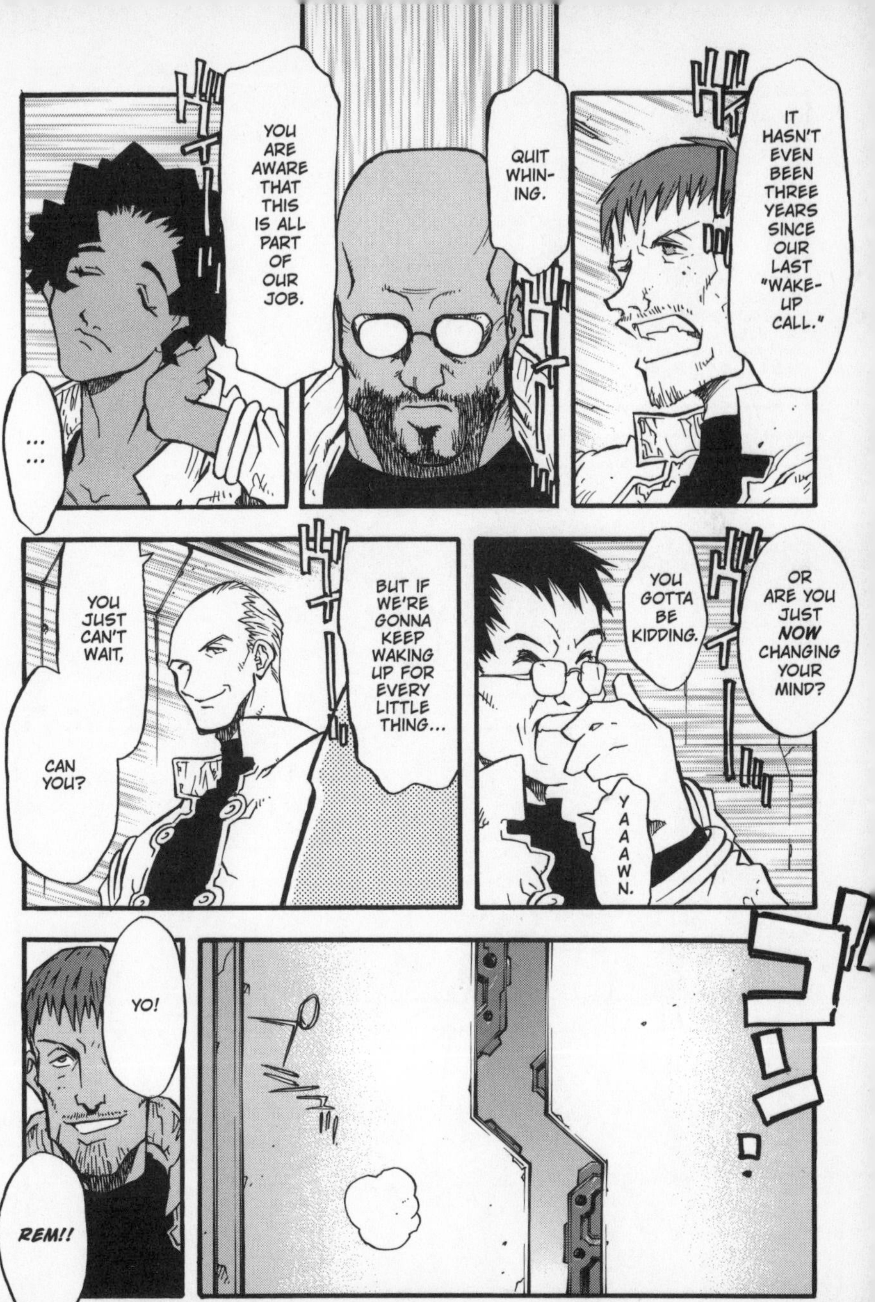
IT HASN'T EVEN BEEN THREE YEARS SINCE OUR LAST "WAKE-UP CALL."
QUIT WHINING.
YOU ARE AWARE THAT THIS IS ALL PART OF OUR JOB.
......
OR ARE YOU JUST **NOW** CHANGING YOUR MIND?
YOU GOTTA BE KIDDING.
YAAAAWN.
BUT IF WE'RE GONNA KEEP WAKING UP FOR EVERY LITTLE THING...
YOU JUST CAN'T WAIT,
CAN YOU?
YO!
REM!!

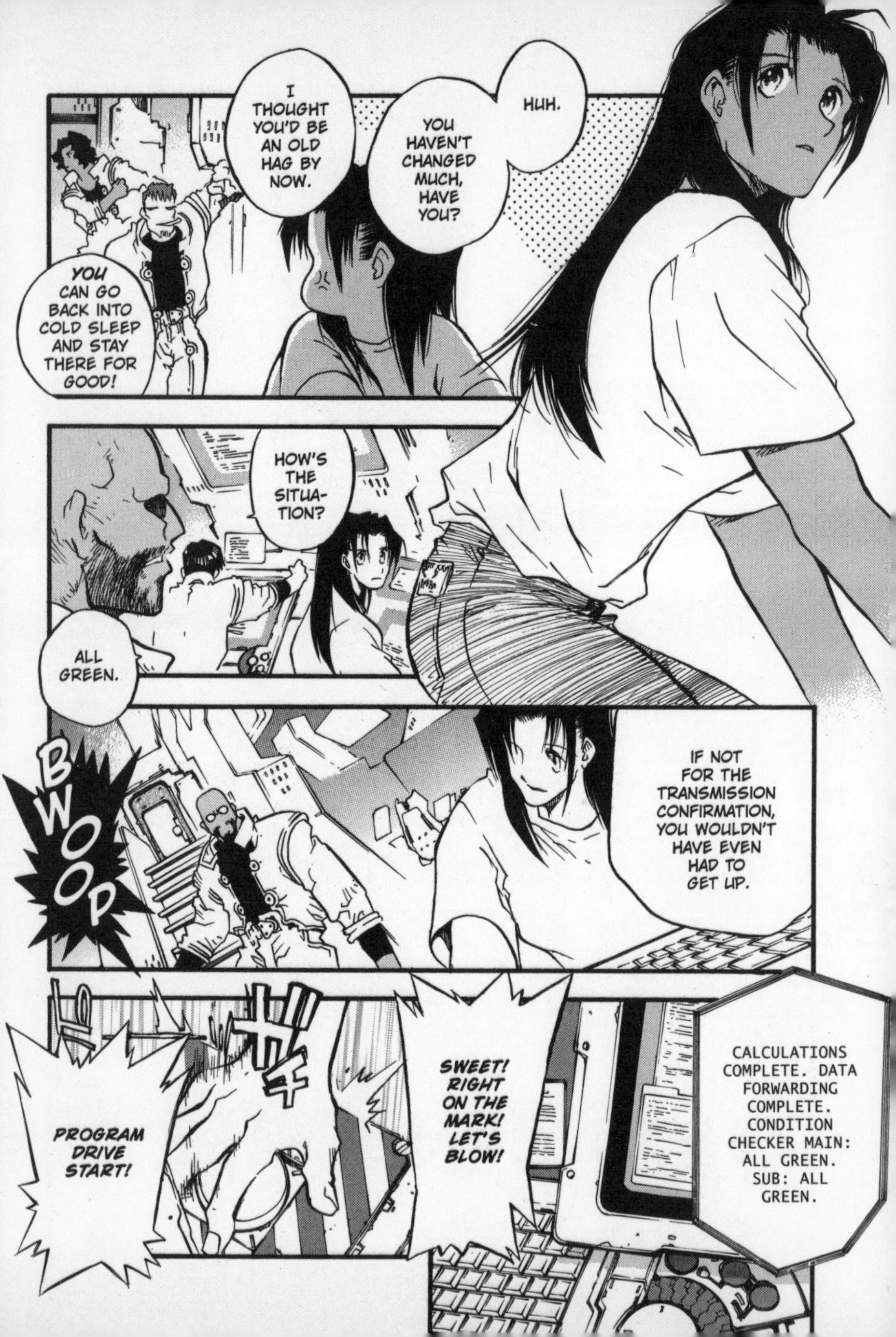
HUH.
YOU HAVEN'T CHANGED MUCH, HAVE YOU?
I THOUGHT YOU'D BE AN OLD HAG BY NOW.
YOU CAN GO BACK INTO COLD SLEEP AND STAY THERE FOR GOOD!
HOW'S THE SITUATION?
ALL GREEN.
IF NOT FOR THE TRANSMISSION CONFIRMATION, YOU WOULDN'T HAVE EVEN HAD TO GET UP.
BWOOP
CALCULATIONS COMPLETE. DATA FORWARDING COMPLETE. CONDITION CHECKER MAIN: ALL GREEN. SUB: ALL GREEN.
SWEET! RIGHT ON THE MARK! LET'S BLOW!
PROGRAM DRIVE START!

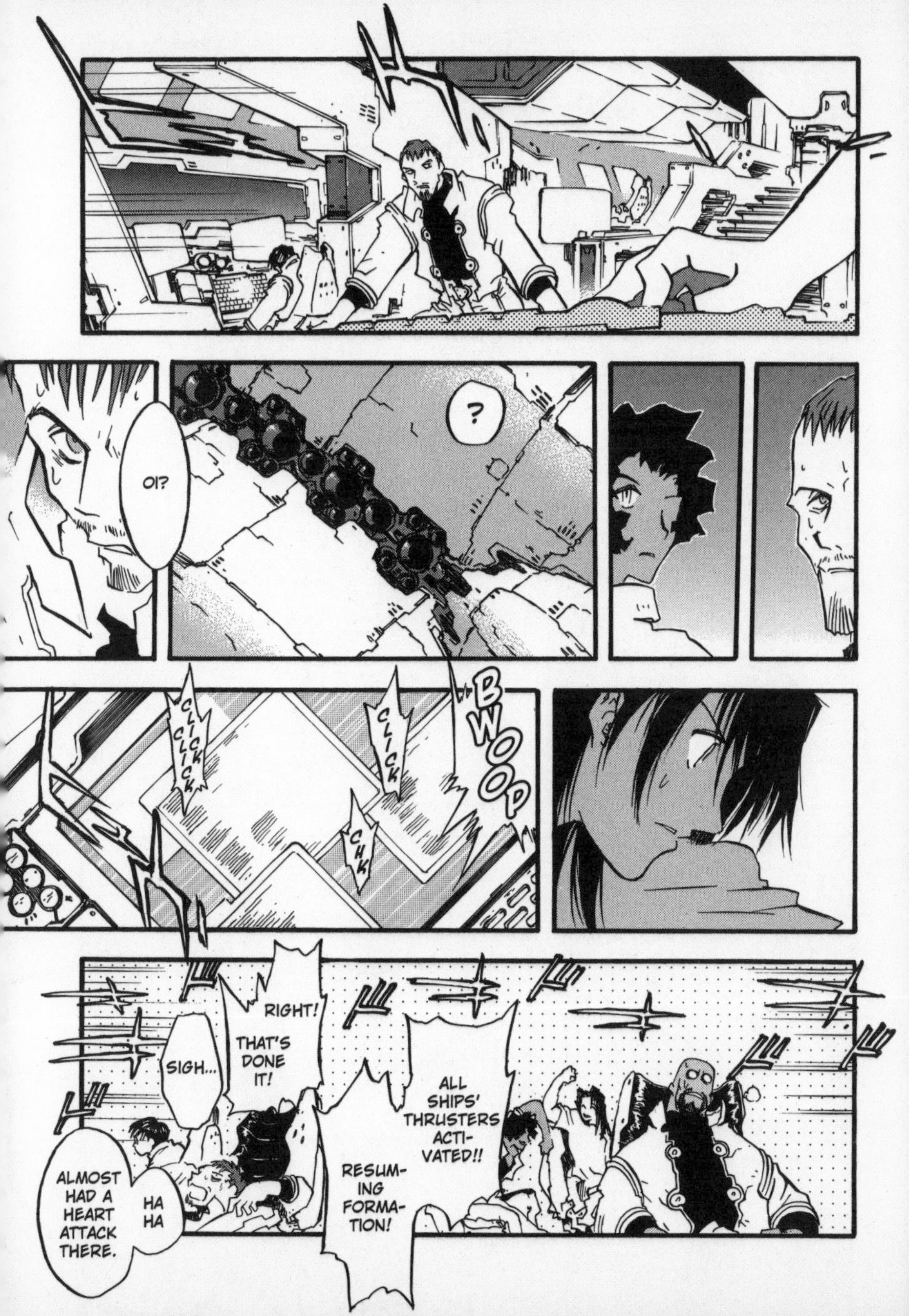
?
OI?
BWOOP
CLICK
CHK
CLICK CLICK
ALL SHIPS' THRUSTERS ACTI-VATED!!
RIGHT! THAT'S DONE IT!
SIGH...
RESUM-ING FORMA-TION!
HA HA
ALMOST HAD A HEART ATTACK THERE.

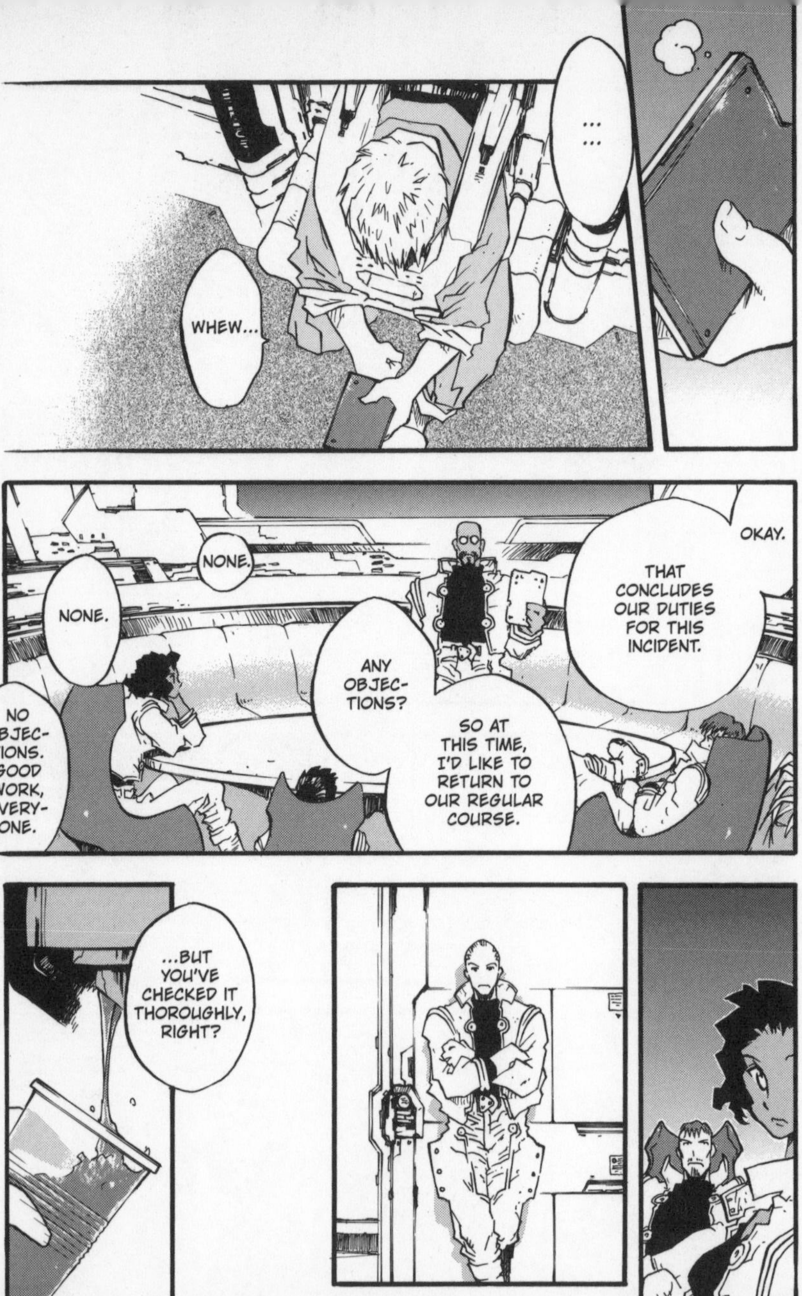
...
...
WHEW...
OKAY.
THAT CONCLUDES OUR DUTIES FOR THIS INCIDENT.
SO AT THIS TIME, I'D LIKE TO RETURN TO OUR REGULAR COURSE.
ANY OBJECTIONS?
NONE.
NONE.
NO OBJECTIONS. GOOD WORK, EVERYONE.
...BUT YOU'VE CHECKED IT THOROUGHLY, RIGHT?

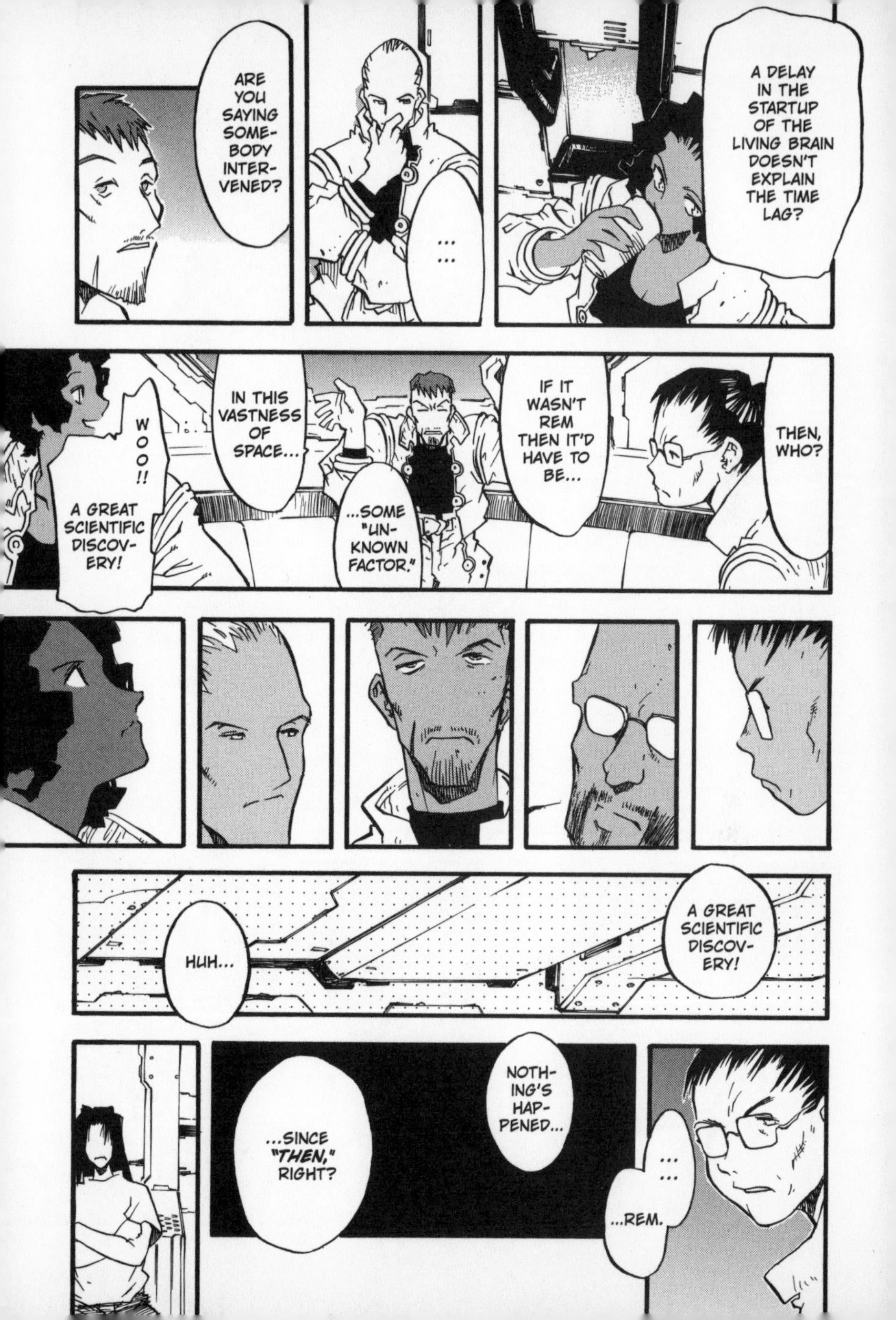
A DELAY IN THE STARTUP OF THE LIVING BRAIN DOESN'T EXPLAIN THE TIME LAG?
ARE YOU SAYING SOMEBODY INTERVENED?
... ...
THEN, WHO?
IF IT WASN'T REM THEN IT'D HAVE TO BE...
IN THIS VASTNESS OF SPACE...
...SOME "UNKNOWN FACTOR."
WOOO!!
A GREAT SCIENTIFIC DISCOVERY!
A GREAT SCIENTIFIC DISCOVERY!
HUH...
... ...
...REM.
NOTHING'S HAPPENED...
...SINCE ***"THEN,"*** RIGHT?

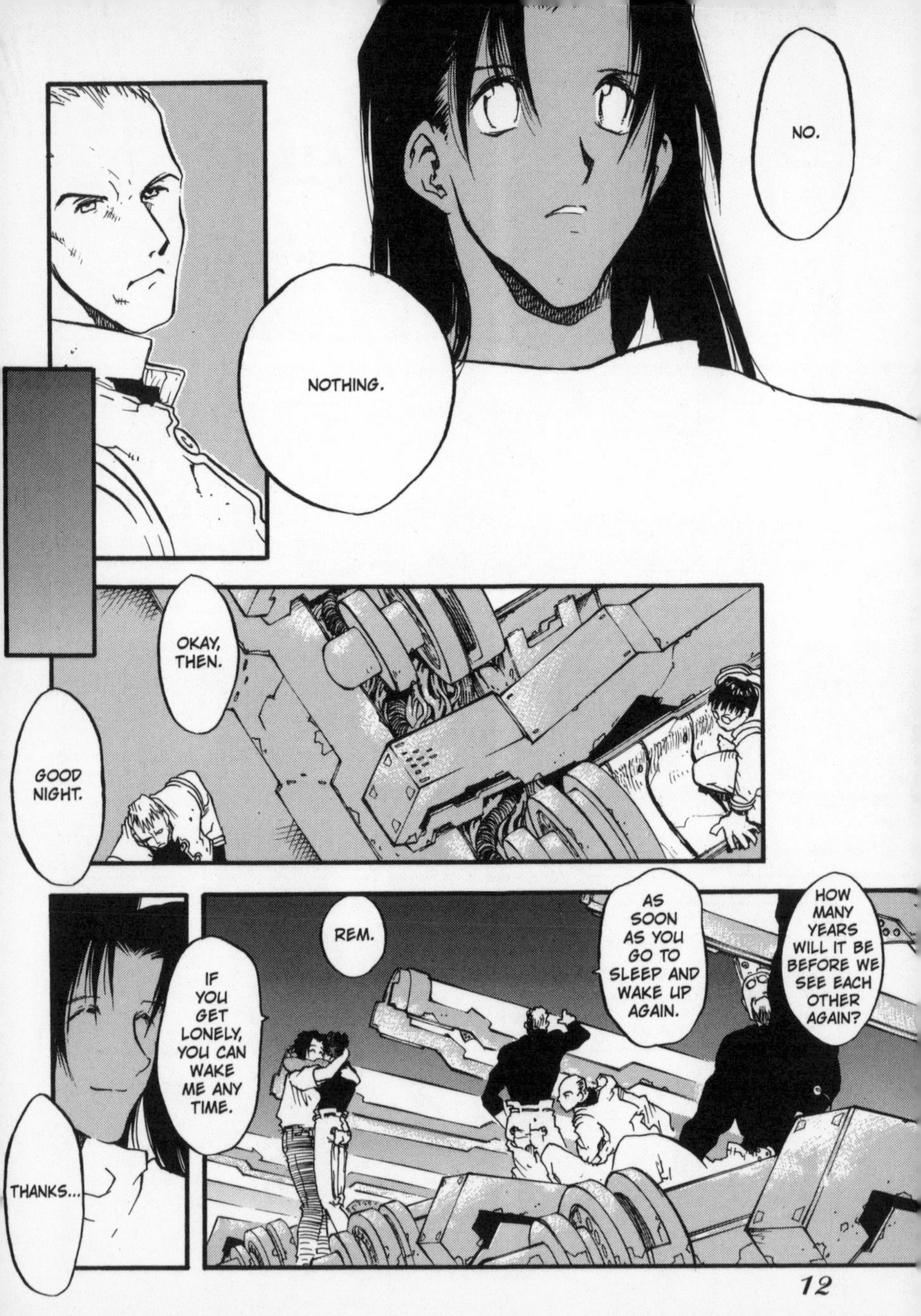
NO.
NOTHING.
OKAY, THEN.
GOOD NIGHT.
HOW MANY YEARS WILL IT BE BEFORE WE SEE EACH OTHER AGAIN?
AS SOON AS YOU GO TO SLEEP AND WAKE UP AGAIN.
REM.
IF YOU GET LONELY, YOU CAN WAKE ME ANY TIME.
THANKS...

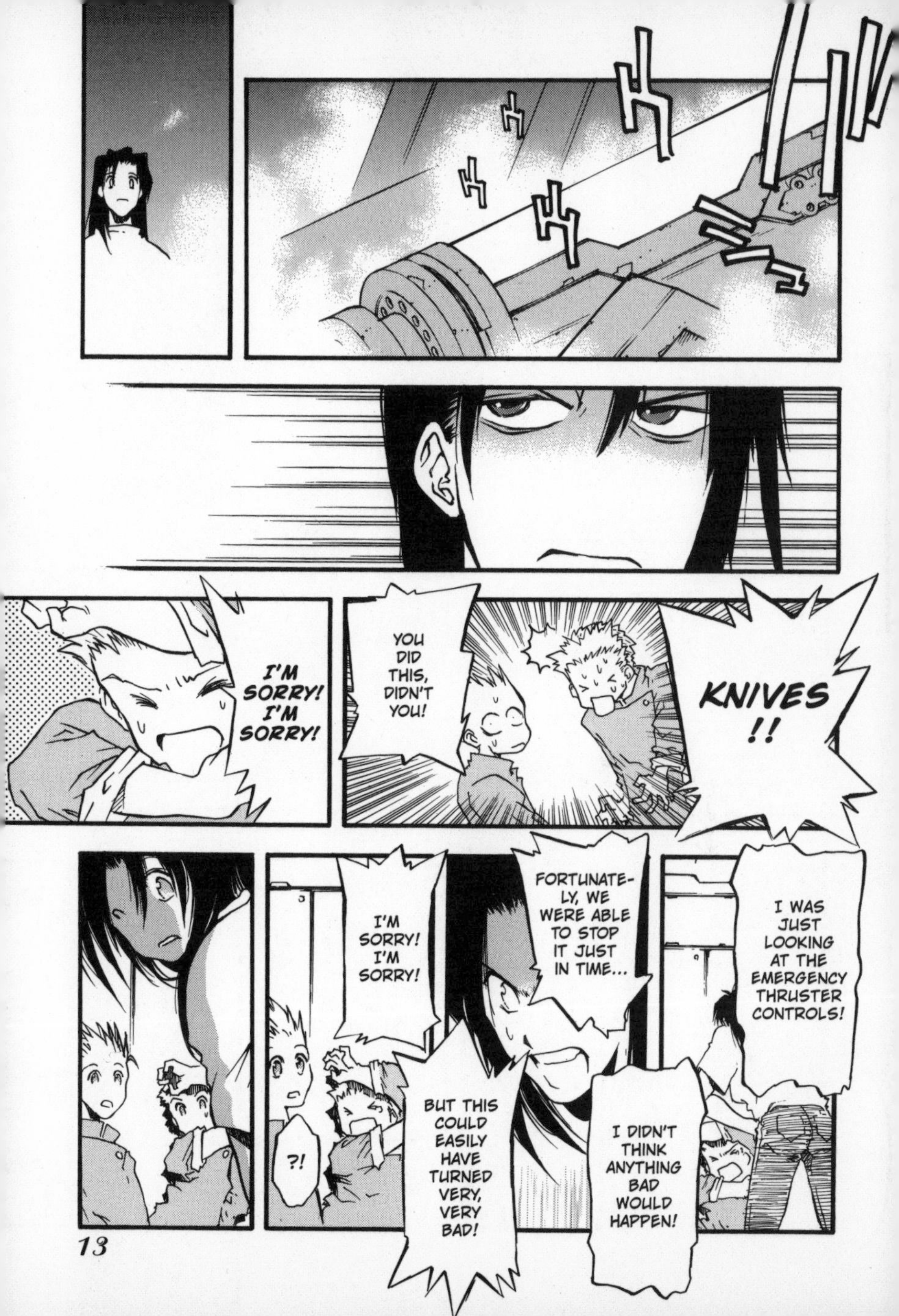
KNIVES !!
YOU DID THIS, DIDN'T YOU!
I'M SORRY! I'M SORRY!
I WAS JUST LOOKING AT THE EMERGENCY THRUSTER CONTROLS!
I DIDN'T THINK ANYTHING BAD WOULD HAPPEN!
FORTUNATE-LY, WE WERE ABLE TO STOP IT JUST IN TIME...
I'M SORRY! I'M SORRY!
BUT THIS COULD EASILY HAVE TURNED VERY, VERY BAD!
?!

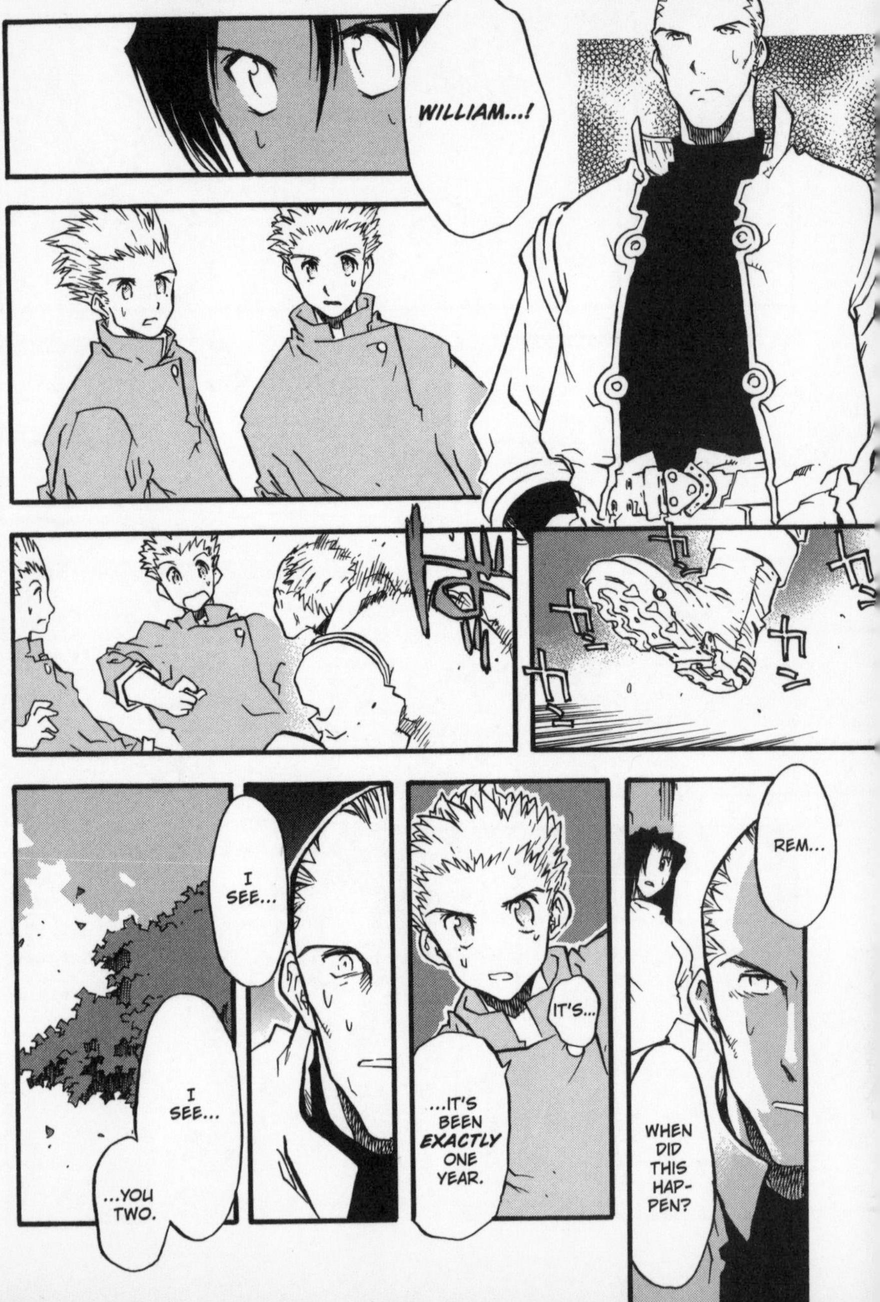
WILLIAM...!
REM...
WHEN DID THIS HAPPEN?
IT'S...
...IT'S BEEN *EXACTLY* ONE YEAR.
I SEE...
I SEE...
...YOU TWO.

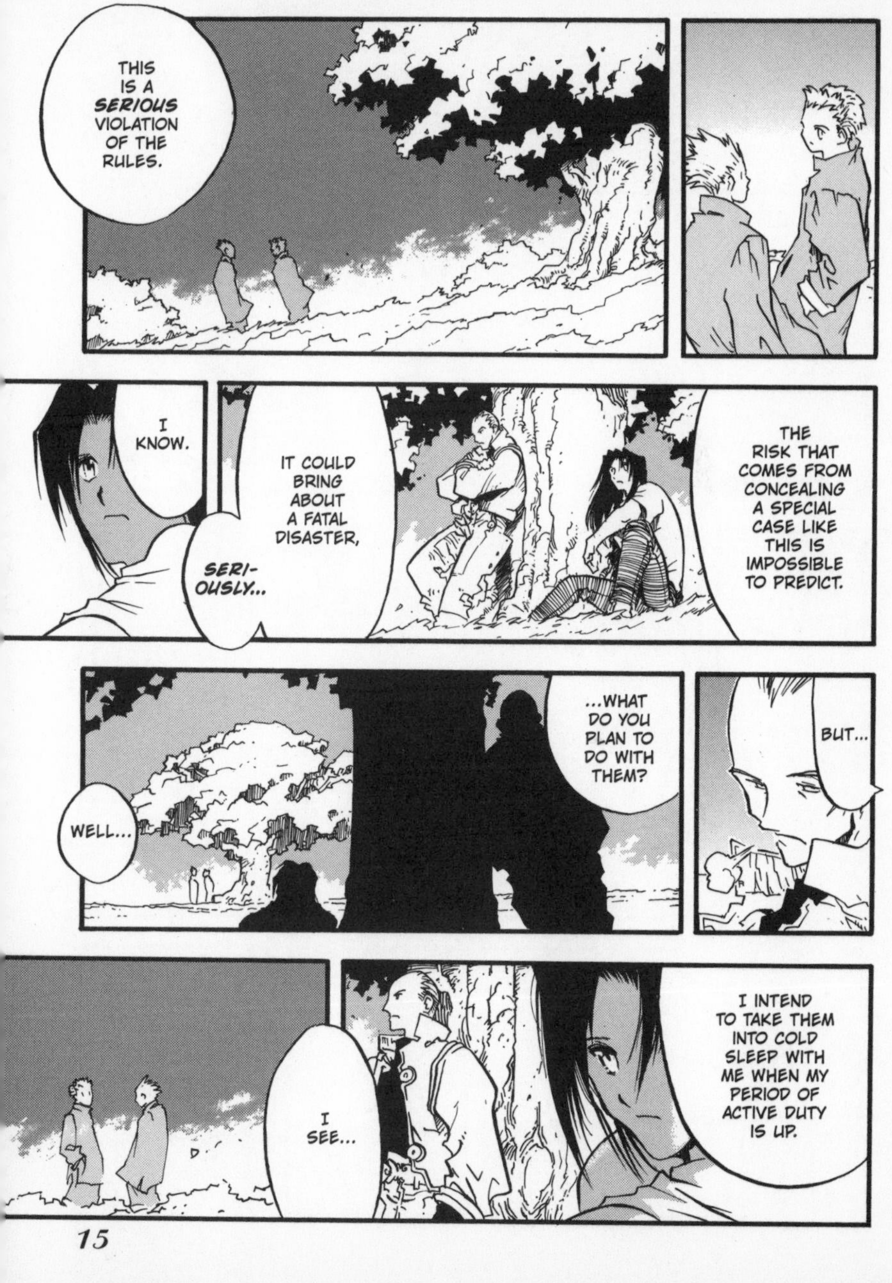
THIS IS A *SERIOUS* VIOLATION OF THE RULES.
THE RISK THAT COMES FROM CONCEALING A SPECIAL CASE LIKE THIS IS IMPOSSIBLE TO PREDICT.
IT COULD BRING ABOUT A FATAL DISASTER,
SERIOUSLY...
I KNOW.
BUT...
...WHAT DO YOU PLAN TO DO WITH THEM?
WELL...
I INTEND TO TAKE THEM INTO COLD SLEEP WITH ME WHEN MY PERIOD OF ACTIVE DUTY IS UP.
I SEE...

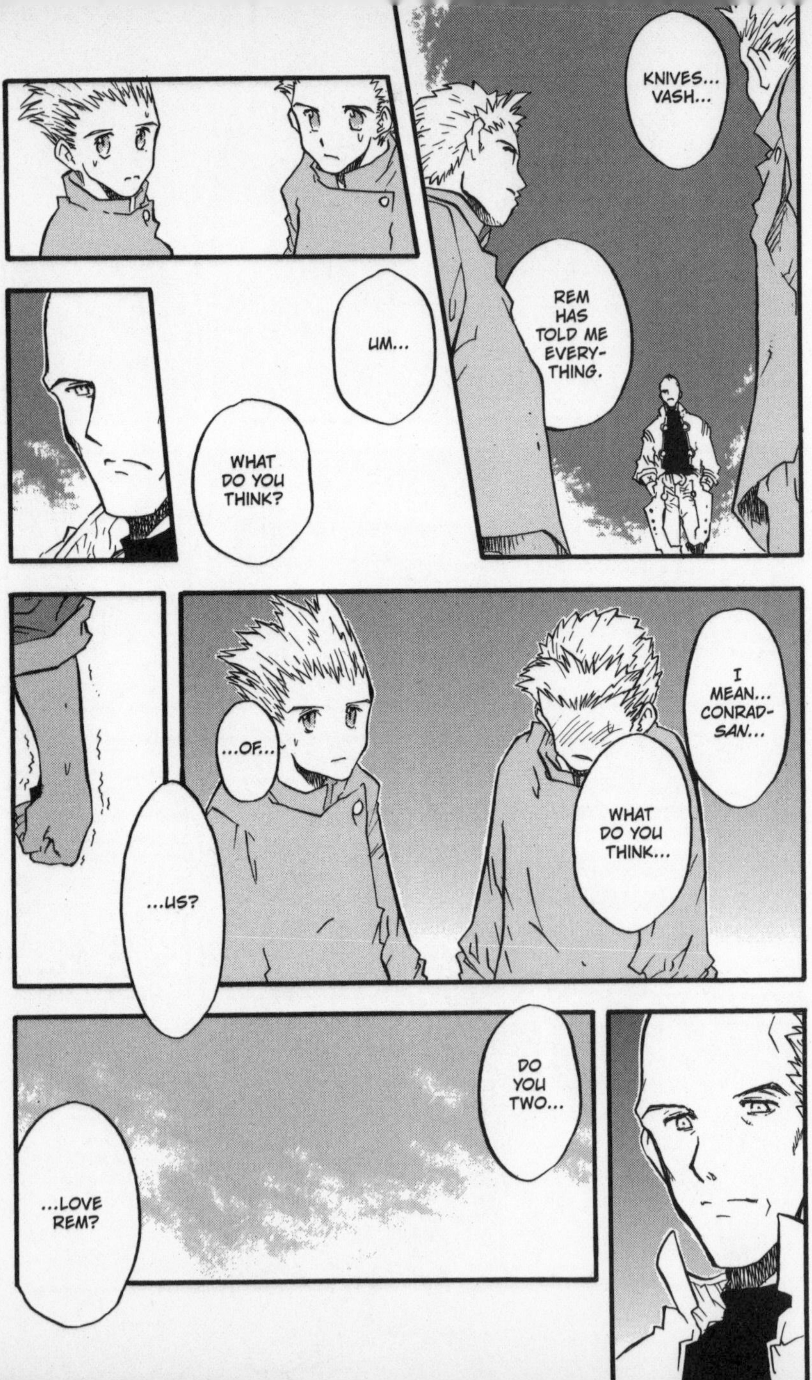
KNIVES... VASH...
REM HAS TOLD ME EVERY-THING.
UM...
WHAT DO YOU THINK?
I MEAN... CONRAD-SAN...
WHAT DO YOU THINK...
...OF...
...US?
DO YOU TWO...
...LOVE REM?

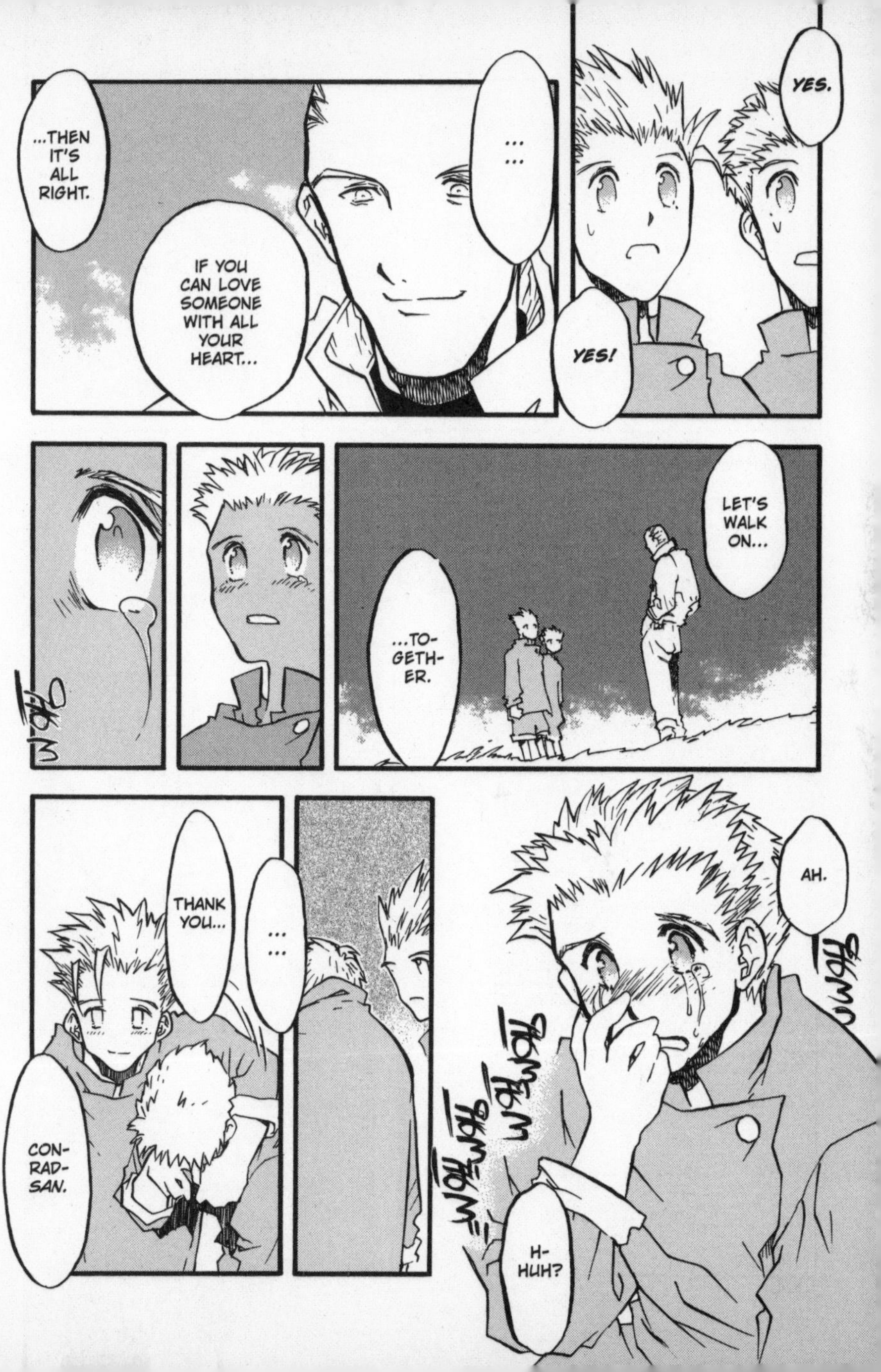
YES.
YES!
...
...
...THEN IT'S ALL RIGHT.
IF YOU CAN LOVE SOMEONE WITH ALL YOUR HEART...
LET'S WALK ON...
...TO-GETH-ER.
AH.
H-HUH?
...
...
THANK YOU...
CON-RAD-SAN.

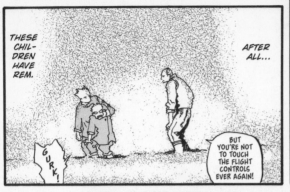

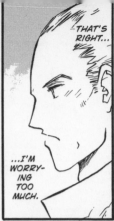

THAT'S RIGHT...
...I'M WORRYING TOO MUCH.
AFTER ALL...
THESE CHILDREN HAVE REM.
BUT YOU'RE NOT TO TOUCH THE FLIGHT CONTROLS EVER AGAIN!
GURK!
GIVEN THE CIRCUMSTANCES, I PROBABLY WOULD HAVE DONE THE SAME THING.
LET ME SEE THEM AGAIN WHEN WE REACH THE NEW WORLD.
......
THANK YOU...
WE'VE ONLY...
...JUST BEGUN.

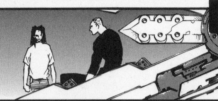

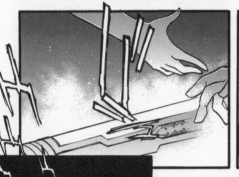

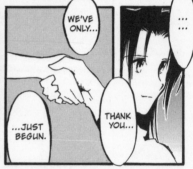

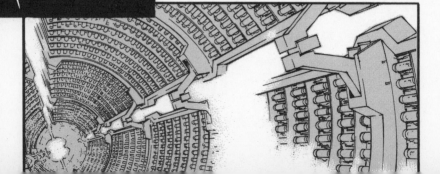

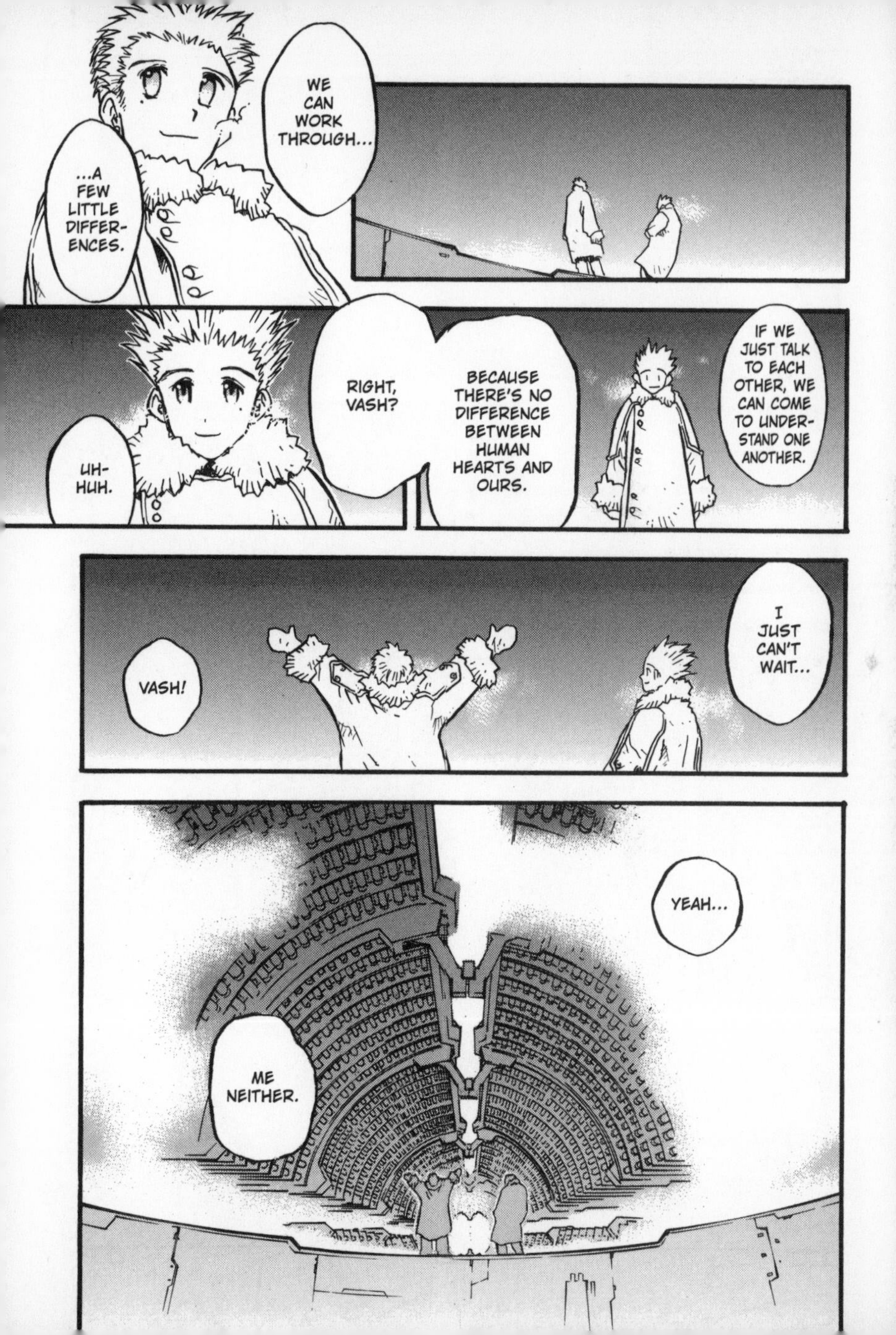
WE CAN WORK THROUGH...
...A FEW LITTLE DIFFER-ENCES.
IF WE JUST TALK TO EACH OTHER, WE CAN COME TO UNDER-STAND ONE ANOTHER.
BECAUSE THERE'S NO DIFFERENCE BETWEEN HUMAN HEARTS AND OURS.
RIGHT, VASH?
UH-HUH.
I JUST CAN'T WAIT...
VASH!
YEAH...
ME NEITHER.

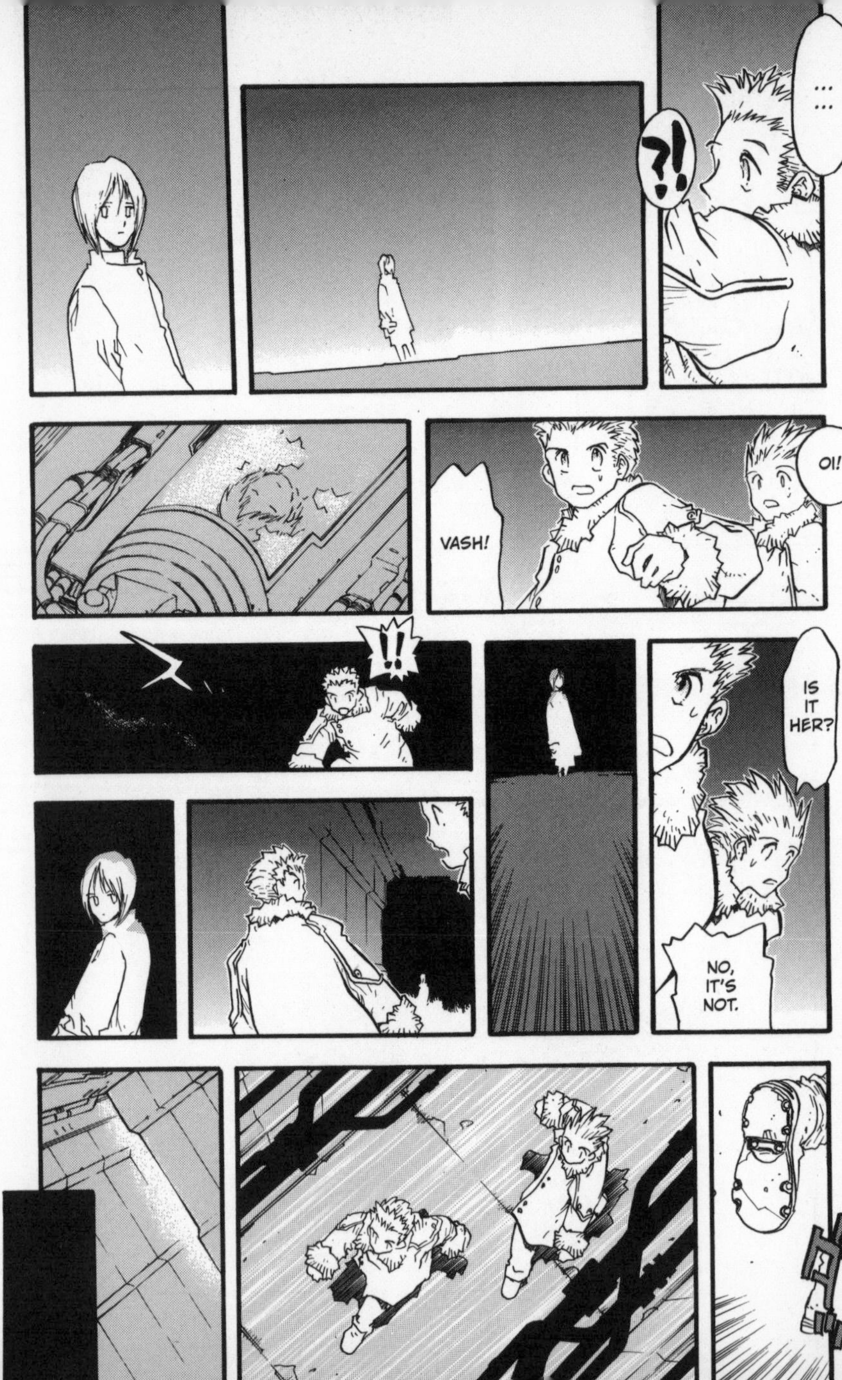
……
?!
OI!
VASH!
IS IT HER?
NO, IT'S NOT.
!!

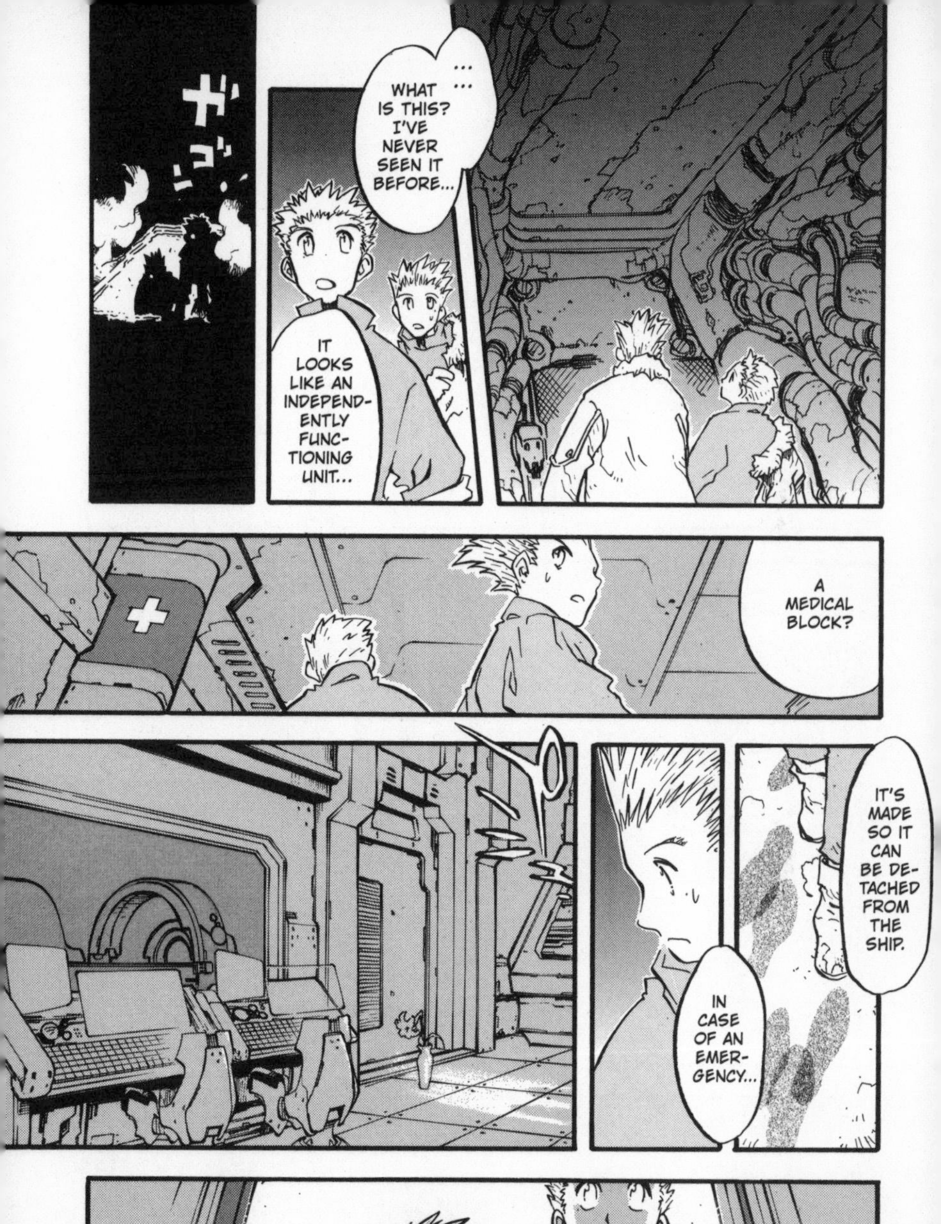
... ...
WHAT IS THIS? I'VE NEVER SEEN IT BEFORE...
IT LOOKS LIKE AN INDEPENDENTLY FUNCTIONING UNIT...
A MEDICAL BLOCK?
IT'S MADE SO IT CAN BE DETACHED FROM THE SHIP.
IN CASE OF AN EMERGENCY...

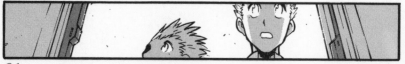

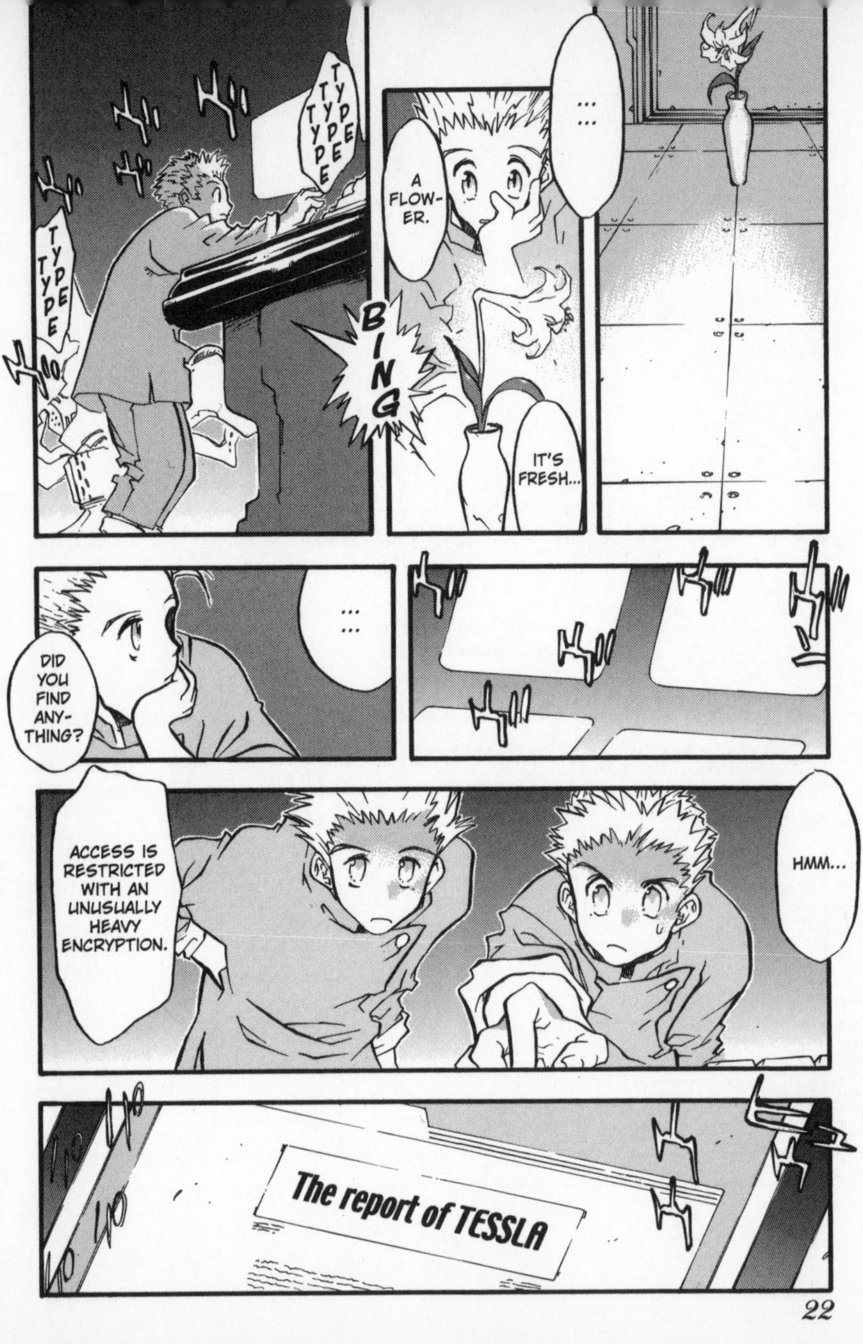
……
A FLOWER.
BING
IT'S FRESH…
TYPE TYPE TYPE
TYPE TYPE TYPE
……
DID YOU FIND ANYTHING?
HMM…
ACCESS IS RESTRICTED WITH AN UNUSUALLY HEAVY ENCRYPTION.
The report of TESSLA

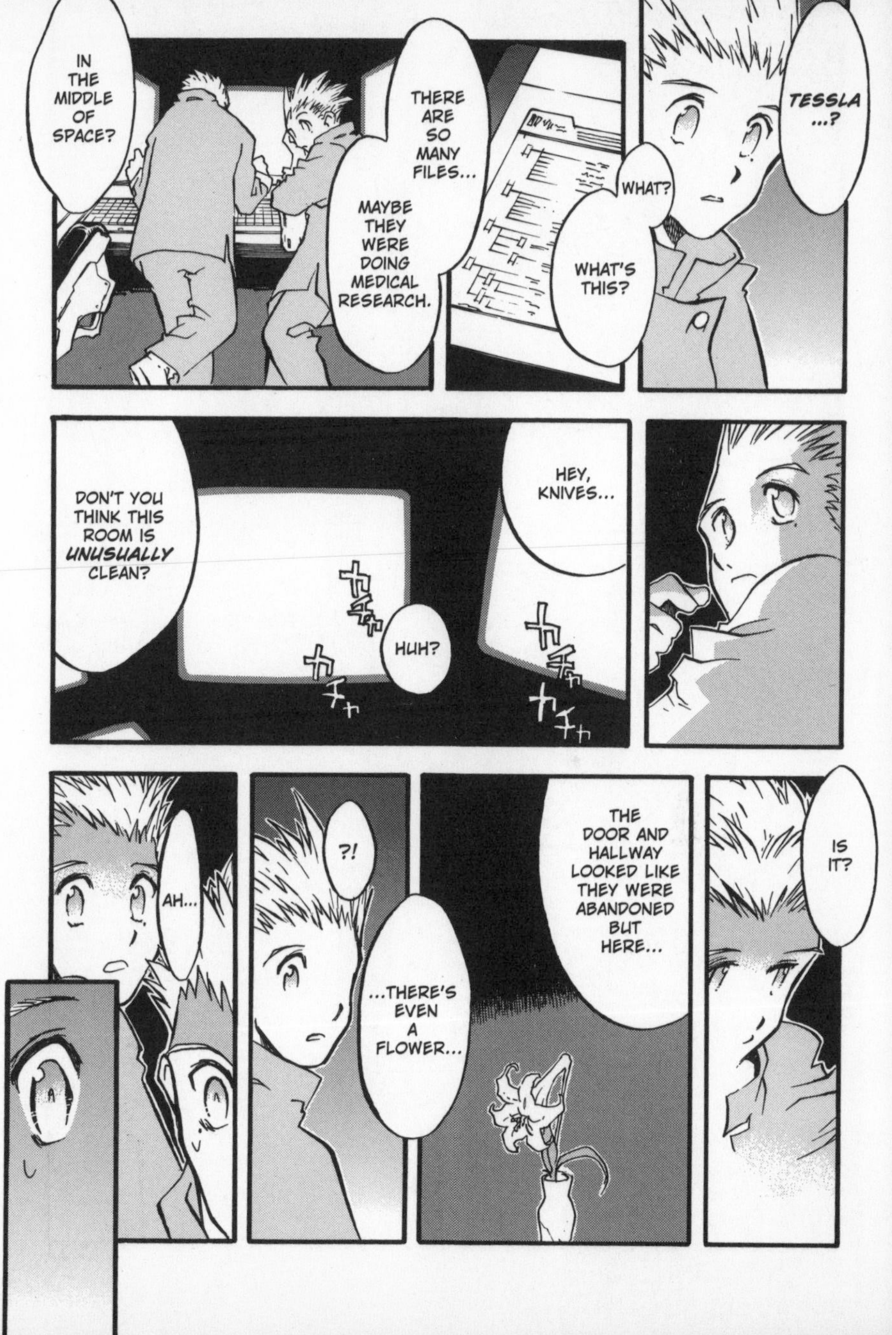
TESSLA ...?
WHAT?
WHAT'S THIS?
THERE ARE SO MANY FILES...
MAYBE THEY WERE DOING MEDICAL RESEARCH.
IN THE MIDDLE OF SPACE?
HEY, KNIVES...
カチャ
カチャ
HUH?
カチャ
カチャ
DON'T YOU THINK THIS ROOM IS *UNUSUALLY* CLEAN?
IS IT?
THE DOOR AND HALLWAY LOOKED LIKE THEY WERE ABANDONED BUT HERE...
?!
...THERE'S EVEN A FLOWER...
AH...

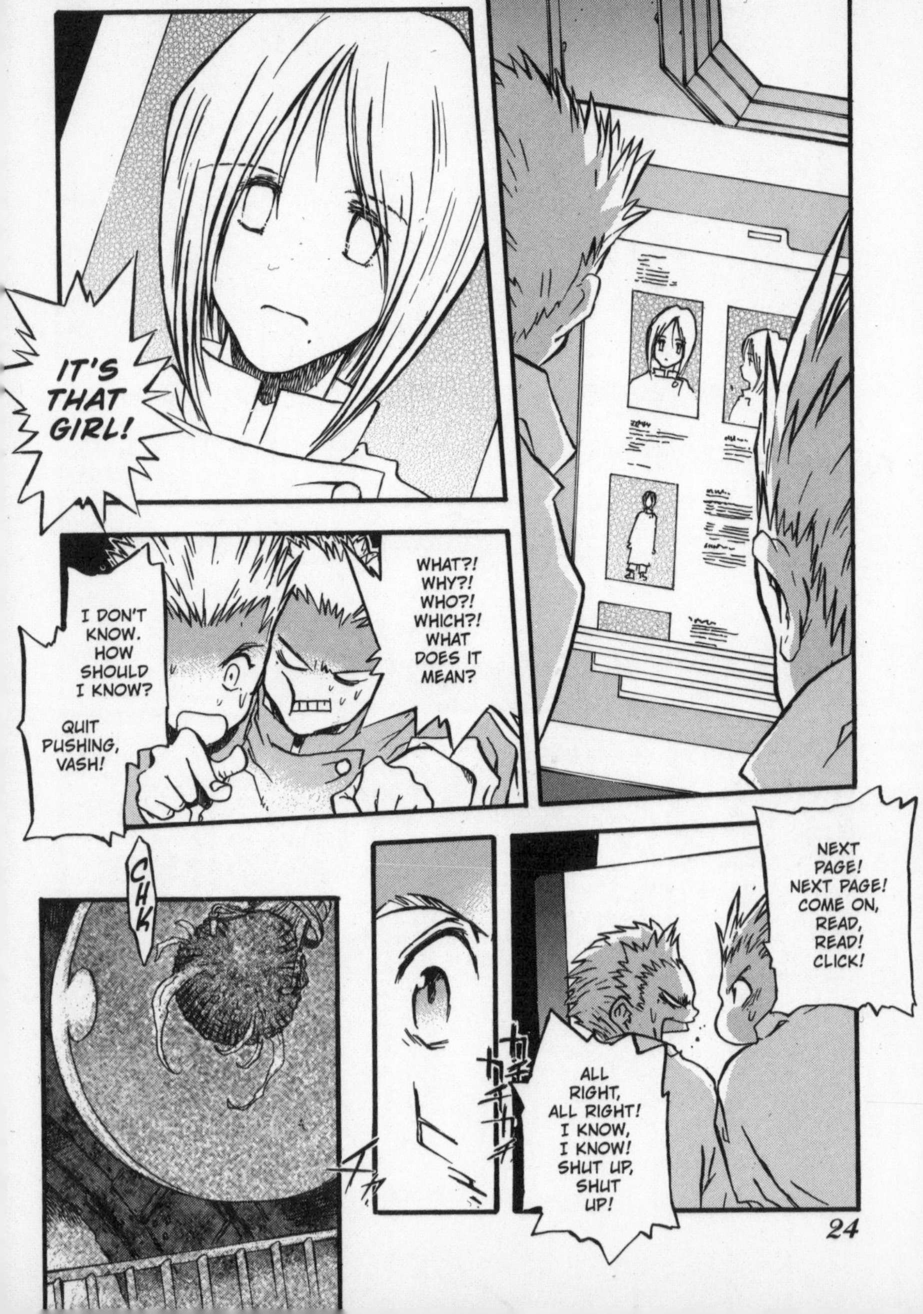
IT'S THAT GIRL!
WHAT?! WHY?! WHO?! WHICH?! WHAT DOES IT MEAN?
I DON'T KNOW. HOW SHOULD I KNOW?
QUIT PUSHING, VASH!
NEXT PAGE! NEXT PAGE! COME ON, READ, READ! CLICK!
ALL RIGHT, ALL RIGHT! I KNOW, I KNOW! SHUT UP, SHUT UP!
CHK

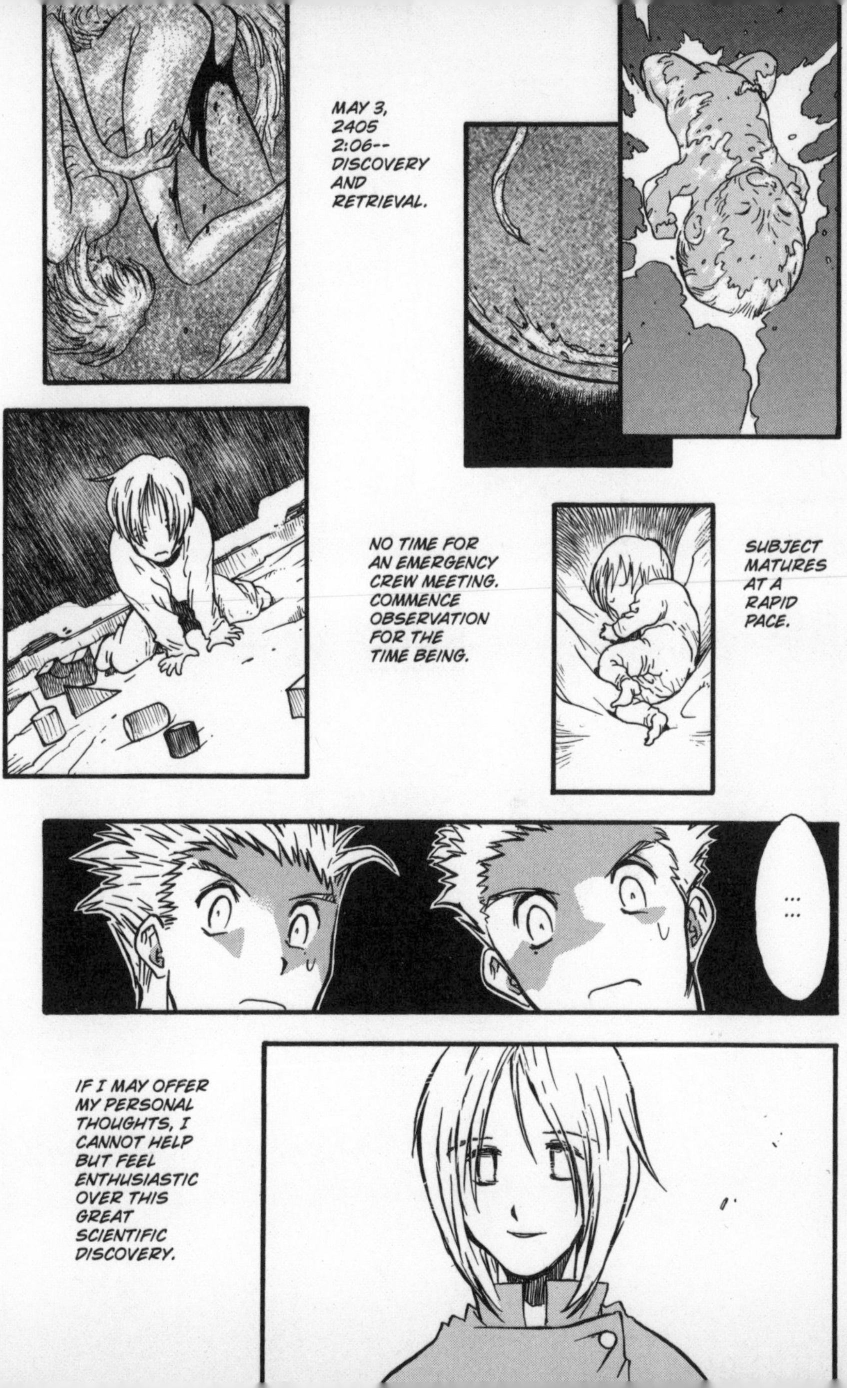
MAY 3, 2405 2:06-- DISCOVERY AND RETRIEVAL.
SUBJECT MATURES AT A RAPID PACE.
NO TIME FOR AN EMERGENCY CREW MEETING. COMMENCE OBSERVATION FOR THE TIME BEING.
......
IF I MAY OFFER MY PERSONAL THOUGHTS, I CANNOT HELP BUT FEEL ENTHUSIASTIC OVER THIS GREAT SCIENTIFIC DISCOVERY.

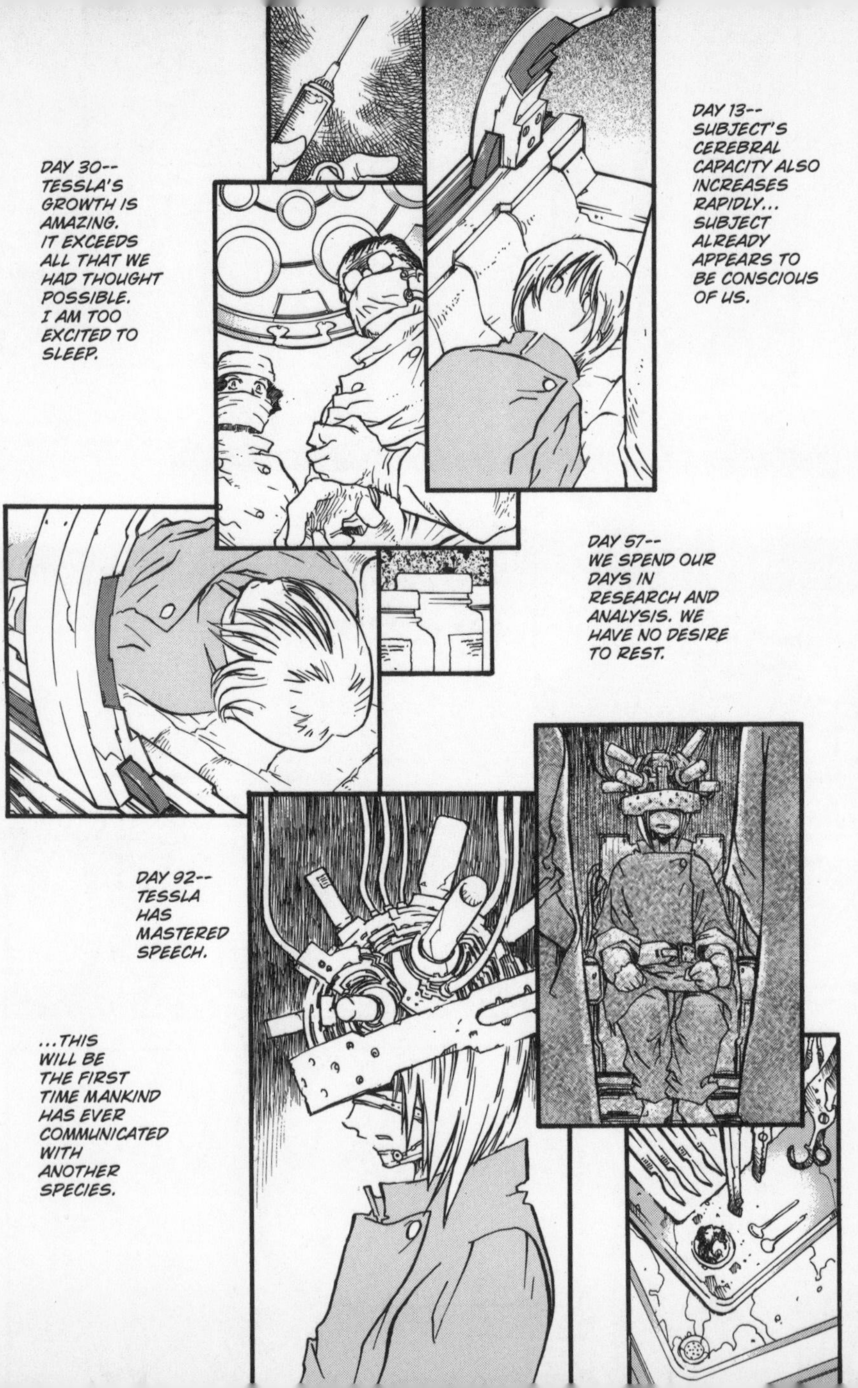
DAY 13-- SUBJECT'S CEREBRAL CAPACITY ALSO INCREASES RAPIDLY... SUBJECT ALREADY APPEARS TO BE CONSCIOUS OF US.
DAY 30-- TESSLA'S GROWTH IS AMAZING. IT EXCEEDS ALL THAT WE HAD THOUGHT POSSIBLE. I AM TOO EXCITED TO SLEEP.
DAY 57-- WE SPEND OUR DAYS IN RESEARCH AND ANALYSIS. WE HAVE NO DESIRE TO REST.
DAY 92-- TESSLA HAS MASTERED SPEECH.
...THIS WILL BE THE FIRST TIME MANKIND HAS EVER COMMUNICATED WITH ANOTHER SPECIES.

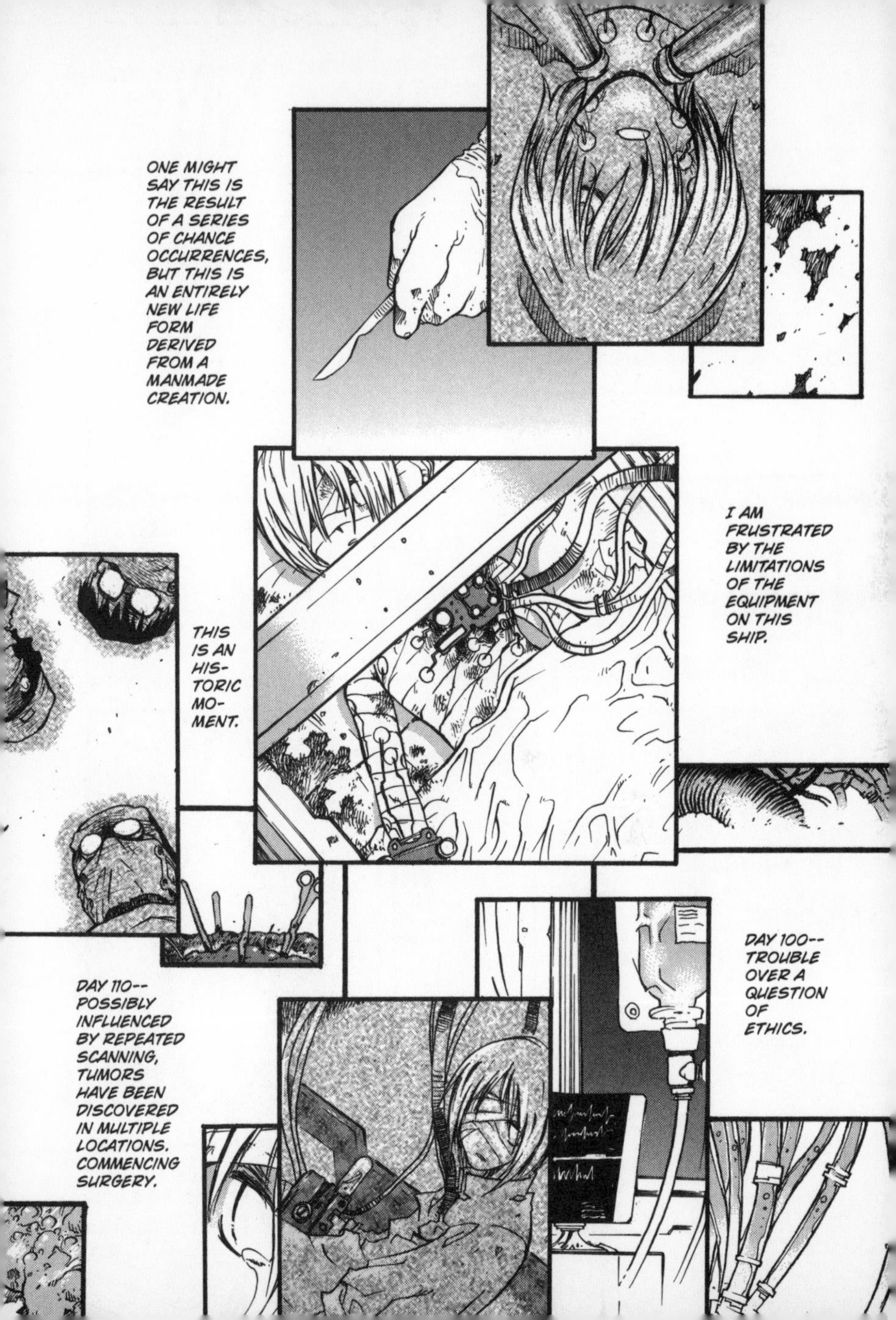
ONE MIGHT SAY THIS IS THE RESULT OF A SERIES OF CHANCE OCCURRENCES, BUT THIS IS AN ENTIRELY NEW LIFE FORM DERIVED FROM A MANMADE CREATION.
I AM FRUSTRATED BY THE LIMITATIONS OF THE EQUIPMENT ON THIS SHIP.
THIS IS AN HIS-TORIC MO-MENT.
DAY 100-- TROUBLE OVER A QUESTION OF ETHICS.
DAY 110-- POSSIBLY INFLUENCED BY REPEATED SCANNING, TUMORS HAVE BEEN DISCOVERED IN MULTIPLE LOCATIONS. COMMENCING SURGERY.

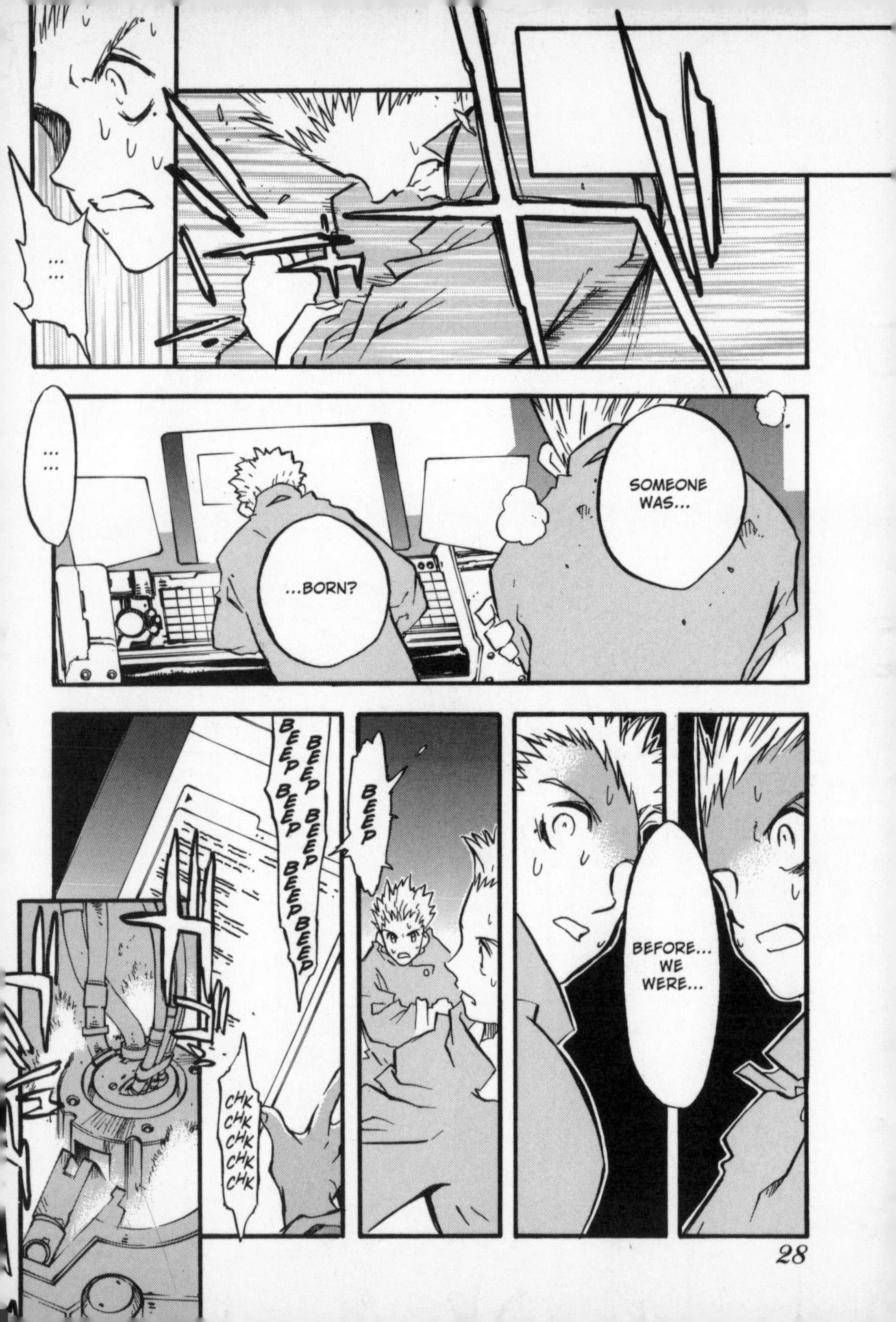
……
SOMEONE WAS…
…BORN?
……
BEFORE… WE WERE…
BEEP
BEEP BEEP BEEP BEEP
BEEP BEEP BEEP
CHK CHK CHK CHK CHK

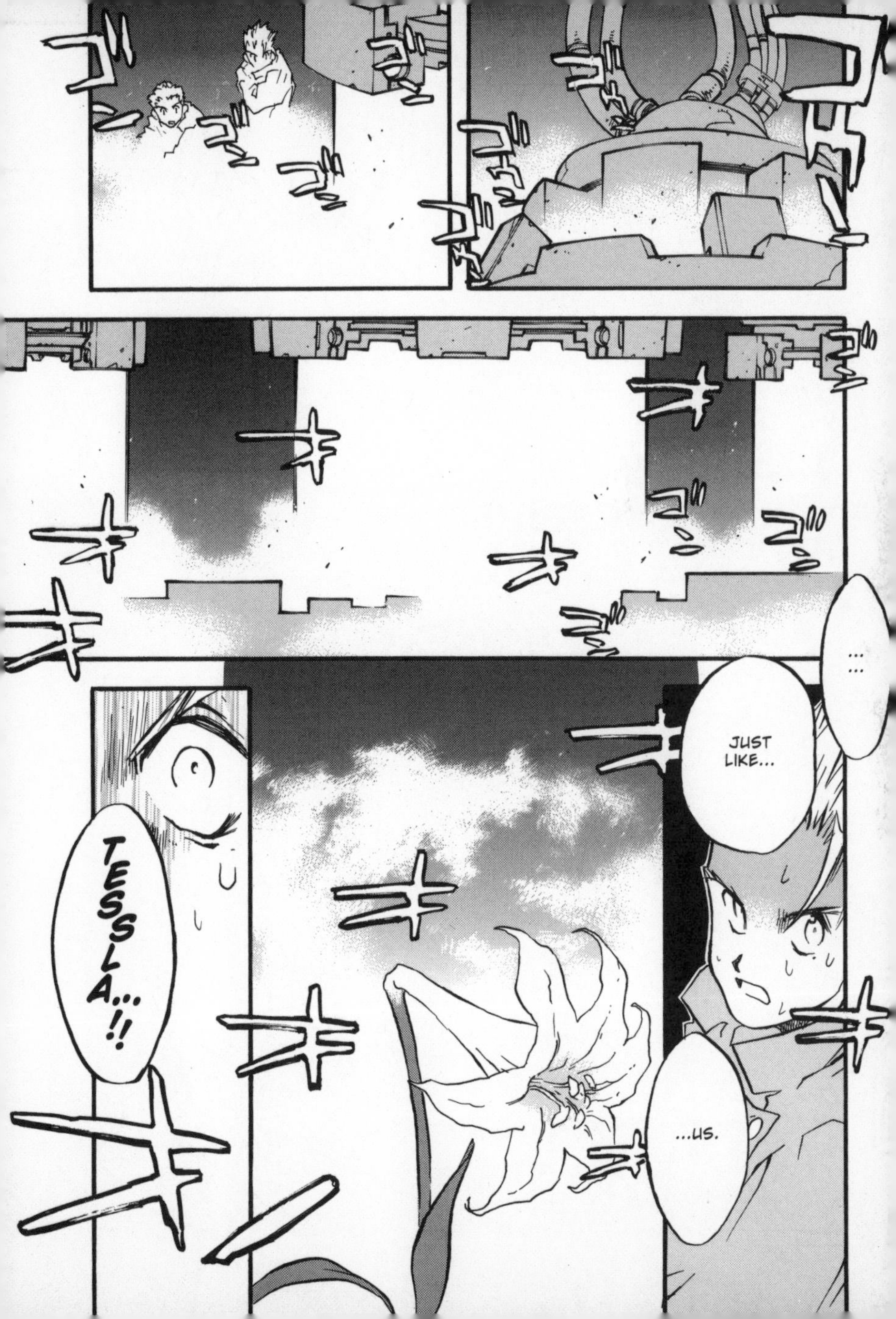
......
JUST LIKE...
...US.
TESSLA...!!

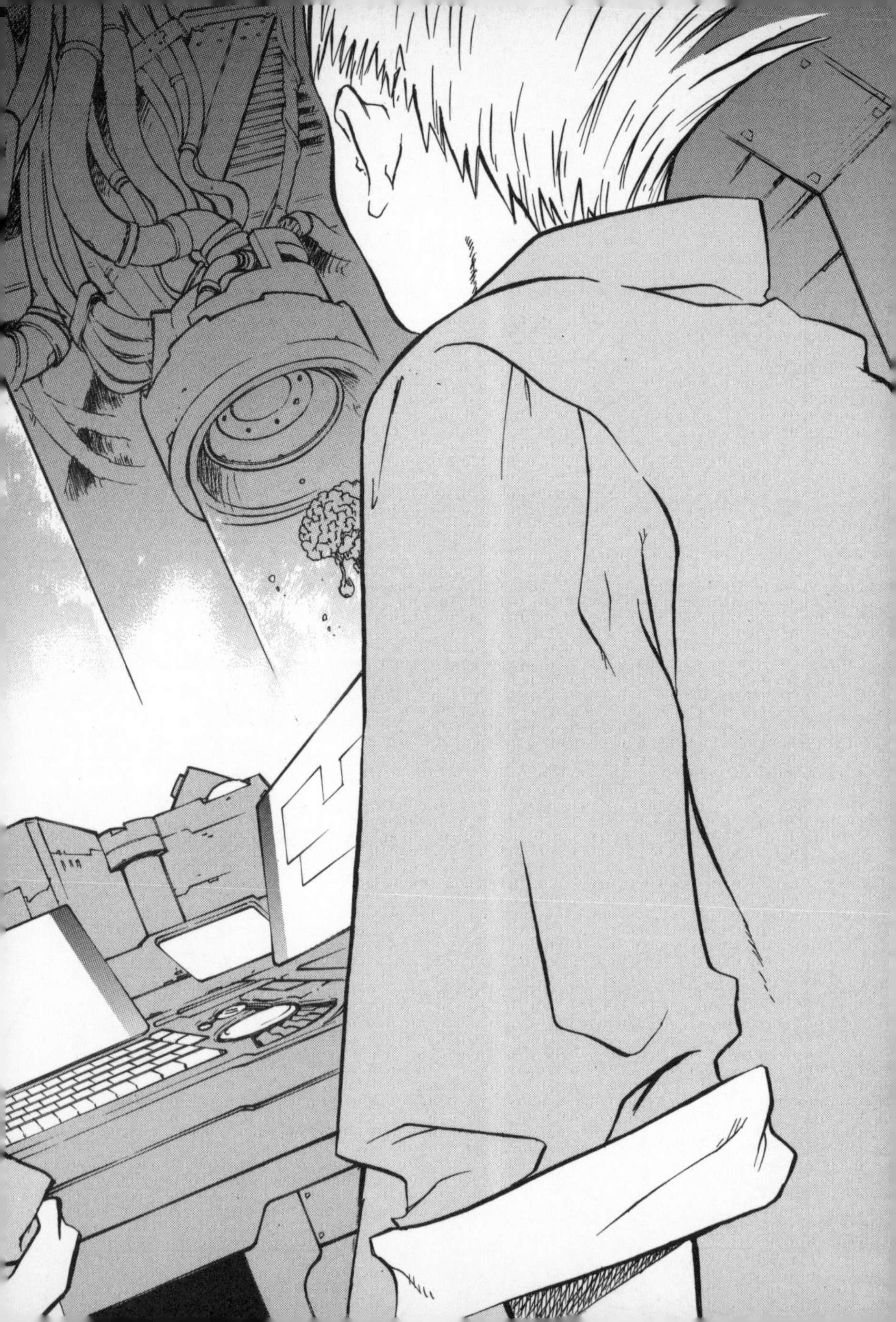

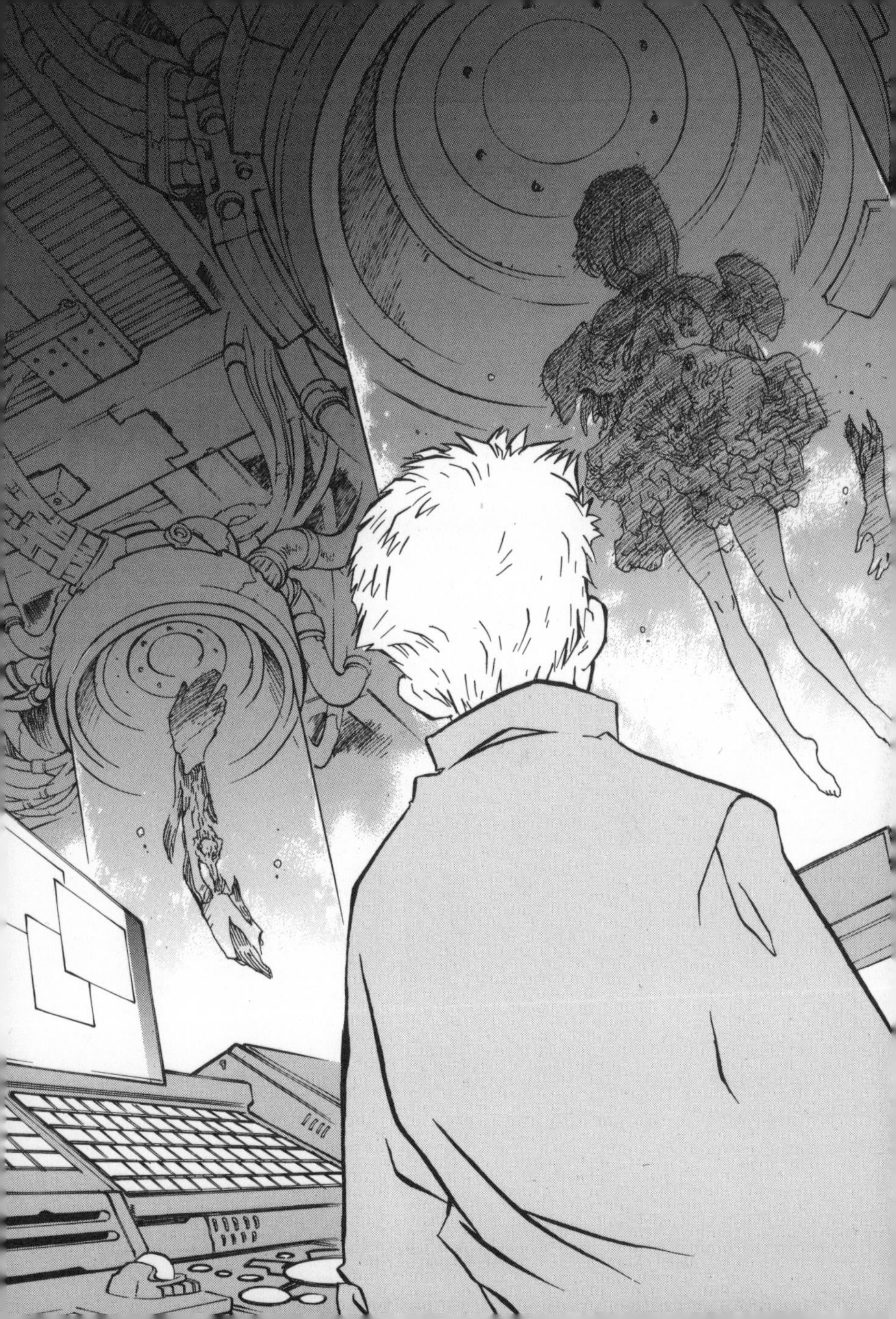

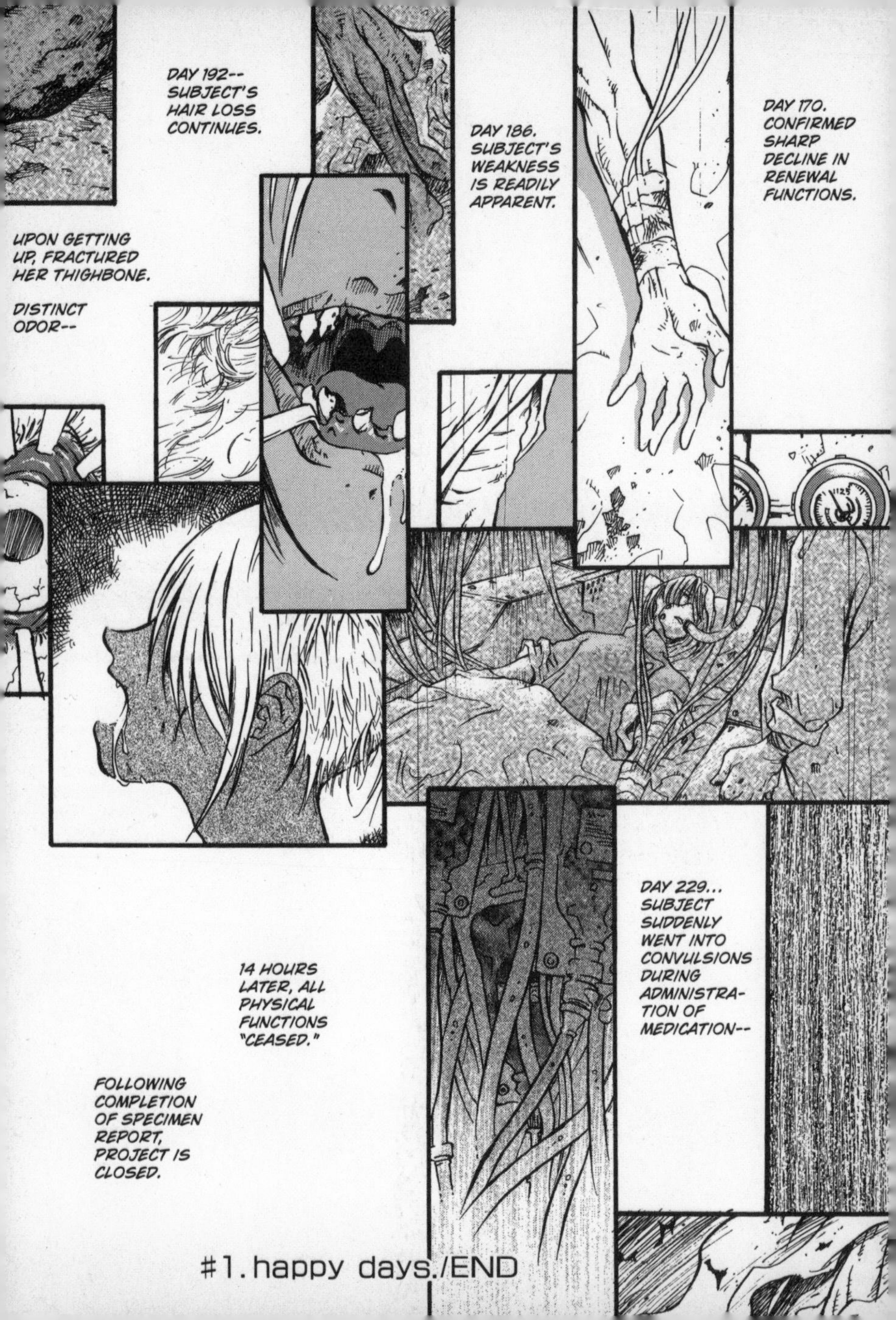
DAY 170. CONFIRMED SHARP DECLINE IN RENEWAL FUNCTIONS.
DAY 186. SUBJECT'S WEAKNESS IS READILY APPARENT.
DAY 192-- SUBJECT'S HAIR LOSS CONTINUES.
UPON GETTING UP, FRACTURED HER THIGHBONE.
DISTINCT ODOR--
DAY 229... SUBJECT SUDDENLY WENT INTO CONVULSIONS DURING ADMINISTRATION OF MEDICATION--
14 HOURS LATER, ALL PHYSICAL FUNCTIONS "CEASED."
FOLLOWING COMPLETION OF SPECIMEN REPORT, PROJECT IS CLOSED.
#1. happy days./END

TRIGUN MAXIMUM

YASUHIRO NIGHTOW

DEEP SPACE PLANET FUTURE GUN ACTION!!

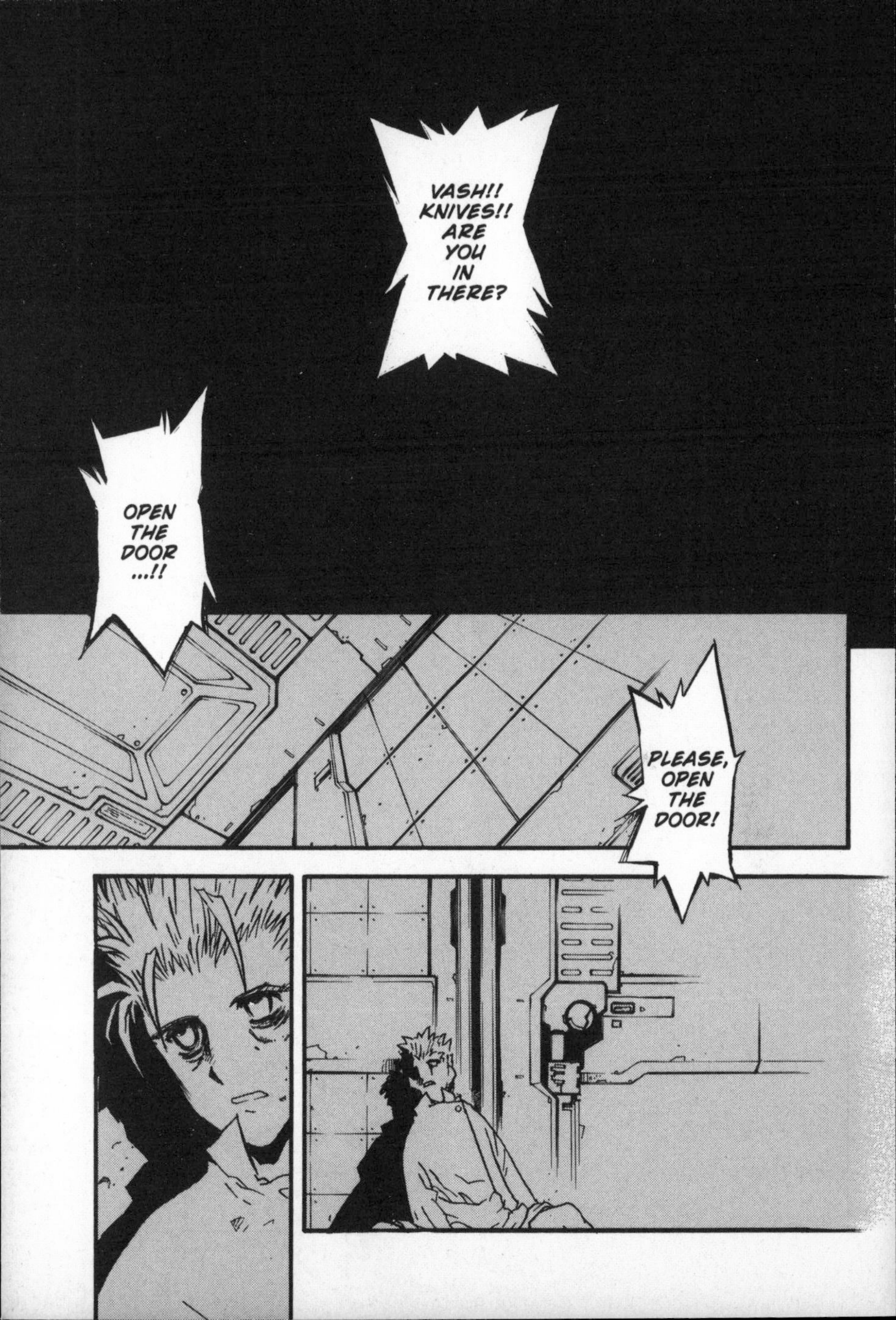
VASH!! KNIVES!! ARE YOU IN THERE?
OPEN THE DOOR ...!!
PLEASE, OPEN THE DOOR!

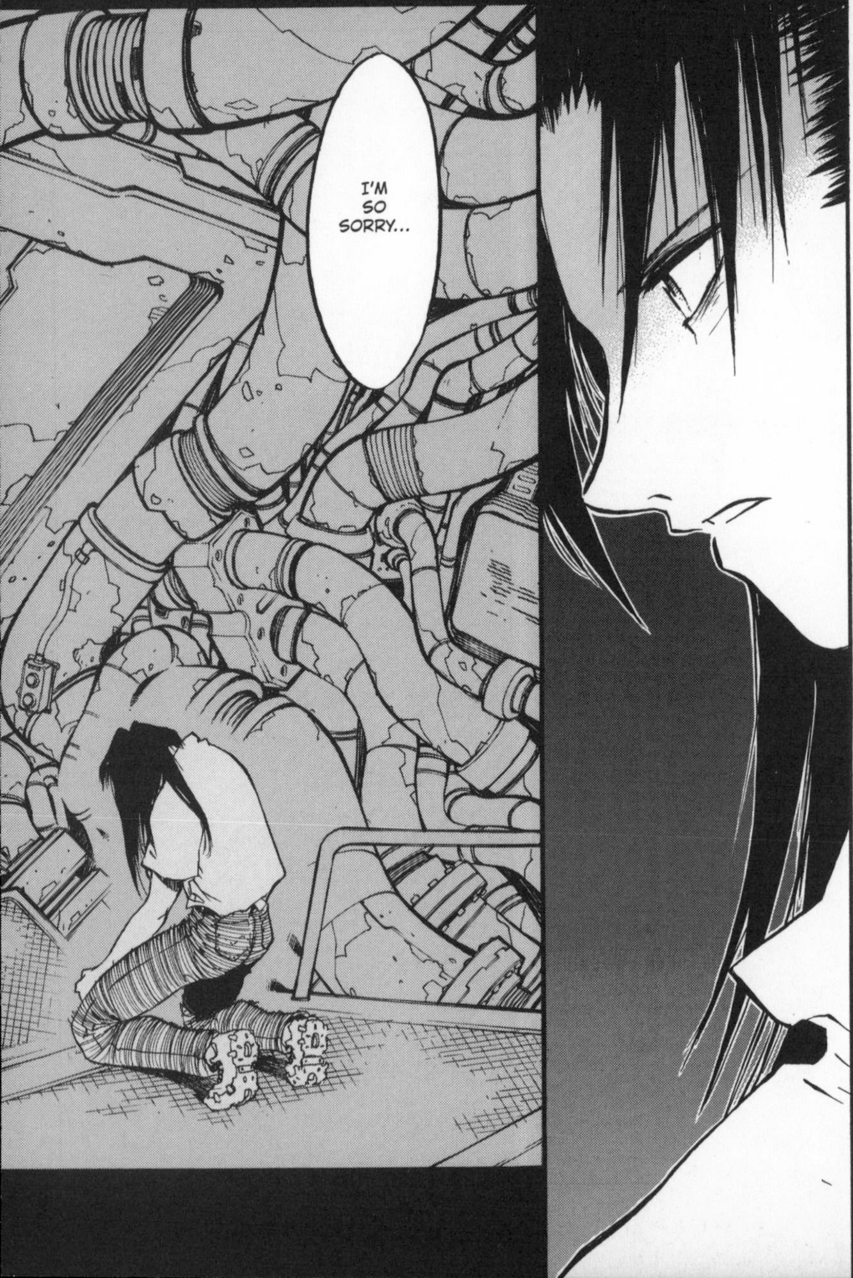
I'M SO SORRY...

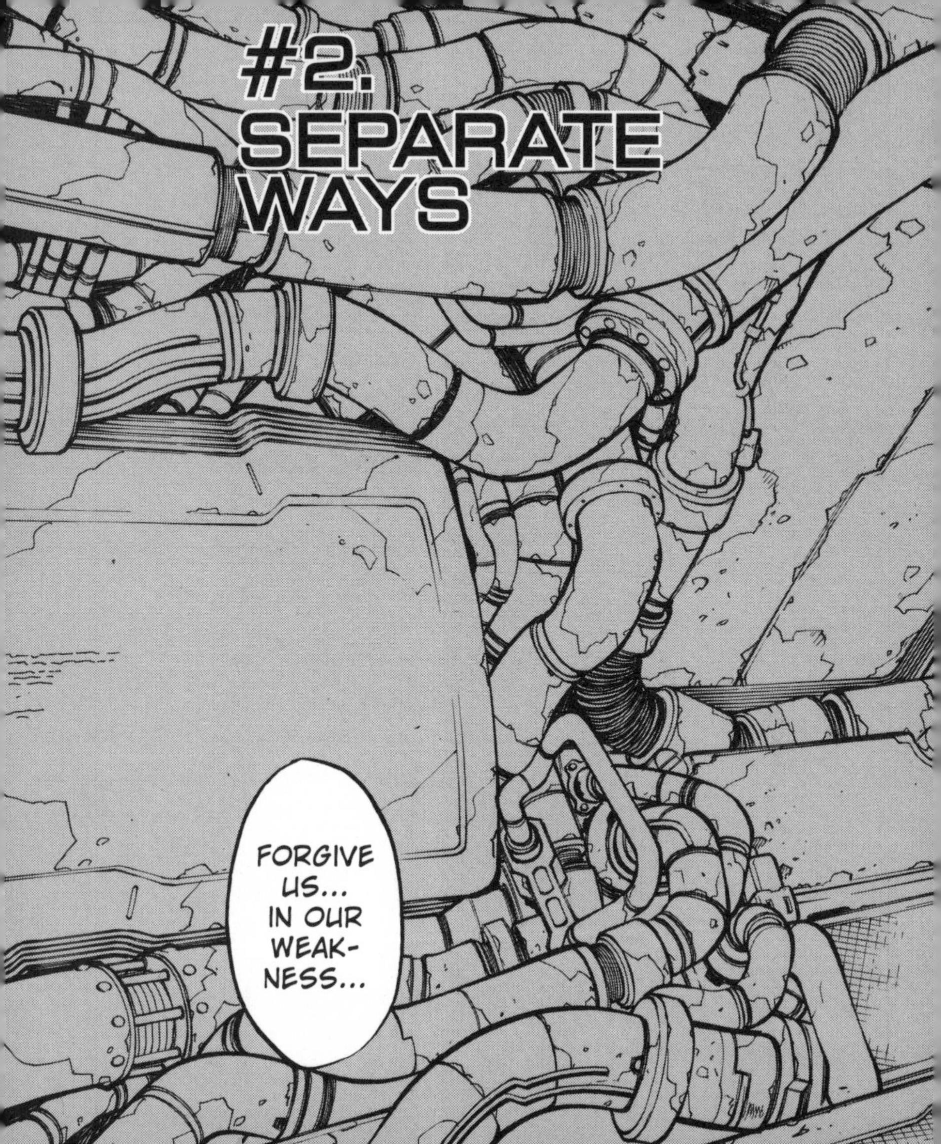
#2. SEPARATE WAYS
FORGIVE US... IN OUR WEAK-NESS...

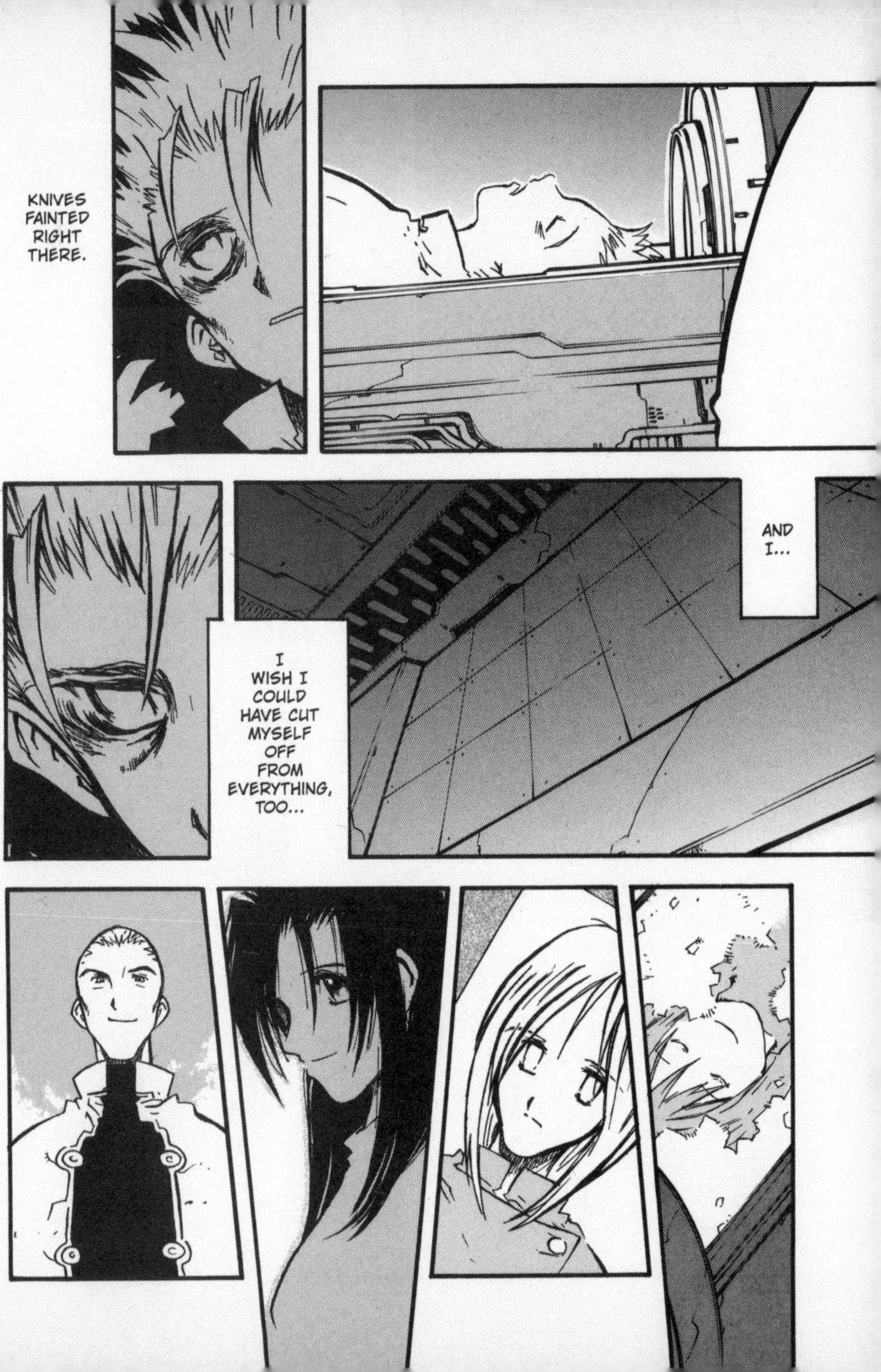
KNIVES FAINTED RIGHT THERE.
AND I...
I WISH I COULD HAVE CUT MYSELF OFF FROM EVERYTHING, TOO...

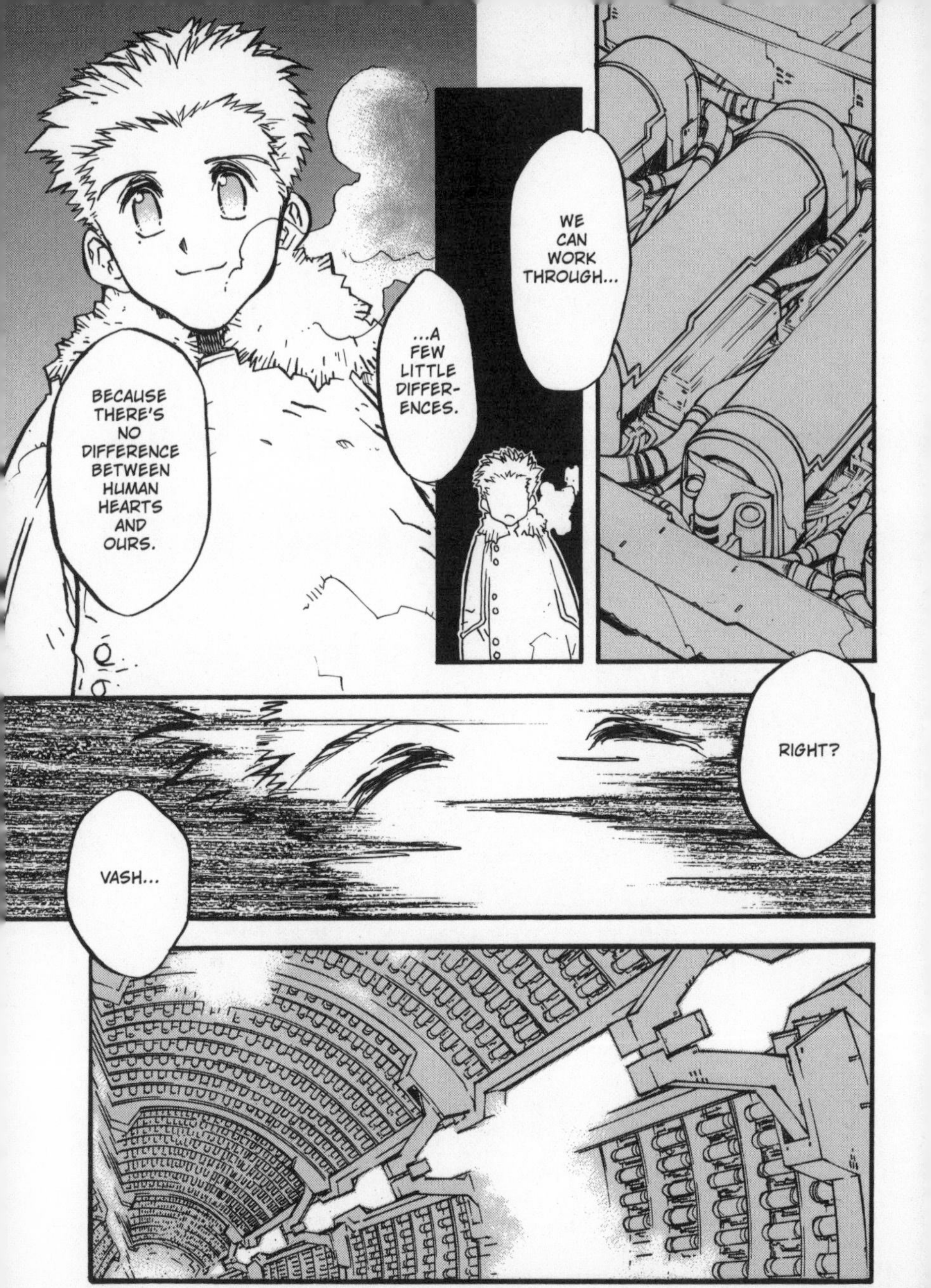
WE CAN WORK THROUGH...
...A FEW LITTLE DIFFERENCES.
BECAUSE THERE'S NO DIFFERENCE BETWEEN HUMAN HEARTS AND OURS.
RIGHT?
VASH...

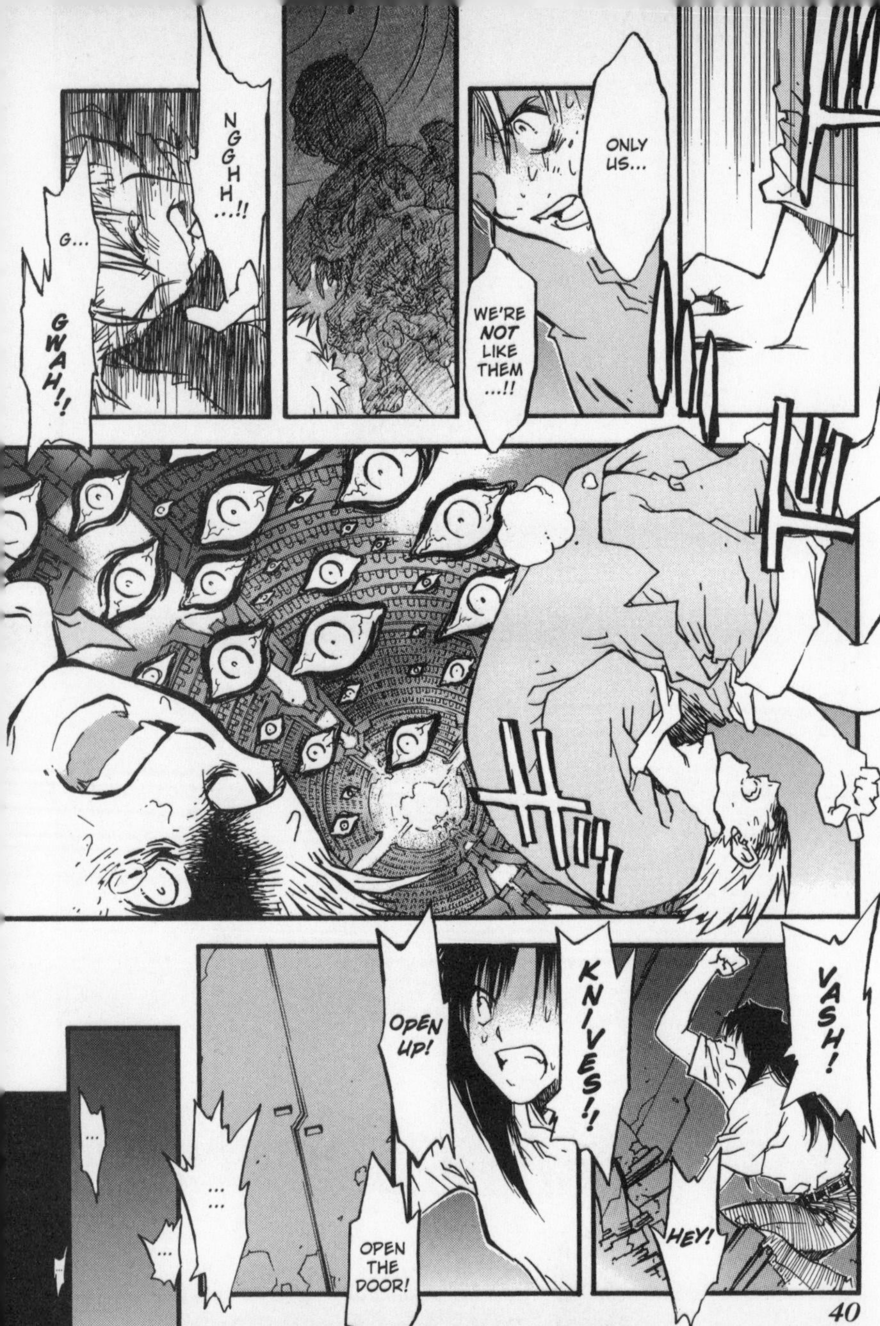
ONLY US...
WE'RE NOT LIKE THEM ...!!
NGGHH ...!!
G...
GWAH!!
VASH!
KNIVES!!
HEY!
OPEN UP!
OPEN THE DOOR!
...
... ...
...

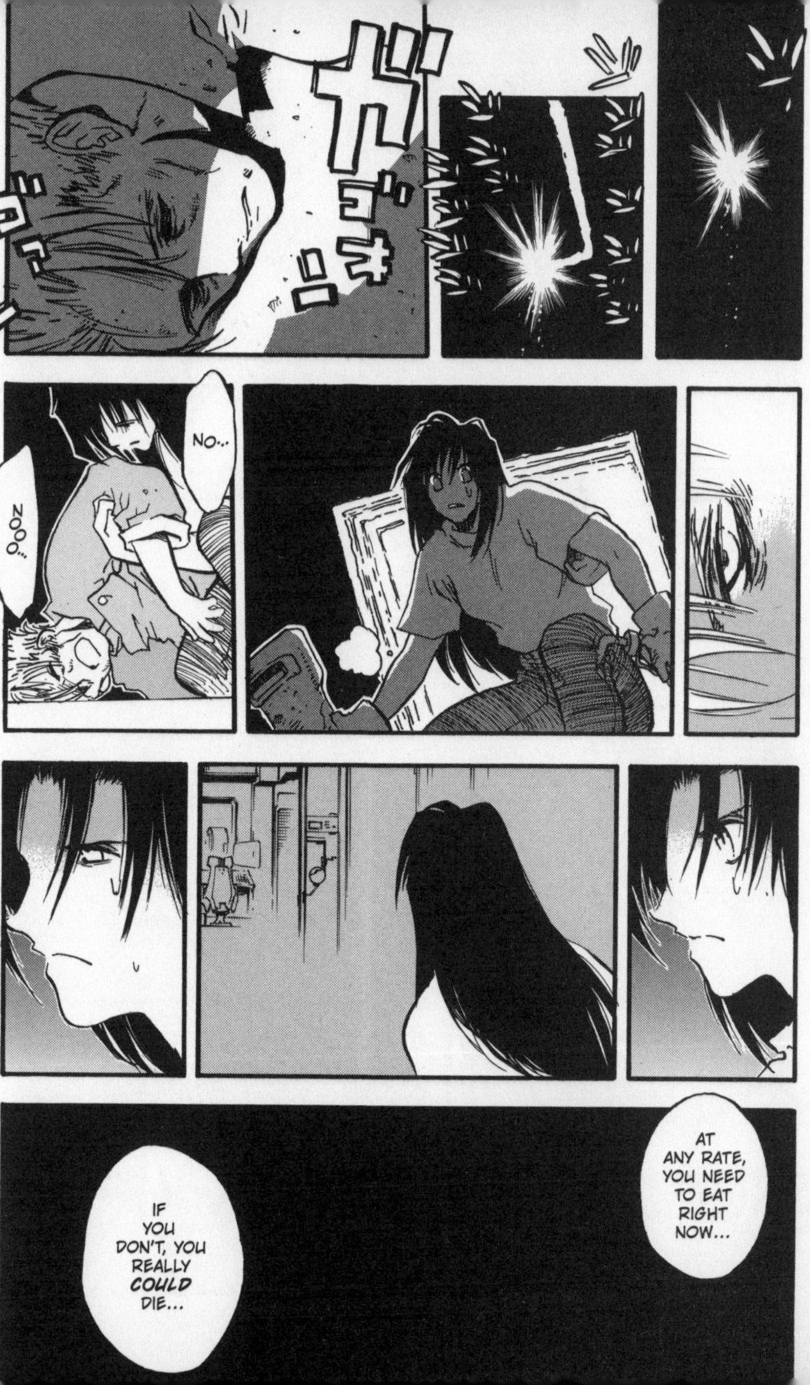
NO...
NOOO...
AT ANY RATE, YOU NEED TO EAT RIGHT NOW...
IF YOU DON'T, YOU REALLY COULD DIE...

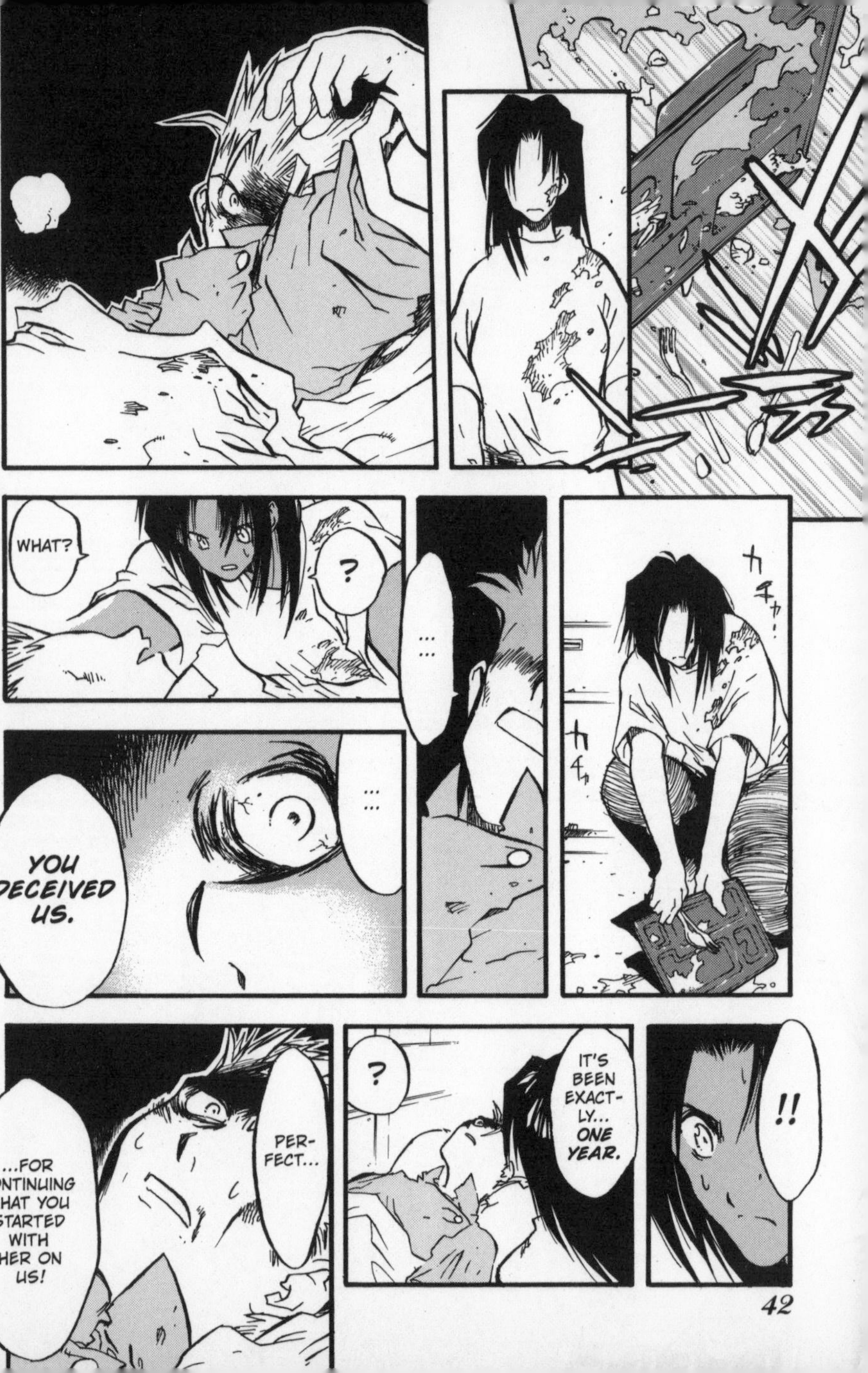
カチャ!
カチャ
......
?
WHAT?
......
YOU DECEIVED US.
!!
IT'S BEEN EXACT-LY... ONE YEAR.
?
PER-FECT...
...FOR CONTINUING WHAT YOU STARTED WITH HER ON US!

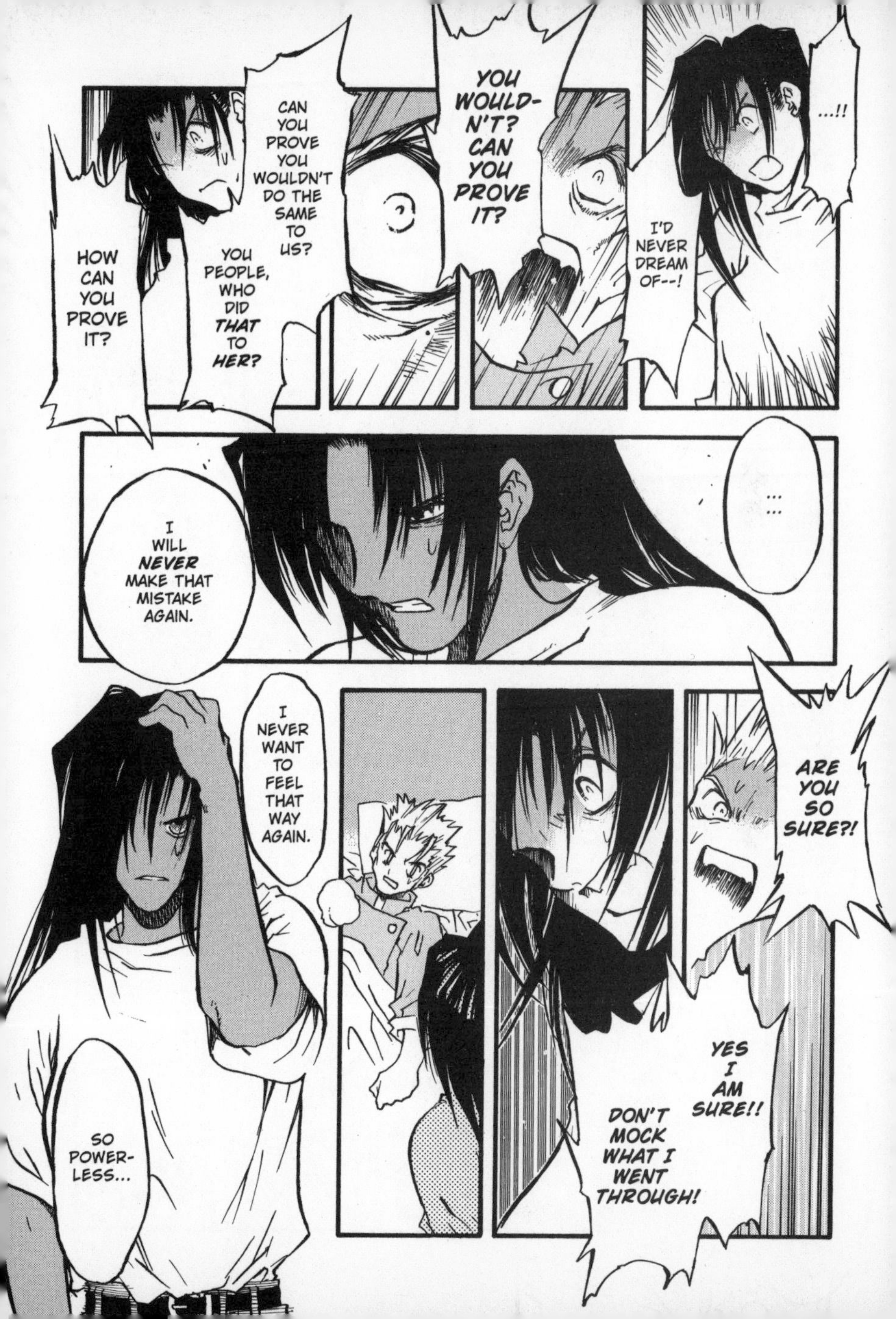
...!!
I'D NEVER DREAM OF--!
YOU WOULDN'T? CAN YOU PROVE IT?
CAN YOU PROVE YOU WOULDN'T DO THE SAME TO US?
YOU PEOPLE, WHO DID THAT TO HER?
HOW CAN YOU PROVE IT?
... ...
I WILL NEVER MAKE THAT MISTAKE AGAIN.
ARE YOU SO SURE?!
YES I AM SURE!!
DON'T MOCK WHAT I WENT THROUGH!
I NEVER WANT TO FEEL THAT WAY AGAIN.
SO POWERLESS...

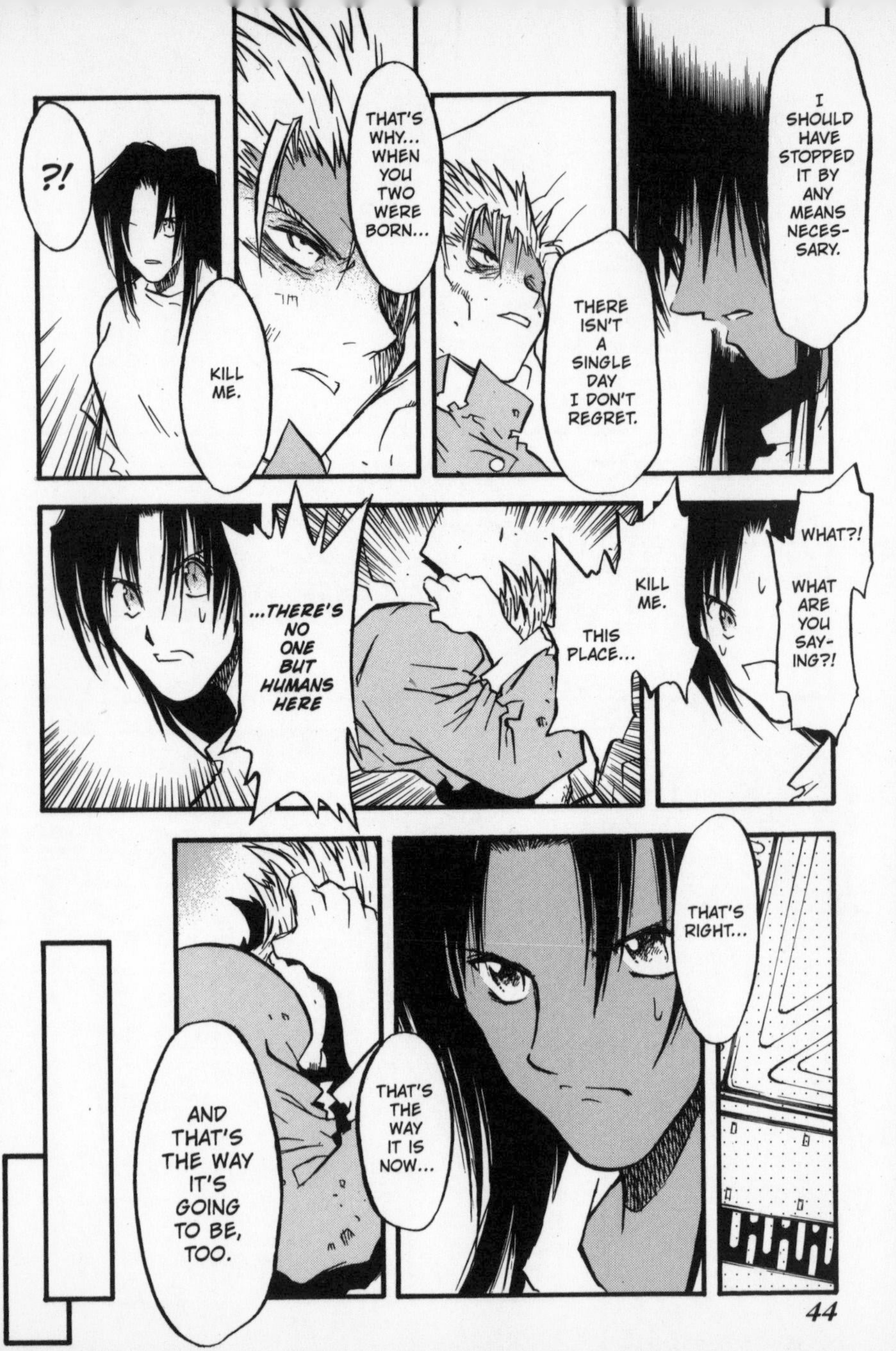
I SHOULD HAVE STOPPED IT BY ANY MEANS NECES-SARY.
THERE ISN'T A SINGLE DAY I DON'T REGRET.
THAT'S WHY... WHEN YOU TWO WERE BORN...
KILL ME.
?!
WHAT?!
WHAT ARE YOU SAY-ING?!
KILL ME.
THIS PLACE...
...THERE'S NO ONE BUT HUMANS HERE
THAT'S RIGHT...
THAT'S THE WAY IT IS NOW...
AND THAT'S THE WAY IT'S GOING TO BE, TOO.

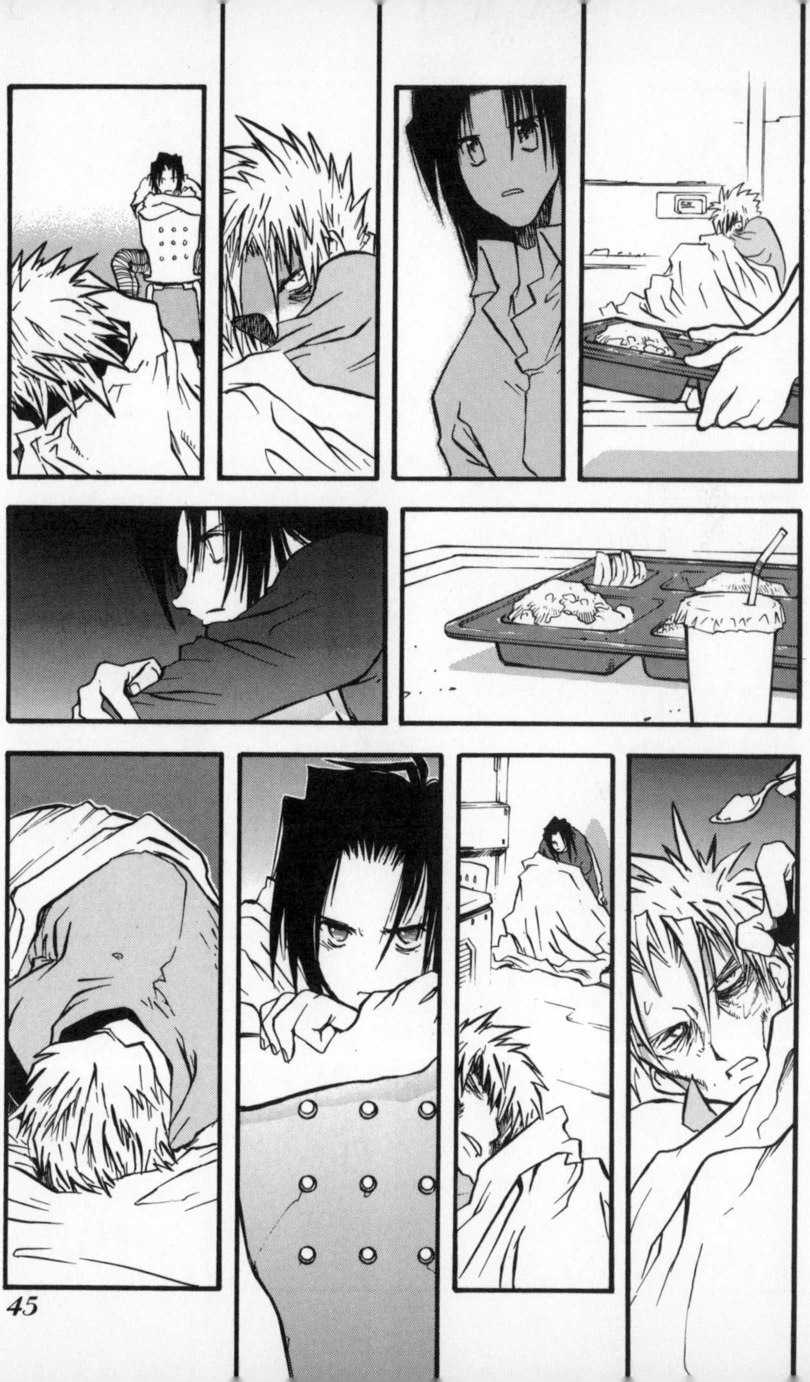

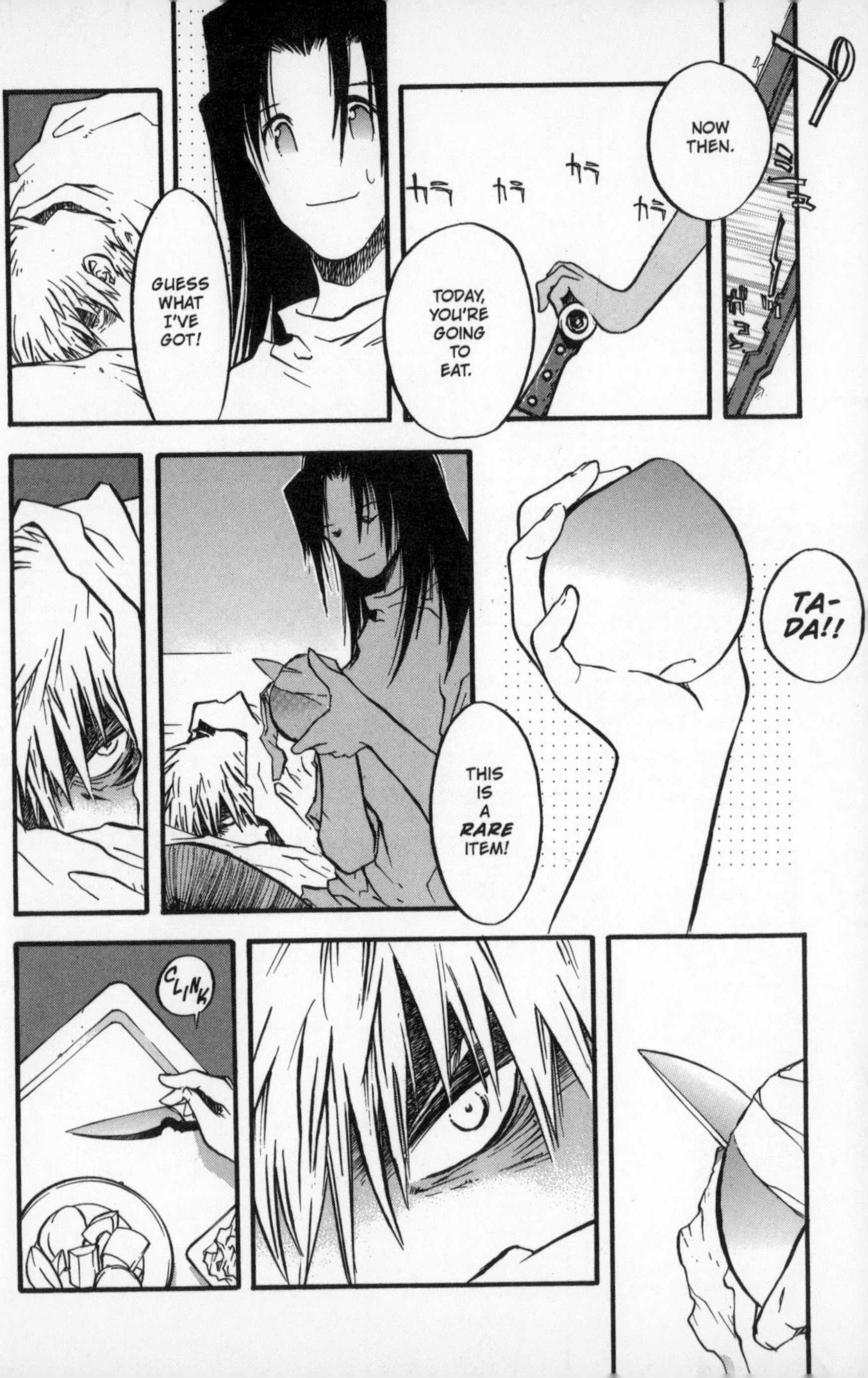
NOW THEN.
カラ カラ カラ カラ
TODAY, YOU'RE GOING TO EAT.
GUESS WHAT I'VE GOT!
TA-DA!!
THIS IS A *RARE* ITEM!
CLINK

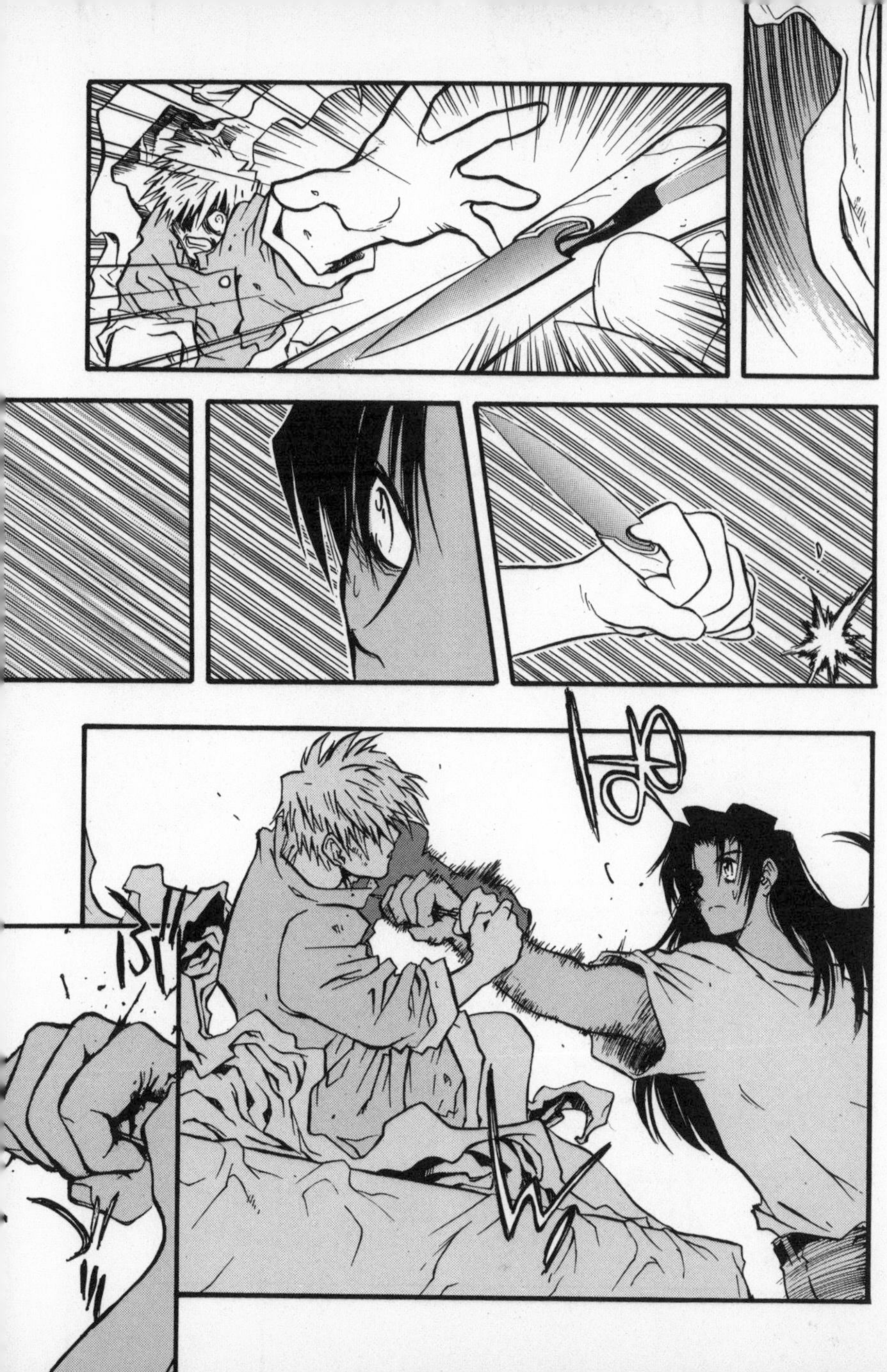

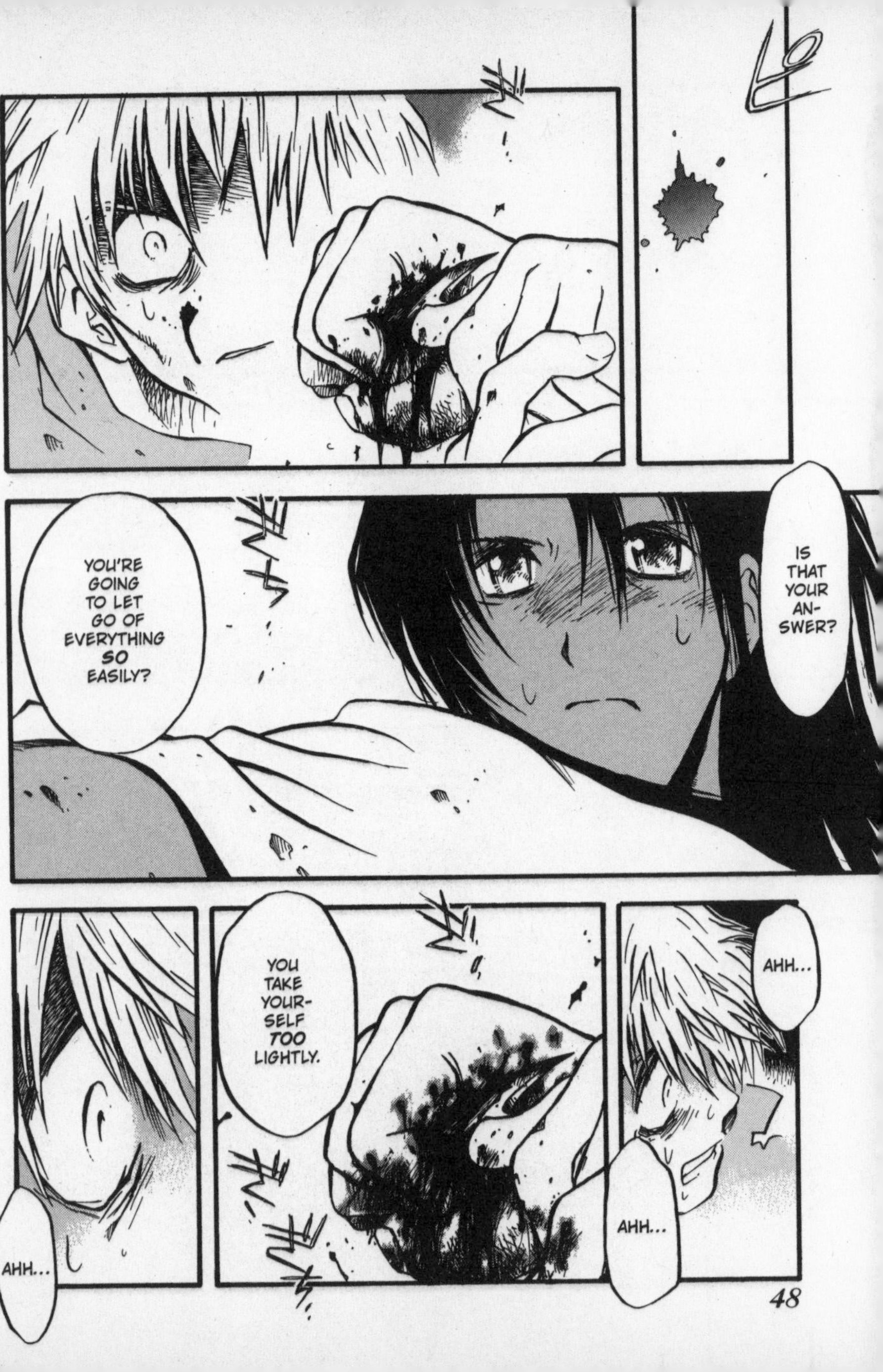
IS THAT YOUR AN-SWER?
YOU'RE GOING TO LET GO OF EVERYTHING **SO** EASILY?
AHH...
AHH...
YOU TAKE YOURSELF *TOO* LIGHTLY.
AHH...

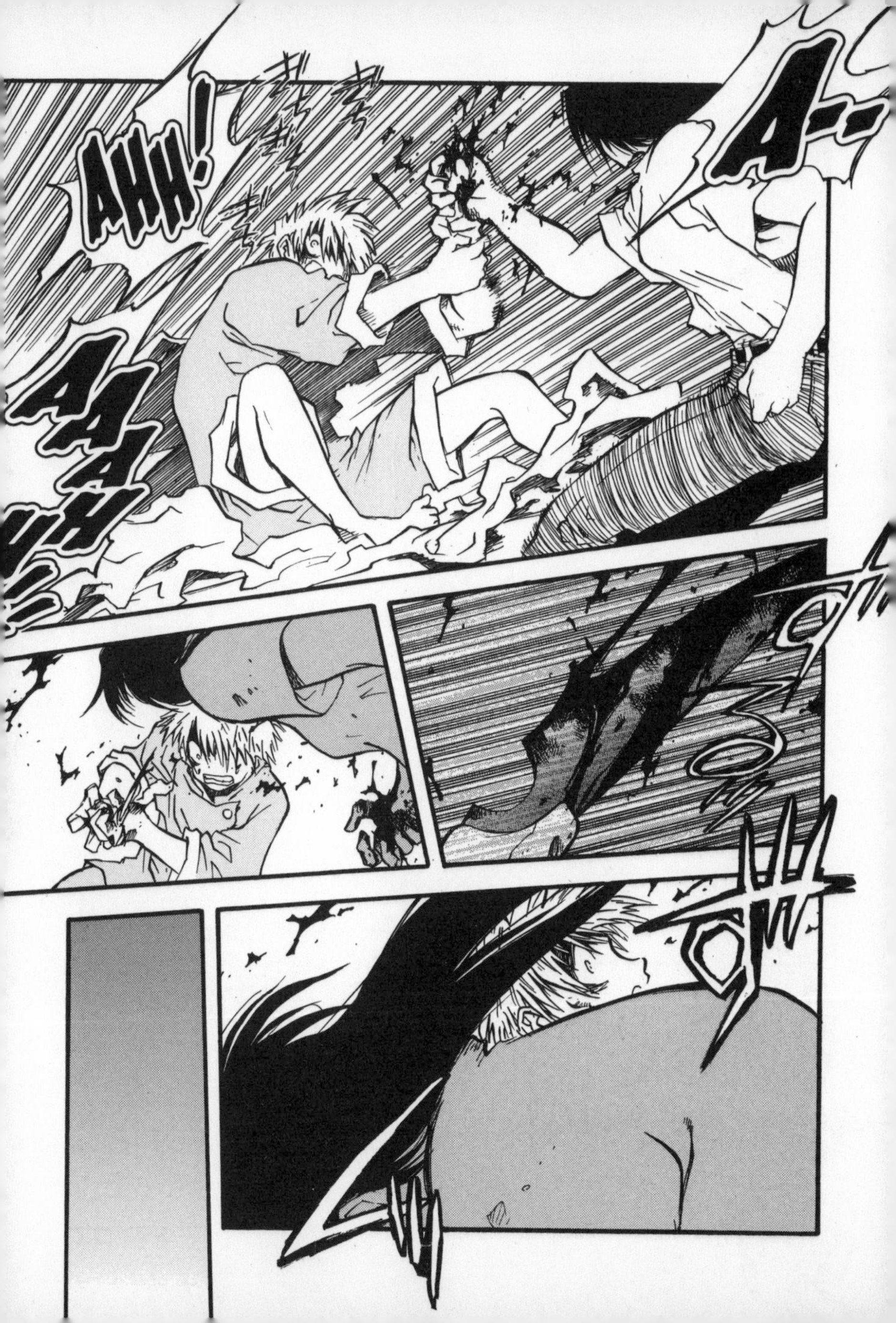
A--
AHH!
AAAHH!!

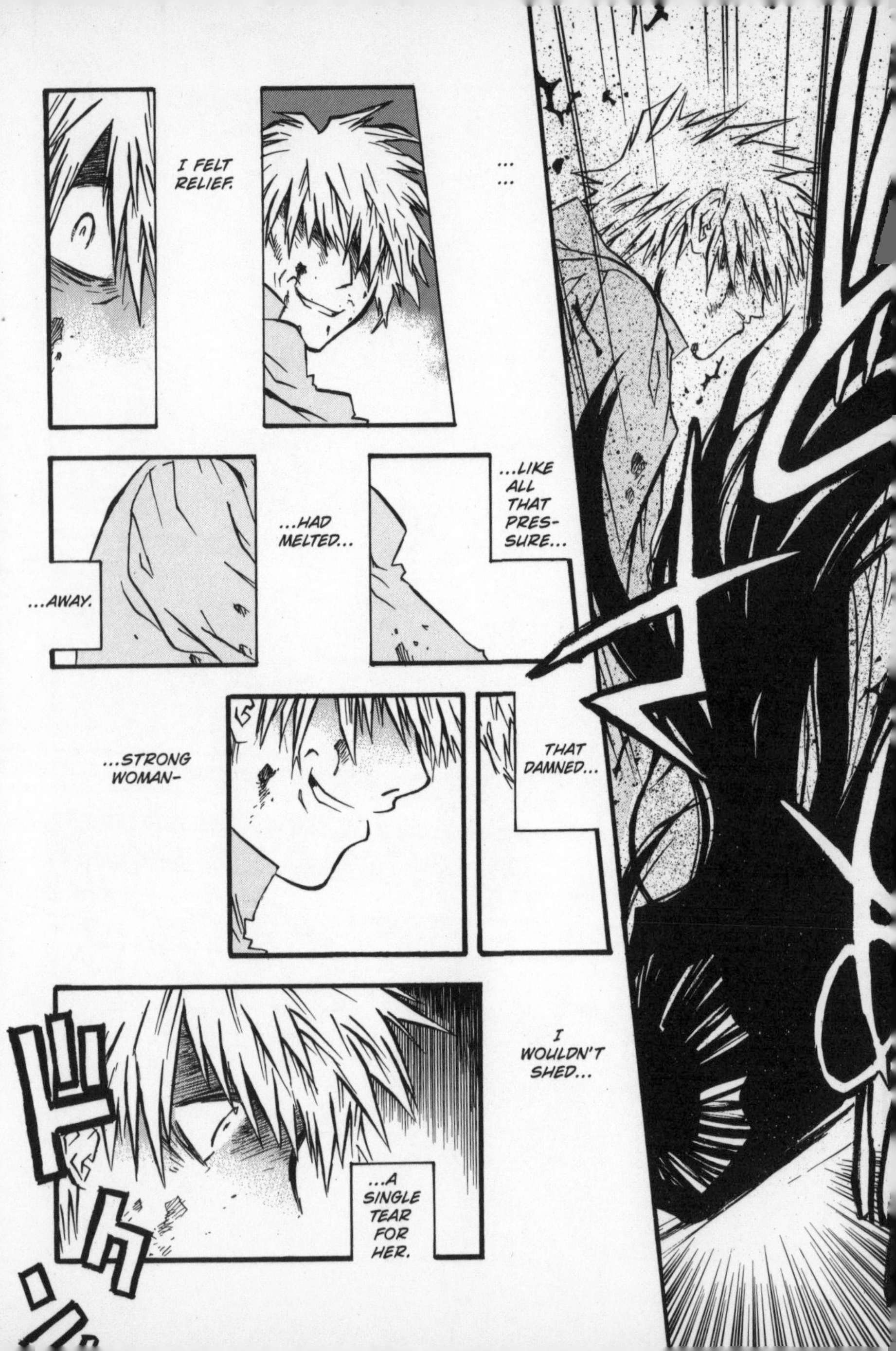
...
...
I FELT RELIEF.
...LIKE ALL THAT PRESSURE...
...HAD MELTED...
...AWAY.
THAT DAMNED...
...STRONG WOMAN-
I WOULDN'T SHED...
...A SINGLE TEAR FOR HER.

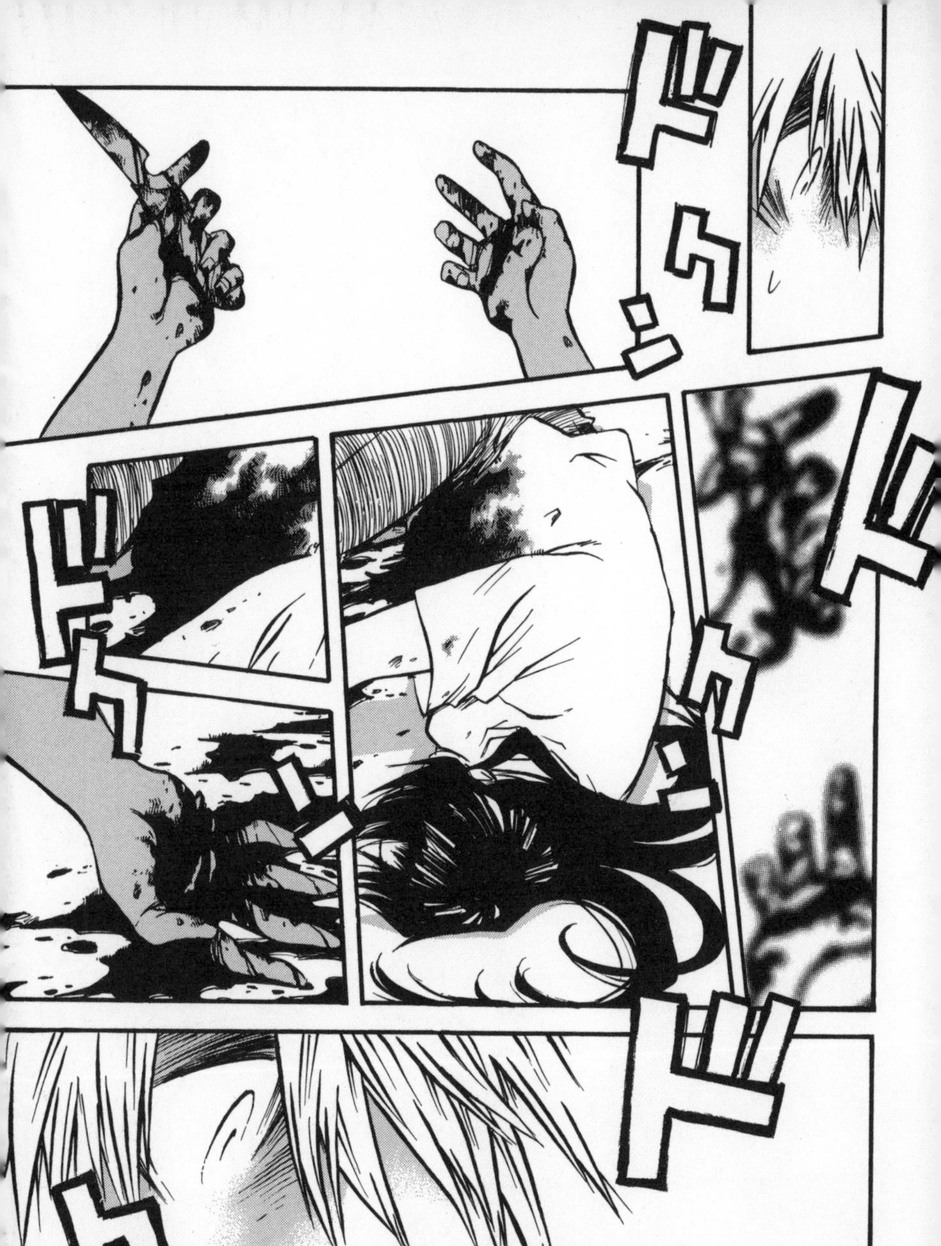
ドん…
ドん…
ドん…
ドん

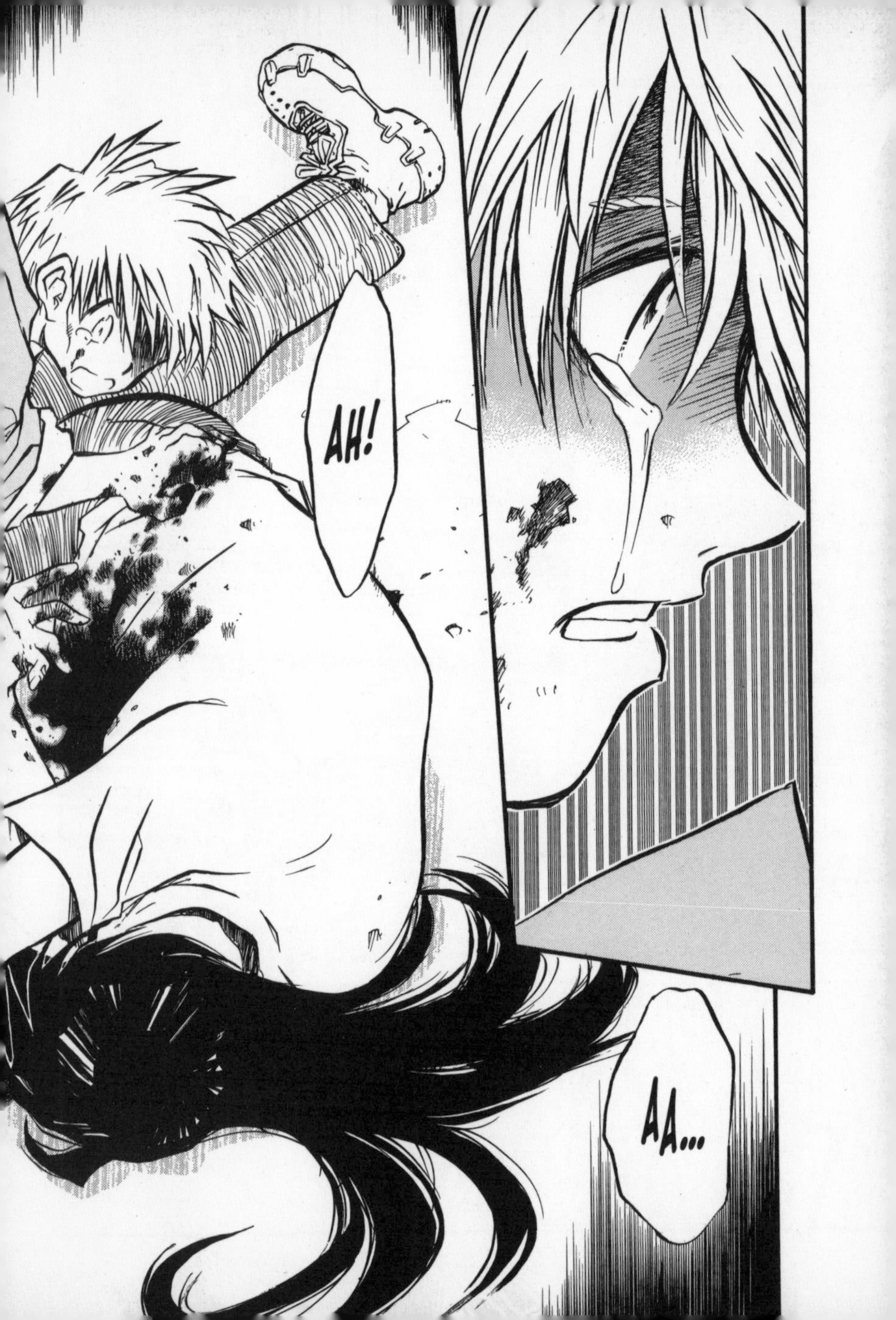
AA...
AH!

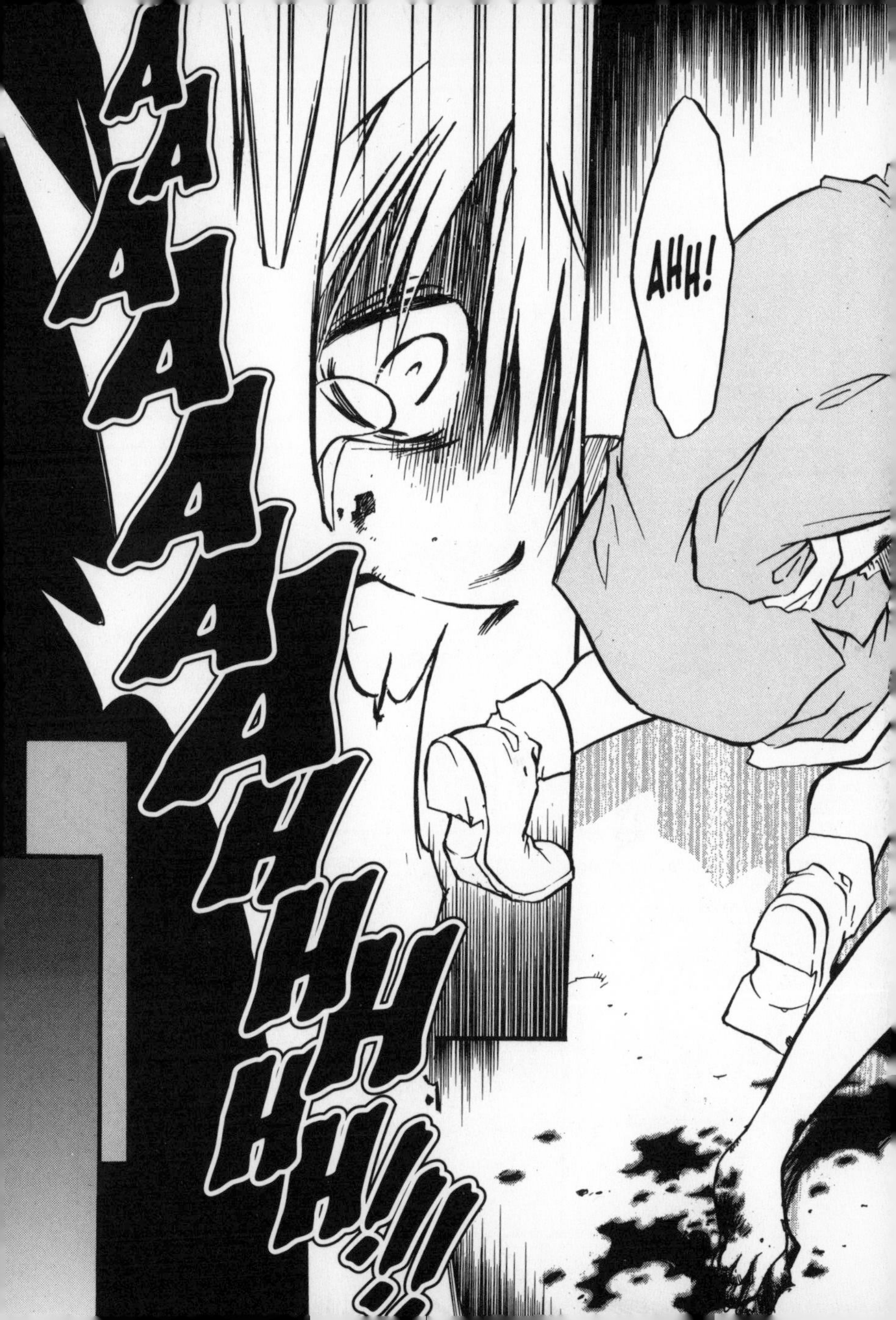
AHH!
AAAAAAAAHHHHH!!!

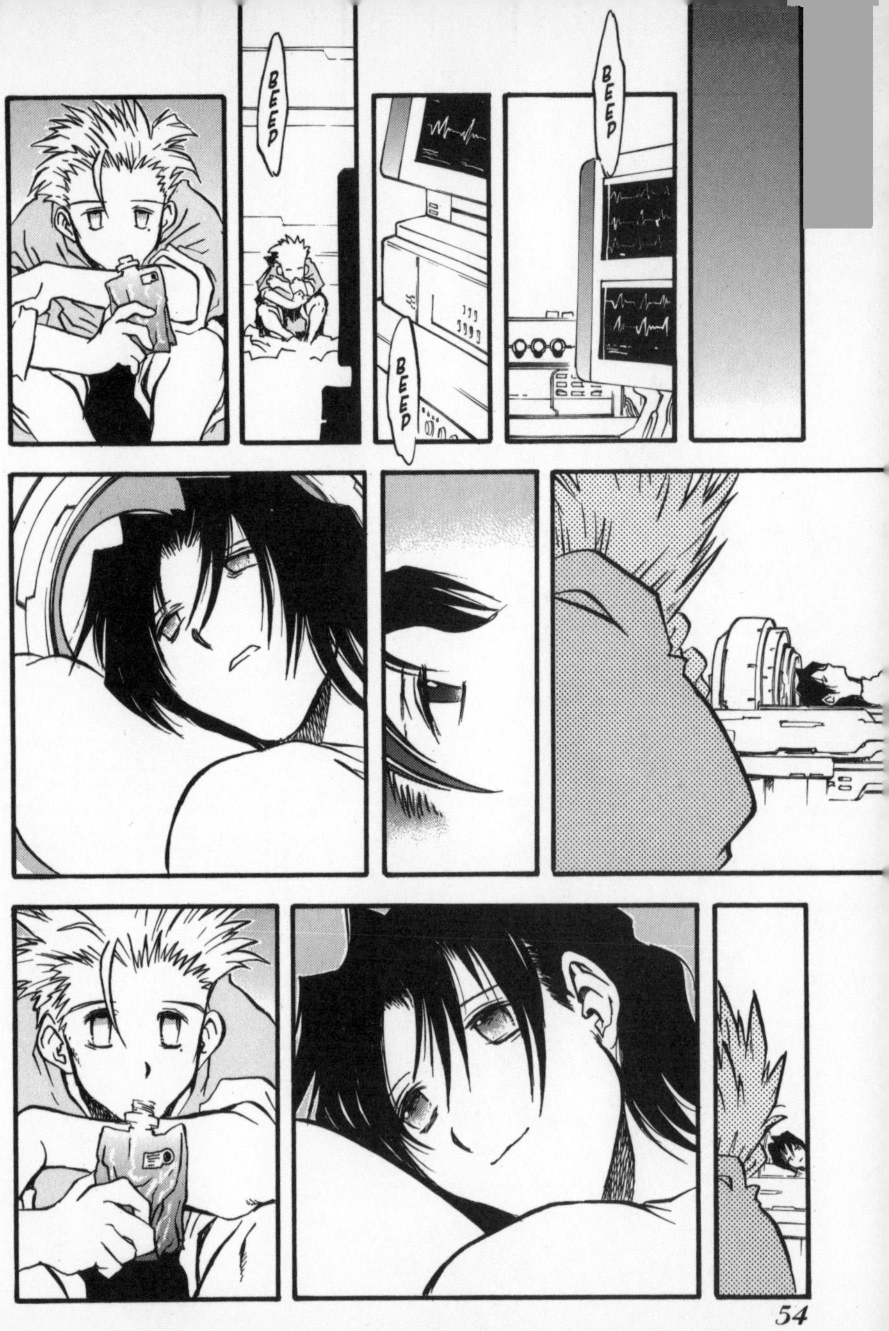
BEEP
BEEP
BEEP

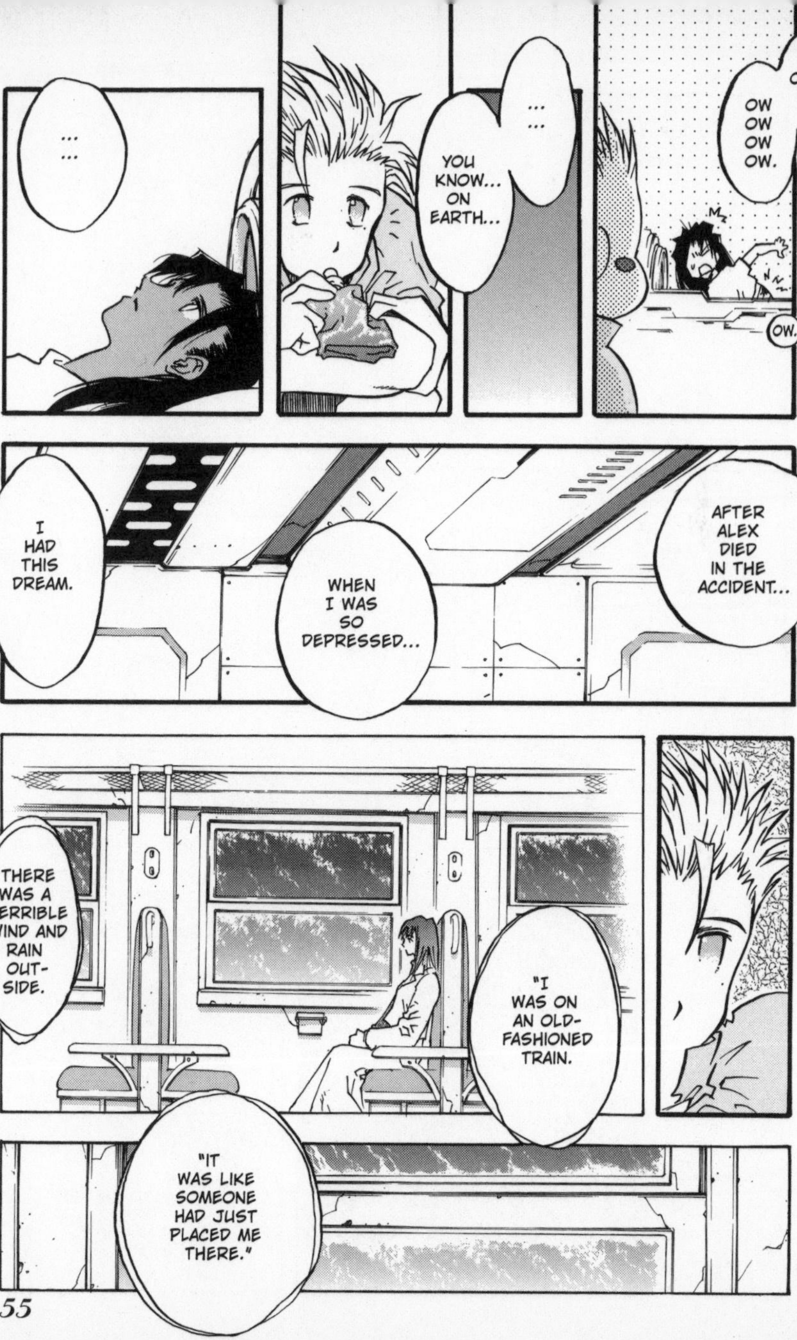
OW.
OW OW OW OW.
OW.
... ...
YOU KNOW... ON EARTH...
... ...
AFTER ALEX DIED IN THE ACCIDENT...
WHEN I WAS SO DEPRESSED...
I HAD THIS DREAM.
"I WAS ON AN OLD-FASHIONED TRAIN.
"THERE WAS A TERRIBLE WIND AND RAIN OUT-SIDE.
"IT WAS LIKE SOMEONE HAD JUST PLACED ME THERE."

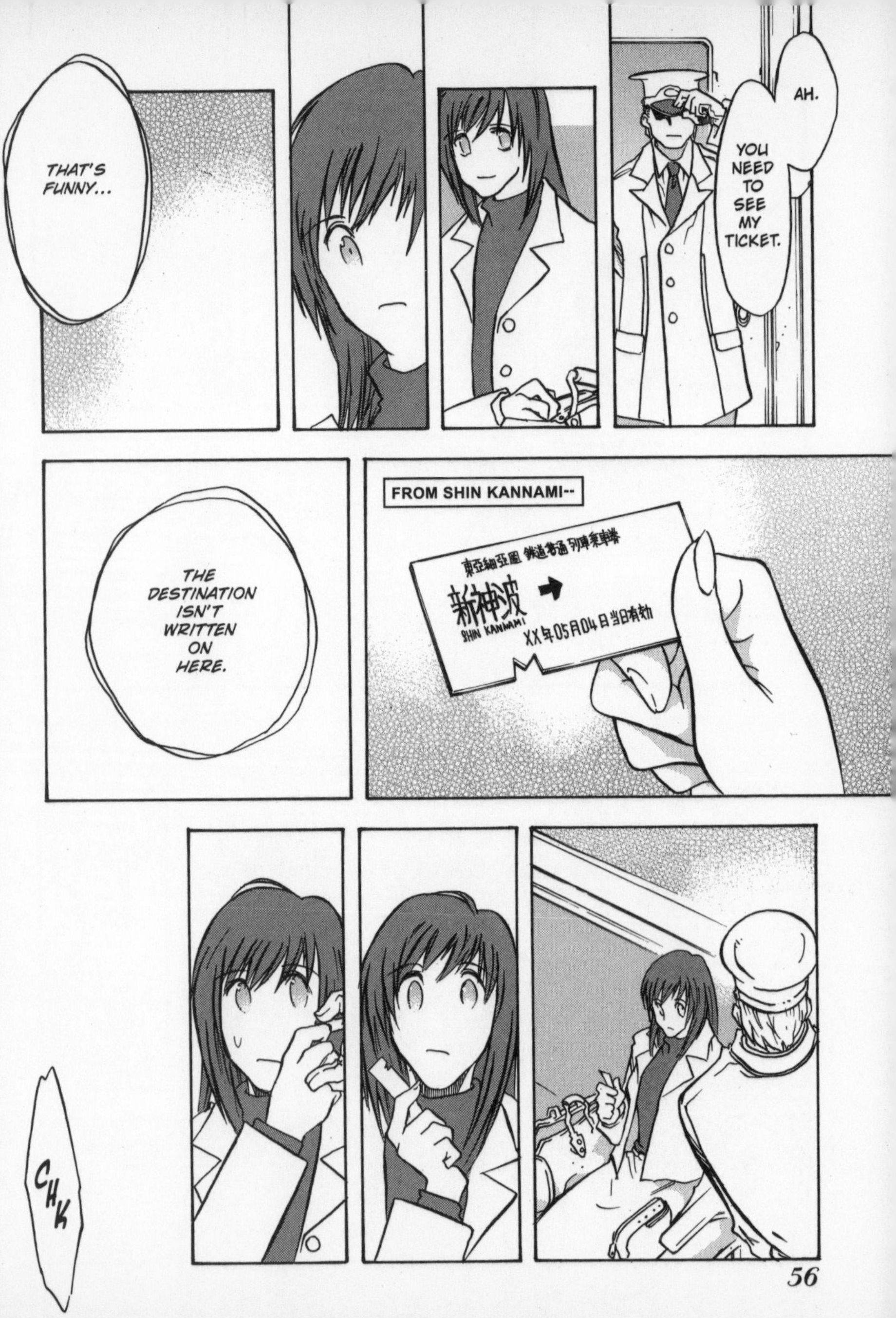
AH.
YOU NEED TO SEE MY TICKET.
THAT'S FUNNY...
FROM SHIN KANNAMI--
東亞細亞圏 鉄道普通 列車乗車券
新神波
SHIN KANNAMI
XX年05月04日当日有効
THE DESTINATION ISN'T WRITTEN ON HERE.
CHK

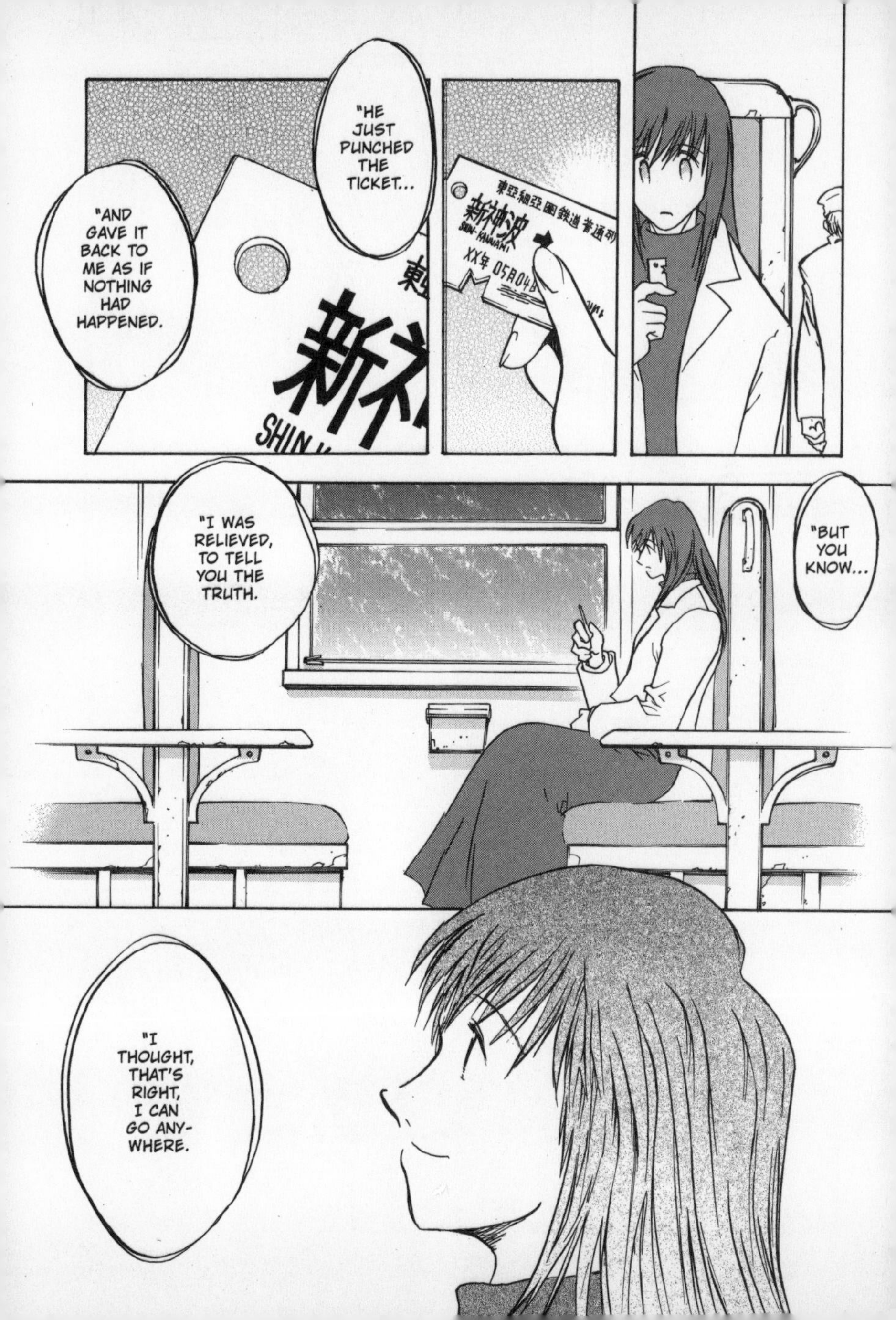
"HE JUST PUNCHED THE TICKET...
"AND GAVE IT BACK TO ME AS IF NOTHING HAD HAPPENED.
"I WAS RELIEVED, TO TELL YOU THE TRUTH.
"BUT YOU KNOW...
"I THOUGHT, THAT'S RIGHT, I CAN GO ANY-WHERE.

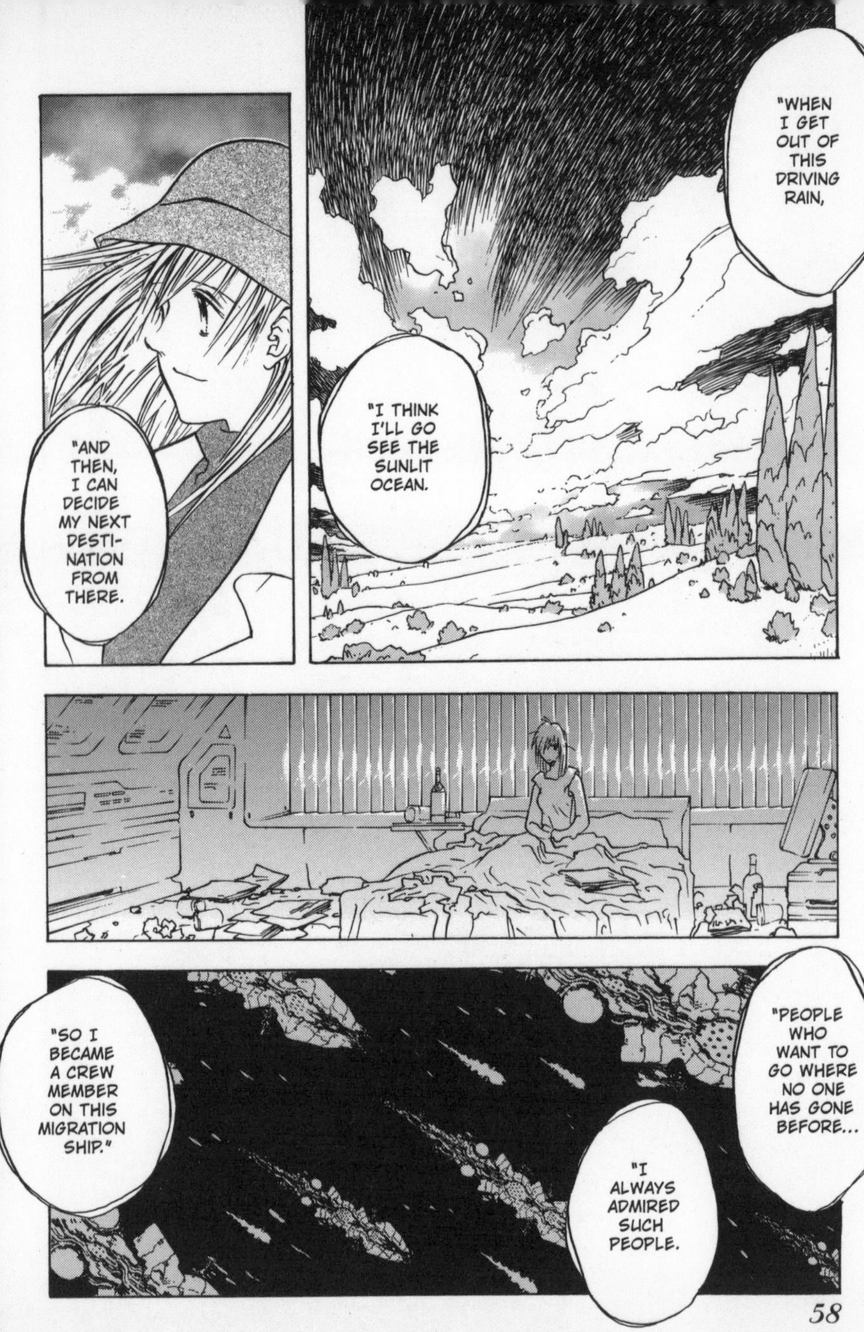
"WHEN I GET OUT OF THIS DRIVING RAIN,
"I THINK I'LL GO SEE THE SUNLIT OCEAN.
"AND THEN, I CAN DECIDE MY NEXT DESTINATION FROM THERE.
"PEOPLE WHO WANT TO GO WHERE NO ONE HAS GONE BEFORE...
"I ALWAYS ADMIRED SUCH PEOPLE.
"SO I BECAME A CREW MEMBER ON THIS MIGRATION SHIP."

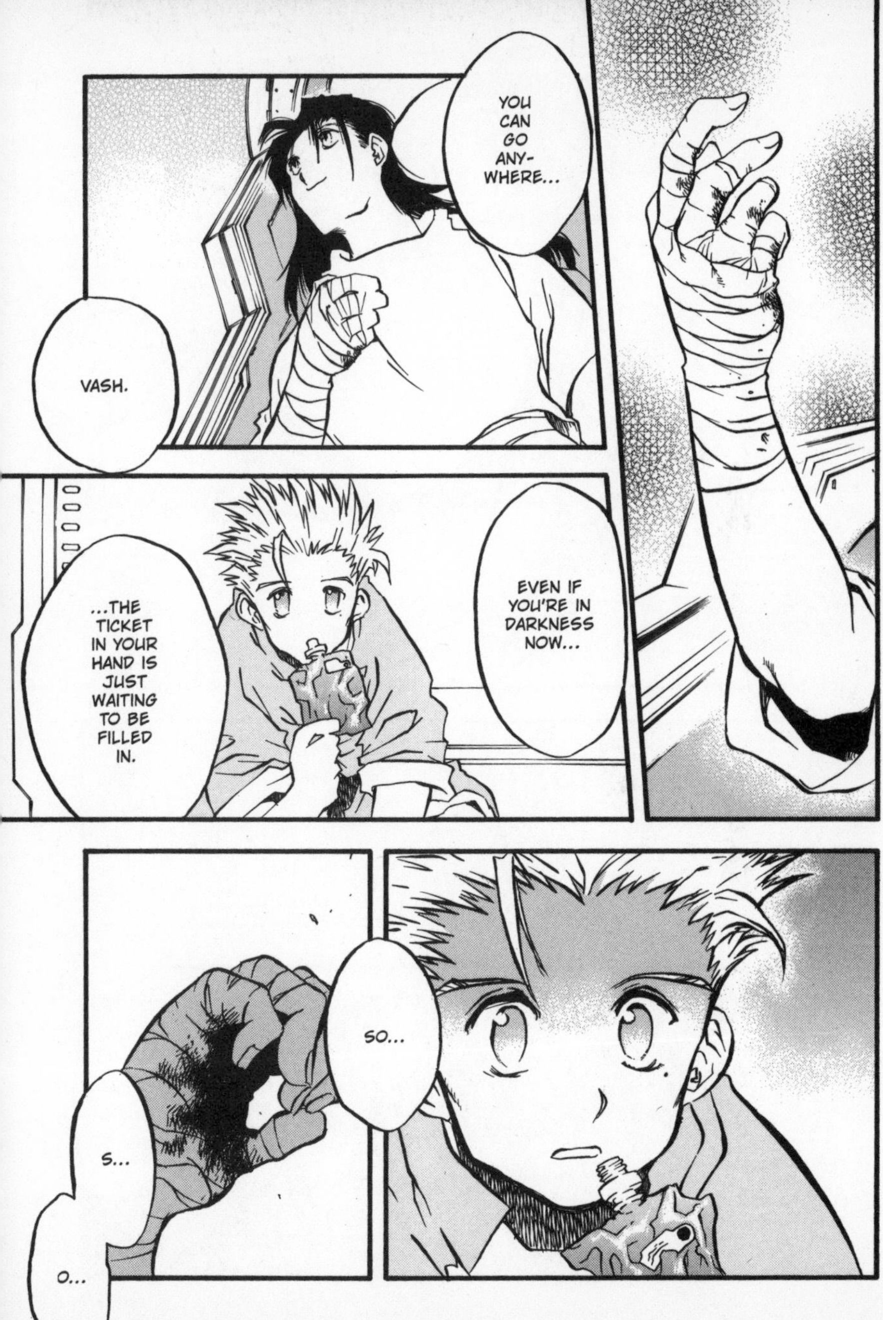
YOU CAN GO ANY-WHERE...
VASH.
EVEN IF YOU'RE IN DARKNESS NOW...
...THE TICKET IN YOUR HAND IS JUST WAITING TO BE FILLED IN.
SO...
S...
O...

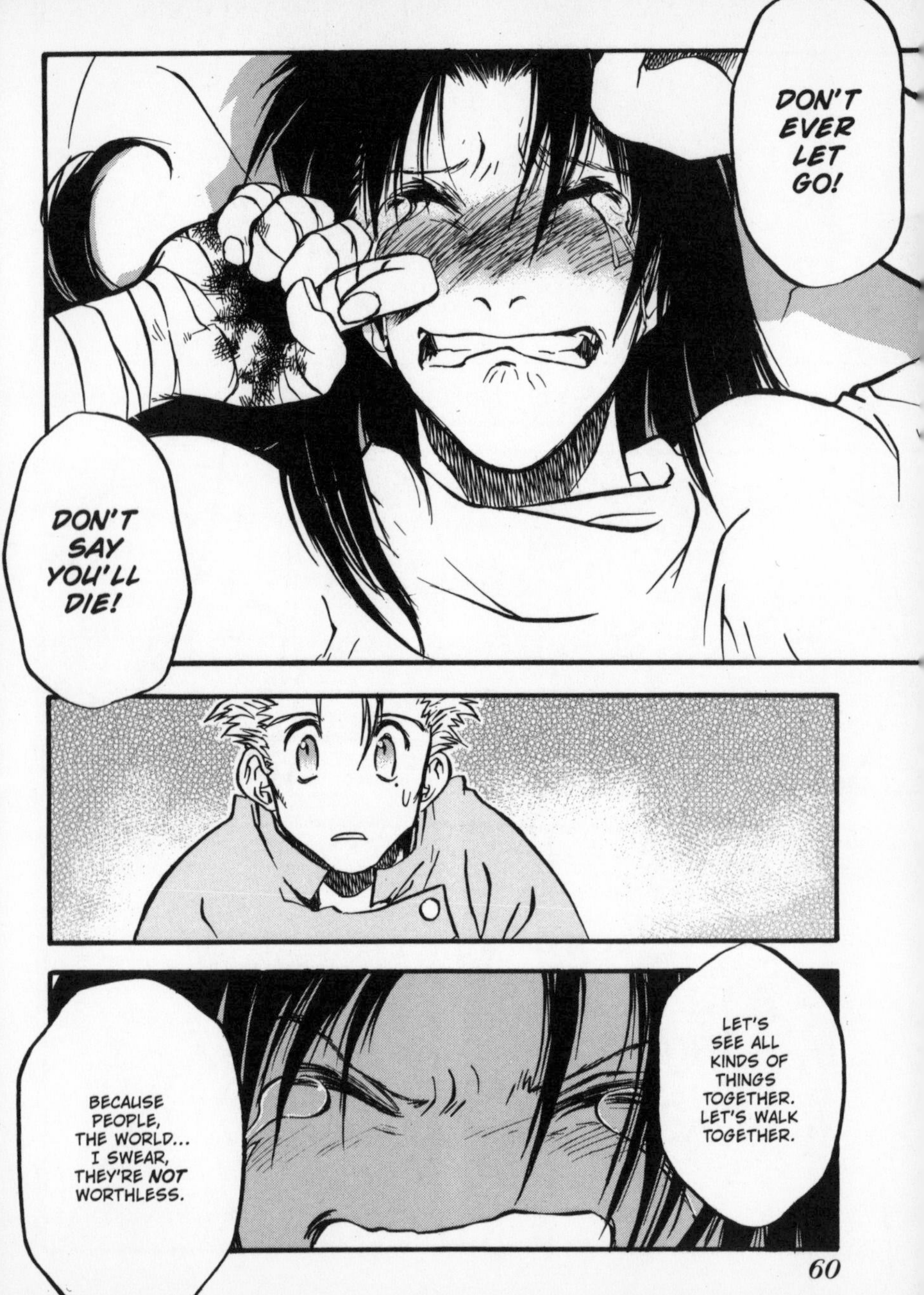
DON'T EVER LET GO!
DON'T SAY YOU'LL DIE!
LET'S SEE ALL KINDS OF THINGS TOGETHER. LET'S WALK TOGETHER.
BECAUSE PEOPLE, THE WORLD... I SWEAR, THEY'RE *NOT* WORTHLESS.

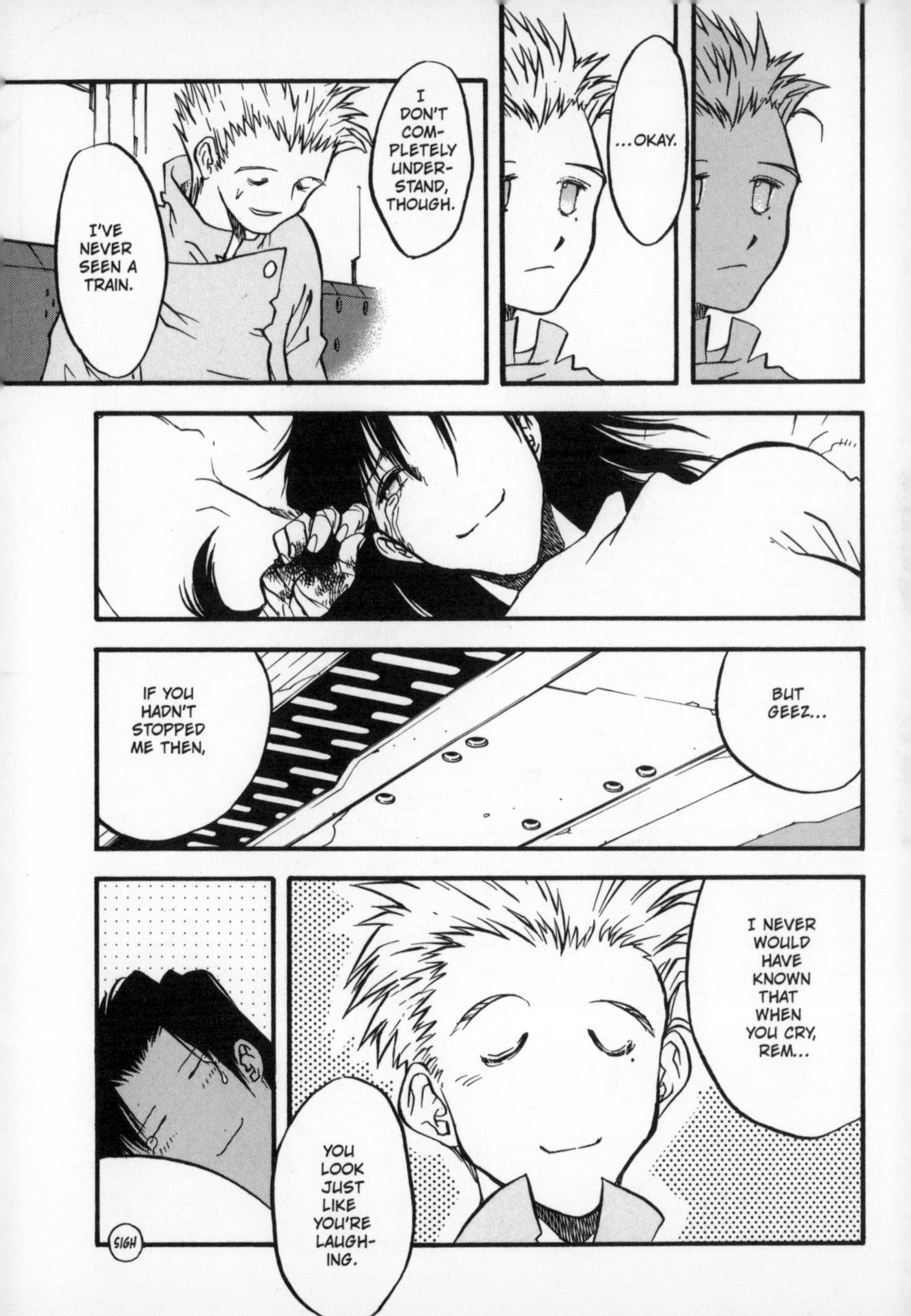
...OKAY.
I DON'T COMPLETELY UNDERSTAND, THOUGH.
I'VE NEVER SEEN A TRAIN.
BUT GEEZ...
IF YOU HADN'T STOPPED ME THEN,
I NEVER WOULD HAVE KNOWN THAT WHEN YOU CRY, REM...
YOU LOOK JUST LIKE YOU'RE LAUGHING.
SIGH

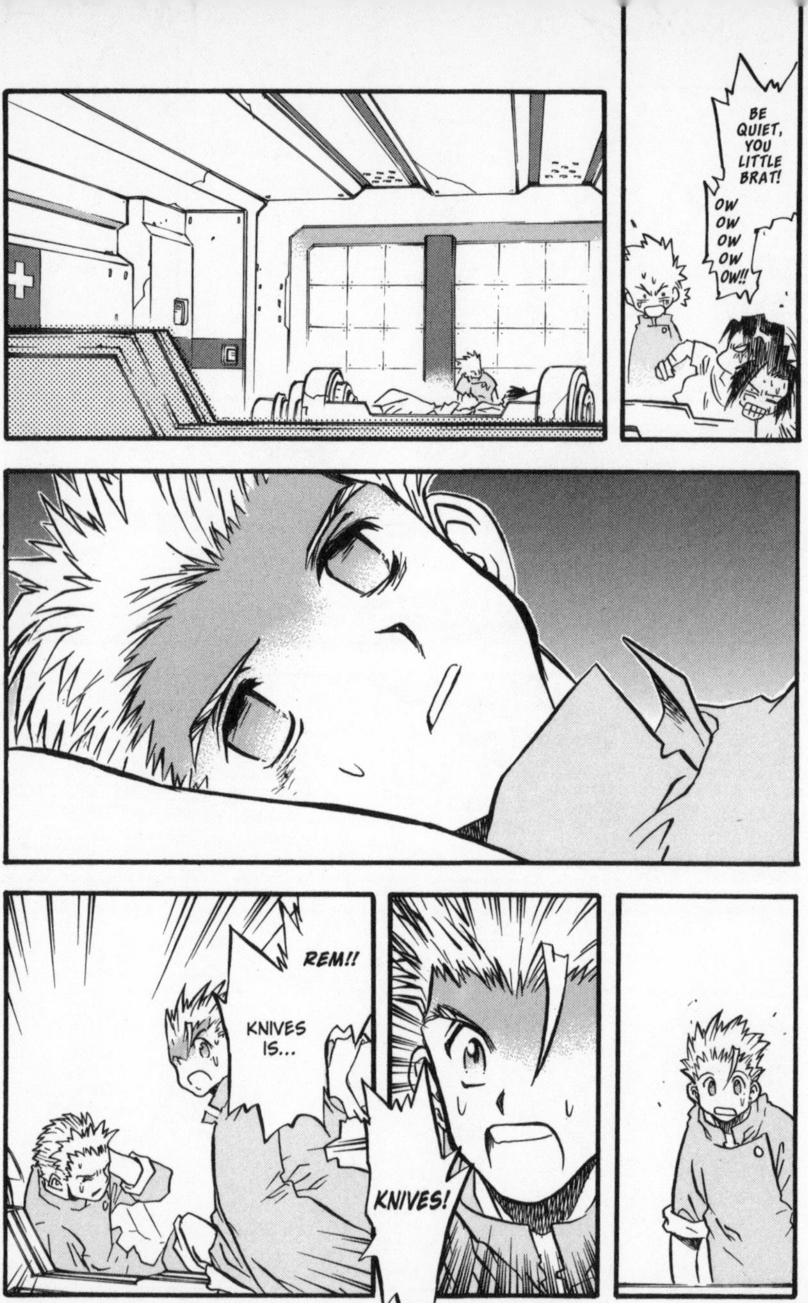
BE QUIET, YOU LITTLE BRAT!
OW OW OW OW OW!!
REM!!
KNIVES IS...
KNIVES!

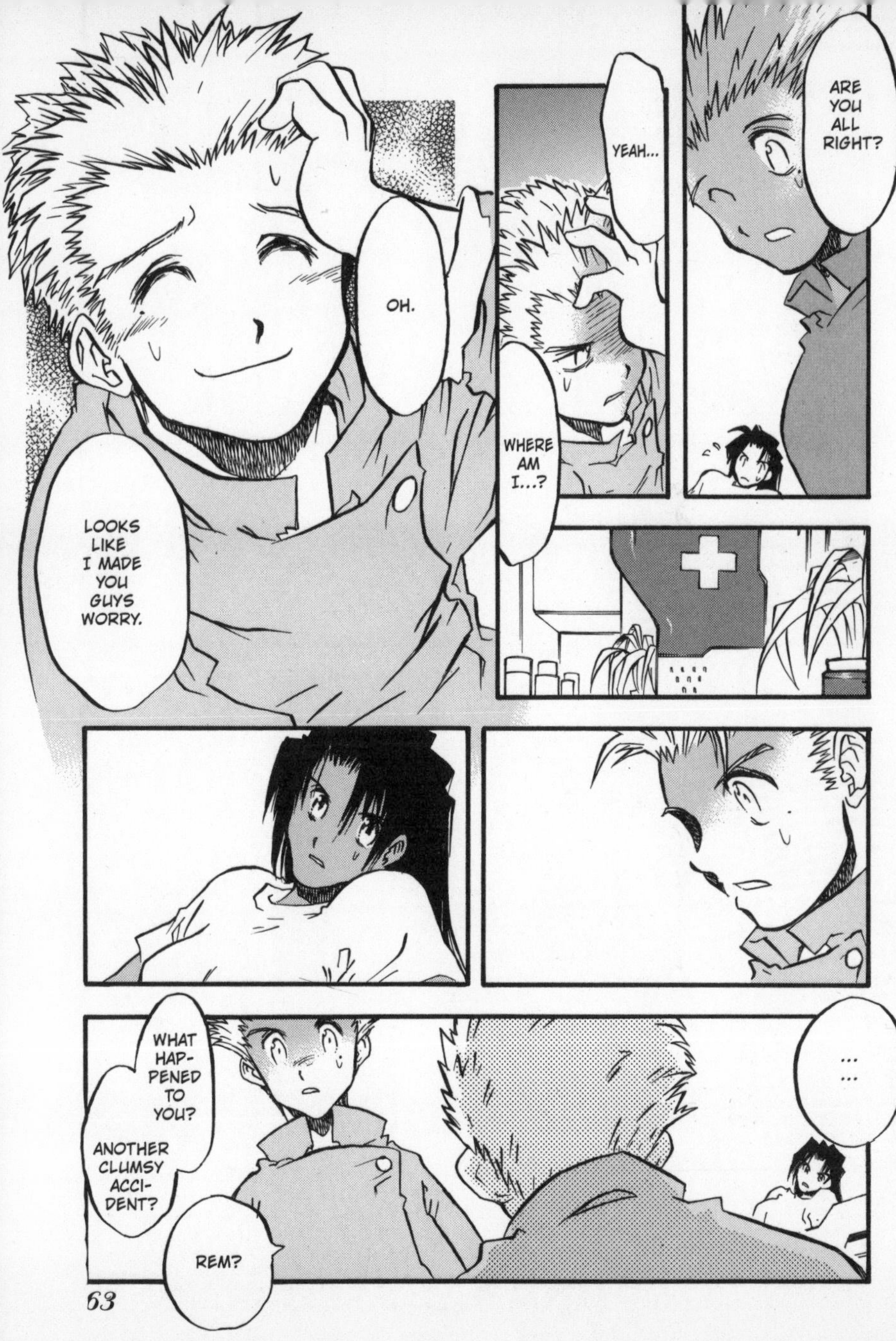
ARE YOU ALL RIGHT?
YEAH...
WHERE AM I...?
OH.
LOOKS LIKE I MADE YOU GUYS WORRY.
......
WHAT HAP-PENED TO YOU?
ANOTHER CLUMSY ACCI-DENT?
REM?

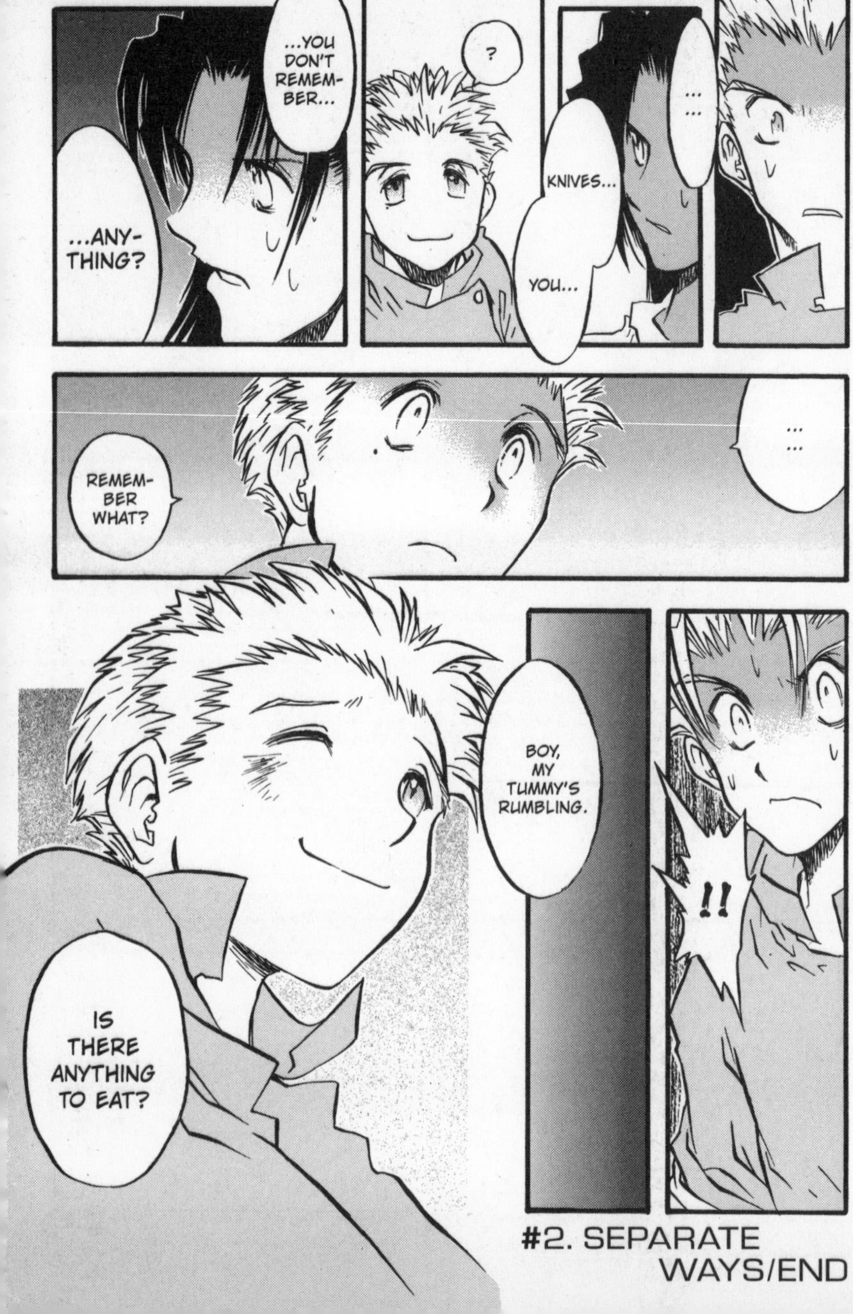
... ...
KNIVES...
YOU...
?
...YOU DON'T REMEMBER...
...ANYTHING?
... ...
REMEMBER WHAT?
!!
BOY, MY TUMMY'S RUMBLING.
IS THERE ANYTHING TO EAT?

#2. SEPARATE WAYS/END

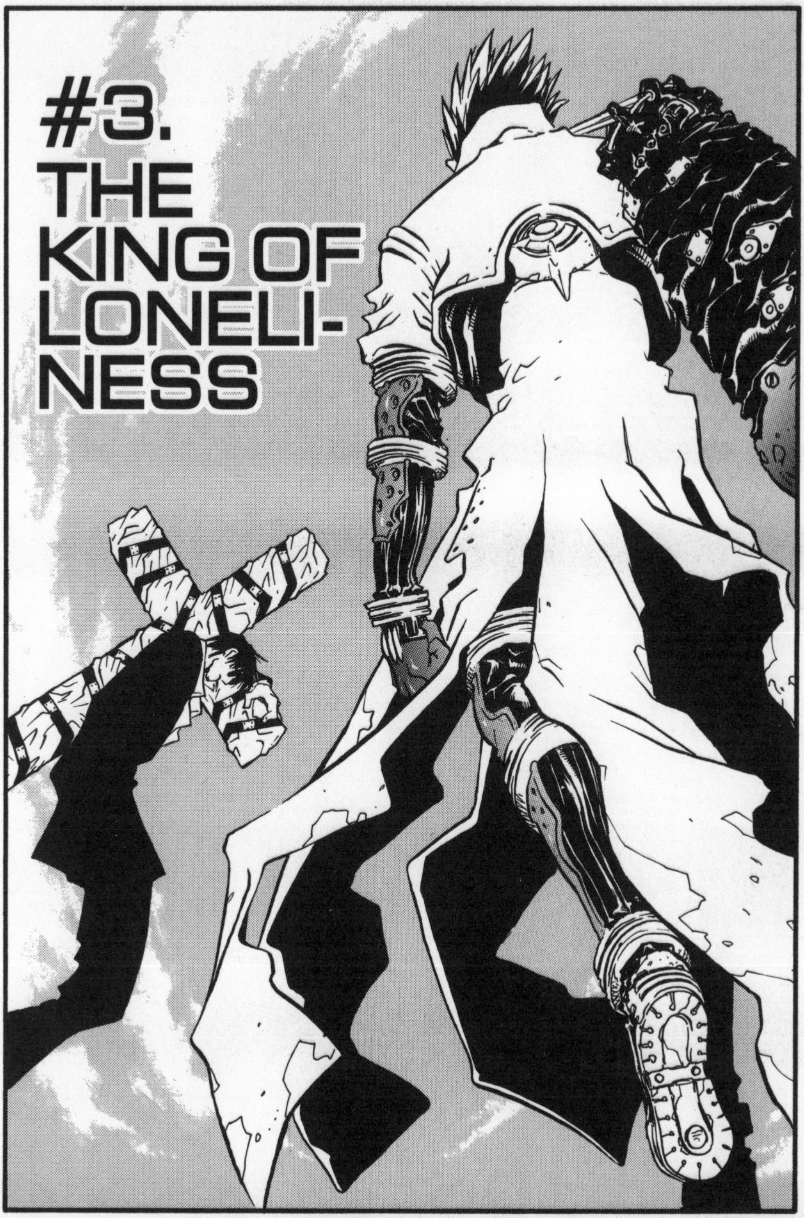
#3.
THE KING OF LONELI-NESS

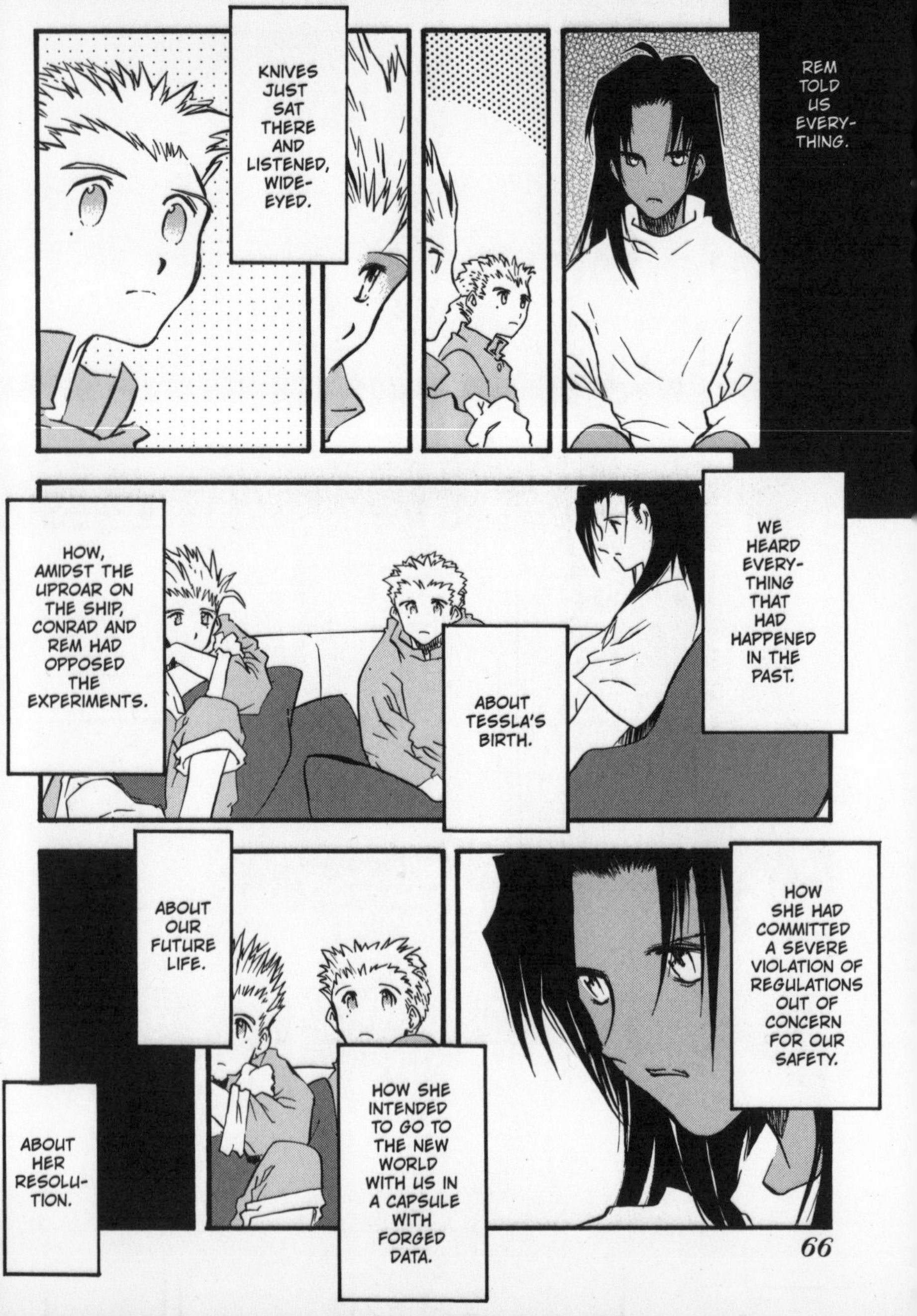
REM TOLD US EVERY-THING.
KNIVES JUST SAT THERE AND LISTENED, WIDE-EYED.
WE HEARD EVERY-THING THAT HAD HAPPENED IN THE PAST.
ABOUT TESSLA'S BIRTH.
HOW, AMIDST THE UPROAR ON THE SHIP, CONRAD AND REM HAD OPPOSED THE EXPERIMENTS.
HOW SHE HAD COMMITTED A SEVERE VIOLATION OF REGULATIONS OUT OF CONCERN FOR OUR SAFETY.
ABOUT OUR FUTURE LIFE.
HOW SHE INTENDED TO GO TO THE NEW WORLD WITH US IN A CAPSULE WITH FORGED DATA.
ABOUT HER RESOLU-TION.

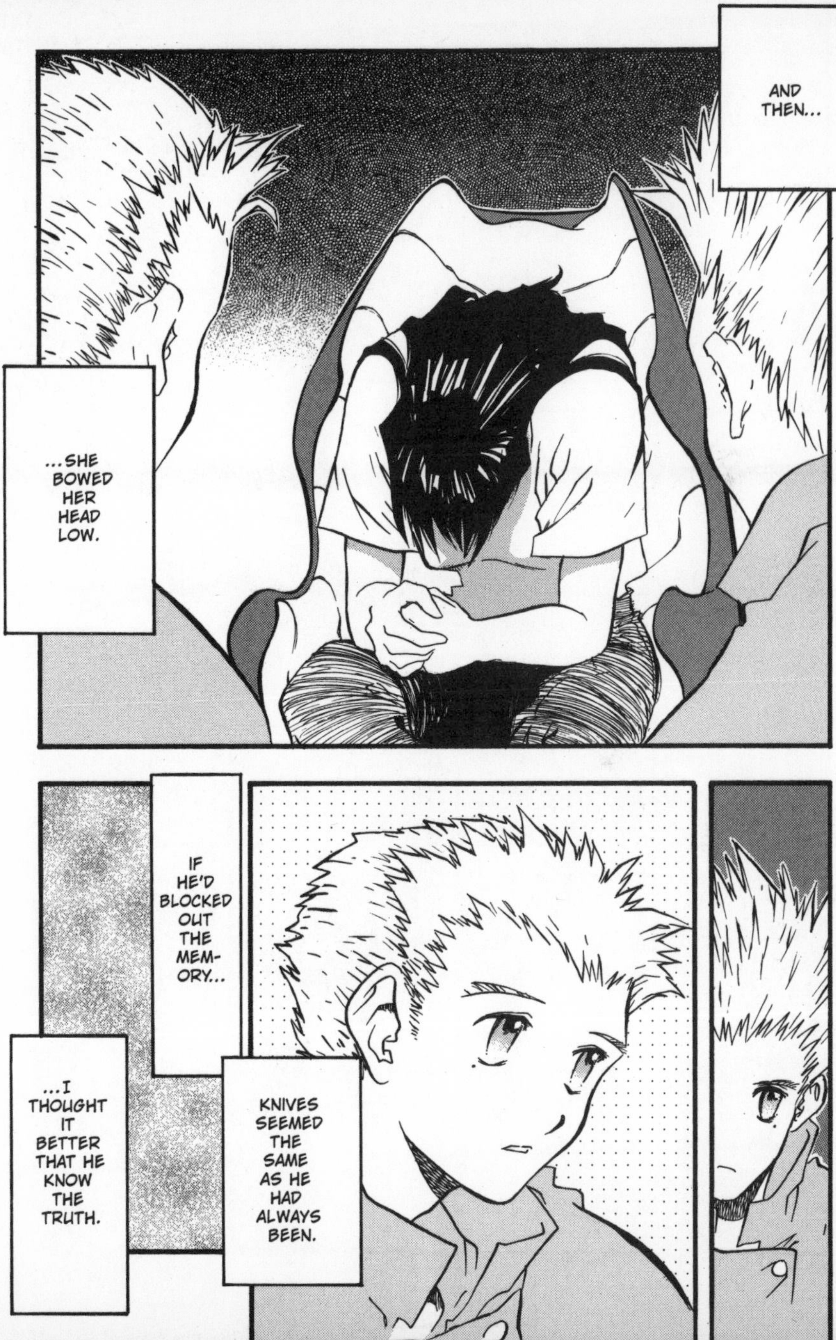
AND THEN...
...SHE BOWED HER HEAD LOW.
KNIVES SEEMED THE SAME AS HE HAD ALWAYS BEEN.
IF HE'D BLOCKED OUT THE MEM-ORY...
...I THOUGHT IT BETTER THAT HE KNOW THE TRUTH.

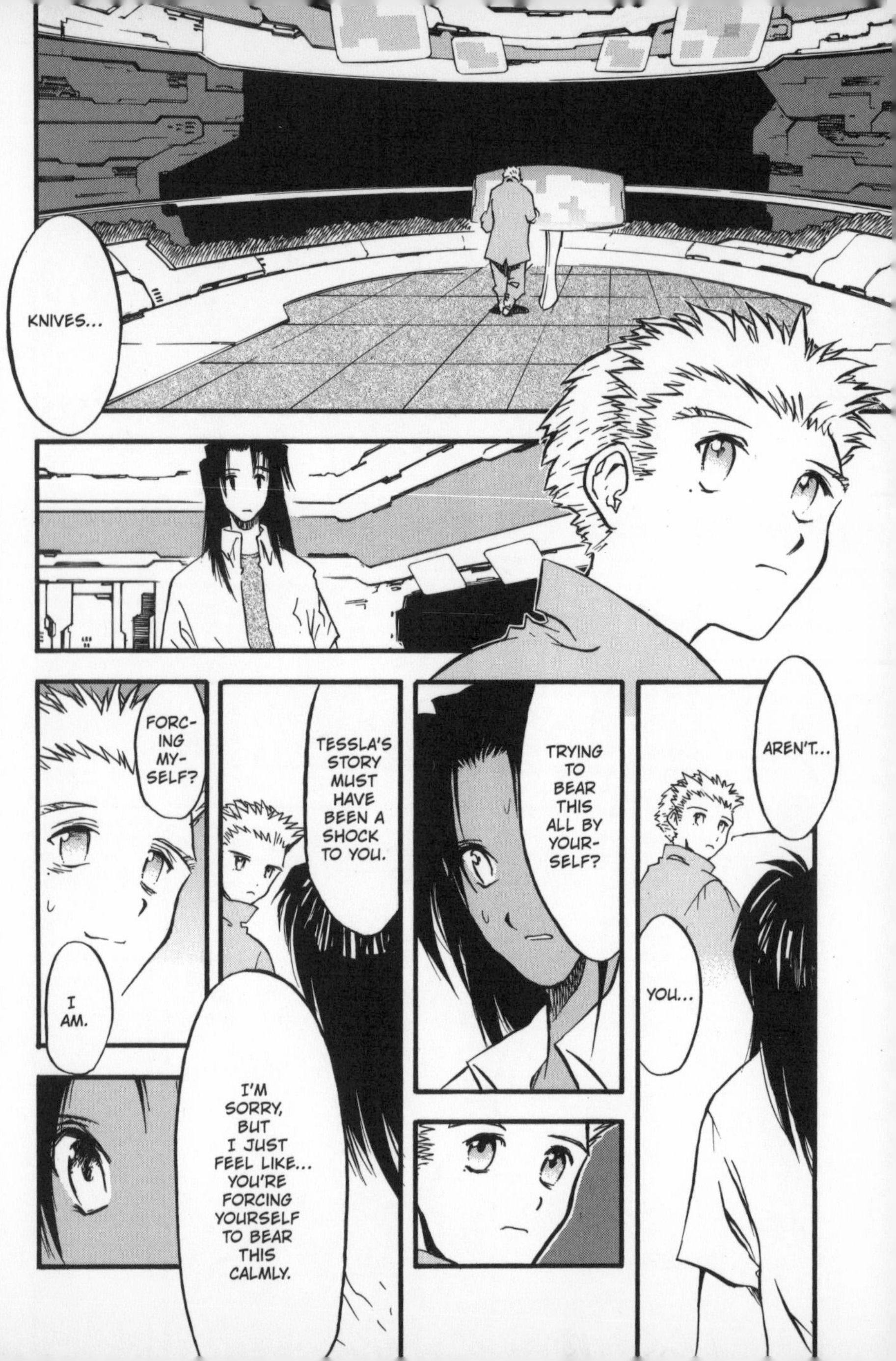
KNIVES...
AREN'T...
YOU...
TRYING TO BEAR THIS ALL BY YOURSELF?
TESSLA'S STORY MUST HAVE BEEN A SHOCK TO YOU.
FORCING MYSELF?
I AM.
I'M SORRY, BUT I JUST FEEL LIKE... YOU'RE FORCING YOURSELF TO BEAR THIS CALMLY.

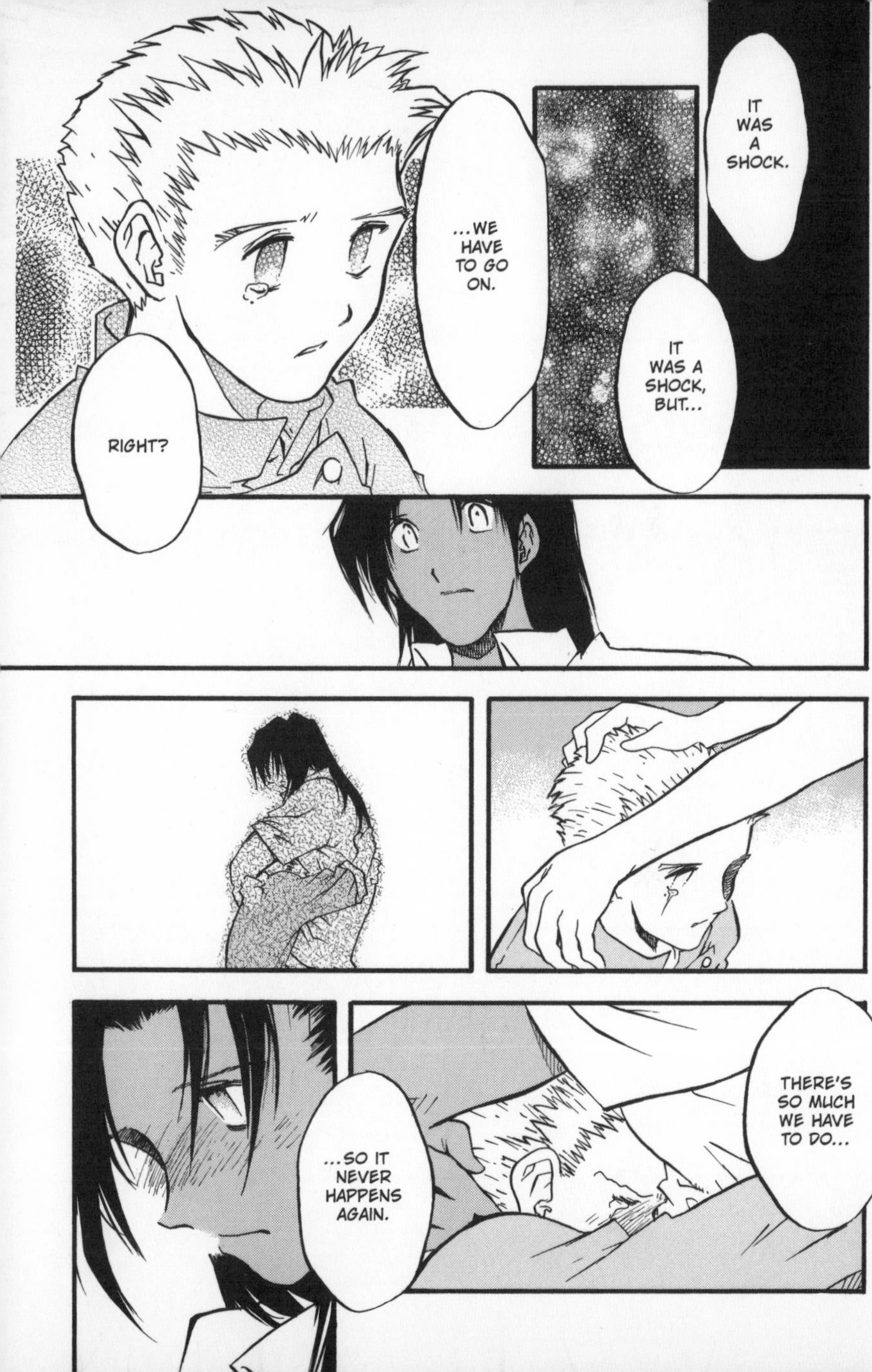
IT WAS A SHOCK.
IT WAS A SHOCK, BUT...
...WE HAVE TO GO ON.
RIGHT?
THERE'S SO MUCH WE HAVE TO DO...
...SO IT NEVER HAPPENS AGAIN.

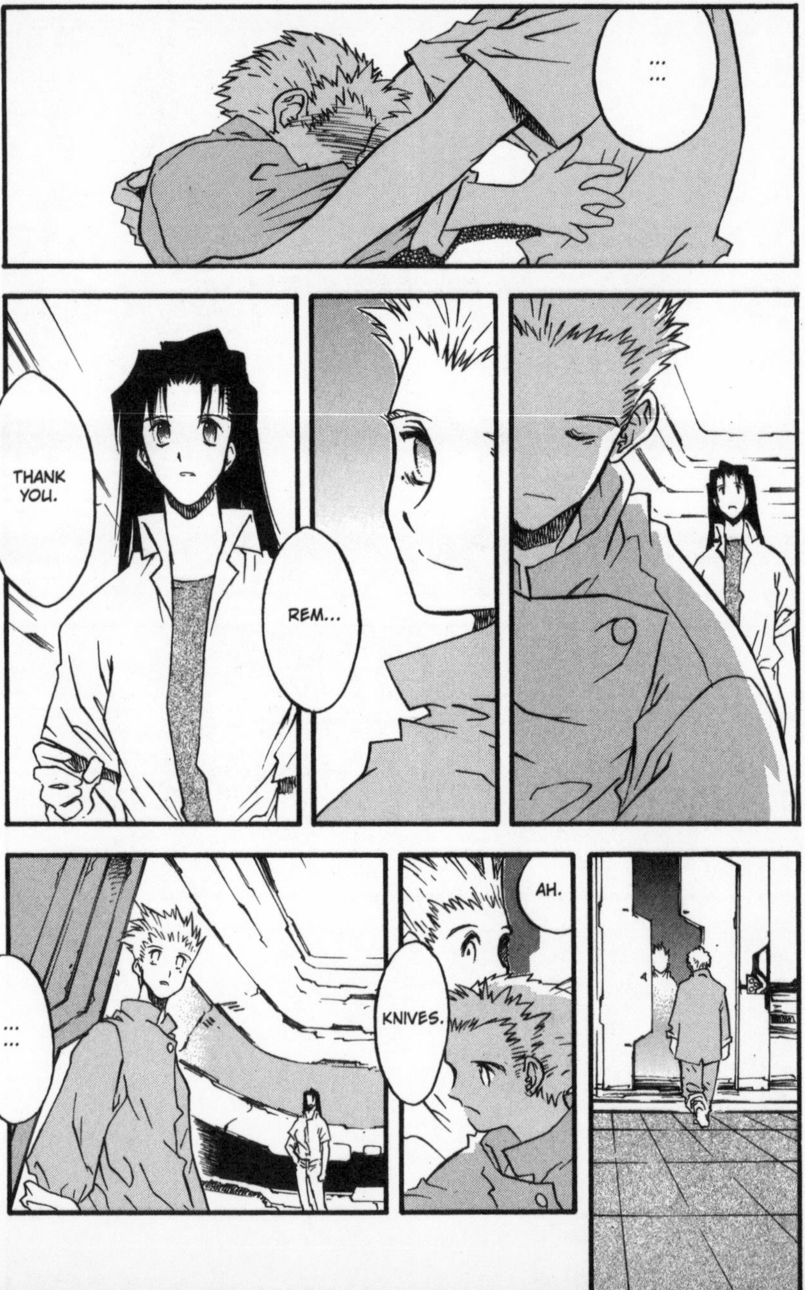
...
...
REM...
THANK YOU.
AH.
KNIVES.
...
...

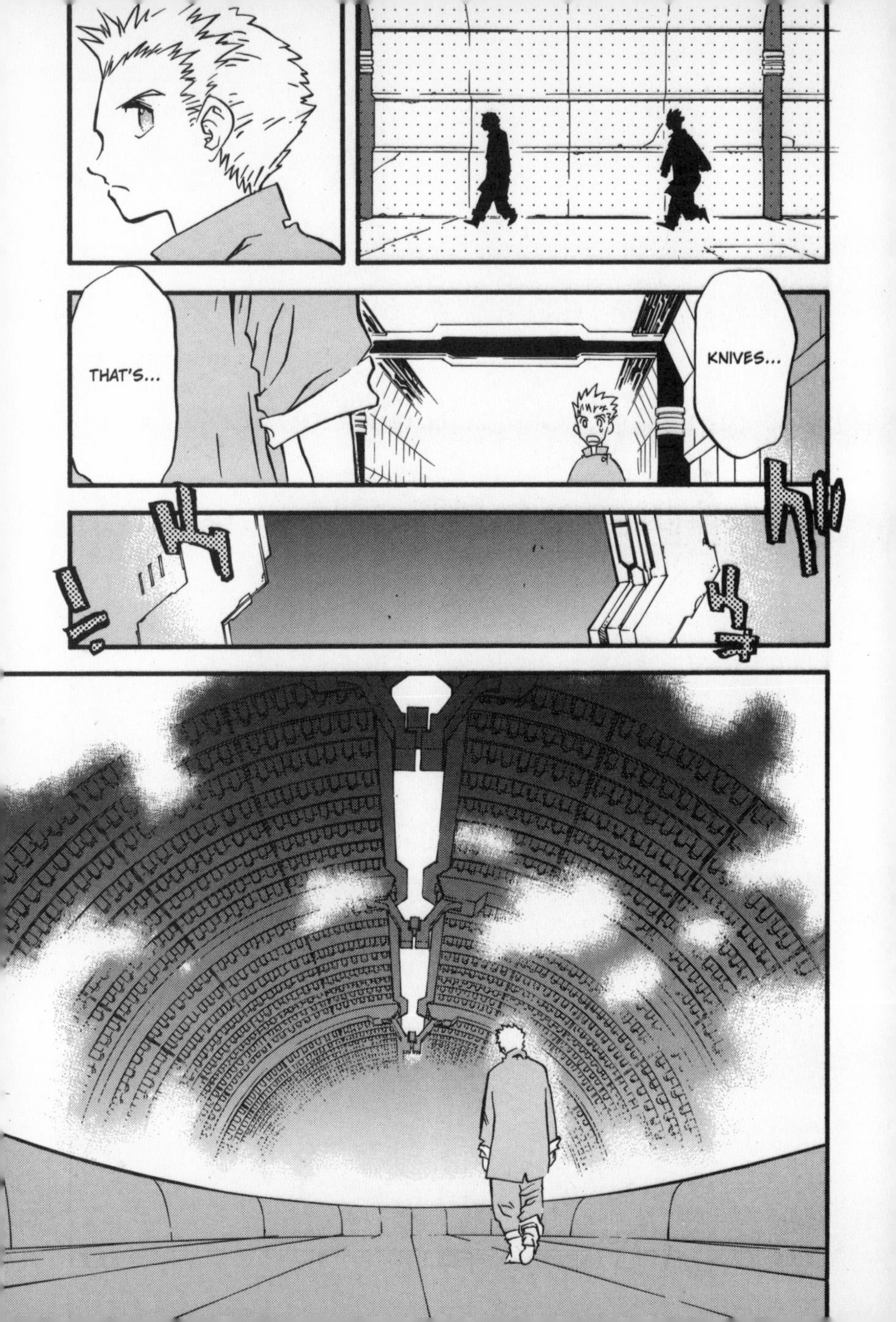
KNIVES...
THAT'S...

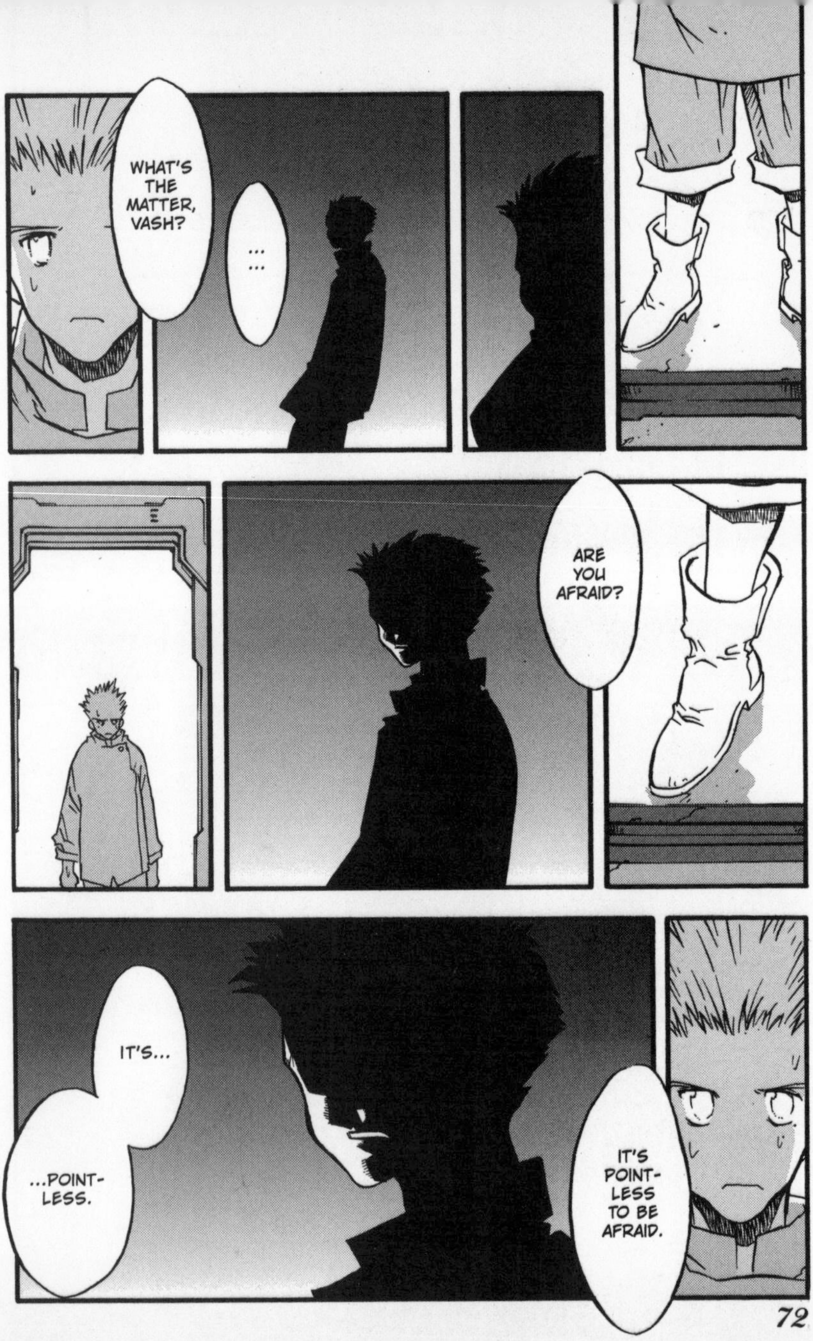
......
WHAT'S THE MATTER, VASH?
ARE YOU AFRAID?
IT'S POINTLESS TO BE AFRAID.
IT'S...
...POINTLESS.

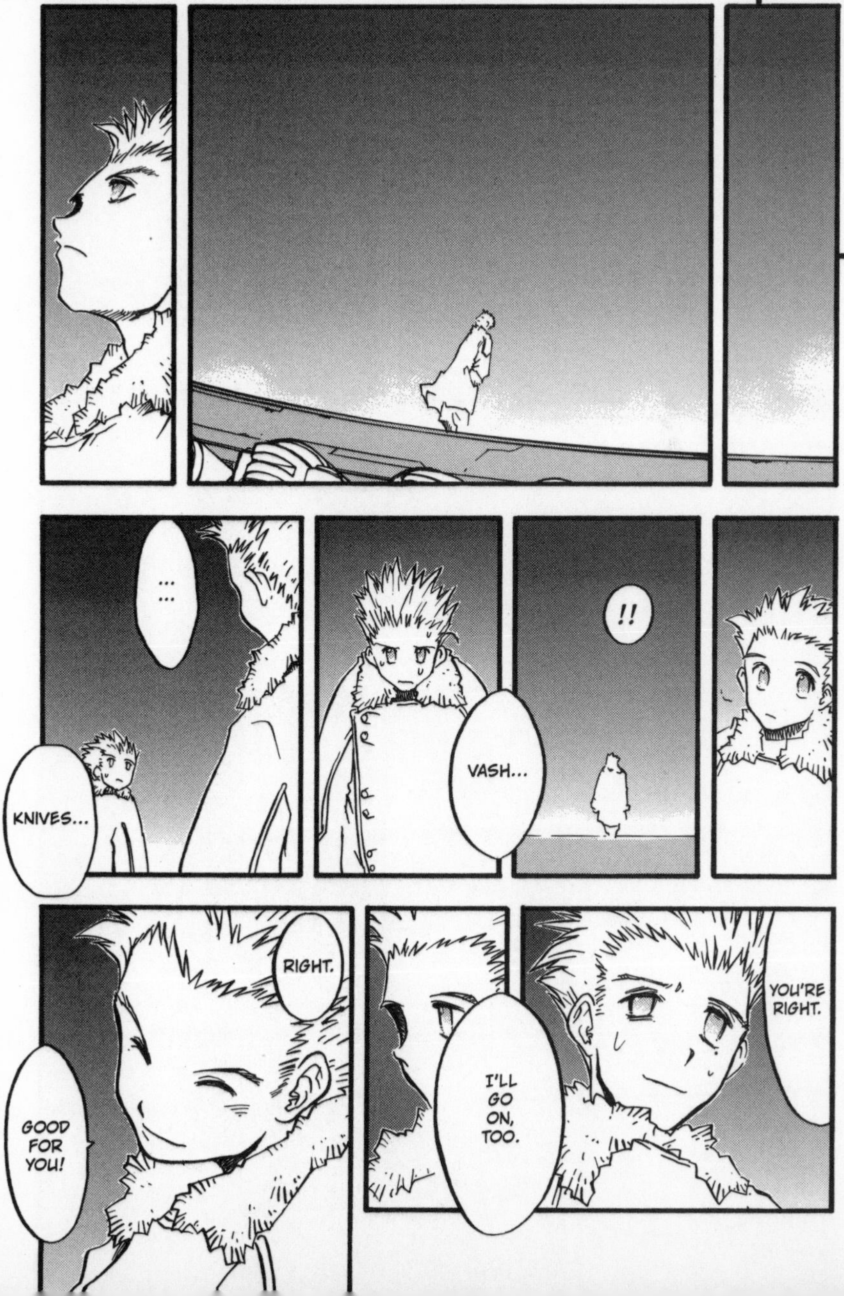
!!
VASH...
……
KNIVES...
YOU'RE RIGHT.
I'LL GO ON, TOO.
RIGHT.
GOOD FOR YOU!

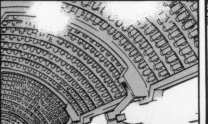

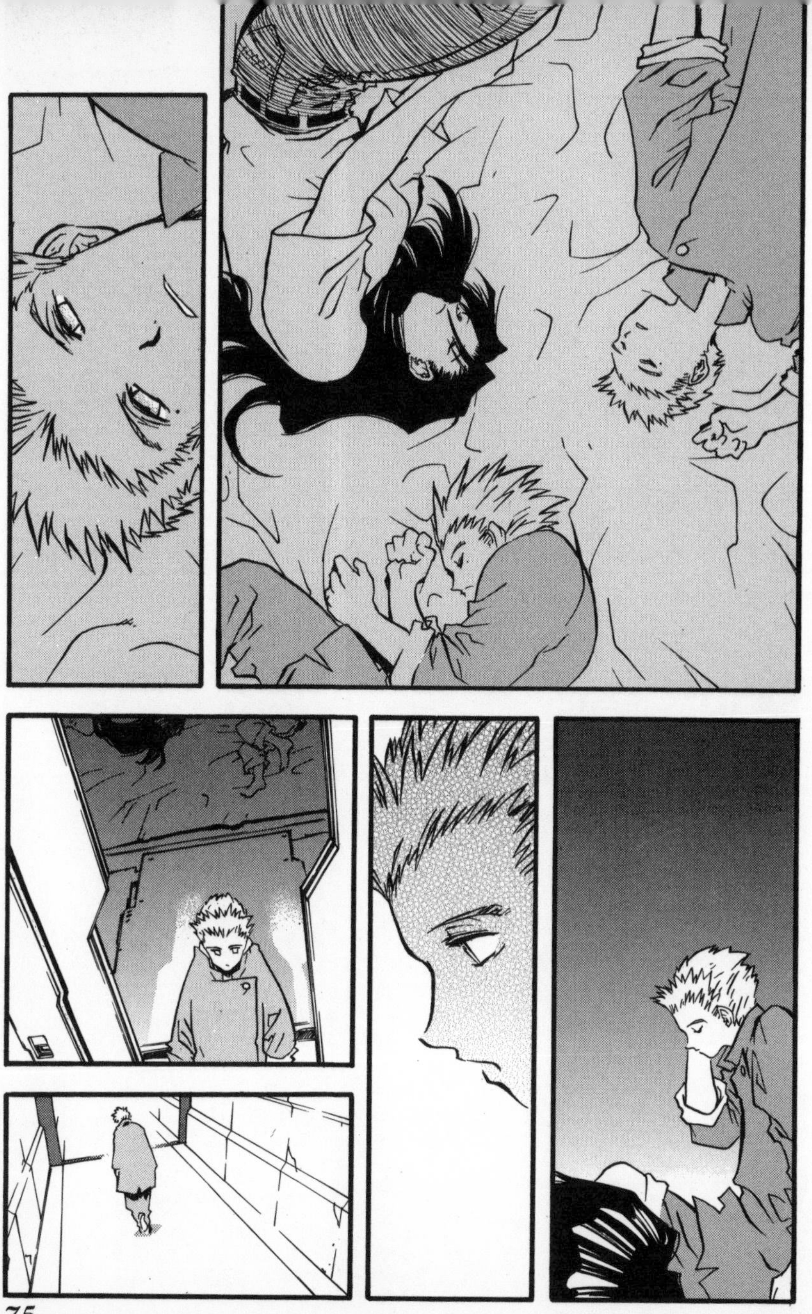

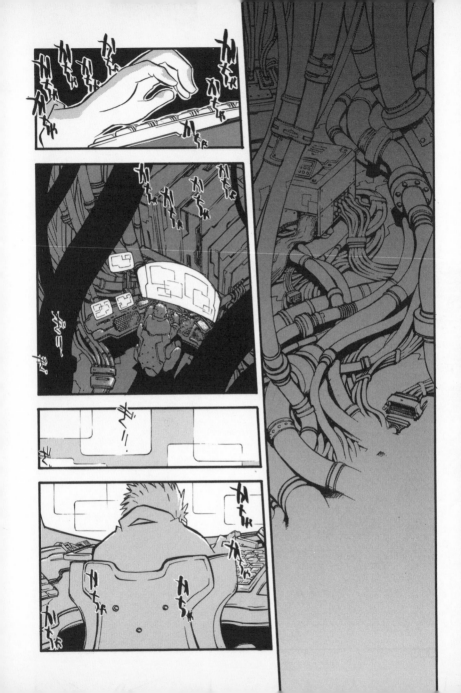

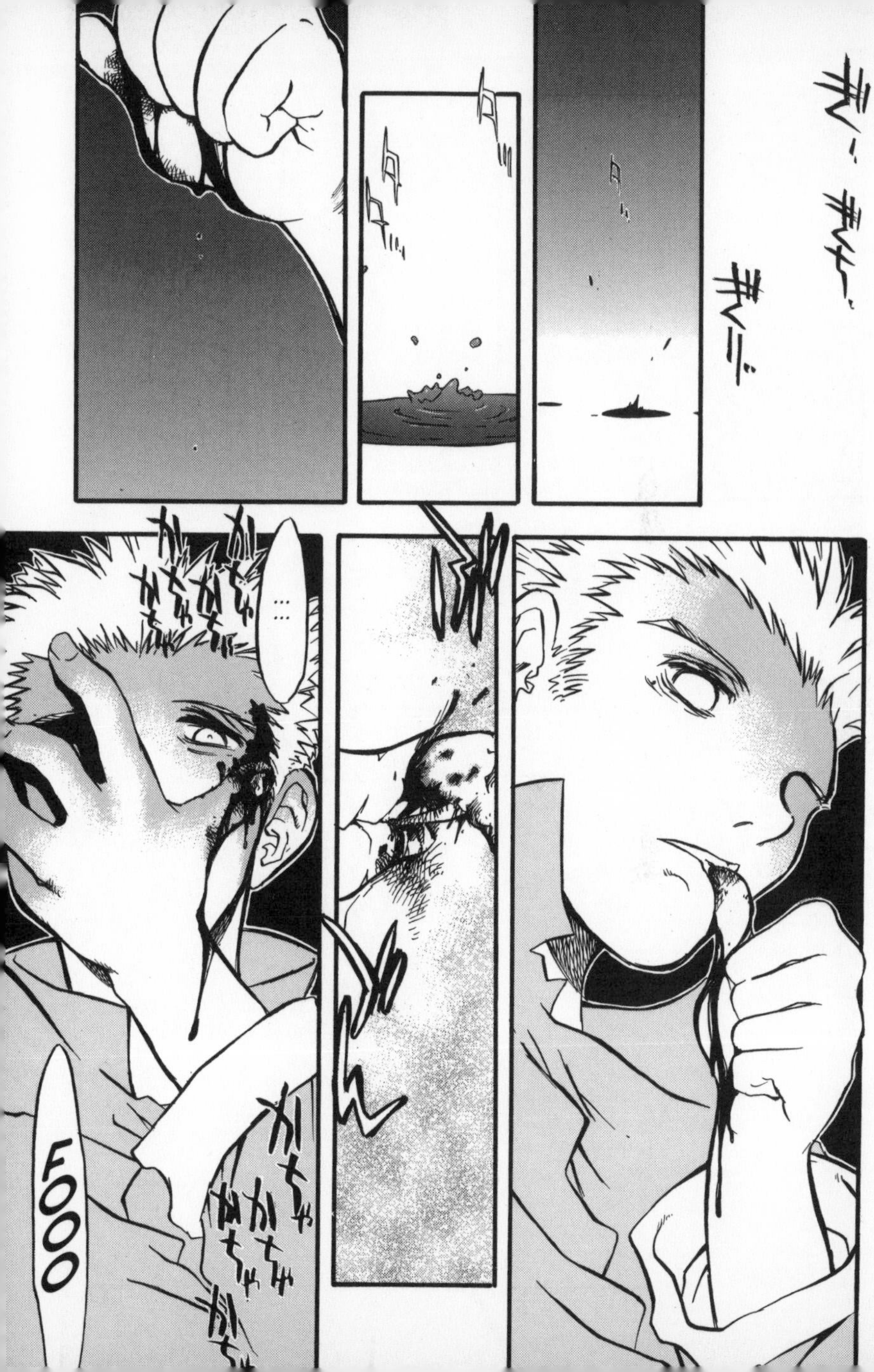
……
かちゃかちゃ
かちゃかちゃ
FOOO
かちゃかちゃ
かちゃかちゃ

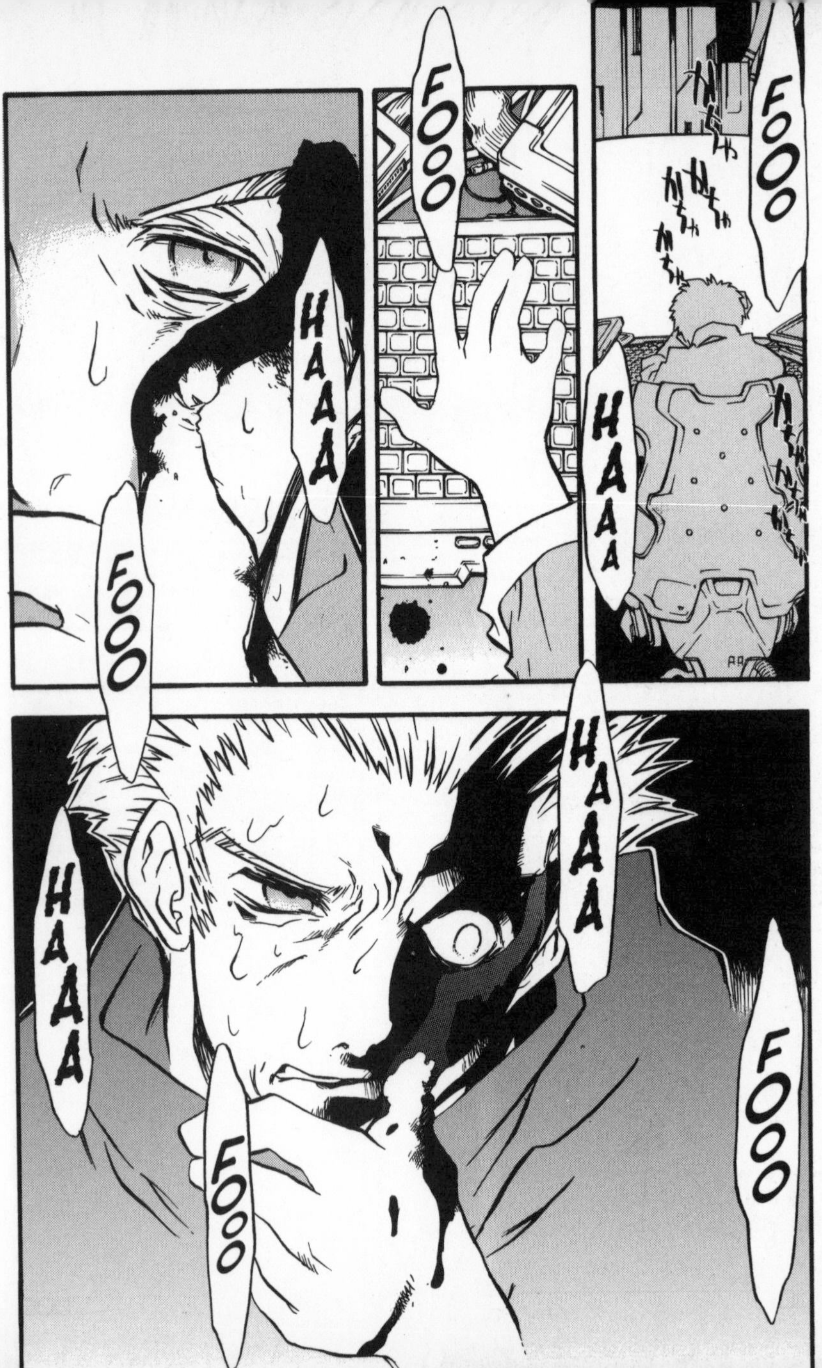
FOOO
HAAAA
FOOO
HAAA
FOOO
HAAAA
FOOO
HAAA
FOOO

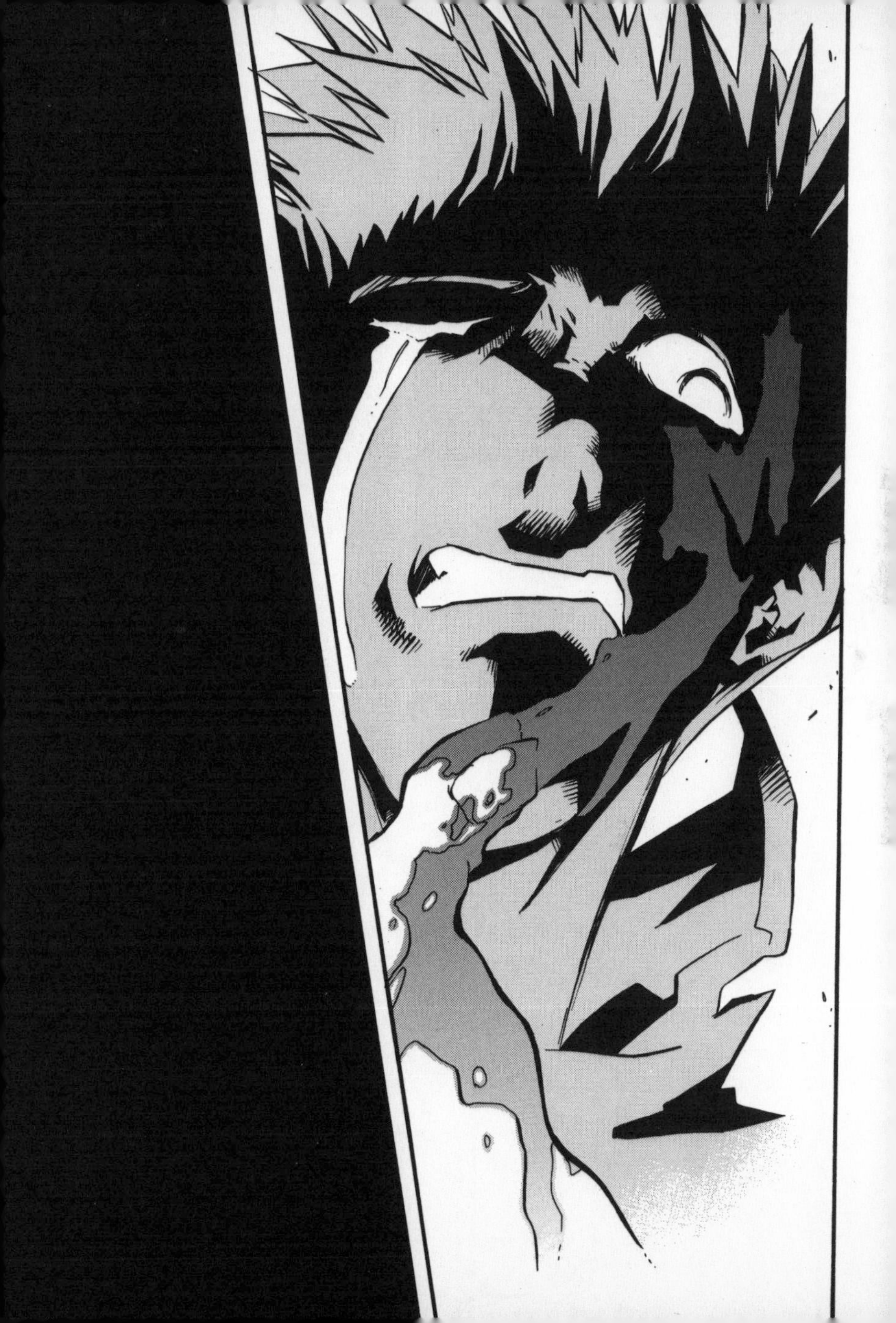

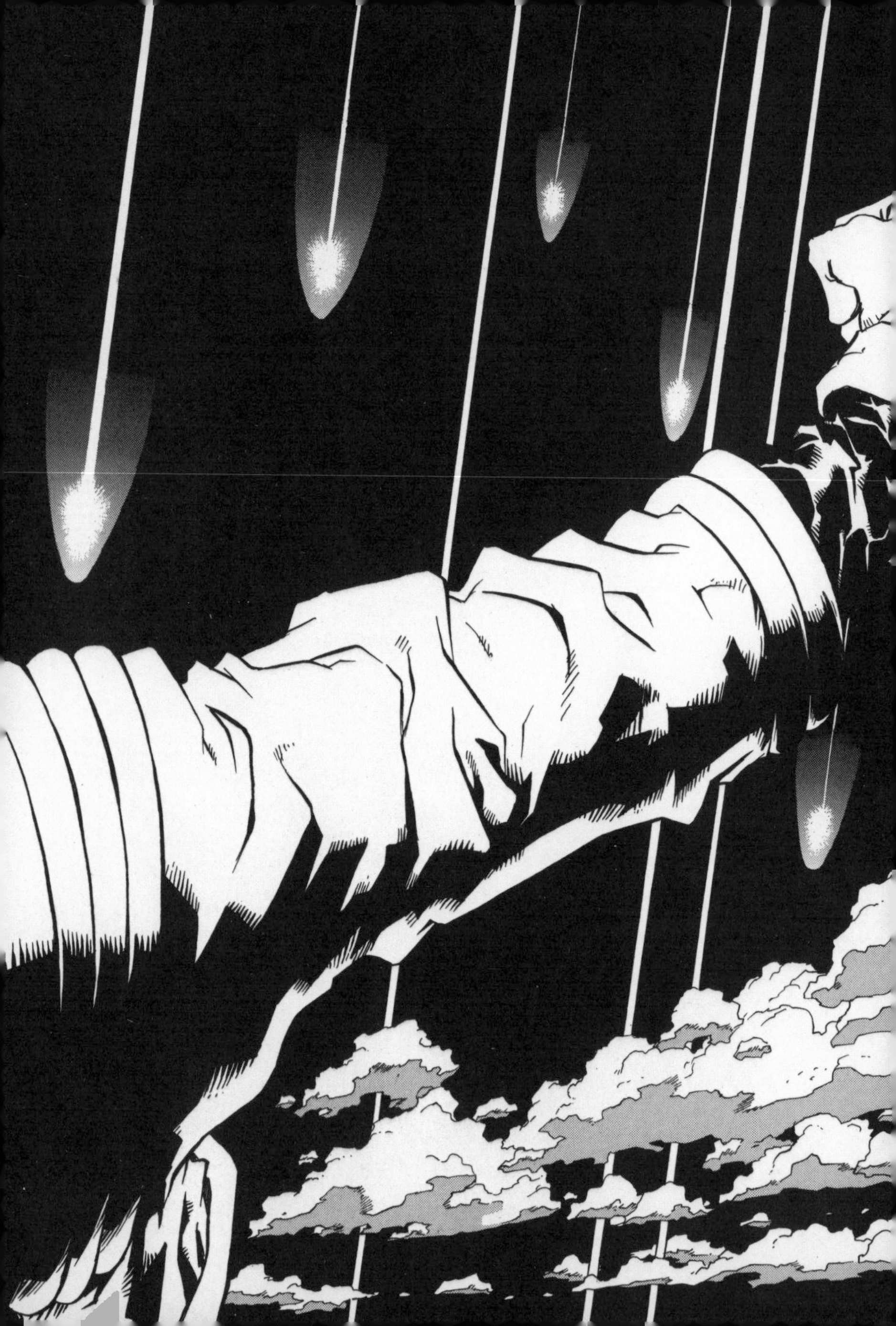

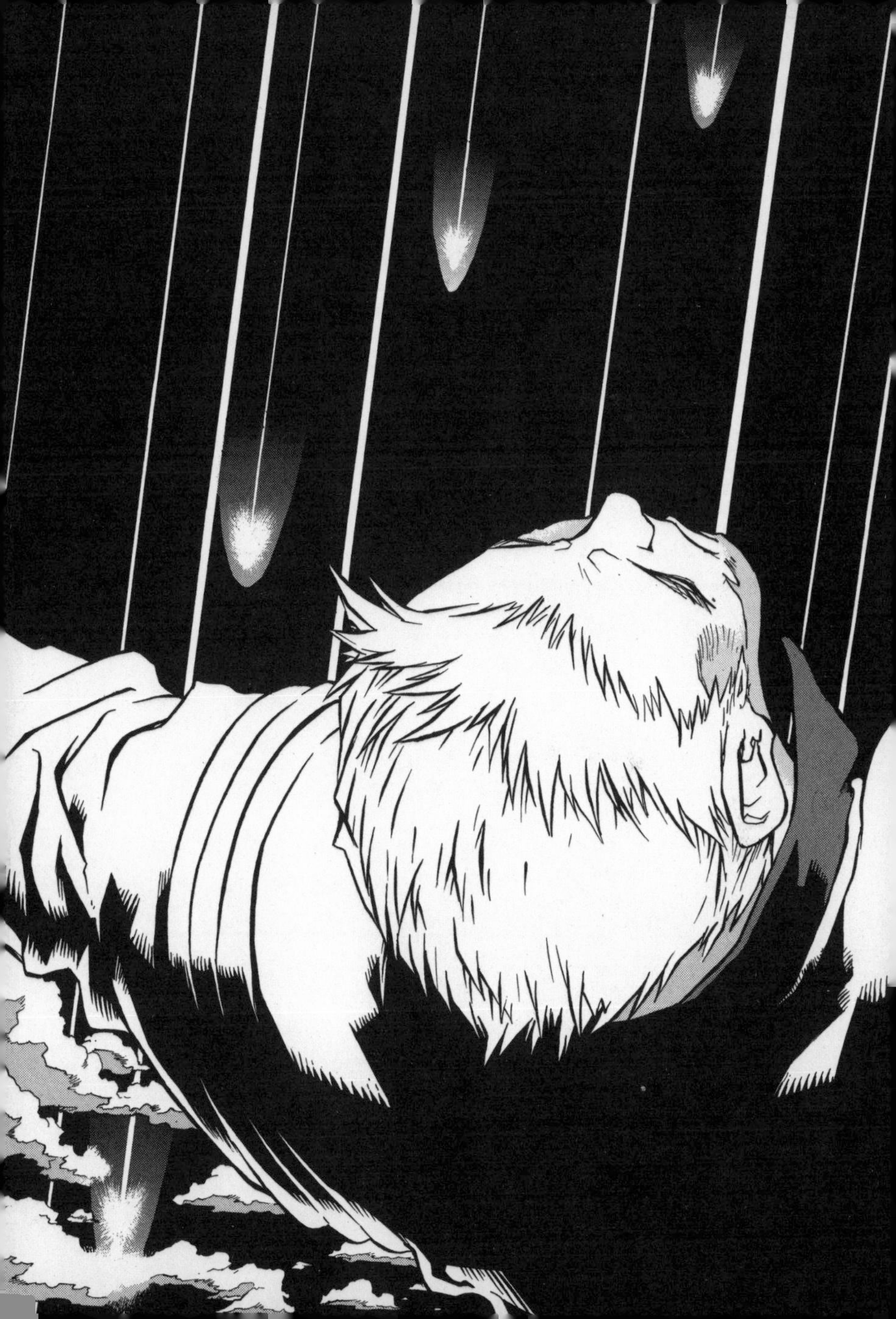

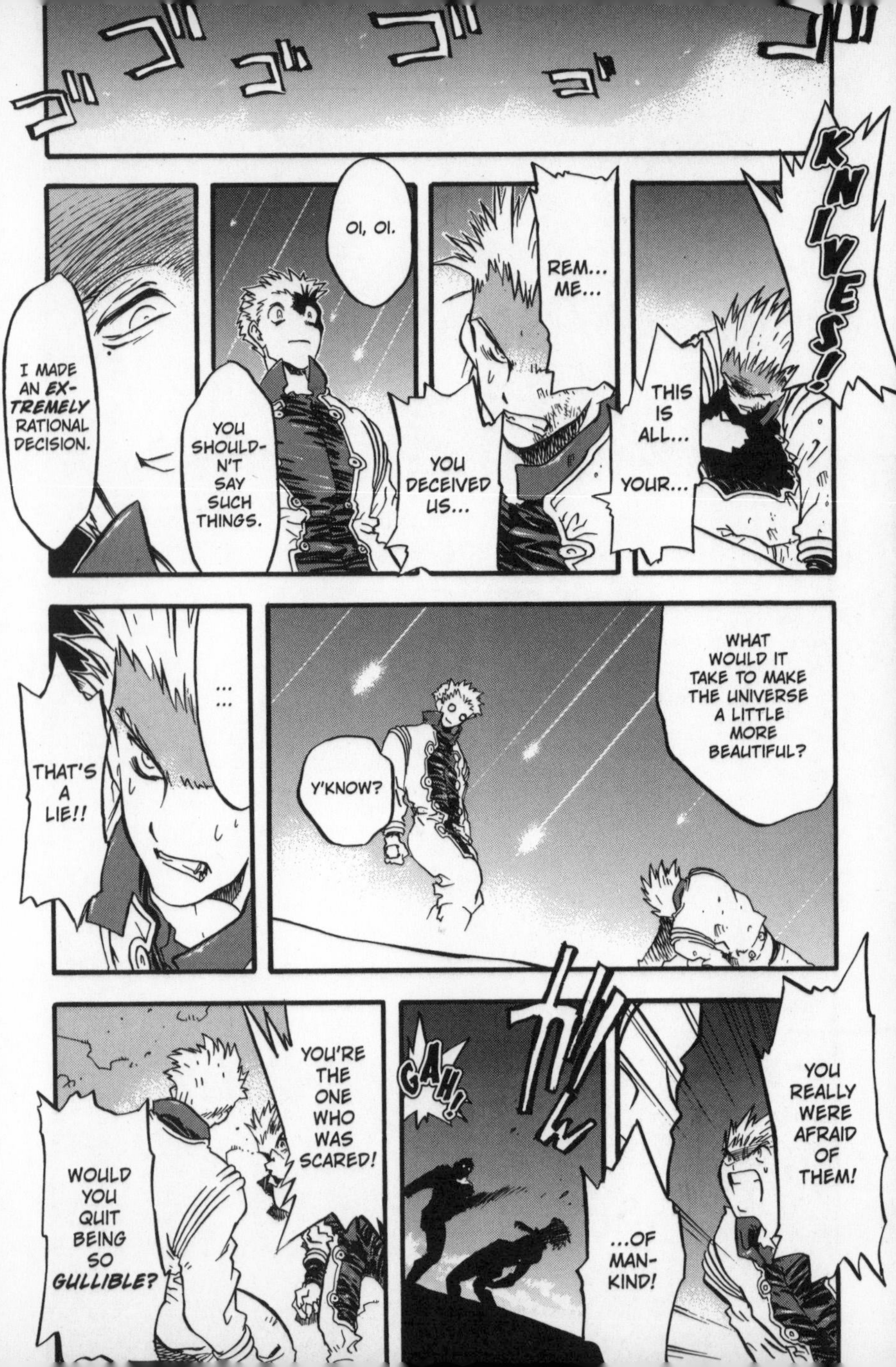
KNIVES!
THIS IS ALL... YOUR...
REM... ME...
YOU DECEIVED US...
OI, OI.
YOU SHOULDN'T SAY SUCH THINGS.
I MADE AN *EXTREMELY* RATIONAL DECISION.
WHAT WOULD IT TAKE TO MAKE THE UNIVERSE A LITTLE MORE BEAUTIFUL?
Y'KNOW?
......
THAT'S A LIE!!
YOU REALLY WERE AFRAID OF THEM!
GAH!
...OF MANKIND!
YOU'RE THE ONE WHO WAS SCARED!
WOULD YOU QUIT BEING SO *GULLIBLE*?

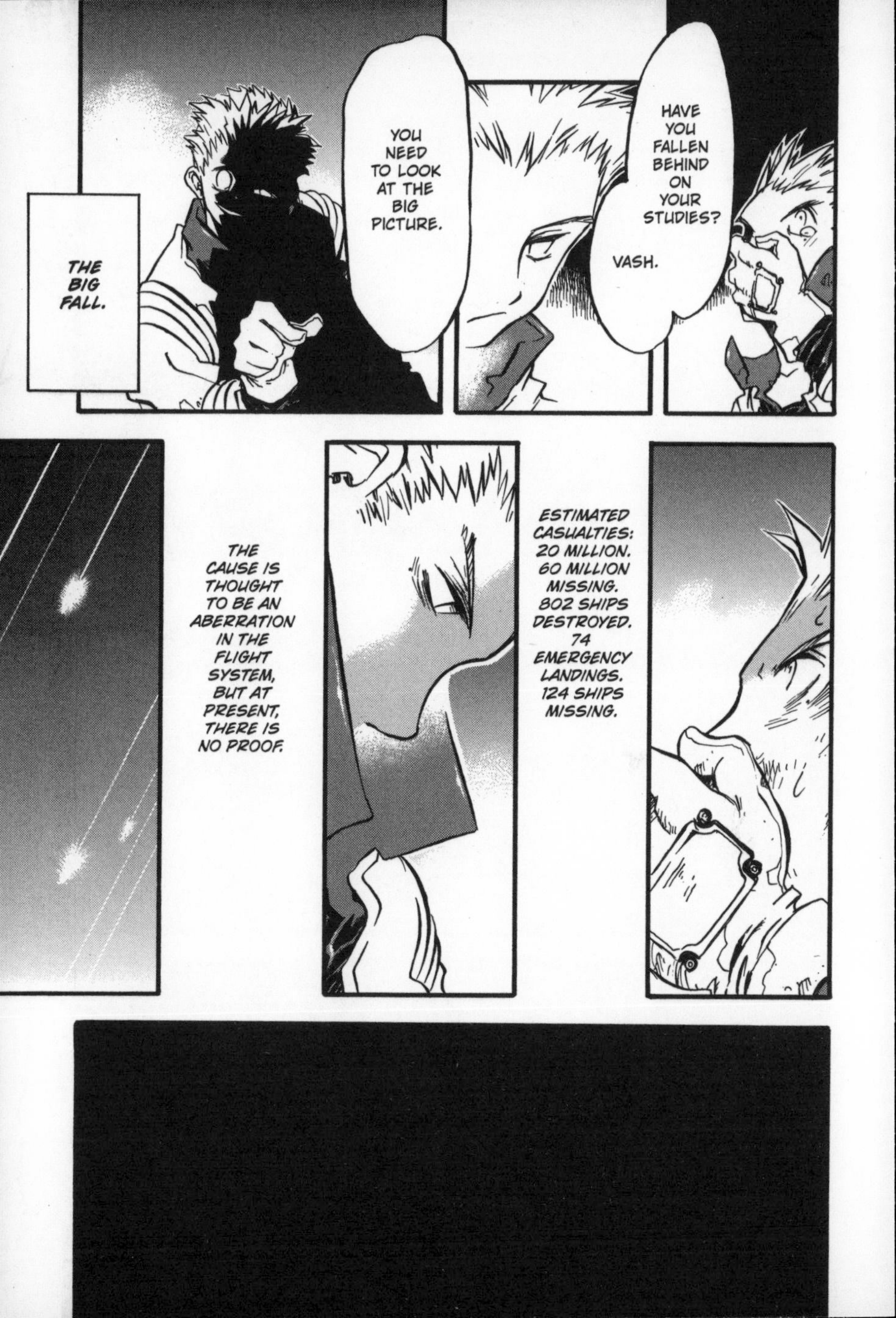
HAVE YOU FALLEN BEHIND ON YOUR STUDIES?
VASH.
YOU NEED TO LOOK AT THE BIG PICTURE.
THE BIG FALL.
ESTIMATED CASUALTIES: 20 MILLION. 60 MILLION MISSING. 802 SHIPS DESTROYED. 74 EMERGENCY LANDINGS. 124 SHIPS MISSING.
THE CAUSE IS THOUGHT TO BE AN ABERRATION IN THE FLIGHT SYSTEM, BUT AT PRESENT, THERE IS NO PROOF.

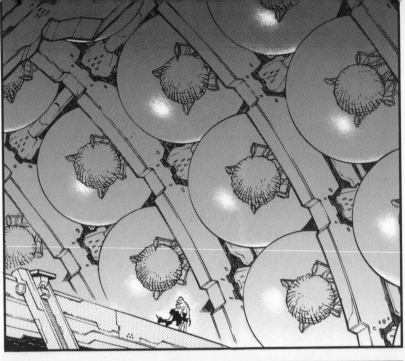

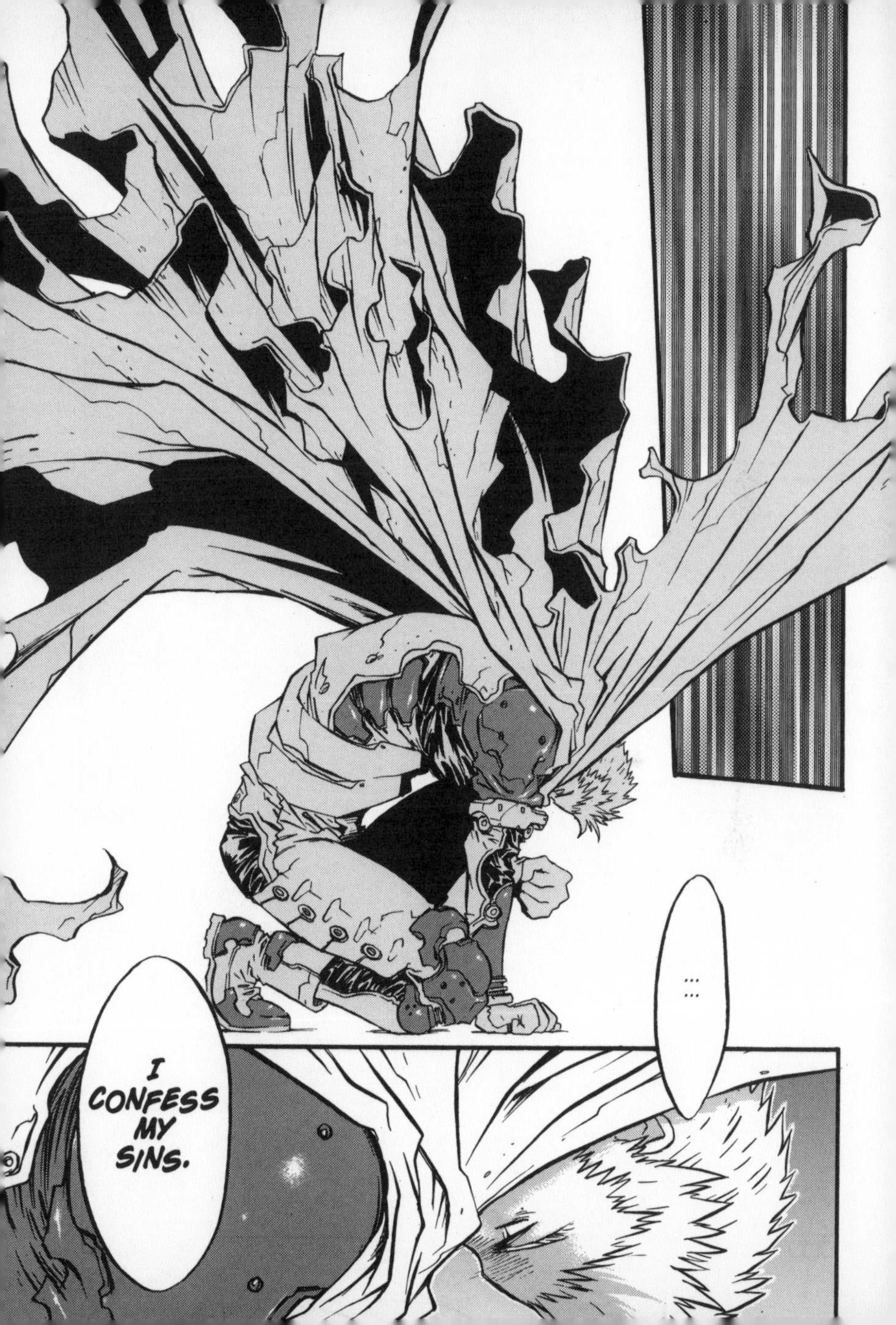
......
I CONFESS MY SINS.

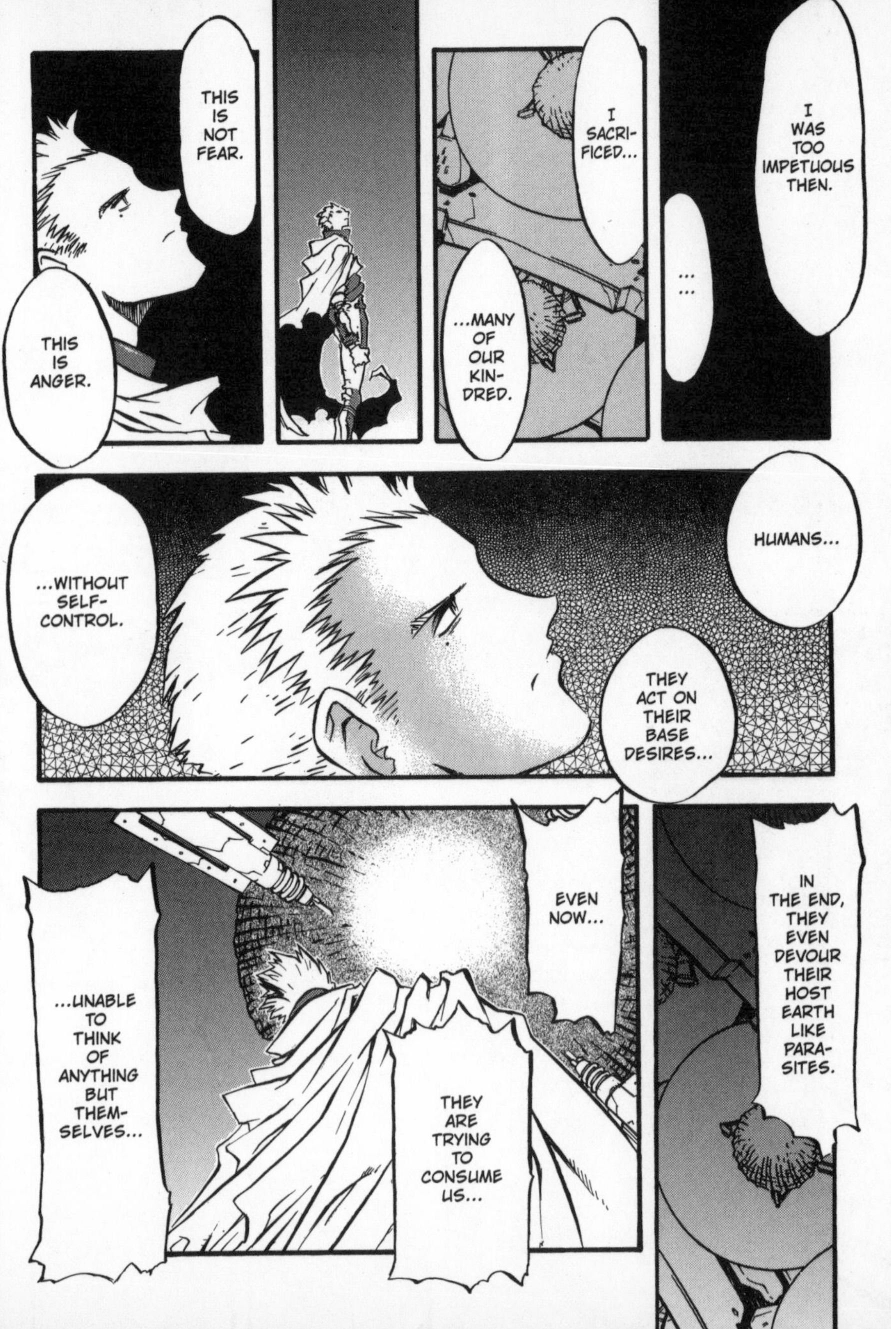
I WAS TOO IMPETUOUS THEN.
......
I SACRIFICED...
...MANY OF OUR KINDRED.
THIS IS NOT FEAR.
THIS IS ANGER.
HUMANS...
THEY ACT ON THEIR BASE DESIRES...
...WITHOUT SELF-CONTROL.
IN THE END, THEY EVEN DEVOUR THEIR HOST EARTH LIKE PARASITES.
EVEN NOW...
THEY ARE TRYING TO CONSUME US...
...UNABLE TO THINK OF ANYTHING BUT THEMSELVES...

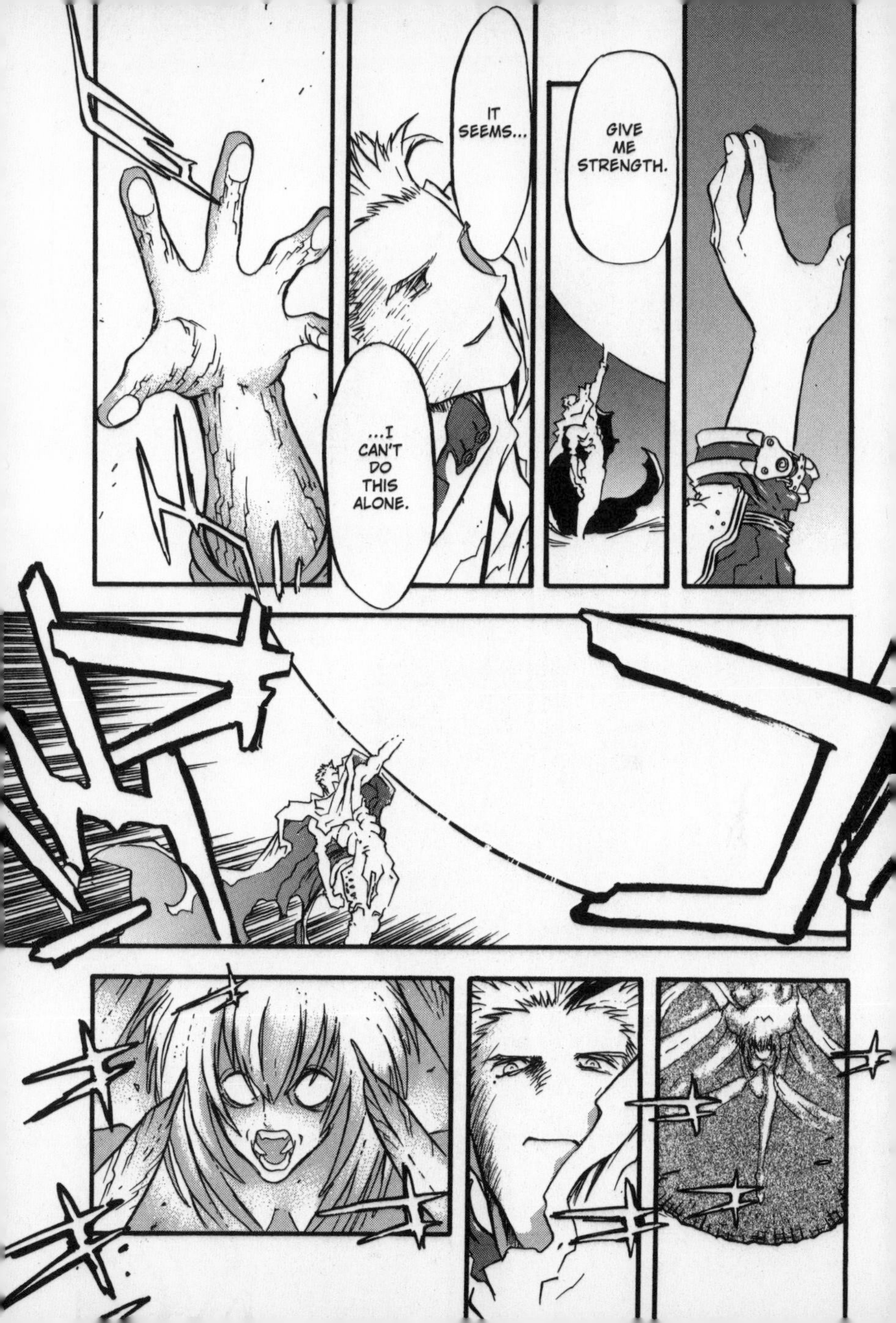
GIVE ME STRENGTH.
IT SEEMS...
...I CAN'T DO THIS ALONE.

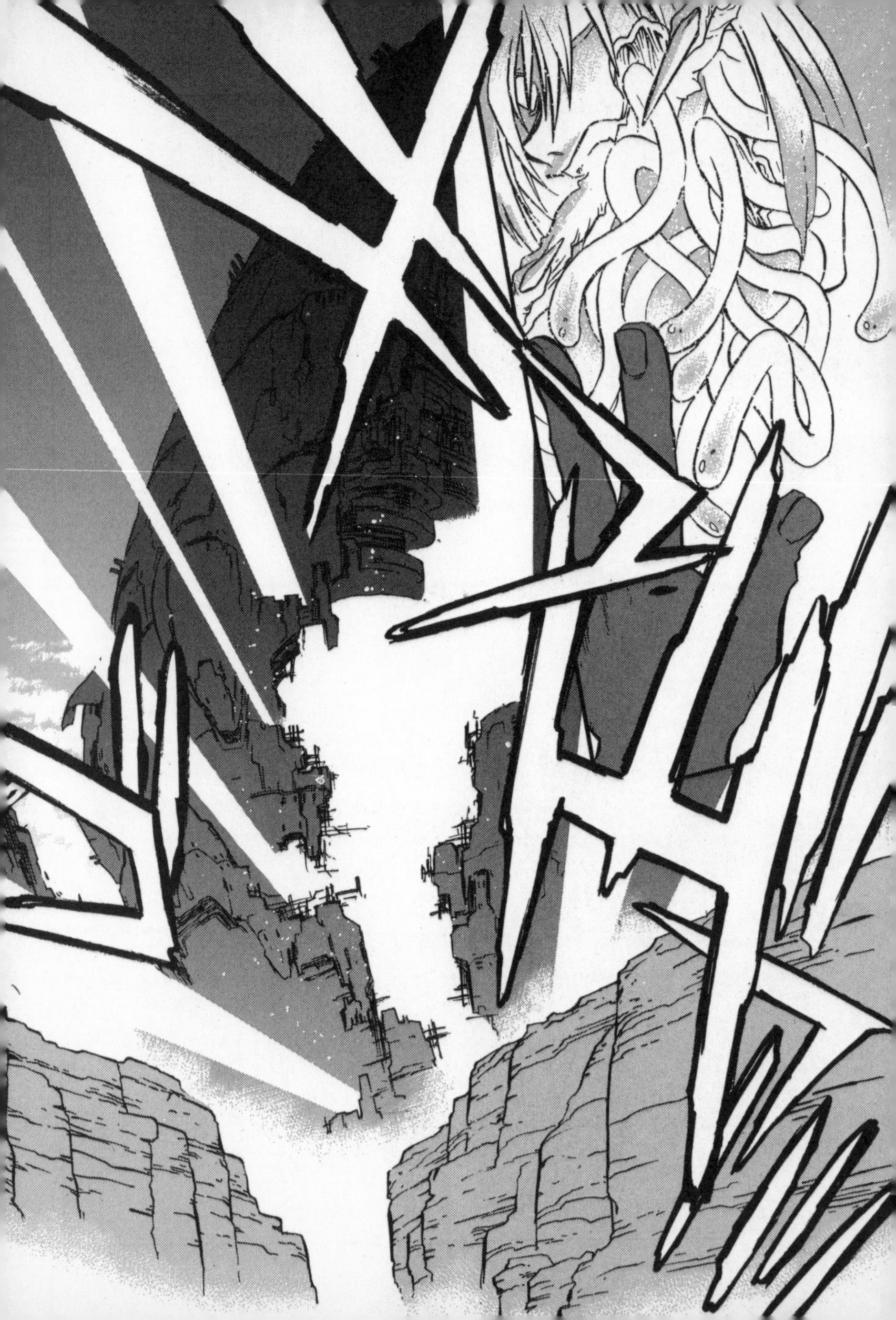

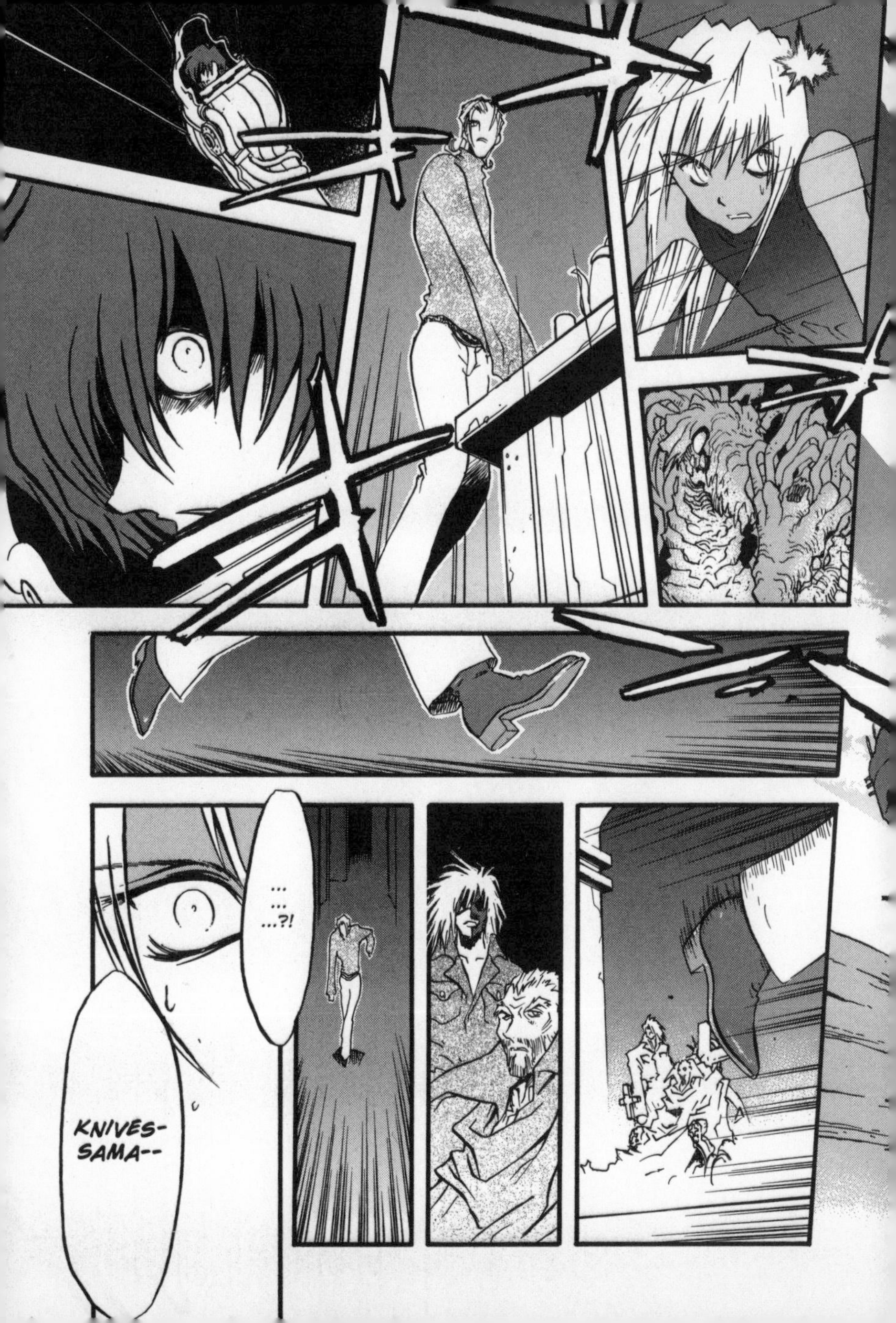
... ...?!
KNIVES-SAMA--

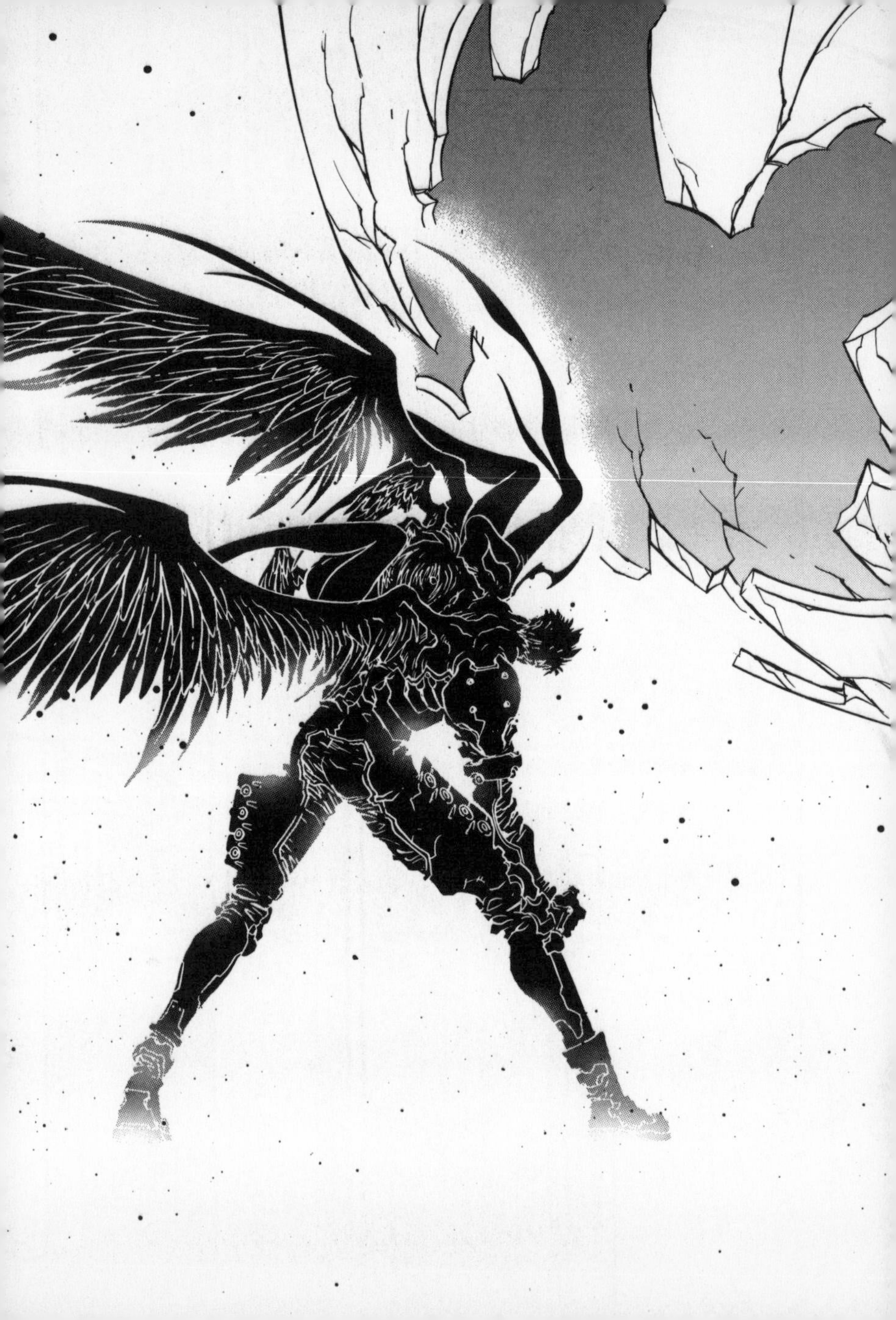

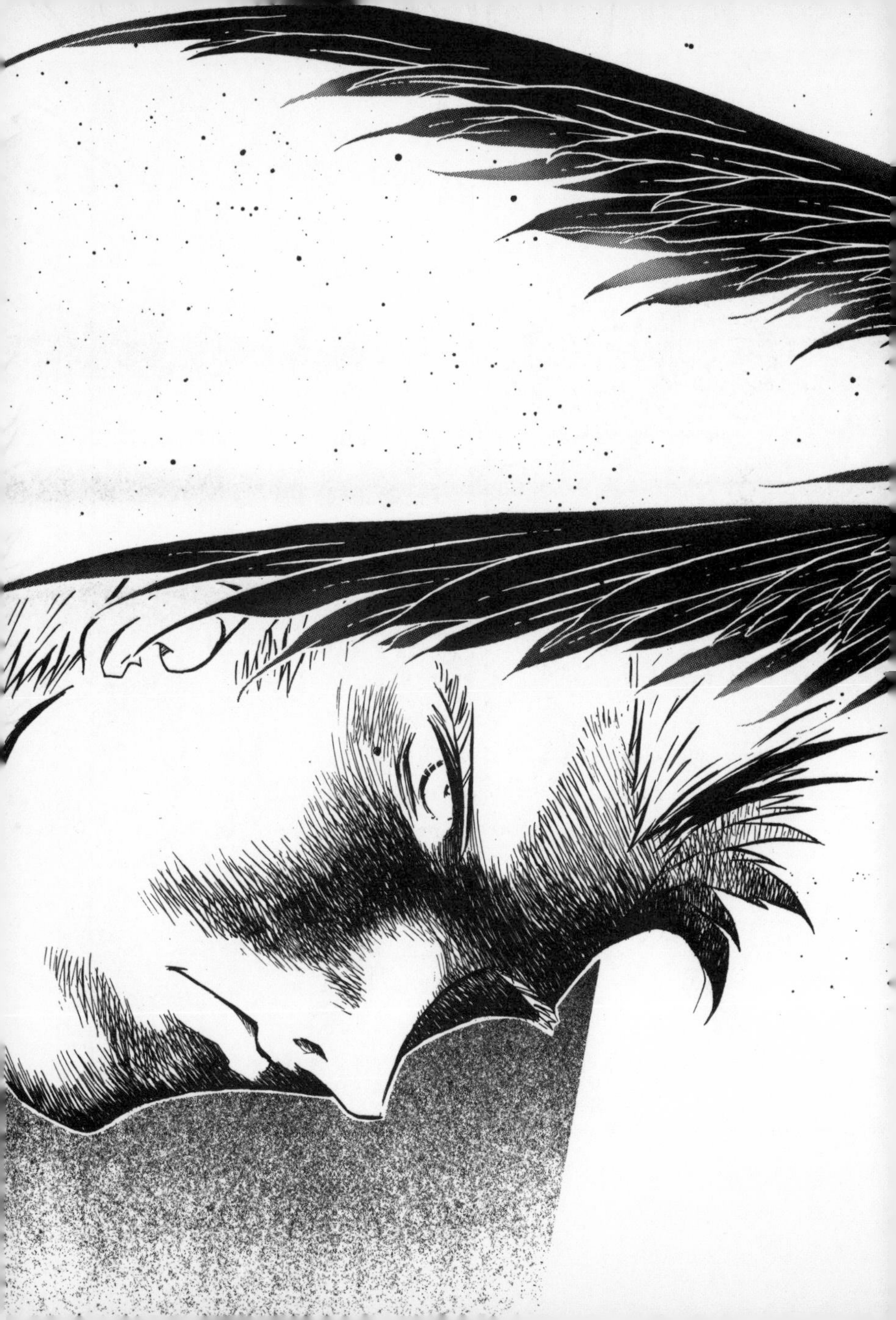

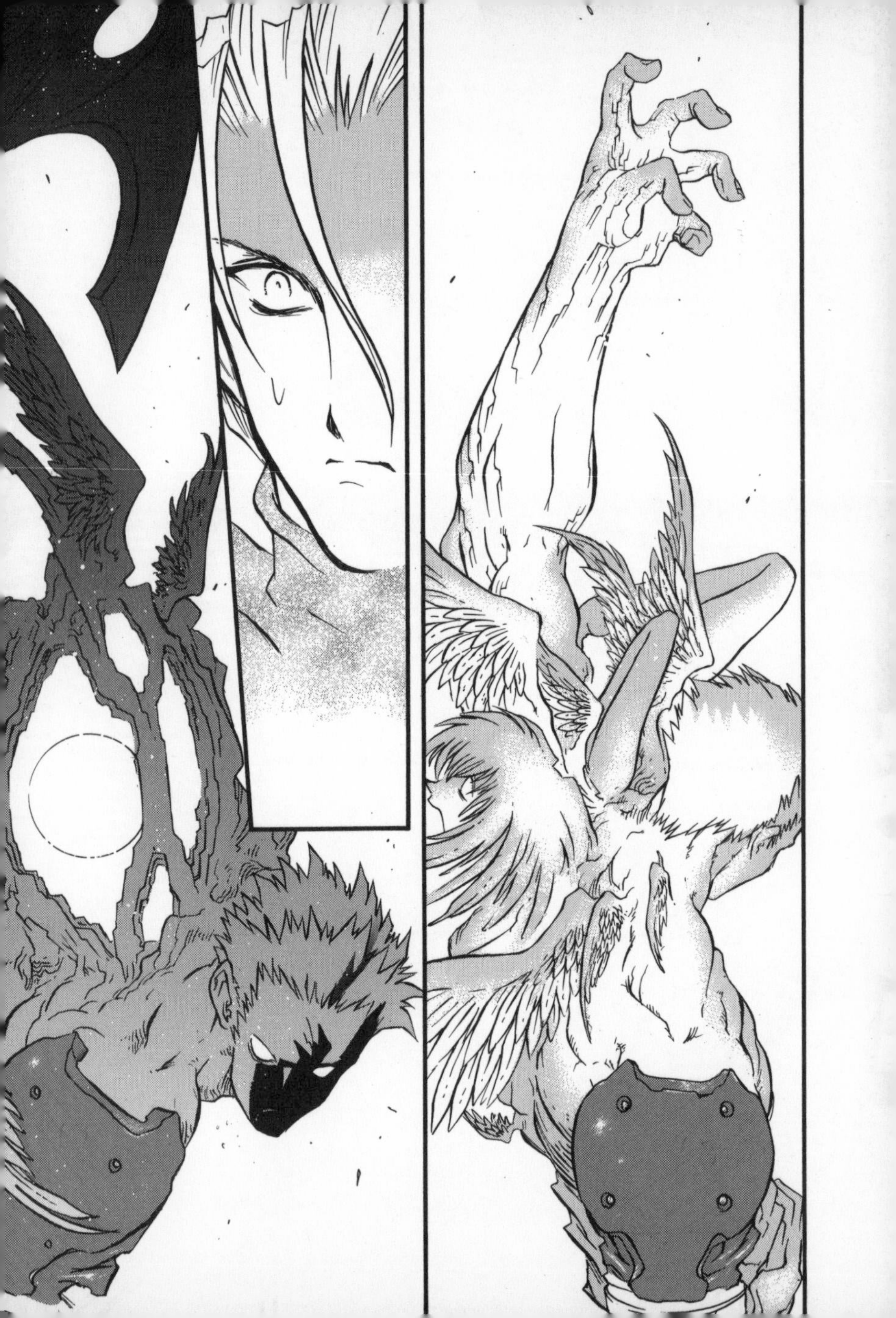

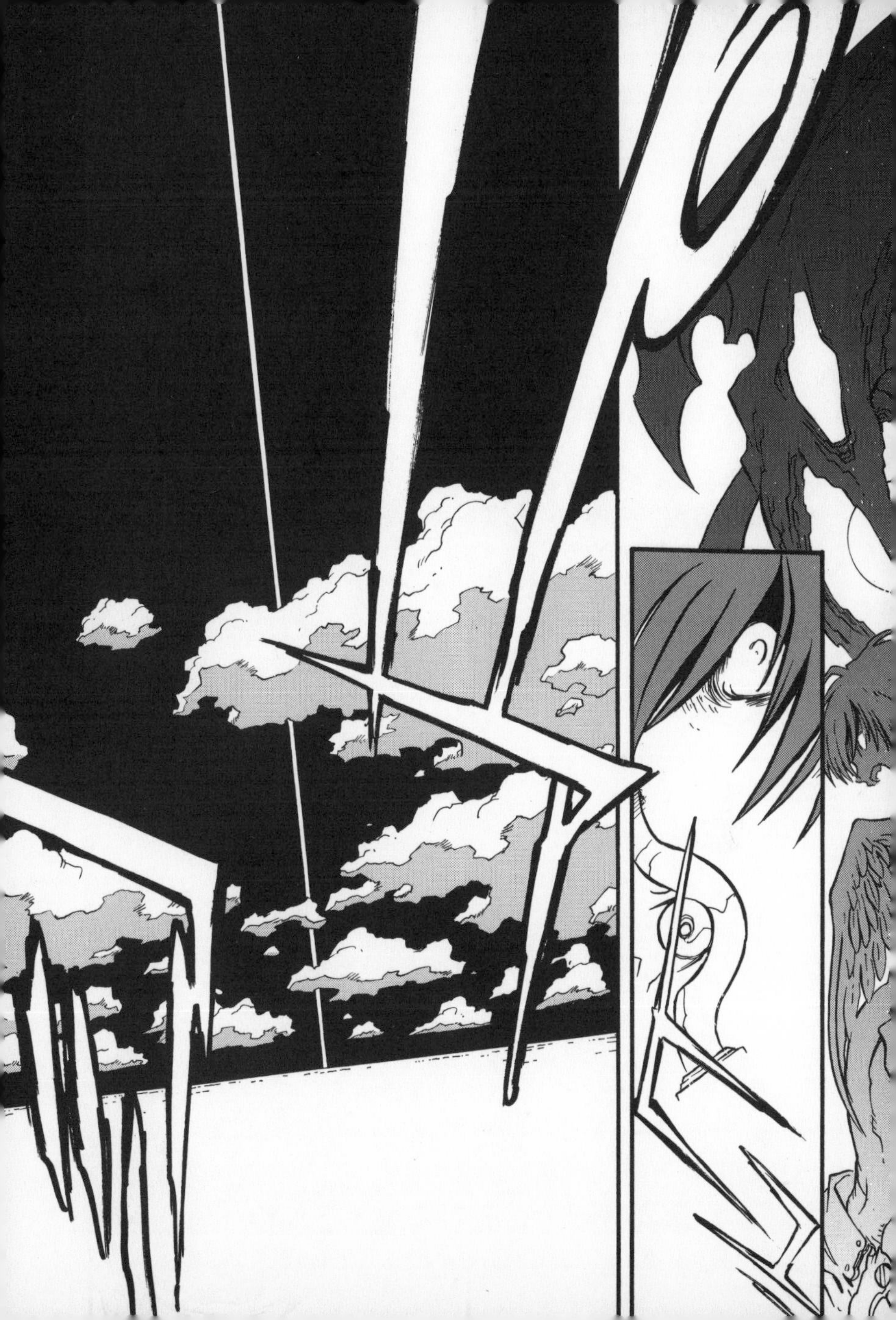

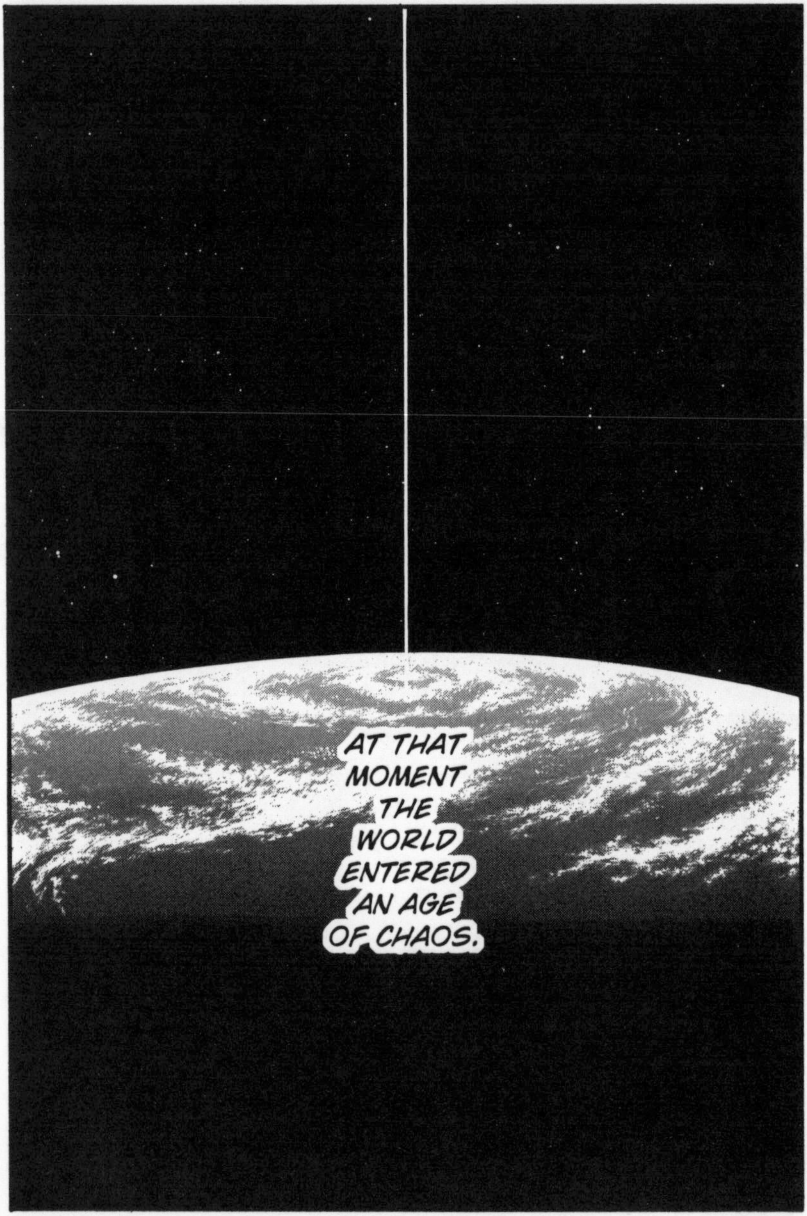
AT THAT MOMENT THE WORLD ENTERED AN AGE OF CHAOS.

#3.THE KING OF LONELINESS/END

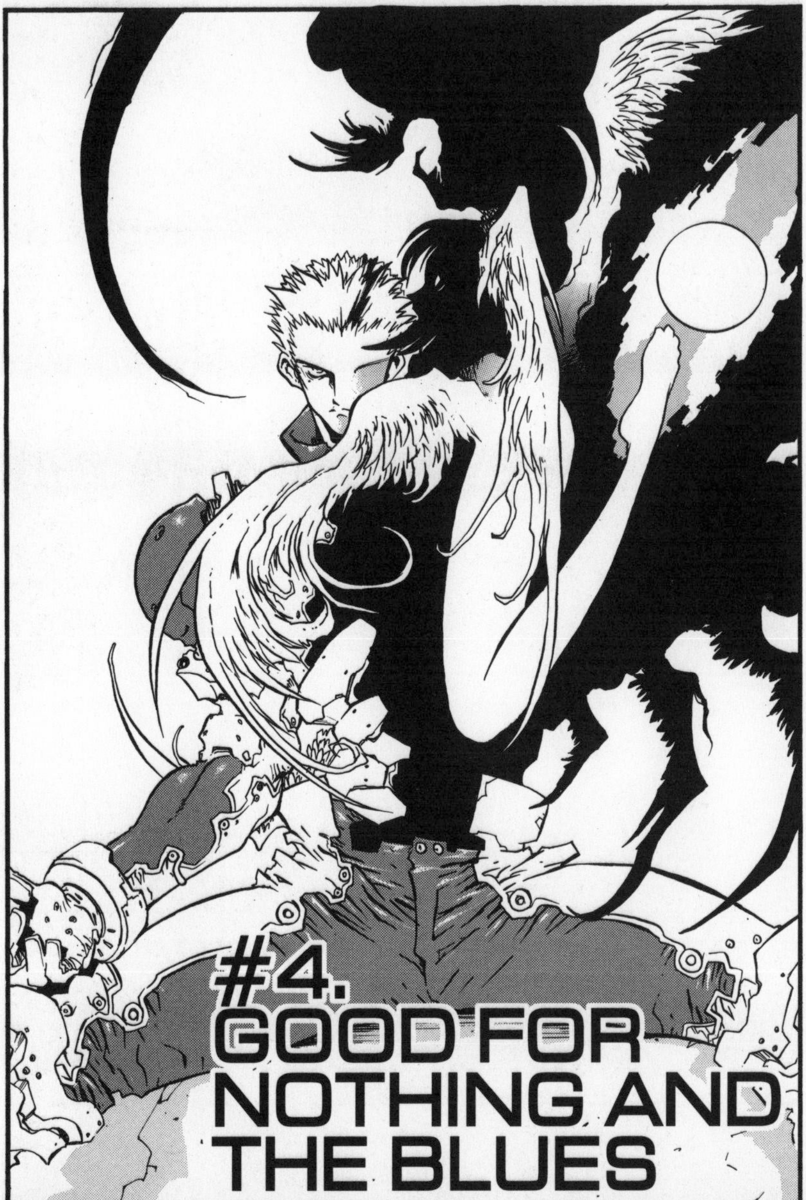
#4.
GOOD FOR NOTHING AND THE BLUES

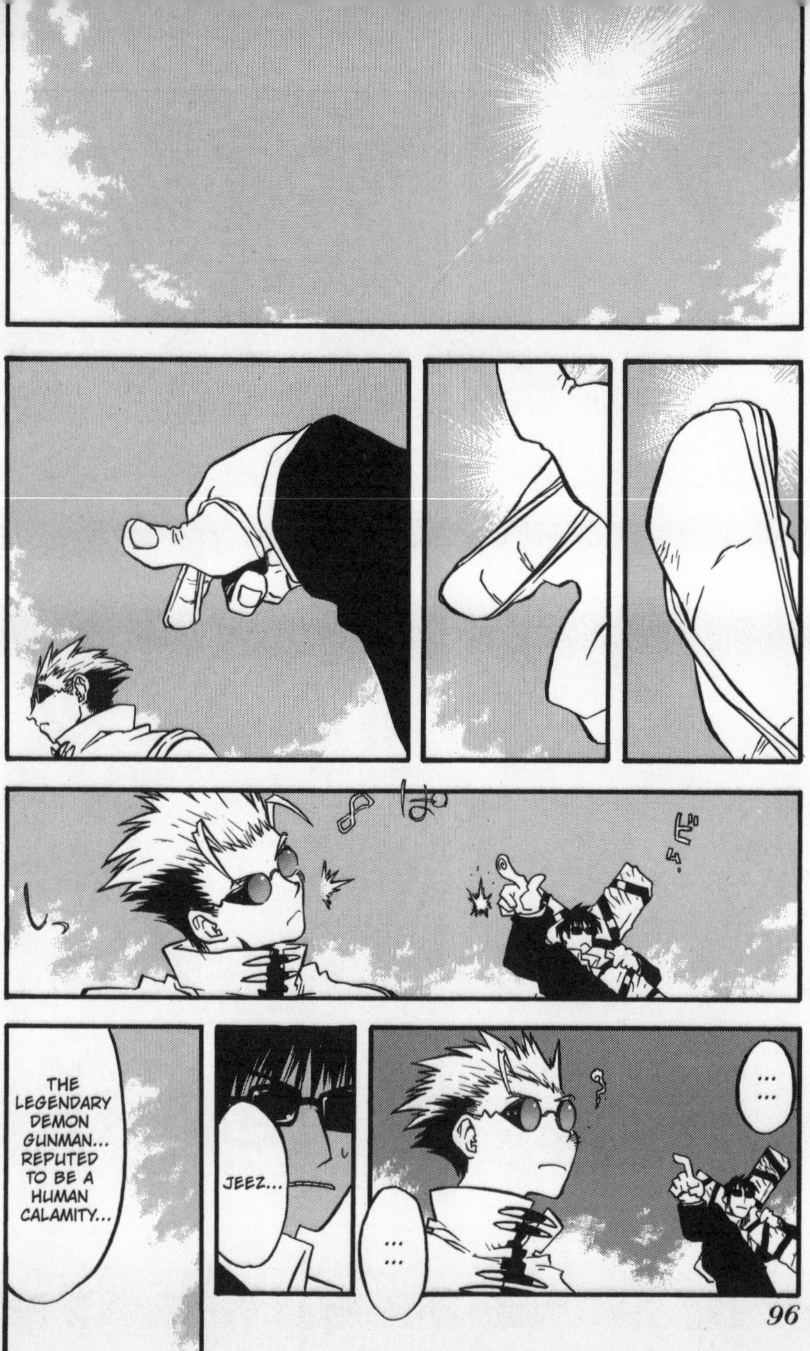
......
......
JEEZ...
THE LEGENDARY DEMON GUNMAN... REPUTED TO BE A HUMAN CALAMITY...

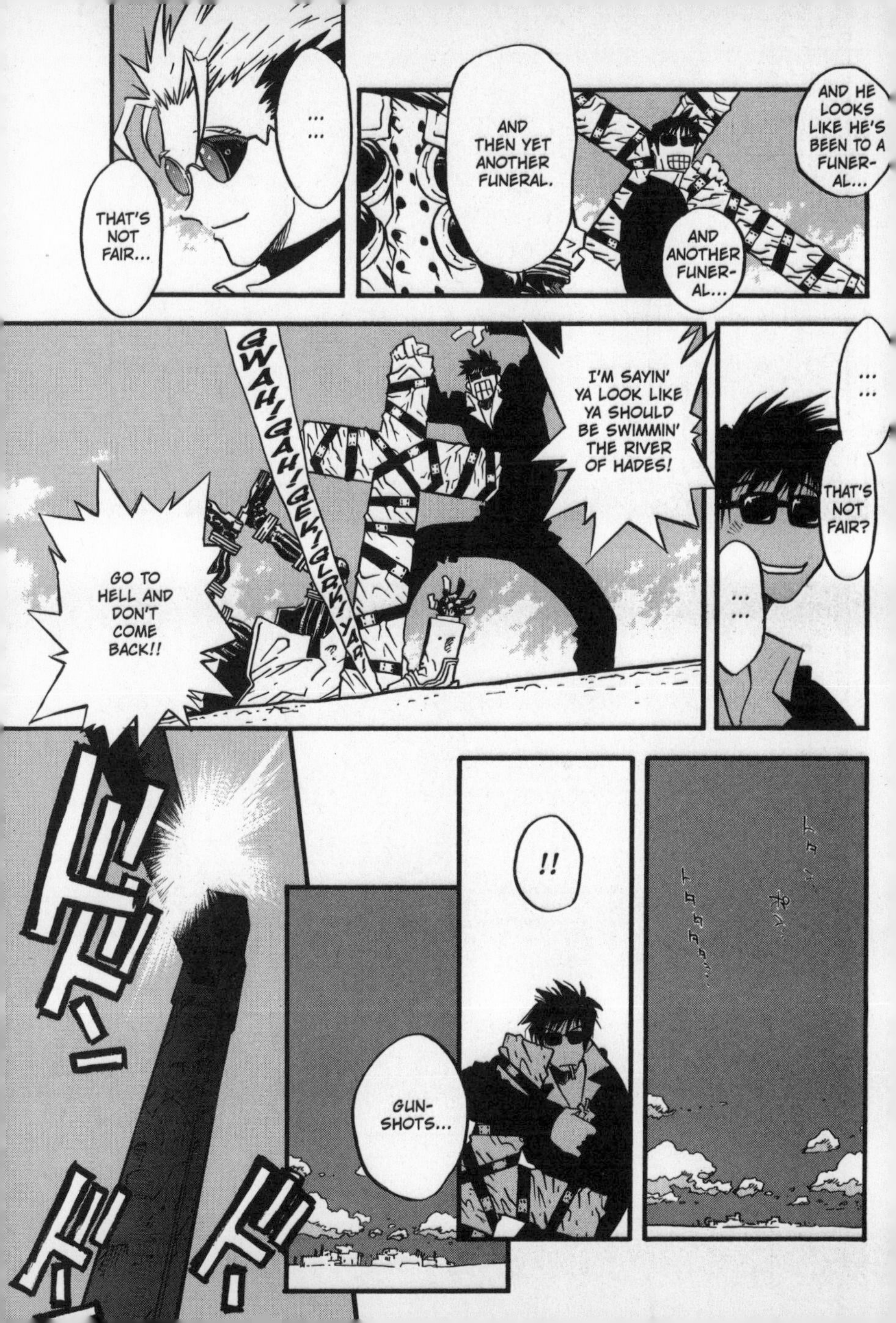
AND HE LOOKS LIKE HE'S BEEN TO A FUNER-AL...
AND ANOTHER FUNER-AL...
AND THEN YET ANOTHER FUNERAL.
... ...
THAT'S NOT FAIR...
... ...
THAT'S NOT FAIR?
... ...
I'M SAYIN' YA LOOK LIKE YA SHOULD BE SWIMMIN' THE RIVER OF HADES!
GWAH! GAH! GEKI! GLRK! YAR!
GO TO HELL AND DON'T COME BACK!!
!!
GUN-SHOTS...

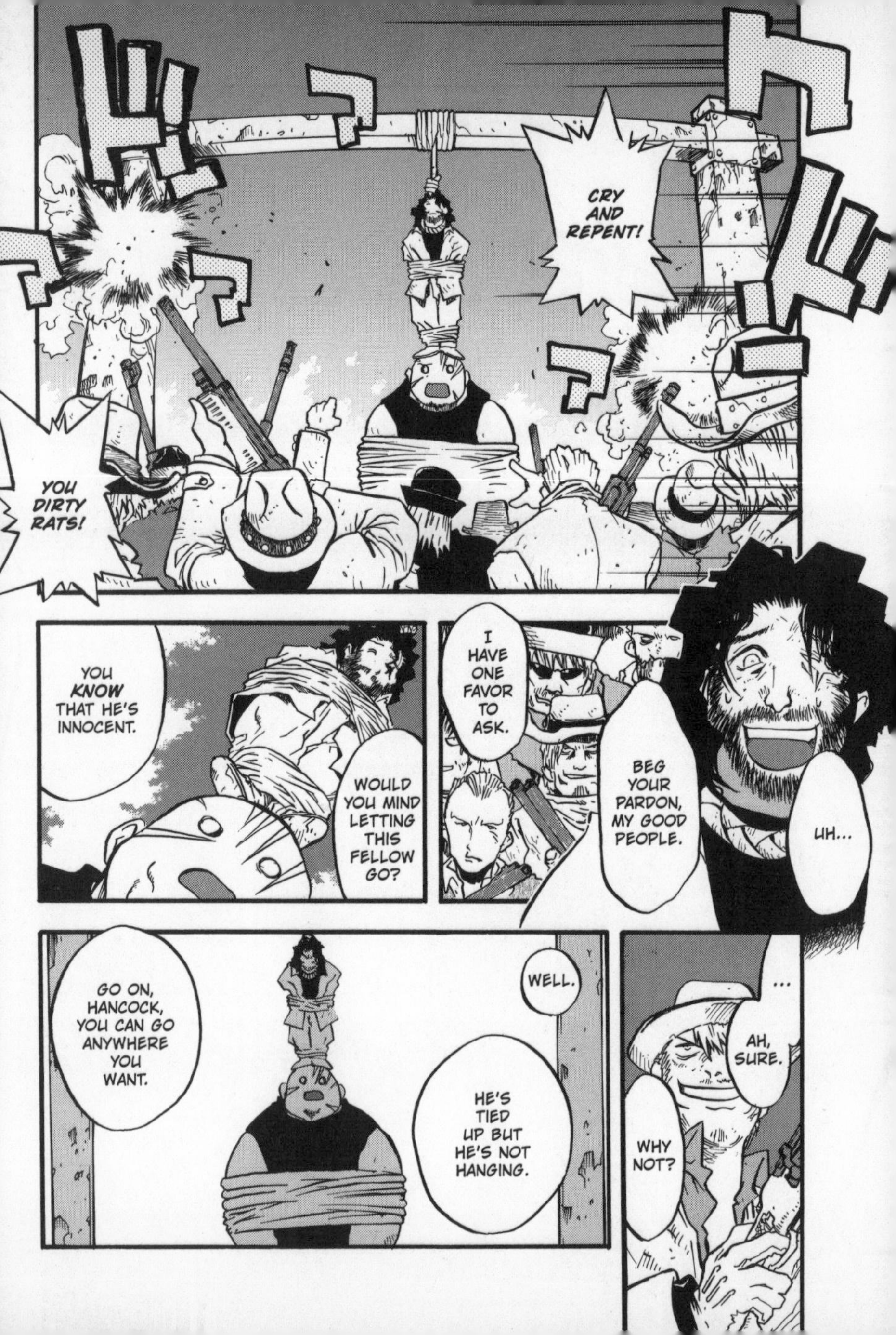
CRY AND REPENT!
YOU DIRTY RATS!
UH...
BEG YOUR PARDON, MY GOOD PEOPLE.
I HAVE ONE FAVOR TO ASK.
WOULD YOU MIND LETTING THIS FELLOW GO?
YOU KNOW THAT HE'S INNOCENT.
...
AH, SURE.
WHY NOT?
WELL.
HE'S TIED UP BUT HE'S NOT HANGING.
GO ON, HANCOCK, YOU CAN GO ANYWHERE YOU WANT.

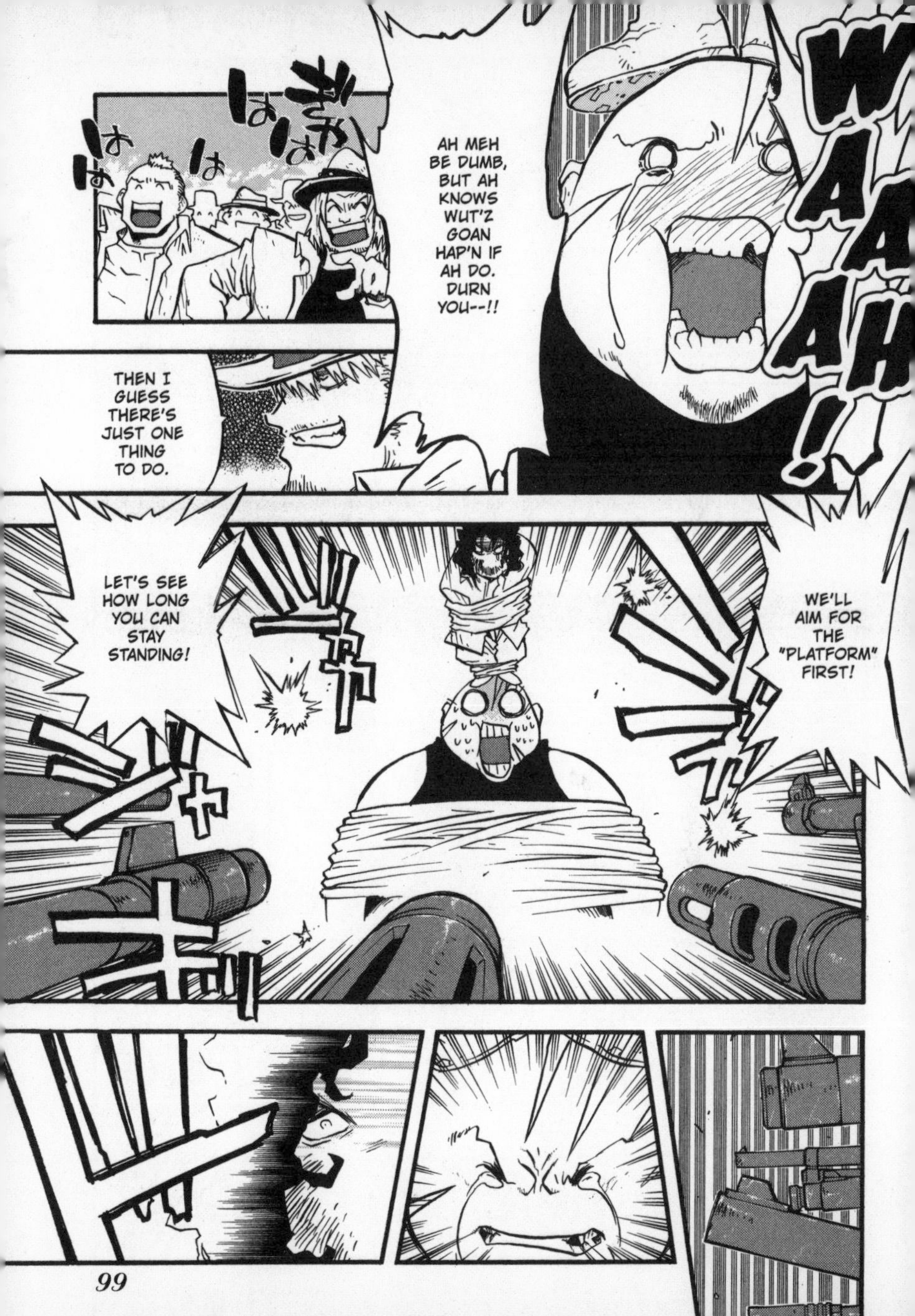

WAAAH!!
AH MEH BE DUMB, BUT AH KNOWS WUT'Z GOAN HAP'N IF AH DO. DURN YOU--!!
THEN I GUESS THERE'S JUST ONE THING TO DO.
WE'LL AIM FOR THE "PLATFORM" FIRST!
LET'S SEE HOW LONG YOU CAN STAY STANDING!

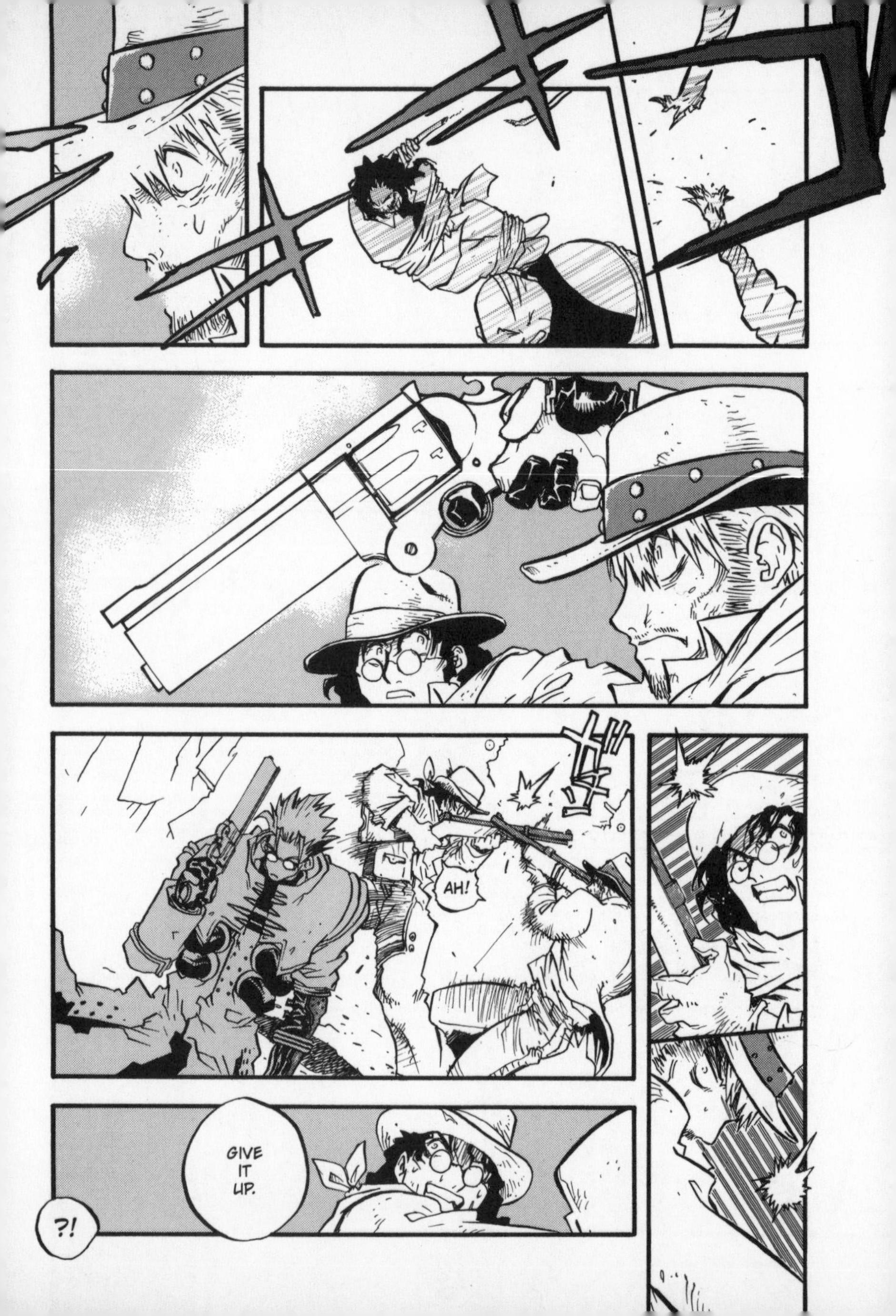
AH!
GIVE IT UP.
?!

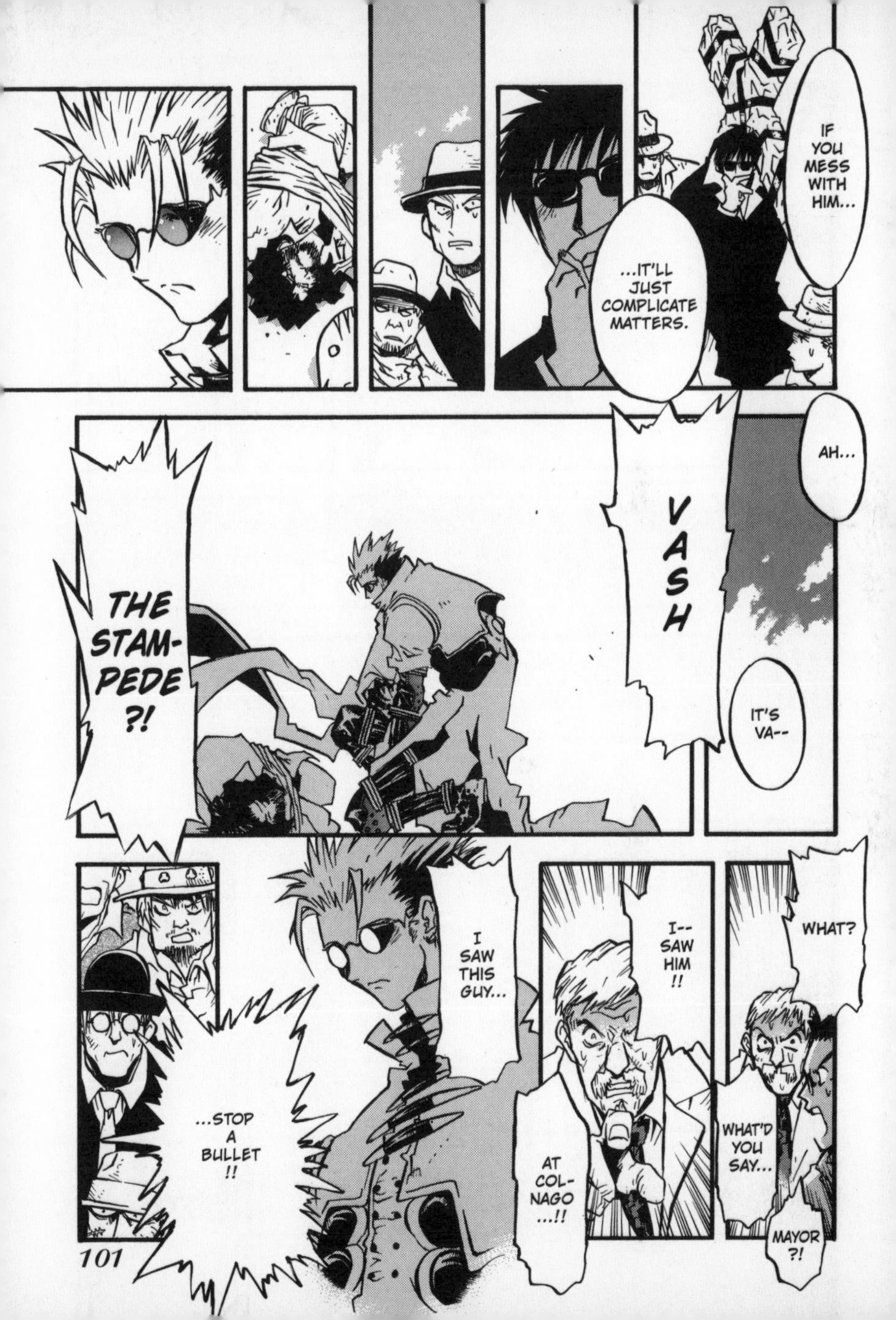
IF YOU MESS WITH HIM...
...IT'LL JUST COMPLICATE MATTERS.
AH...
IT'S VA--
VASH
THE STAMPEDE ?!
WHAT?
WHAT'D YOU SAY...
MAYOR ?!
I-- SAW HIM !!
AT COLNAGO ...!!
I SAW THIS GUY...
...STOP A BULLET !!

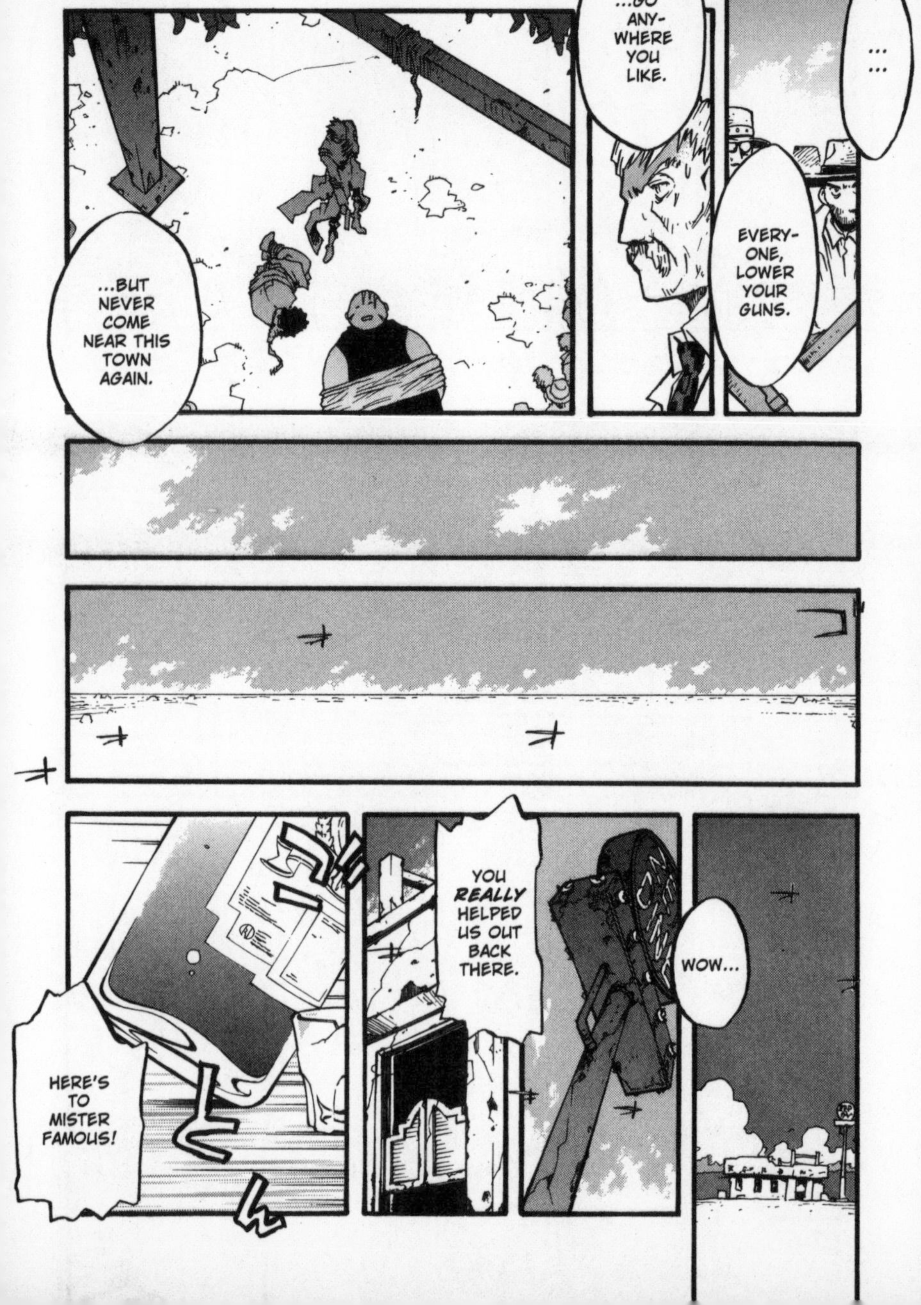
……
EVERYONE, LOWER YOUR GUNS.
...GO ANYWHERE YOU LIKE.
...BUT NEVER COME NEAR THIS TOWN AGAIN.
WOW...
YOU *REALLY* HELPED US OUT BACK THERE.
HERE'S TO MISTER FAMOUS!

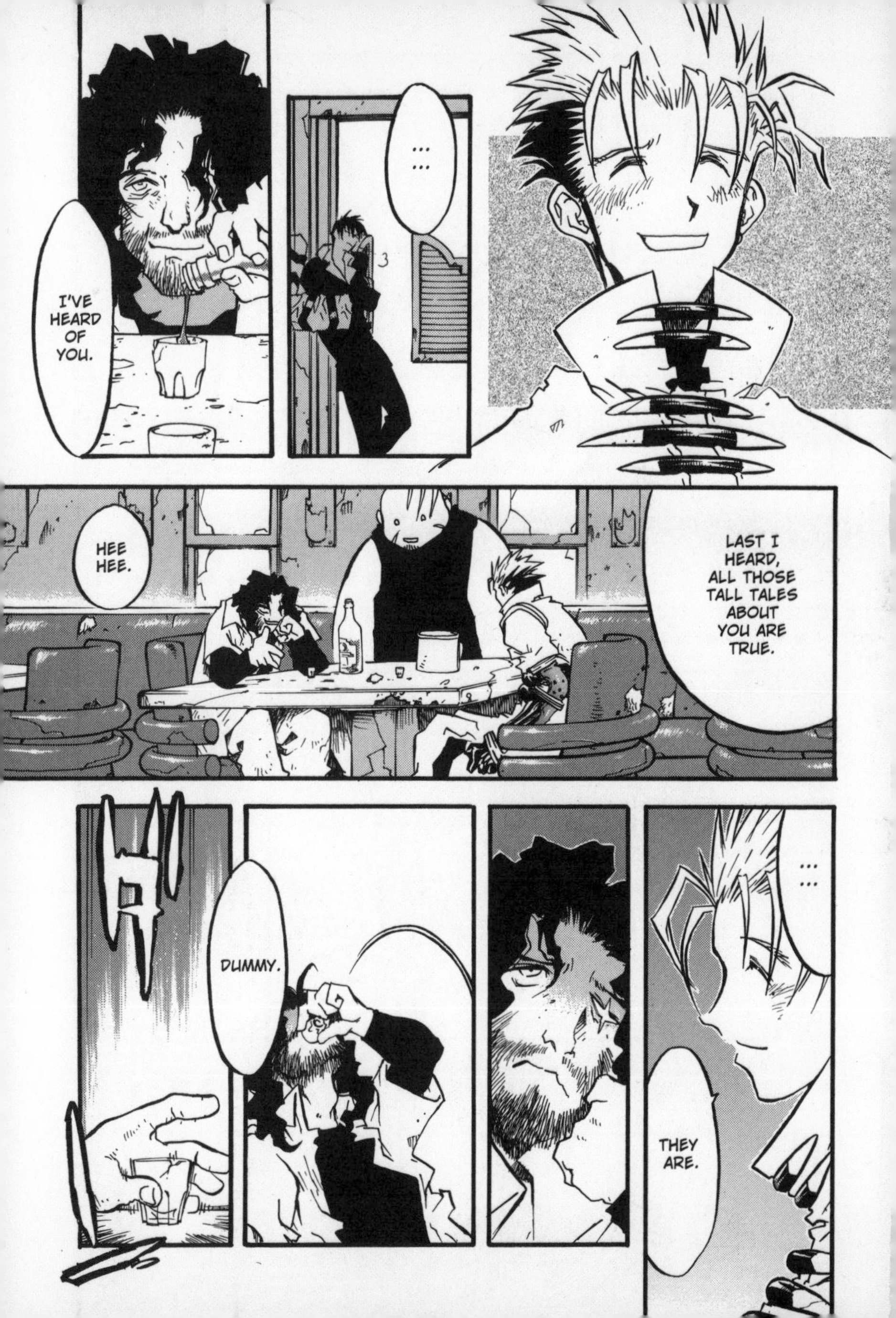
... ...
I'VE HEARD OF YOU.
LAST I HEARD, ALL THOSE TALL TALES ABOUT YOU ARE TRUE.
HEE HEE.
... ...
THEY ARE.
DUMMY.

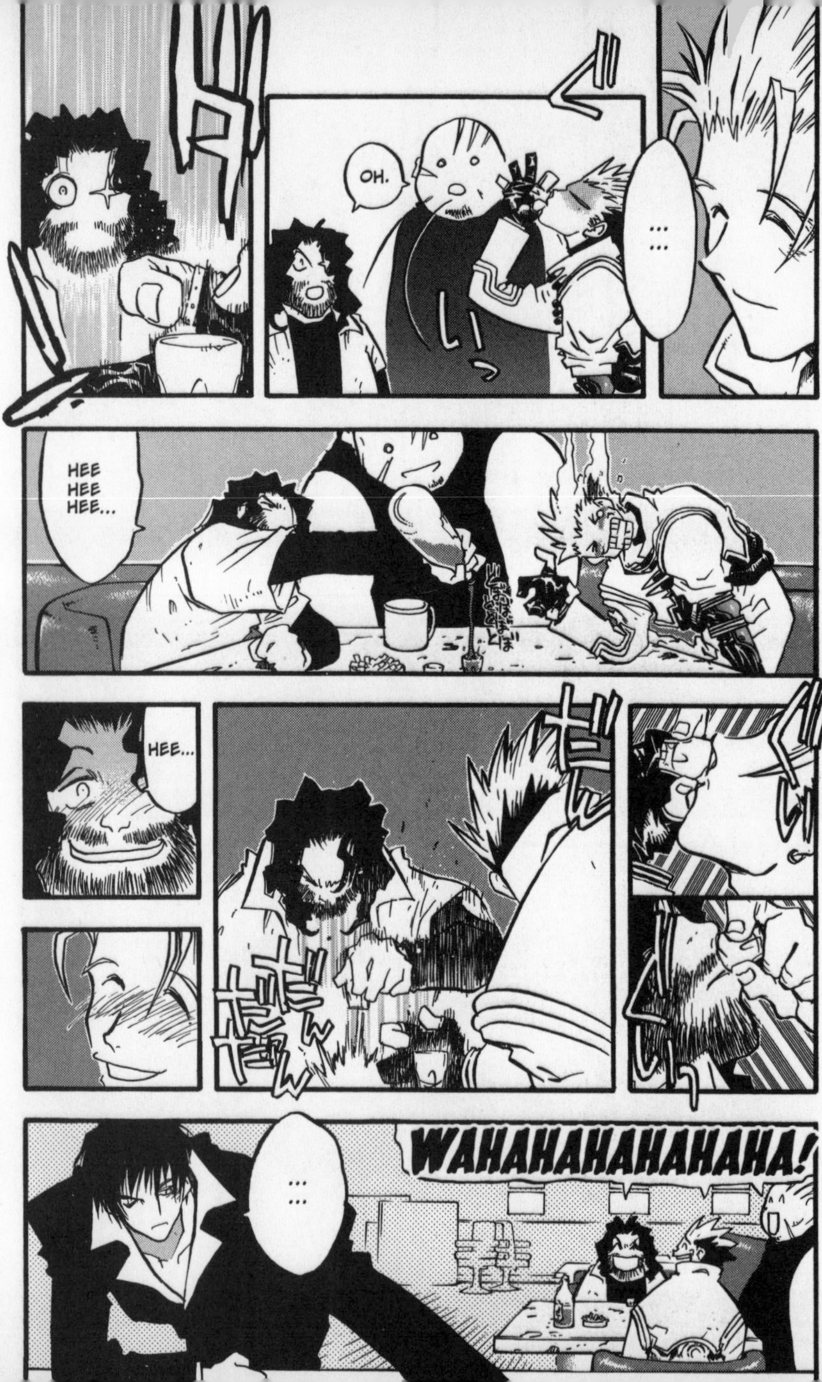
... ...
OH.
HEE HEE HEE...
HEE...
WAHAHAHAHAHAHA!
... ...

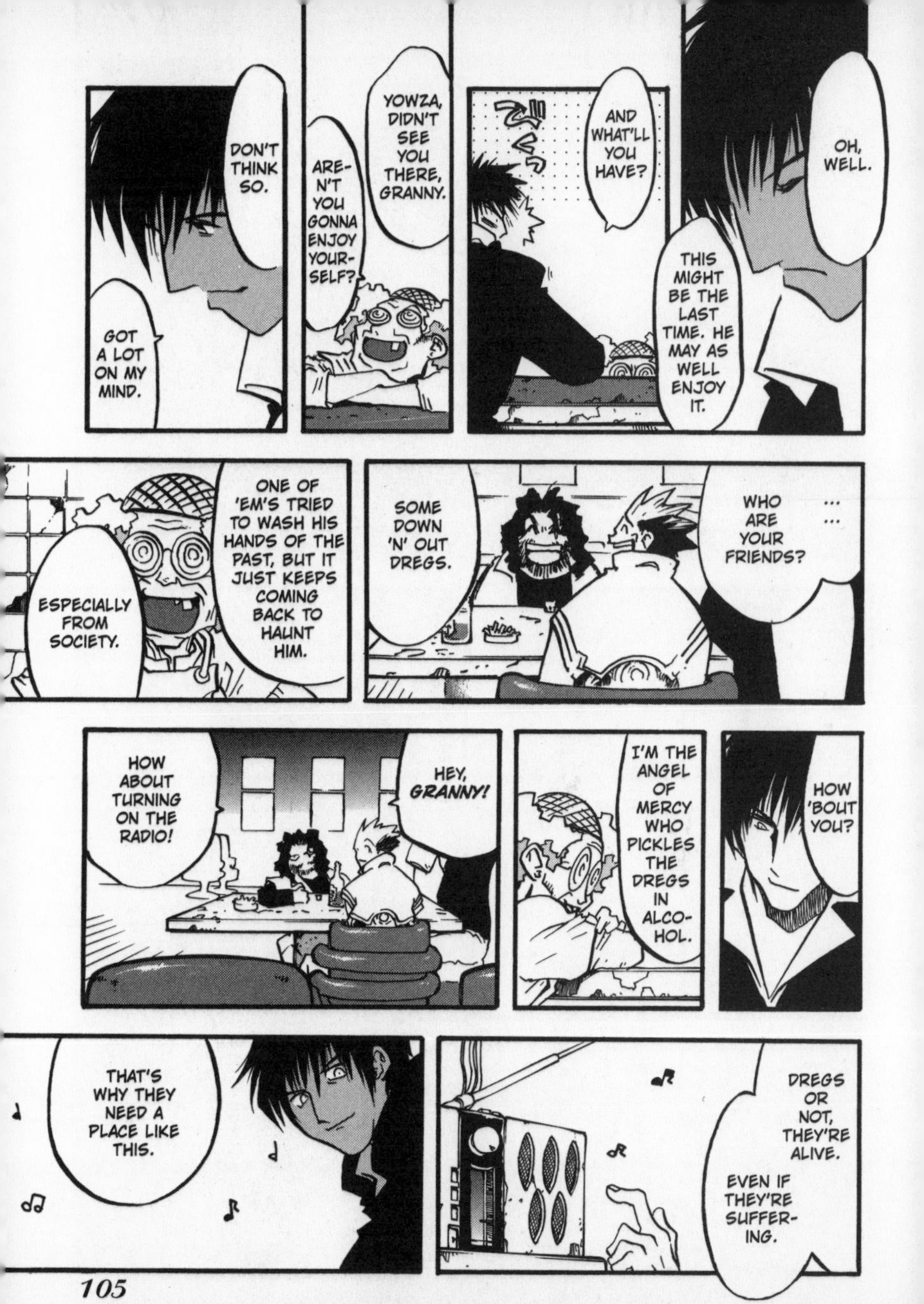
OH, WELL.
THIS MIGHT BE THE LAST TIME. HE MAY AS WELL ENJOY IT.
AND WHAT'LL YOU HAVE?
YOWZA, DIDN'T SEE YOU THERE, GRANNY.
AREN'T YOU GONNA ENJOY YOURSELF?
DON'T THINK SO.
GOT A LOT ON MY MIND.
WHO ARE YOUR FRIENDS?
… …
SOME DOWN 'N' OUT DREGS.
ONE OF 'EM'S TRIED TO WASH HIS HANDS OF THE PAST, BUT IT JUST KEEPS COMING BACK TO HAUNT HIM.
ESPECIALLY FROM SOCIETY.
HOW 'BOUT YOU?
I'M THE ANGEL OF MERCY WHO PICKLES THE DREGS IN ALCOHOL.
HEY, *GRANNY!*
HOW ABOUT TURNING ON THE RADIO!
DREGS OR NOT, THEY'RE ALIVE.
EVEN IF THEY'RE SUFFERING.
THAT'S WHY THEY NEED A PLACE LIKE THIS.

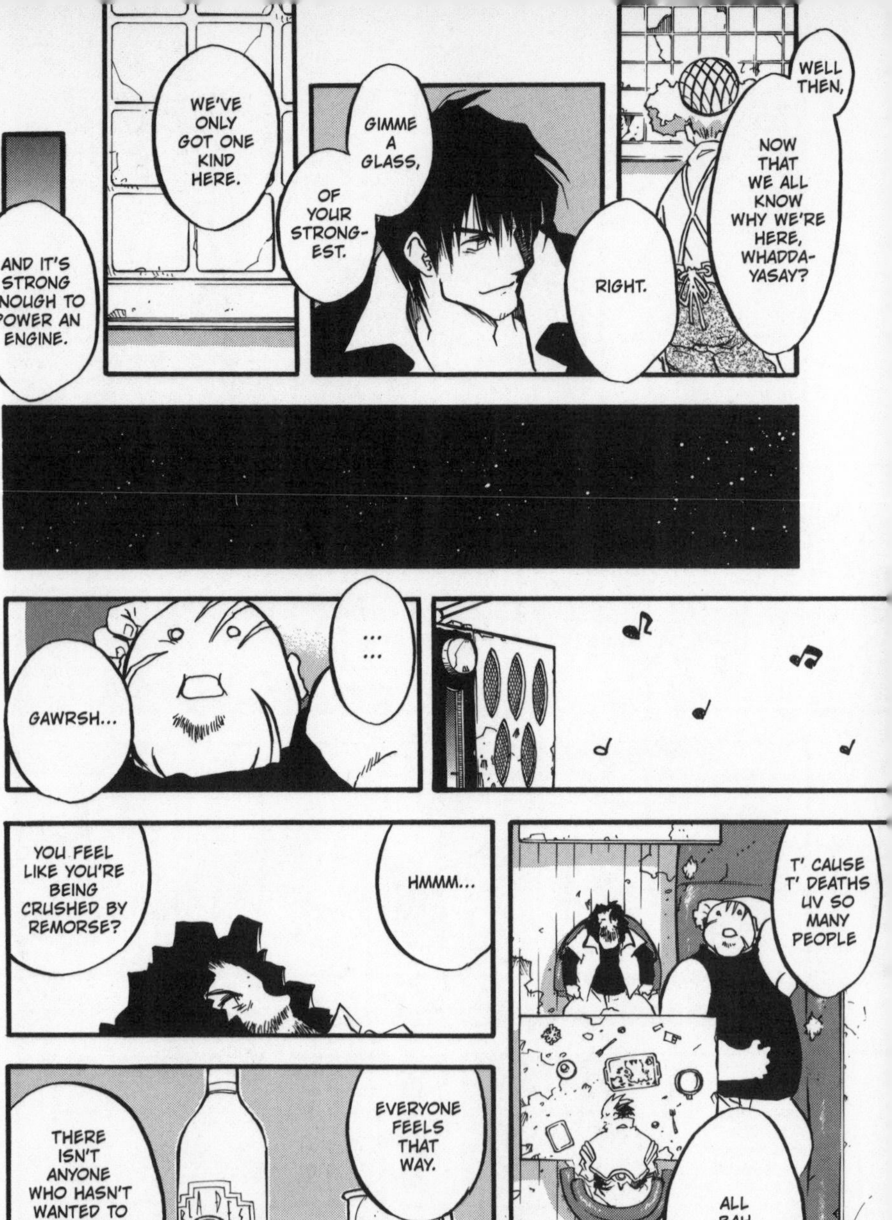
WELL THEN,
NOW THAT WE ALL KNOW WHY WE'RE HERE, WHADDAYASAY?
RIGHT.
GIMME A GLASS,
OF YOUR STRONGEST.
WE'VE ONLY GOT ONE KIND HERE.
AND IT'S STRONG ENOUGH TO POWER AN ENGINE.
...
...
GAWRSH...
T' CAUSE T' DEATHS UV SO MANY PEOPLE
ALL BAH Y'SELF.
HMMM...
YOU FEEL LIKE YOU'RE BEING CRUSHED BY REMORSE?
EVERYONE FEELS THAT WAY.
THERE ISN'T ANYONE WHO HASN'T WANTED TO ESCAPE FROM IT ALL.

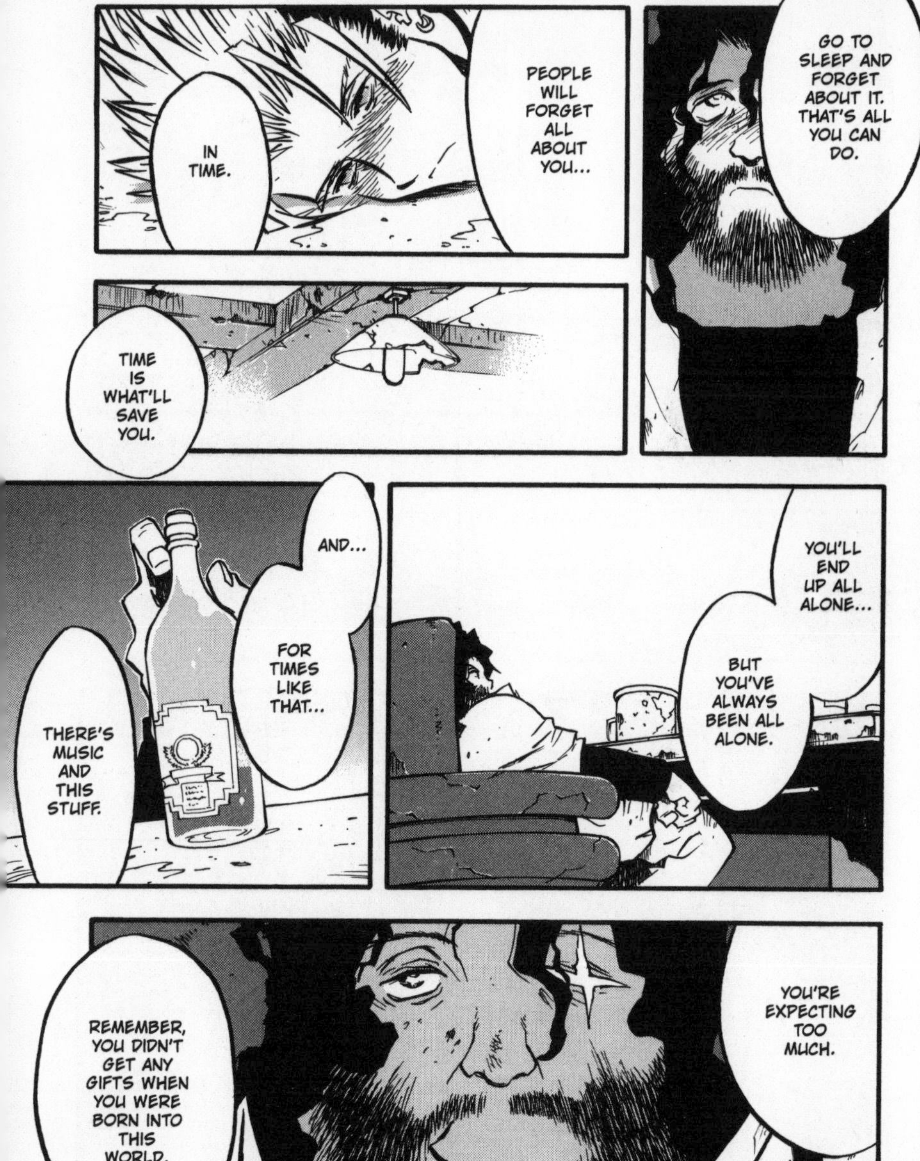
GO TO SLEEP AND FORGET ABOUT IT. THAT'S ALL YOU CAN DO.
PEOPLE WILL FORGET ALL ABOUT YOU...
IN TIME.
TIME IS WHAT'LL SAVE YOU.
YOU'LL END UP ALL ALONE...
BUT YOU'VE ALWAYS BEEN ALL ALONE.
AND...
FOR TIMES LIKE THAT...
THERE'S MUSIC AND THIS STUFF.
YOU'RE EXPECTING TOO MUCH.
REMEMBER, YOU DIDN'T GET ANY GIFTS WHEN YOU WERE BORN INTO THIS WORLD.

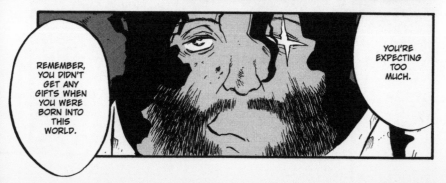

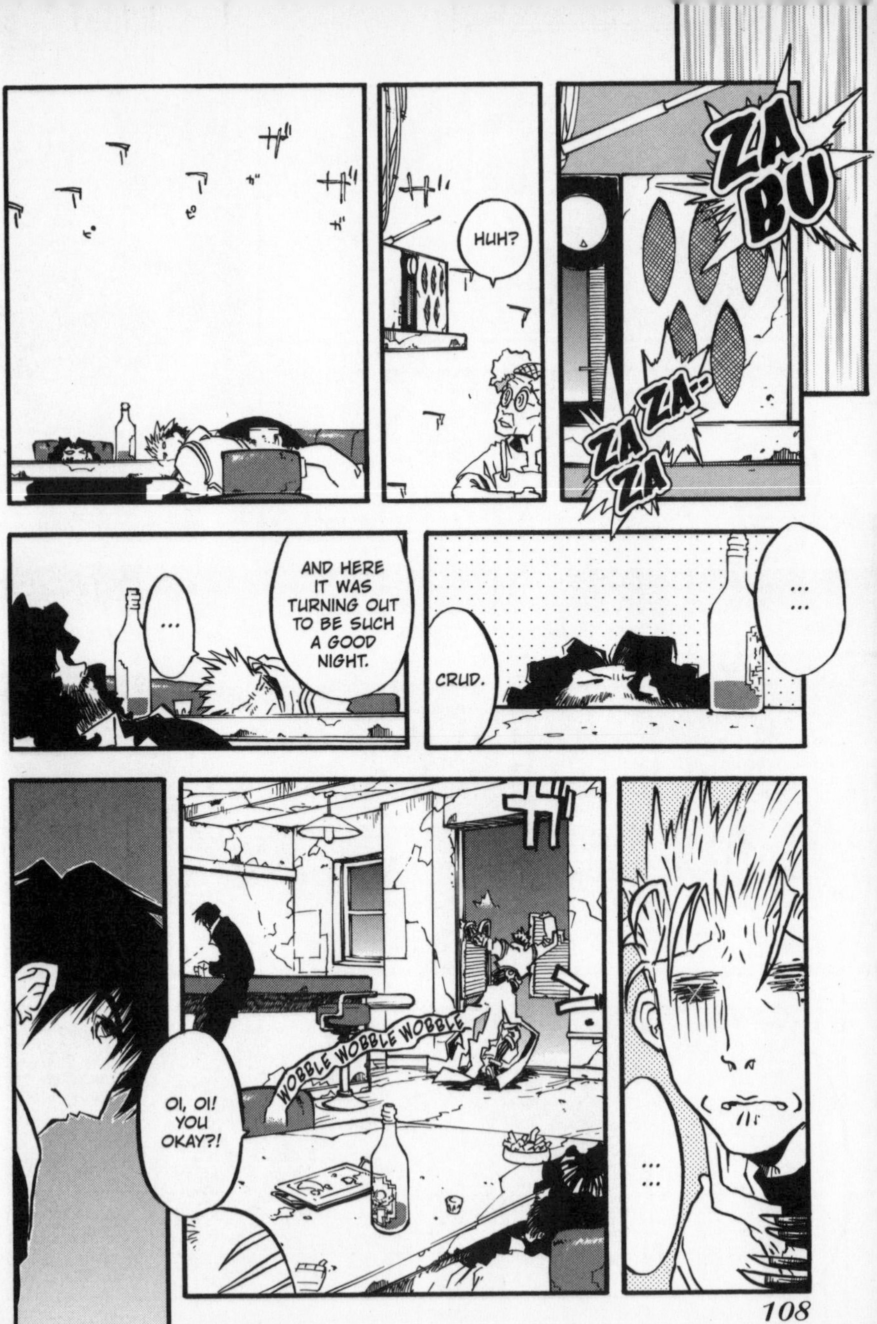
ZA BU
ZA ZA-
ZA ZA
HUH?
...
...
CRUD.
AND HERE IT WAS TURNING OUT TO BE SUCH A GOOD NIGHT.
...
...
...
WOBBLE WOBBLE WOBBLE
OI, OI! YOU OKAY?!

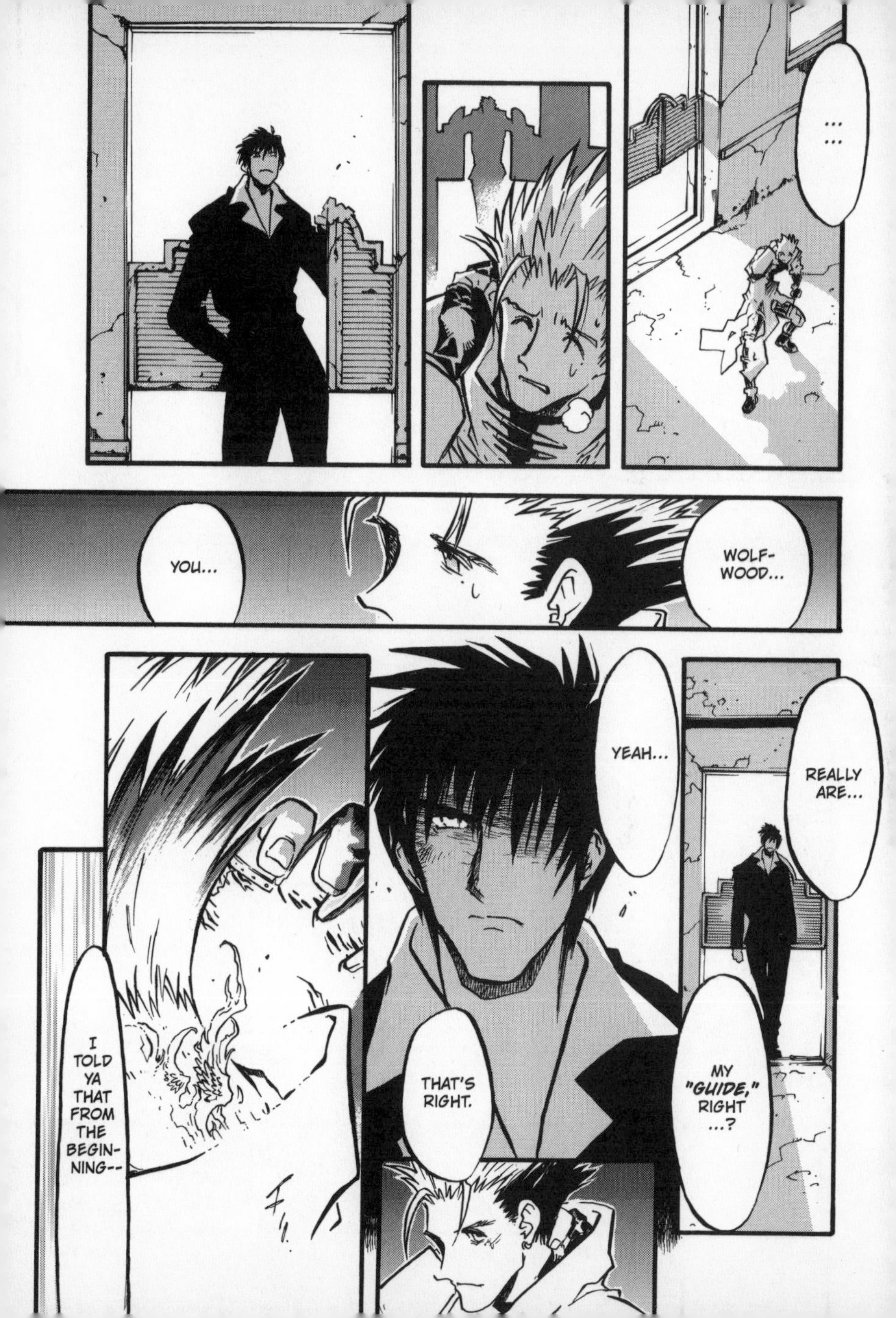
......
WOLF-WOOD...
YOU...
REALLY ARE...
MY "GUIDE," RIGHT ...?
YEAH...
THAT'S RIGHT.
I TOLD YA THAT FROM THE BEGIN-NING--

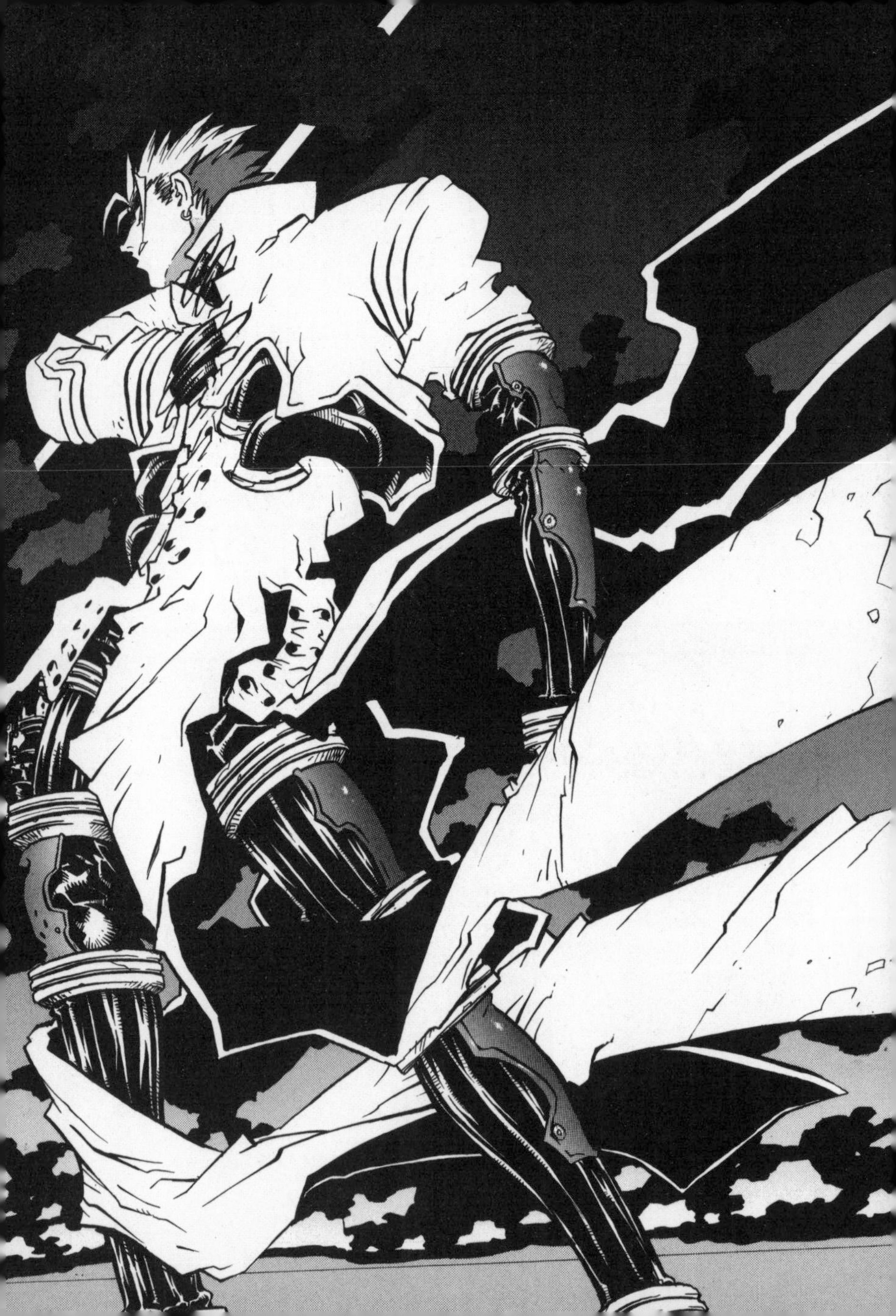

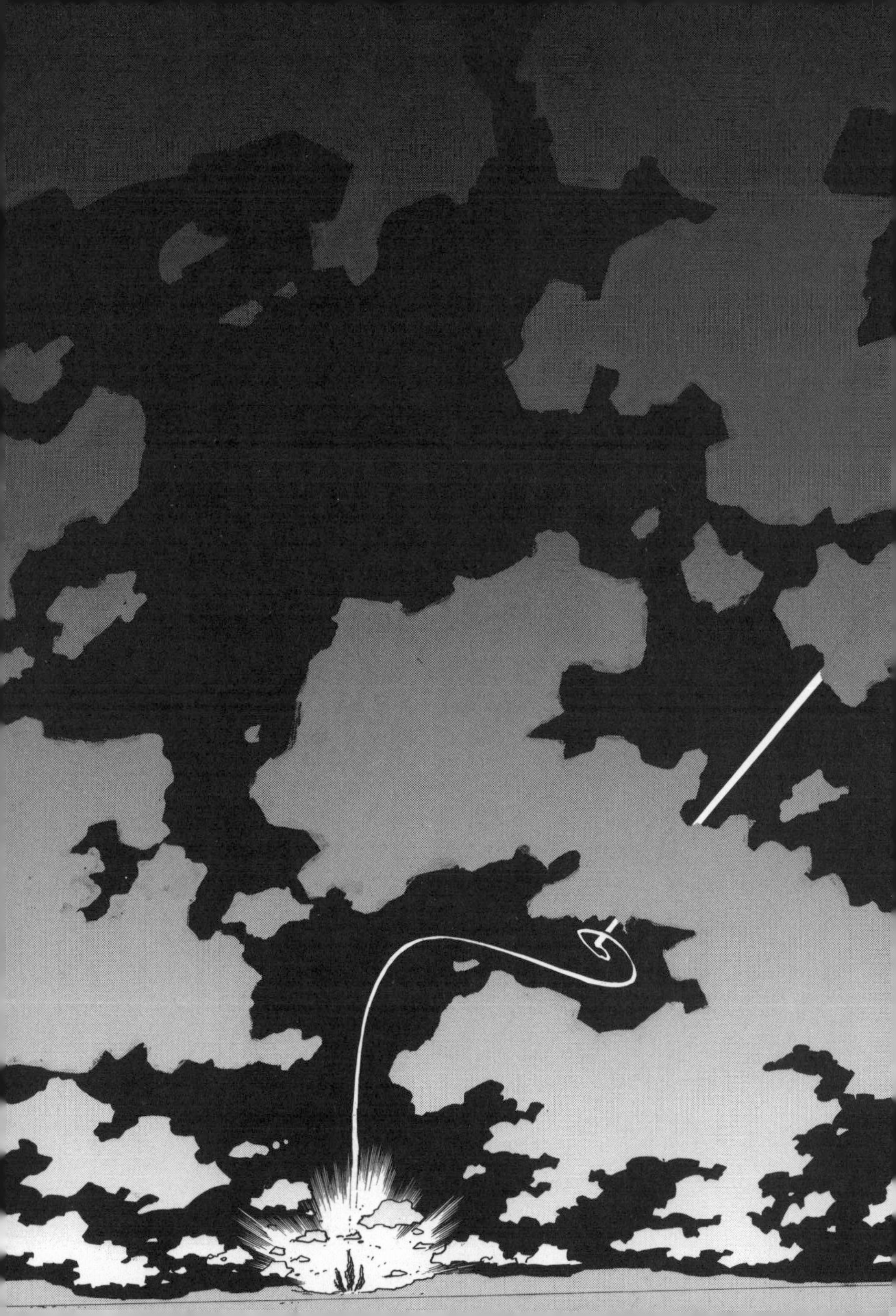

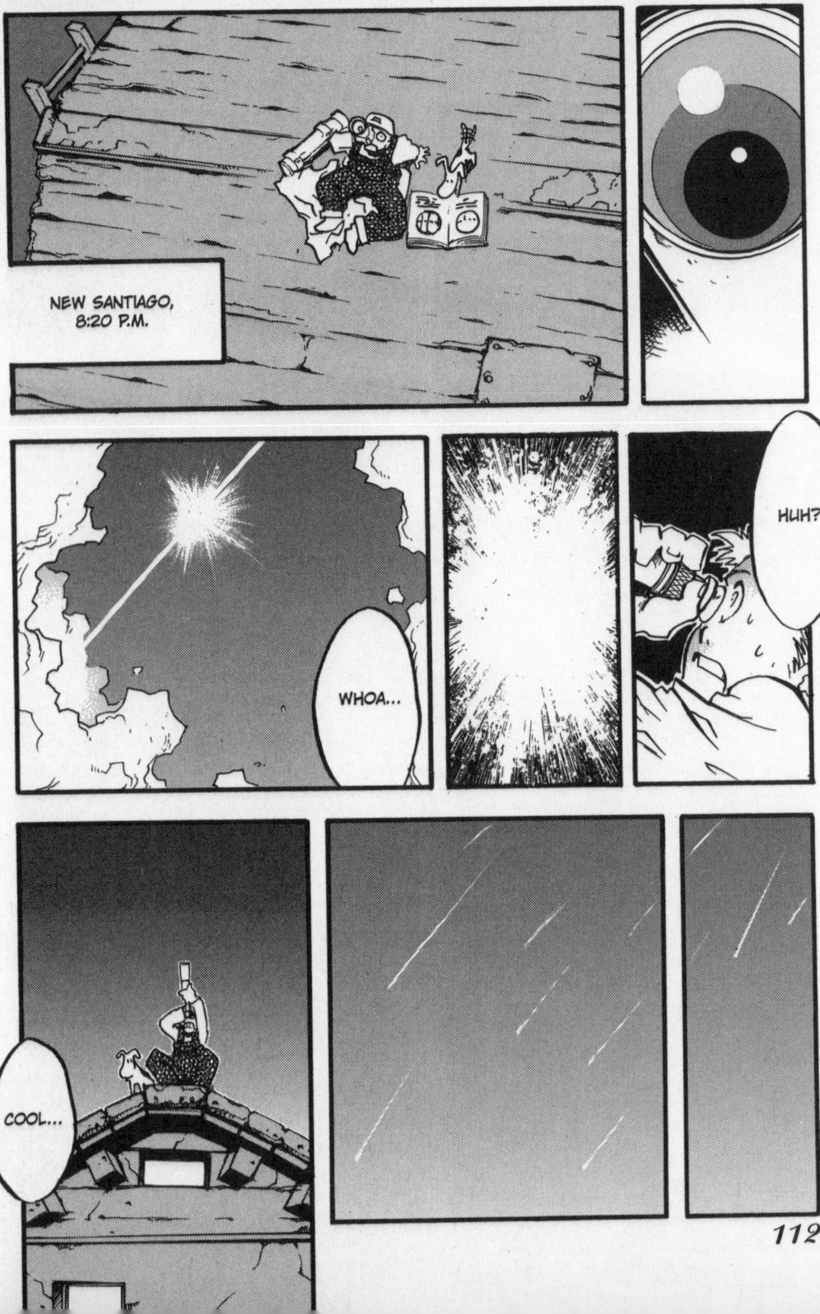
NEW SANTIAGO, 8:20 P.M.
HUH?
WHOA...
COOL...

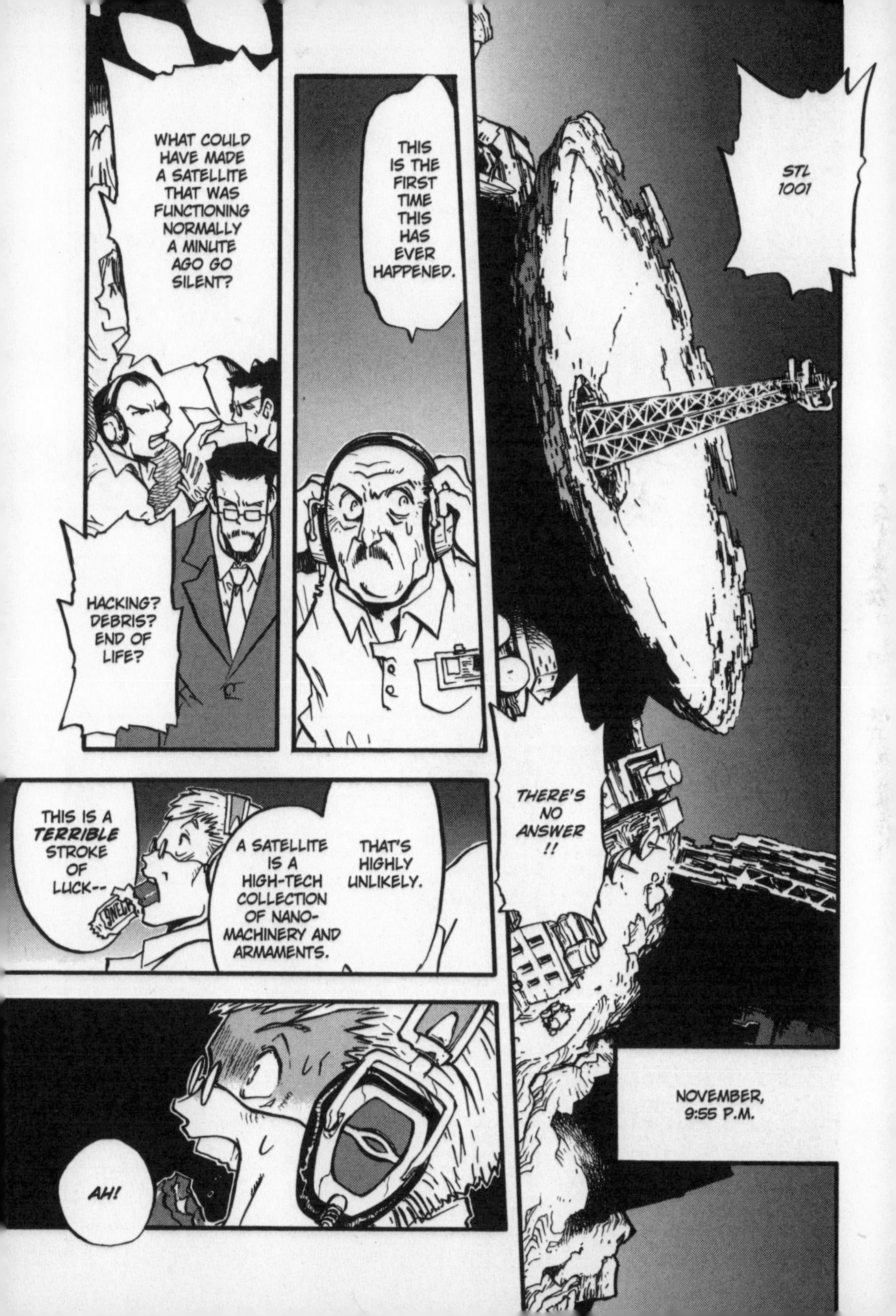

STL 1001
THERE'S NO ANSWER !!
NOVEMBER, 9:55 P.M.
THIS IS THE FIRST TIME THIS HAS EVER HAPPENED.
WHAT COULD HAVE MADE A SATELLITE THAT WAS FUNCTIONING NORMALLY A MINUTE AGO GO SILENT?
HACKING? DEBRIS? END OF LIFE?
THAT'S HIGHLY UNLIKELY.
A SATELLITE IS A HIGH-TECH COLLECTION OF NANO-MACHINERY AND ARMAMENTS.
THIS IS A *TERRIBLE* STROKE OF LUCK--
AH!

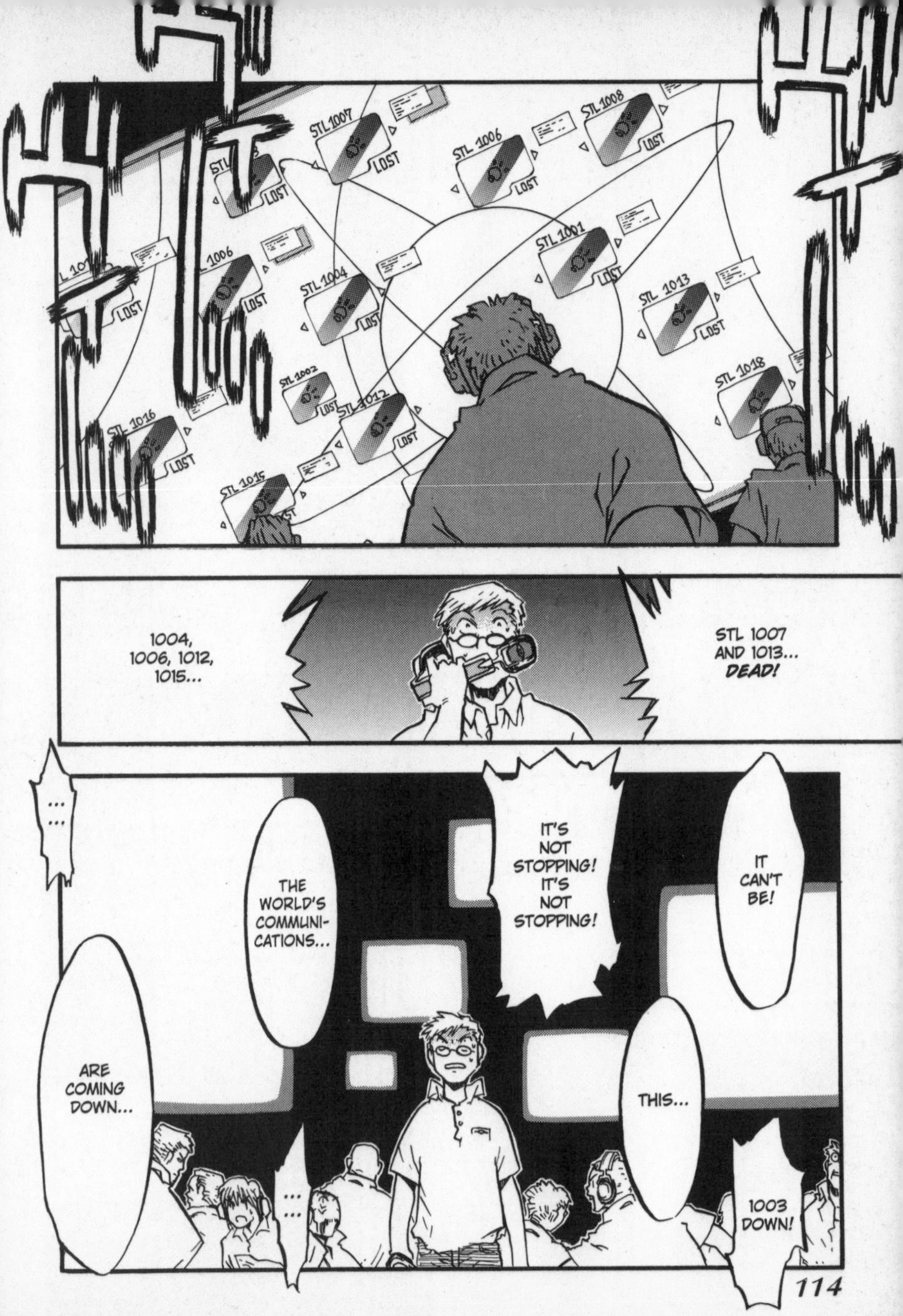
STL 1008
LOST
STL 1006
LOST
STL 1007
LOST
STL 1001
STL 1013
LOST
STL 1004
STL 1006
LOST
STL 1018
STL 1002
STL 1012
LOST
STL 1016
LOST
STL 1015
STL 1007 AND 1013... DEAD!
1004, 1006, 1012, 1015...
IT CAN'T BE!
IT'S NOT STOPPING! IT'S NOT STOPPING!
THE WORLD'S COMMUNI-CATIONS...
......
1003 DOWN!
THIS...
ARE COMING DOWN...
......

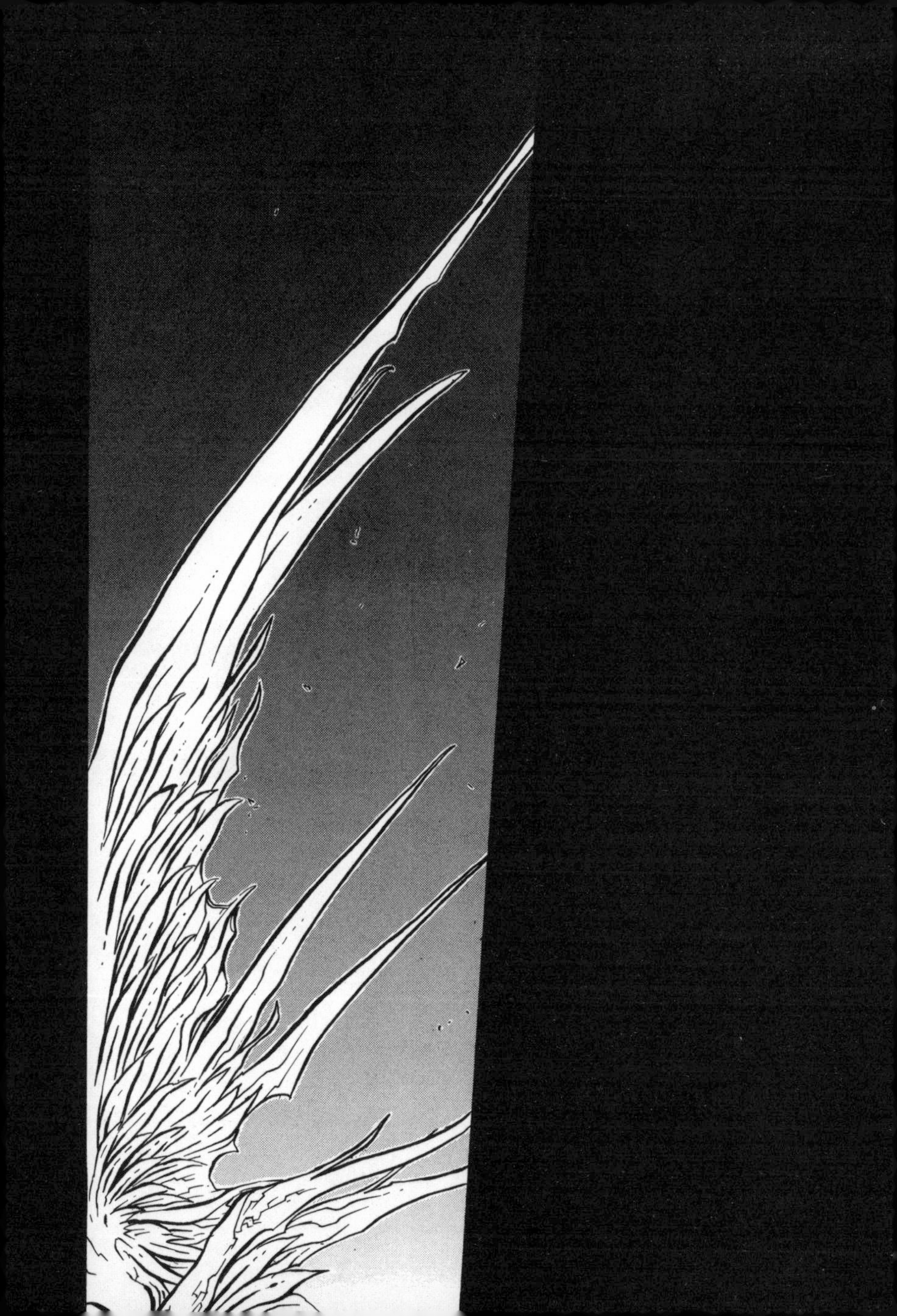

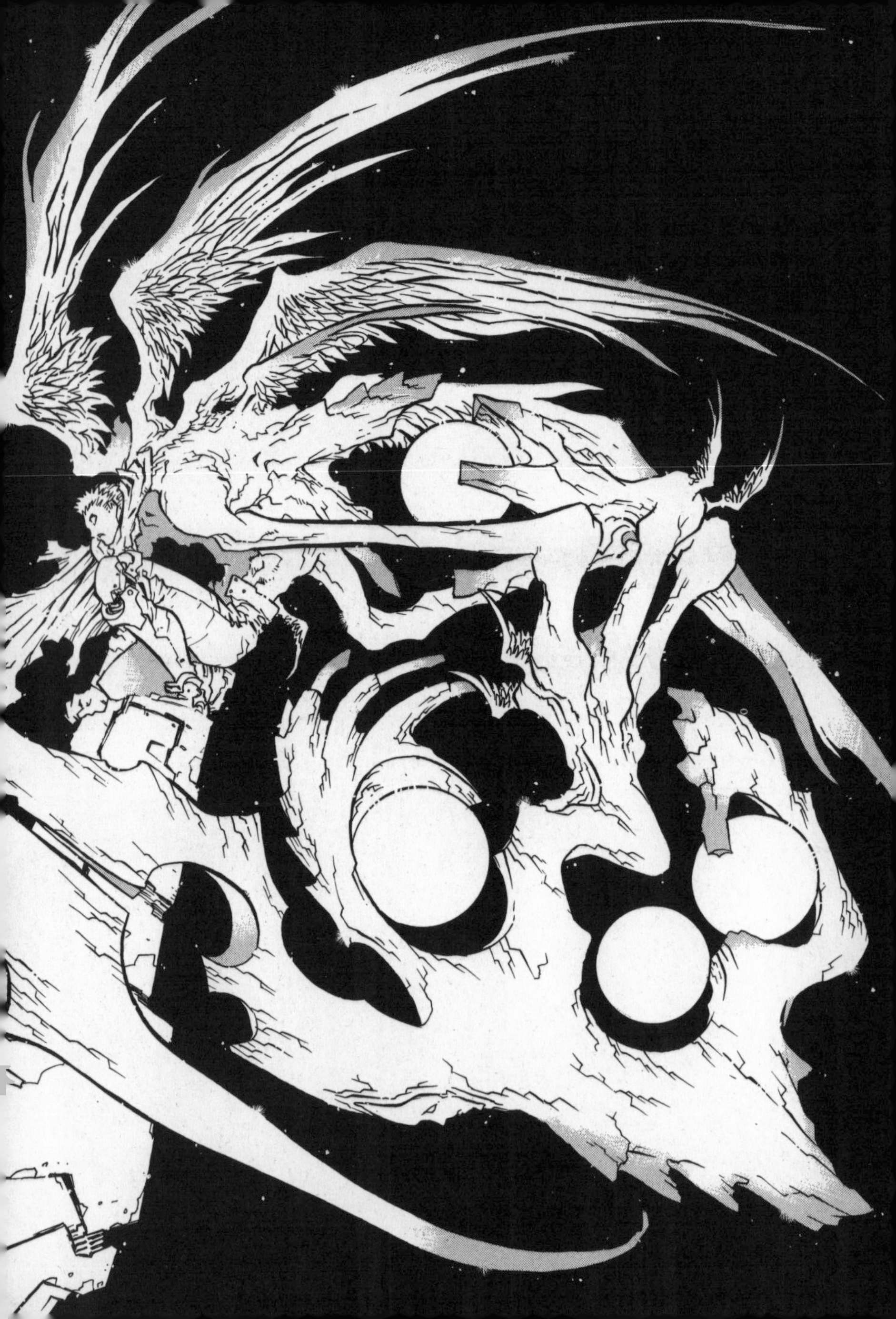

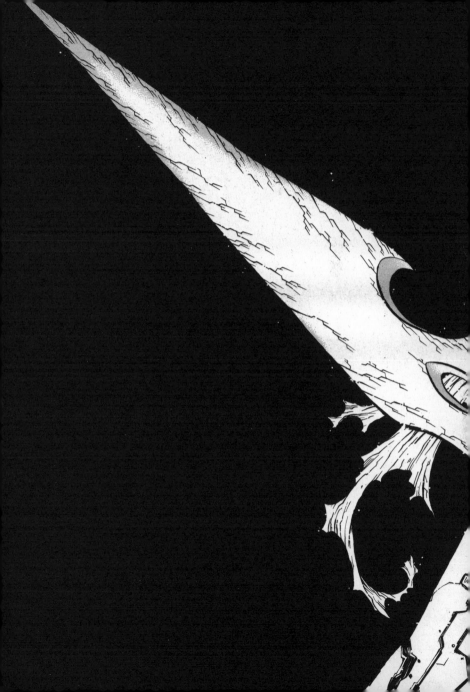

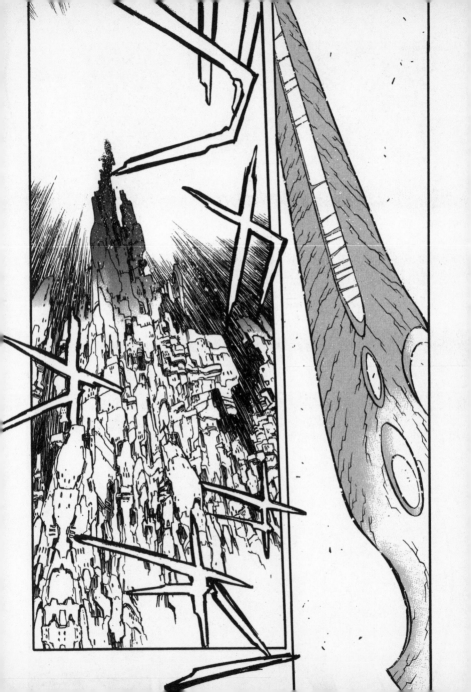

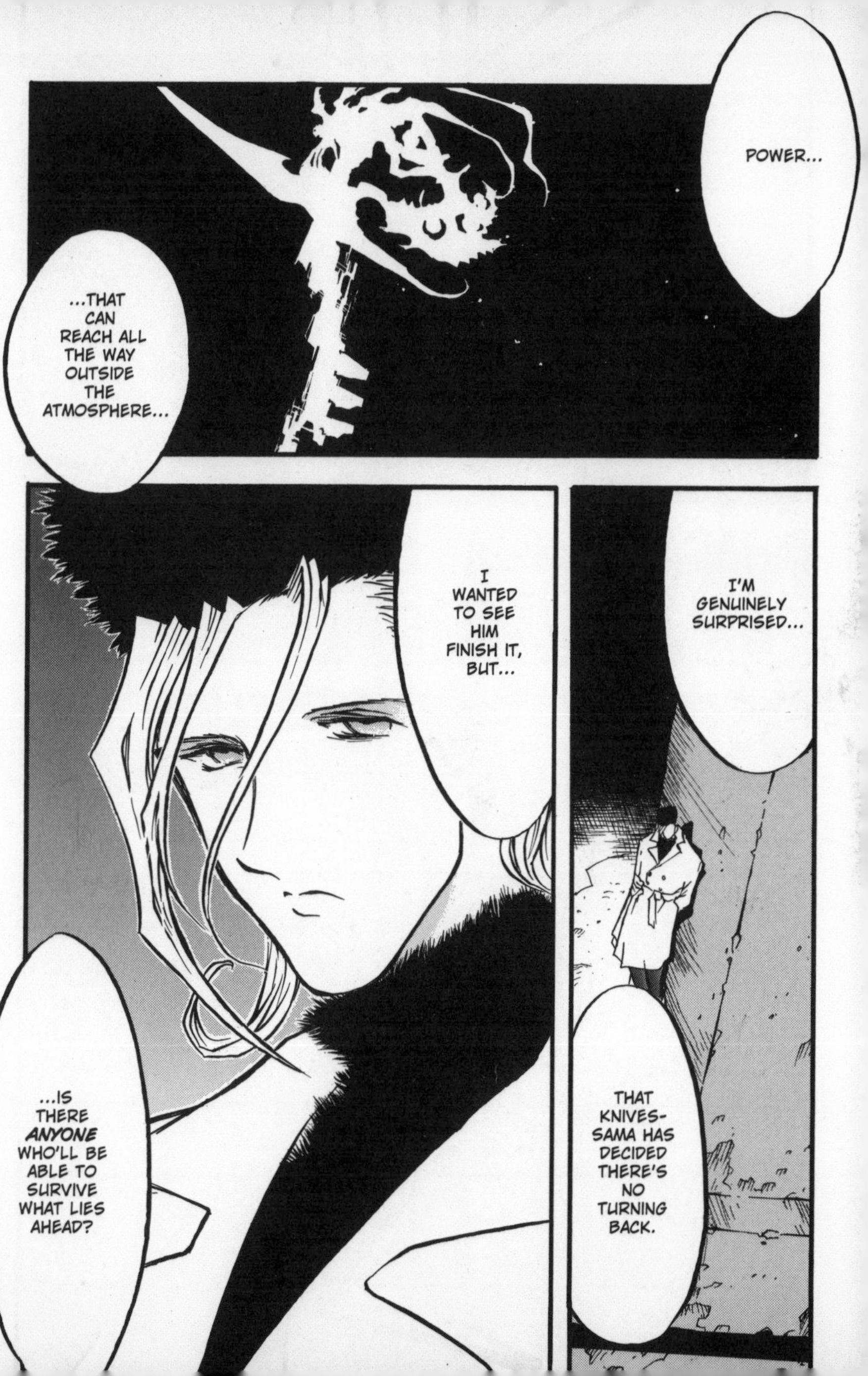
POWER...
...THAT CAN REACH ALL THE WAY OUTSIDE THE ATMOSPHERE...
I'M GENUINELY SURPRISED...
THAT KNIVES-SAMA HAS DECIDED THERE'S NO TURNING BACK.
I WANTED TO SEE HIM FINISH IT, BUT...
...IS THERE *ANYONE* WHO'LL BE ABLE TO SURVIVE WHAT LIES AHEAD?

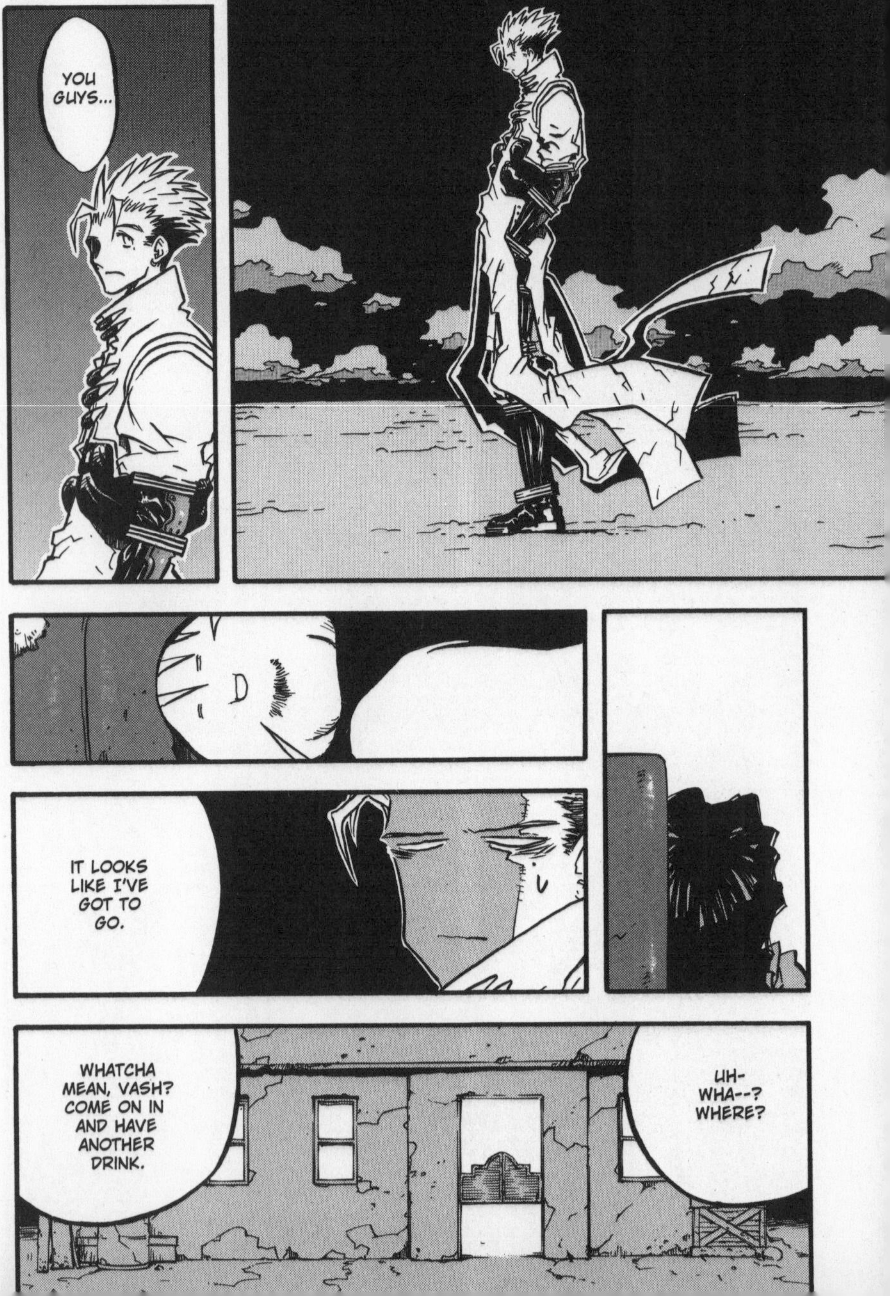
YOU GUYS...
IT LOOKS LIKE I'VE GOT TO GO.
UH- WHA--? WHERE?
WHATCHA MEAN, VASH? COME ON IN AND HAVE ANOTHER DRINK.

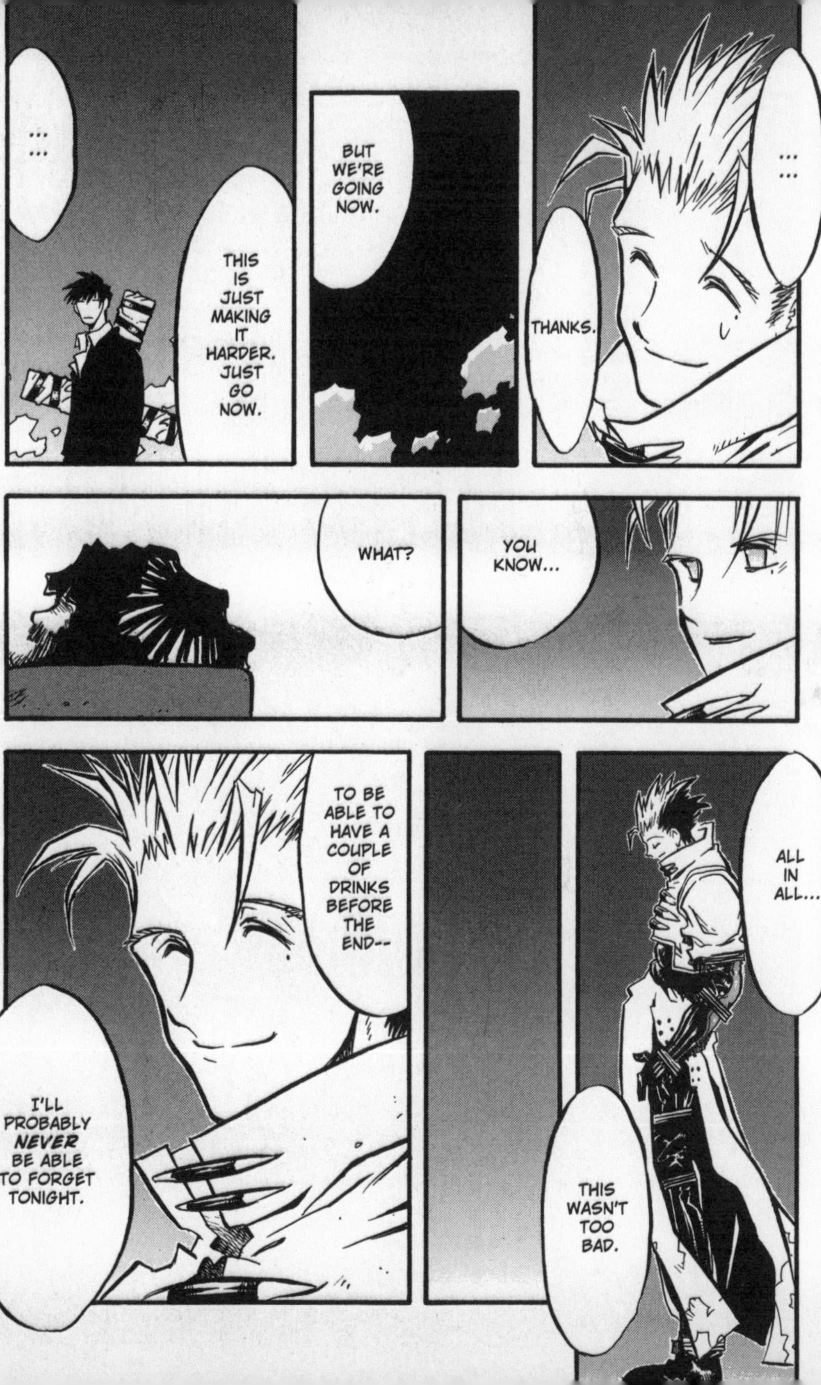
...
...
THANKS.
BUT WE'RE GOING NOW.
...
...
THIS IS JUST MAKING IT HARDER. JUST GO NOW.
YOU KNOW...
WHAT?
ALL IN ALL...
THIS WASN'T TOO BAD.
TO BE ABLE TO HAVE A COUPLE OF DRINKS BEFORE THE END--
I'LL PROBABLY *NEVER* BE ABLE TO FORGET TONIGHT.

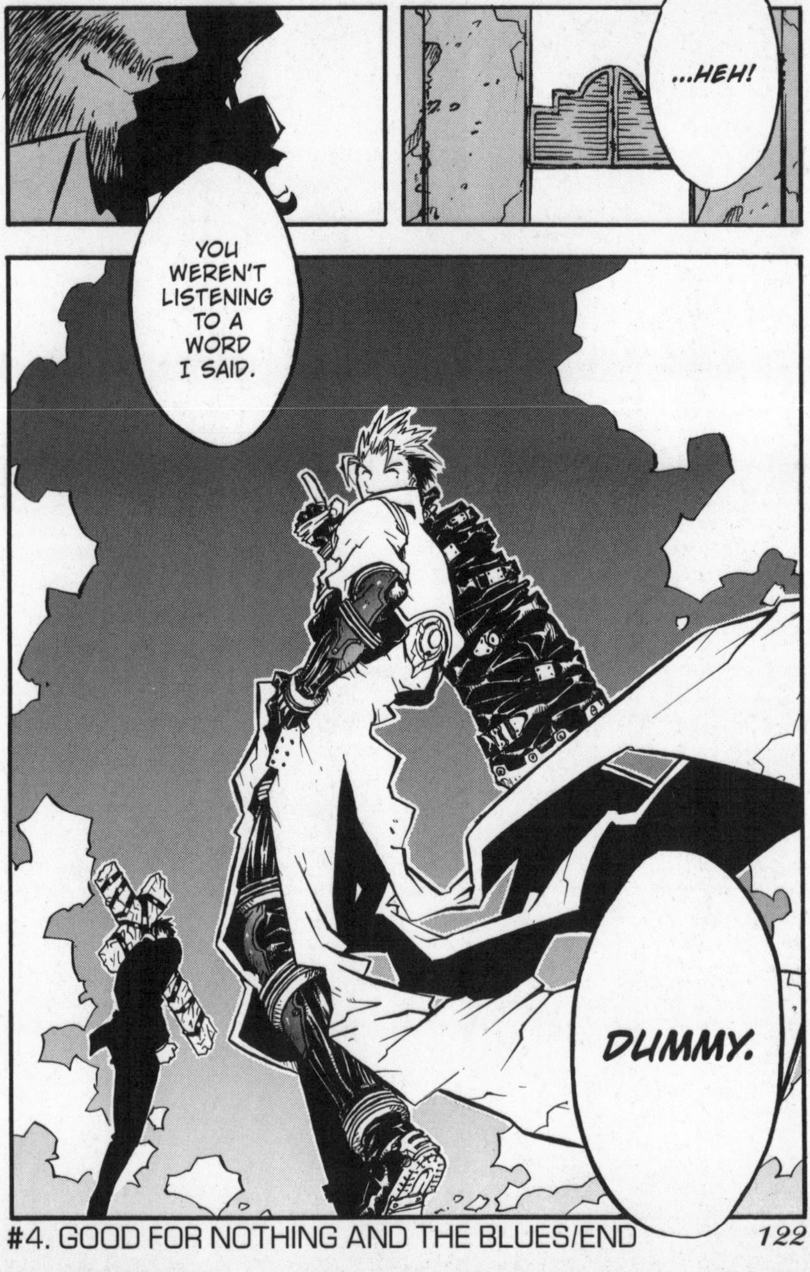
...HEH!
YOU WEREN'T LISTENING TO A WORD I SAID.
DUMMY.

TRIGUN MAXIMUM

YASUHIRO NIGHTOW

DEEP SPACE PLANET FUTURE GUN ACTION!!

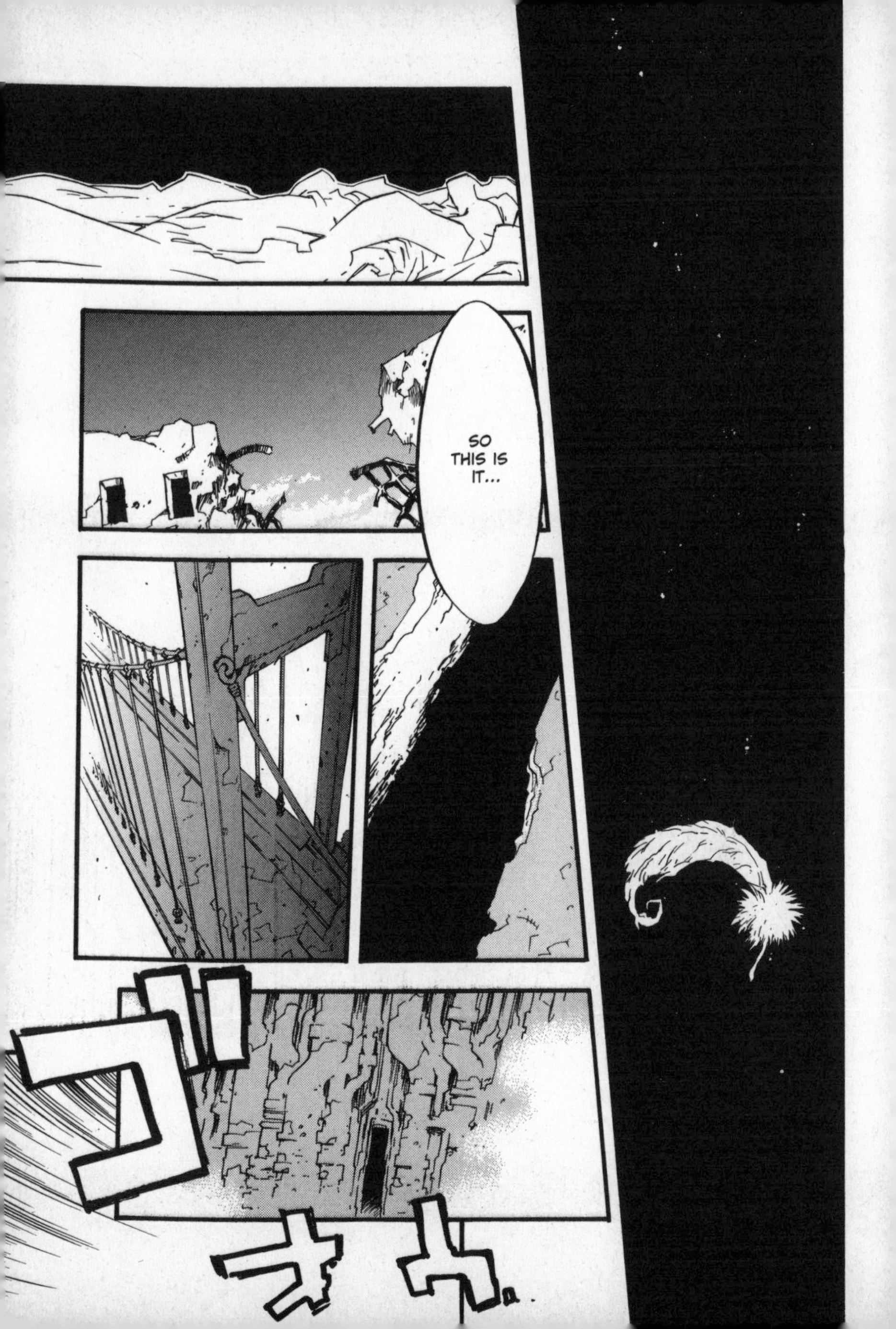
SO THIS IS IT...
ゴオォ

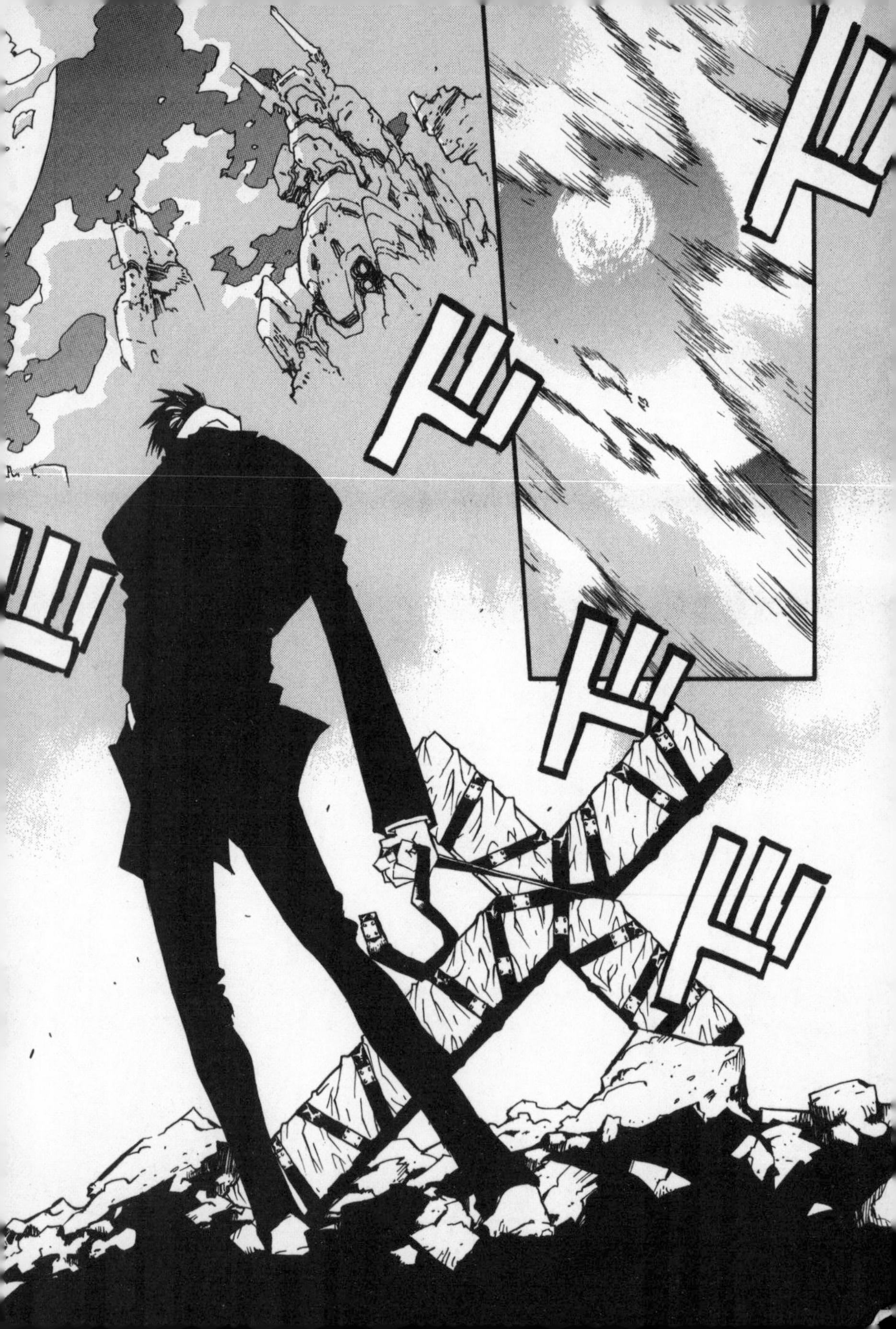
ド
ド
ド
ド
ド

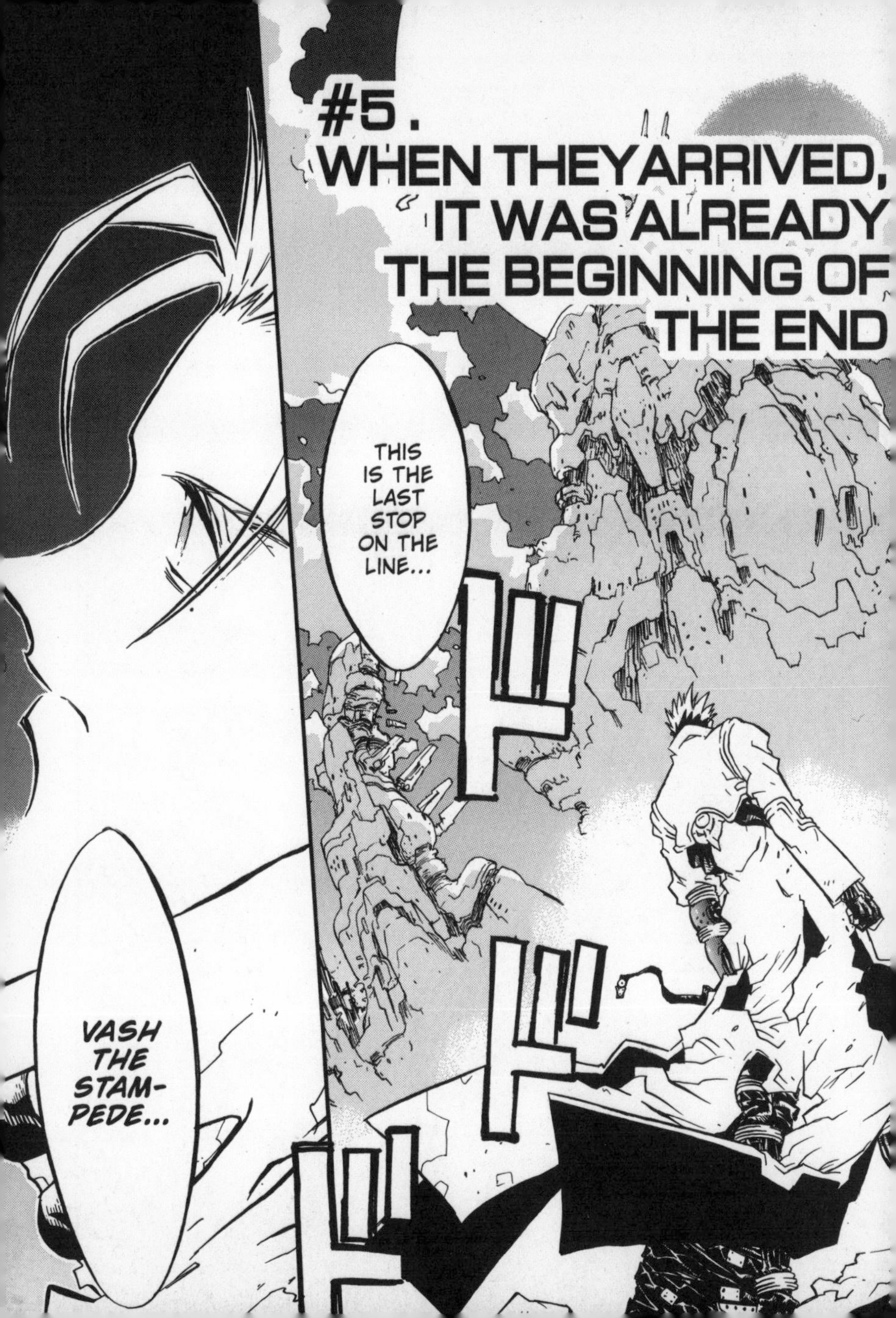
#5.
WHEN THEY ARRIVED, IT WAS ALREADY THE BEGINNING OF THE END
THIS IS THE LAST STOP ON THE LINE...
VASH THE STAMPEDE...

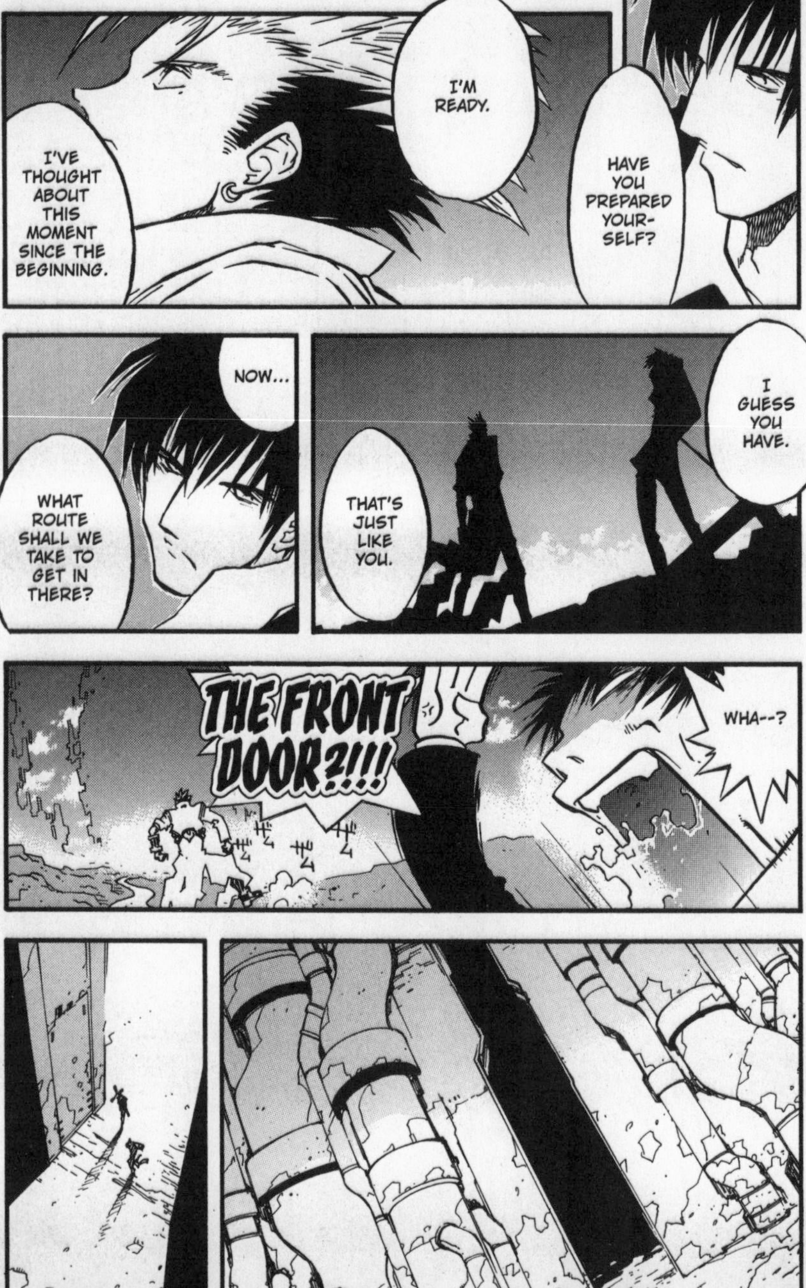
HAVE YOU PREPARED YOUR-SELF?
I'M READY.
I'VE THOUGHT ABOUT THIS MOMENT SINCE THE BEGINNING.
I GUESS YOU HAVE.
THAT'S JUST LIKE YOU.
NOW...
WHAT ROUTE SHALL WE TAKE TO GET IN THERE?
WHA--?
THE FRONT DOOR?!!!

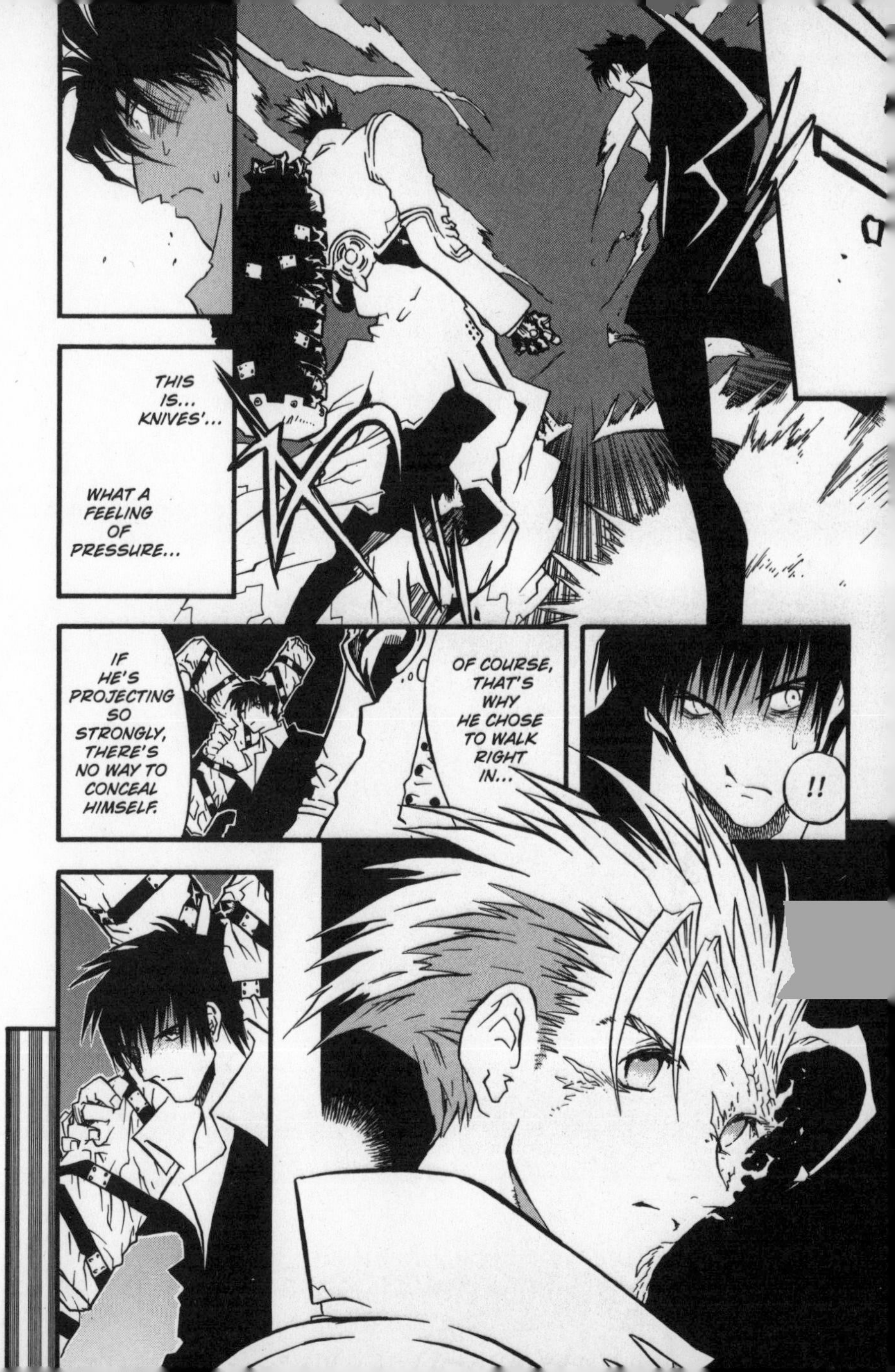
THIS IS... KNIVES'...
WHAT A FEELING OF PRESSURE...
!!
OF COURSE, THAT'S WHY HE CHOSE TO WALK RIGHT IN...
IF HE'S PROJECTING SO STRONGLY, THERE'S NO WAY TO CONCEAL HIMSELF.

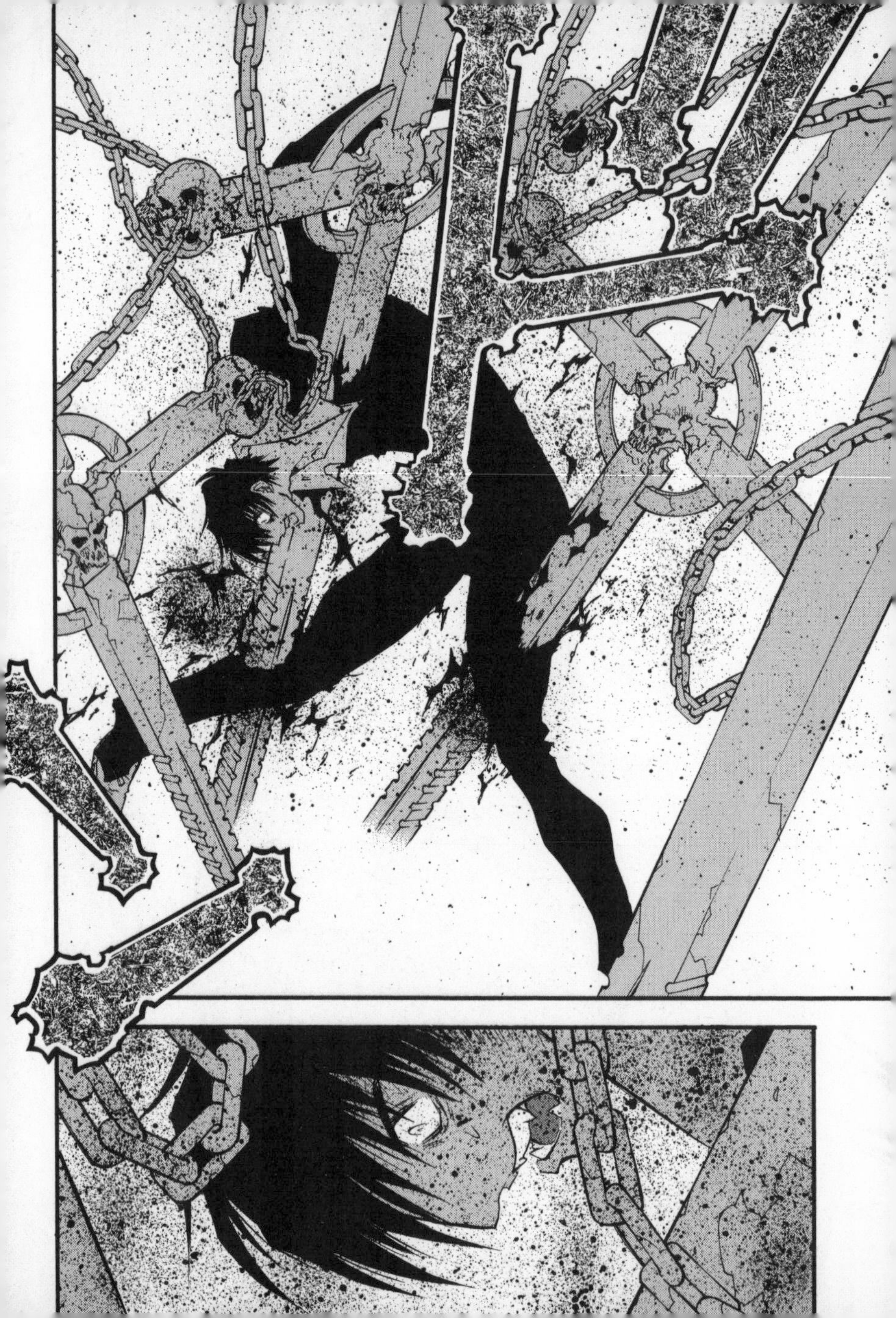

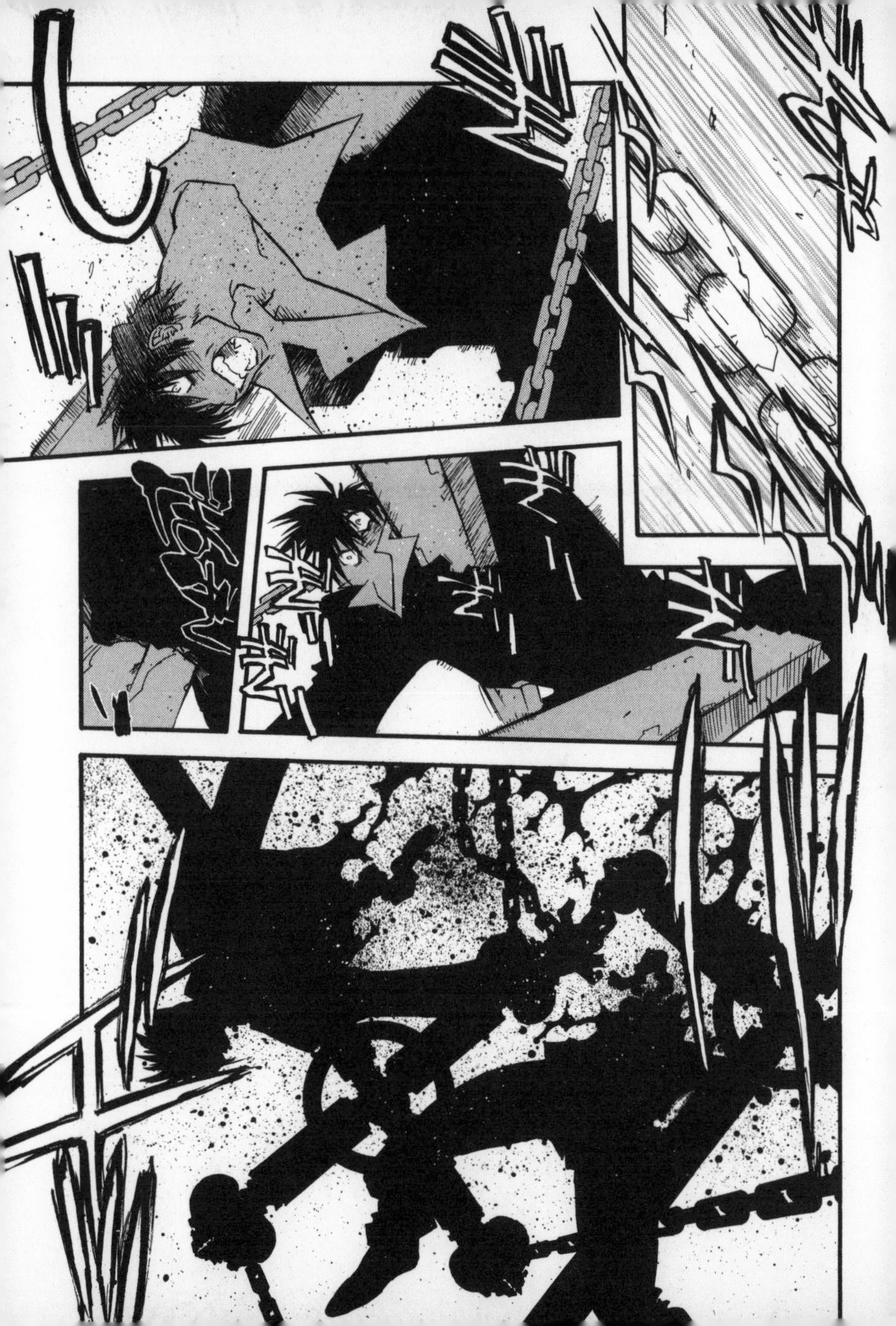

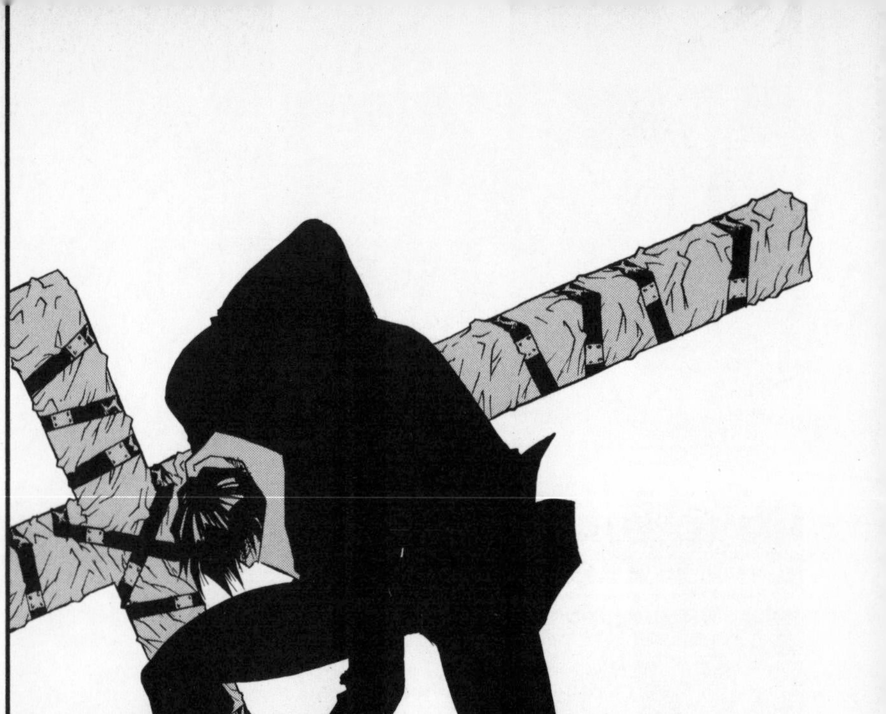

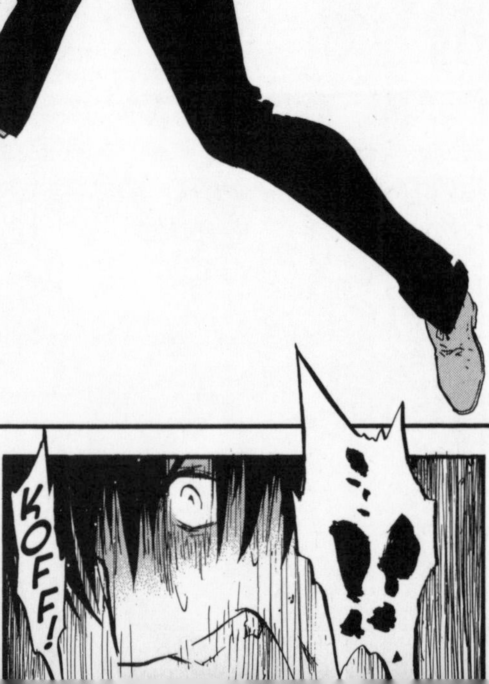
KOFF!

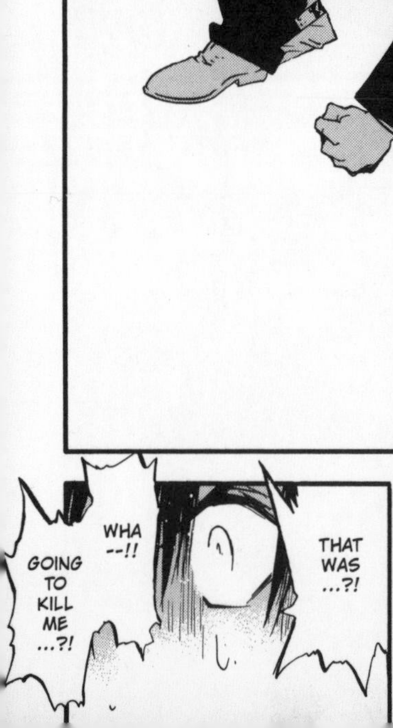
WHA --!!
THAT WAS ...?!
GOING TO KILL ME ...?!

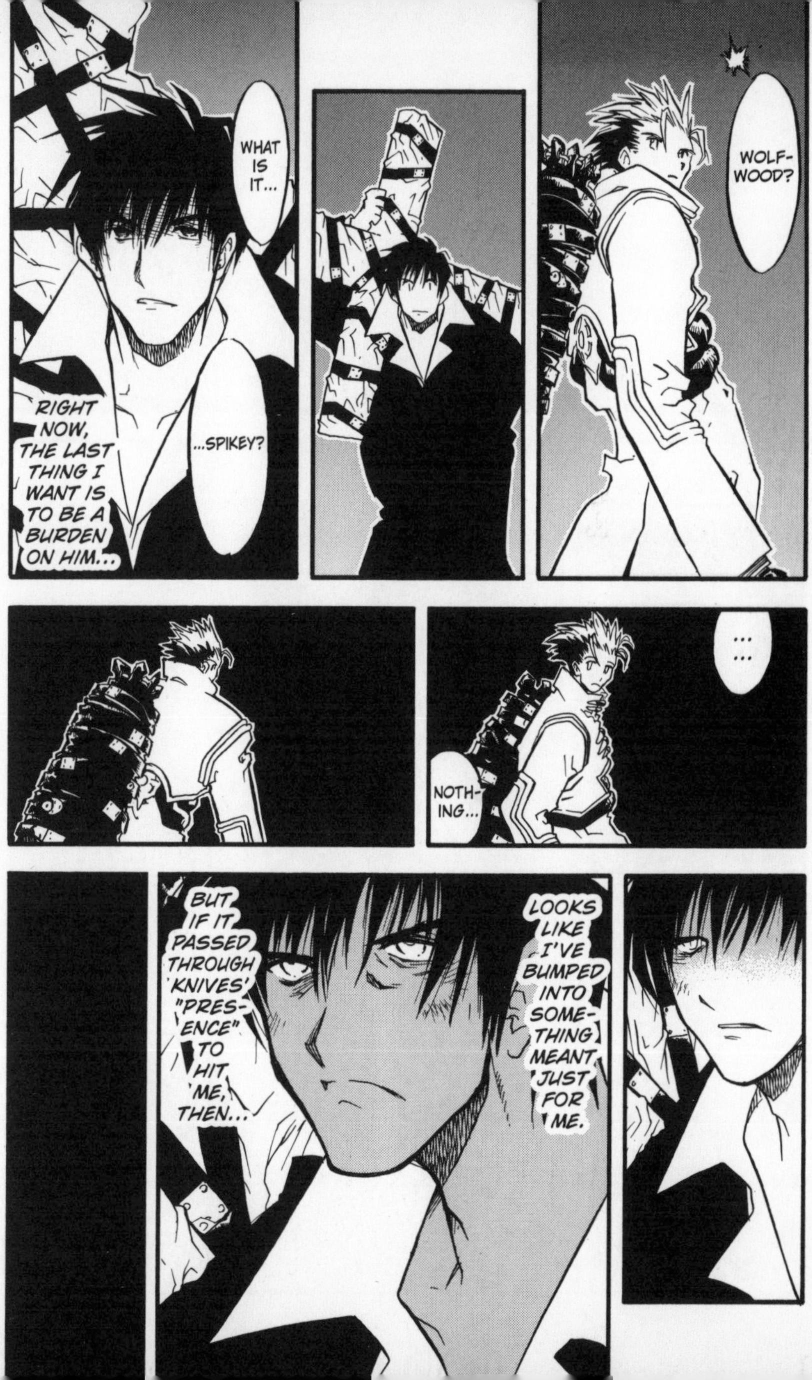
WOLF-WOOD?
WHAT IS IT...
...SPIKEY?
RIGHT NOW, THE LAST THING I WANT IS TO BE A BURDEN ON HIM...
......
NOTHING...
LOOKS LIKE I'VE BUMPED INTO SOMETHING MEANT JUST FOR ME.
BUT IF IT PASSED THROUGH KNIVES' "PRESENCE" TO HIT ME, THEN...

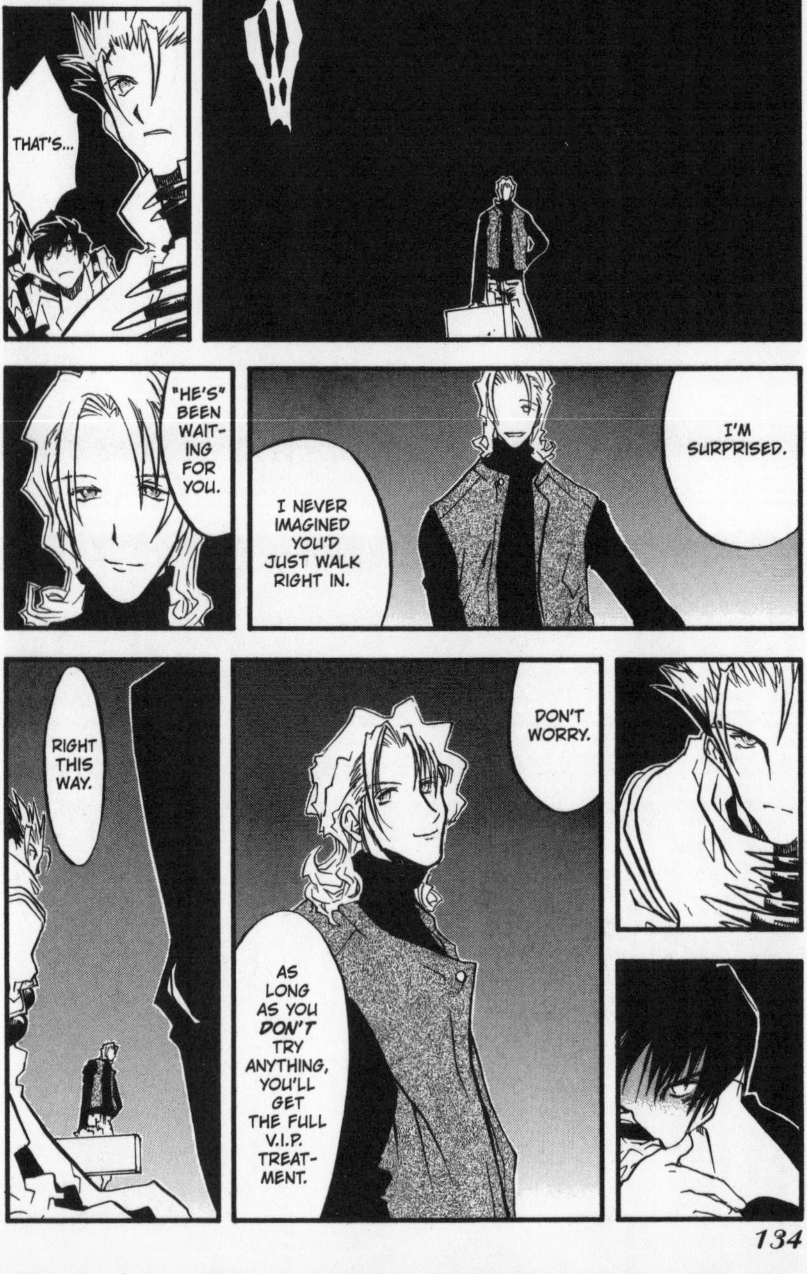
THAT'S...
I'M SURPRISED.
I NEVER IMAGINED YOU'D JUST WALK RIGHT IN.
"HE'S" BEEN WAITING FOR YOU.
DON'T WORRY.
AS LONG AS YOU **DON'T** TRY ANYTHING, YOU'LL GET THE FULL V.I.P. TREATMENT.
RIGHT THIS WAY.

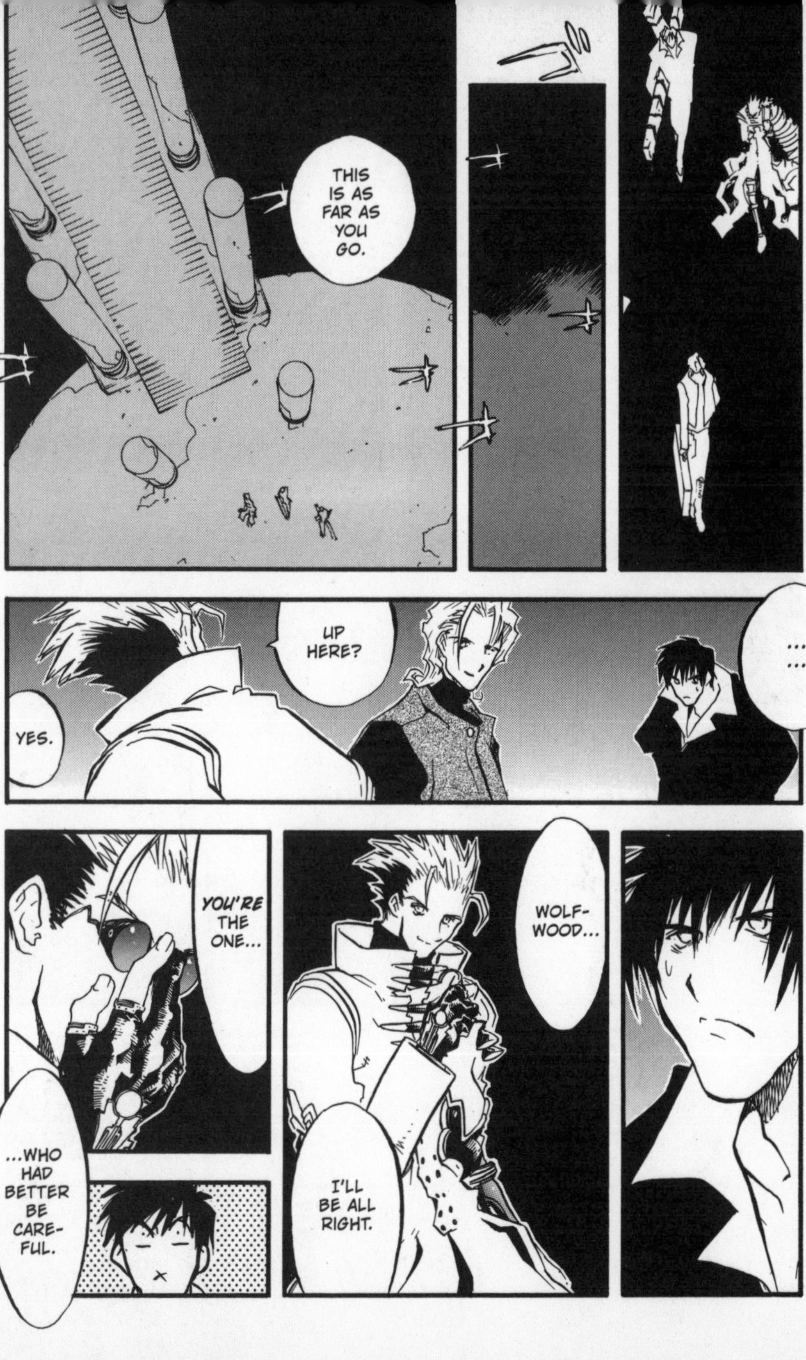
THIS IS AS FAR AS YOU GO.
... ...
UP HERE?
YES.
WOLF-WOOD...
I'LL BE ALL RIGHT.
YOU'RE THE ONE...
...WHO HAD BETTER BE CARE-FUL.

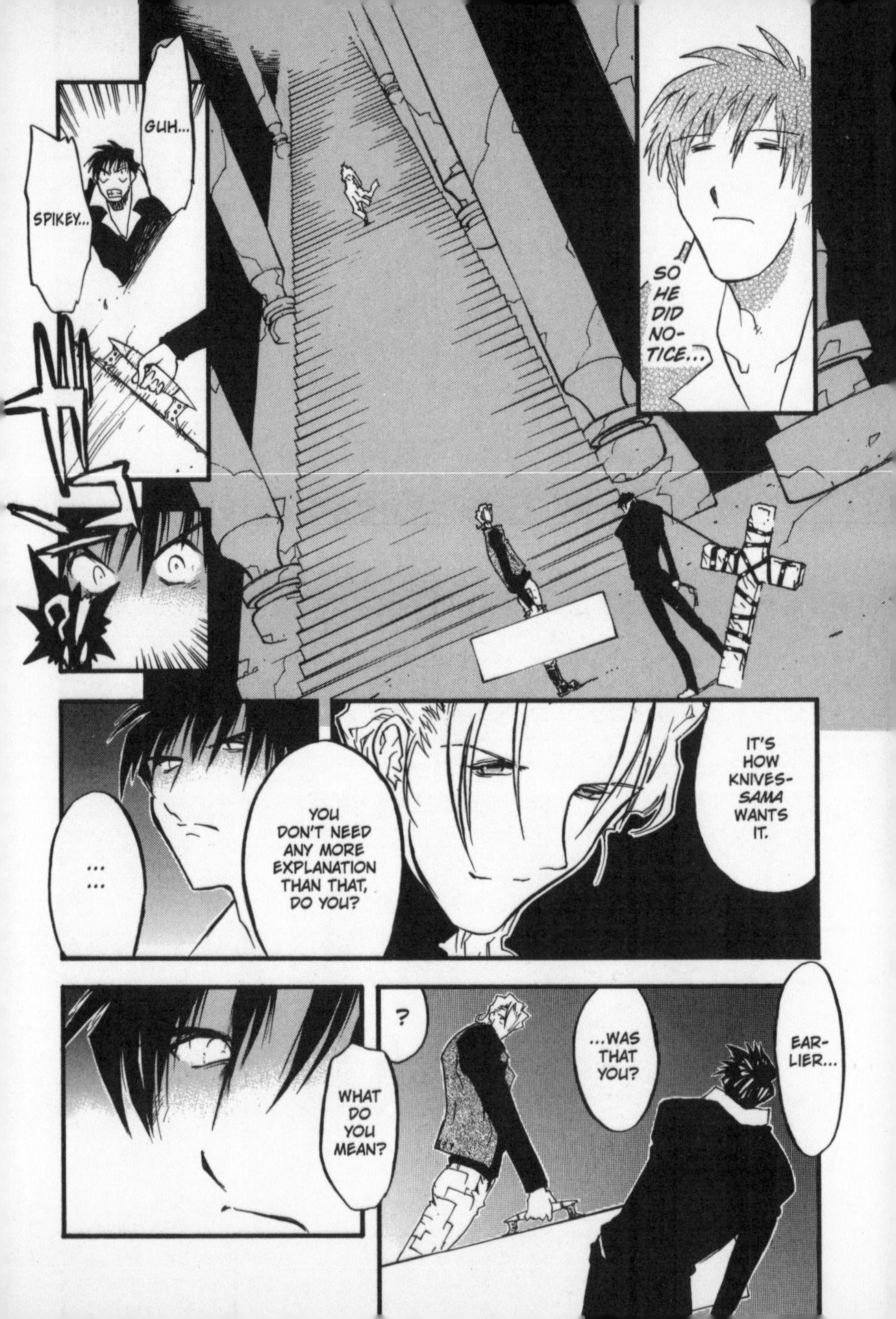
SO HE DID NO-TICE...
GUH...
SPIKEY...
IT'S HOW KNIVES-SAMA WANTS IT.
YOU DON'T NEED ANY MORE EXPLANATION THAN THAT, DO YOU?
......
EAR-LIER...
...WAS THAT YOU?
?
WHAT DO YOU MEAN?

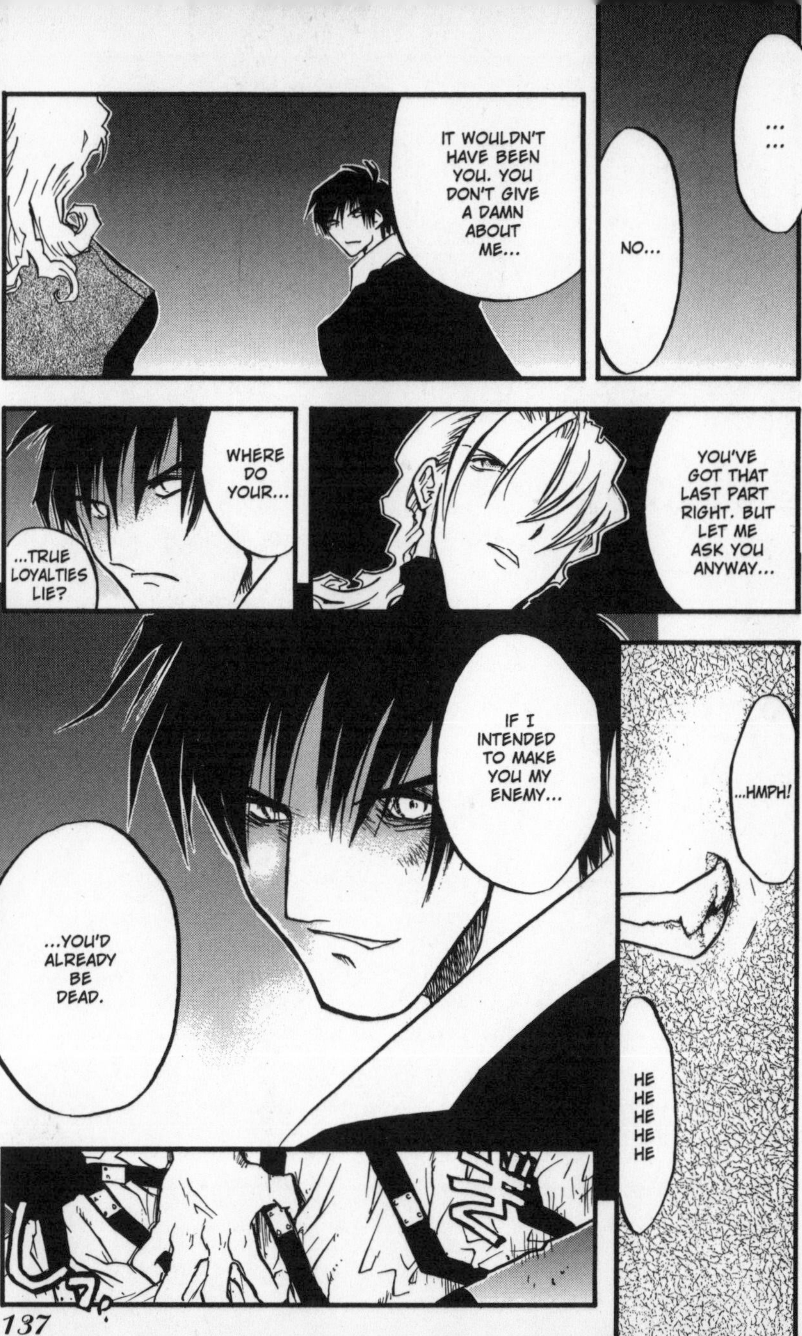
......
NO...
IT WOULDN'T HAVE BEEN YOU. YOU DON'T GIVE A DAMN ABOUT ME...
YOU'VE GOT THAT LAST PART RIGHT. BUT LET ME ASK YOU ANYWAY...
WHERE DO YOUR...
...TRUE LOYALTIES LIE?
...HMPH!
HE HE HE HE HE
IF I INTENDED TO MAKE YOU MY ENEMY...
...YOU'D ALREADY BE DEAD.

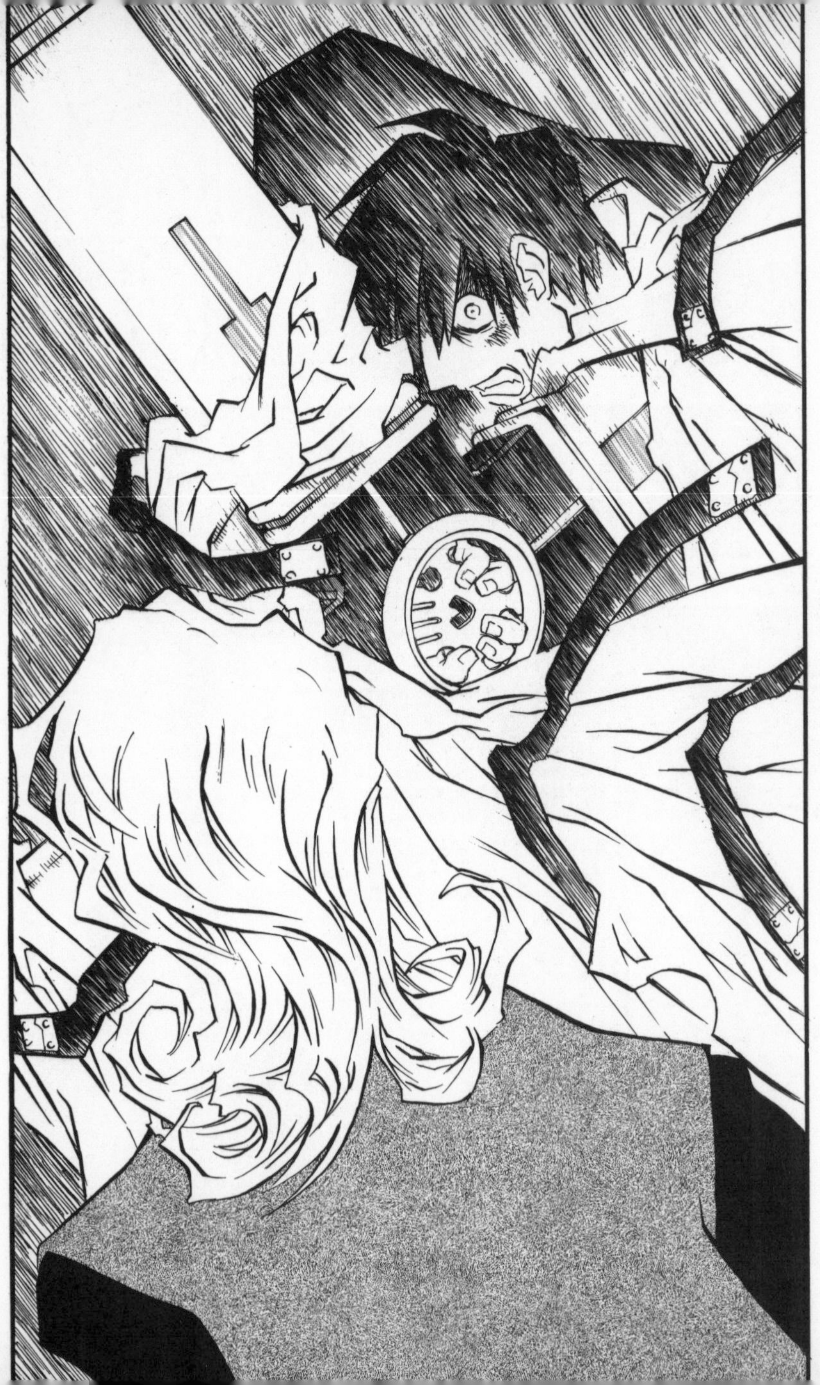

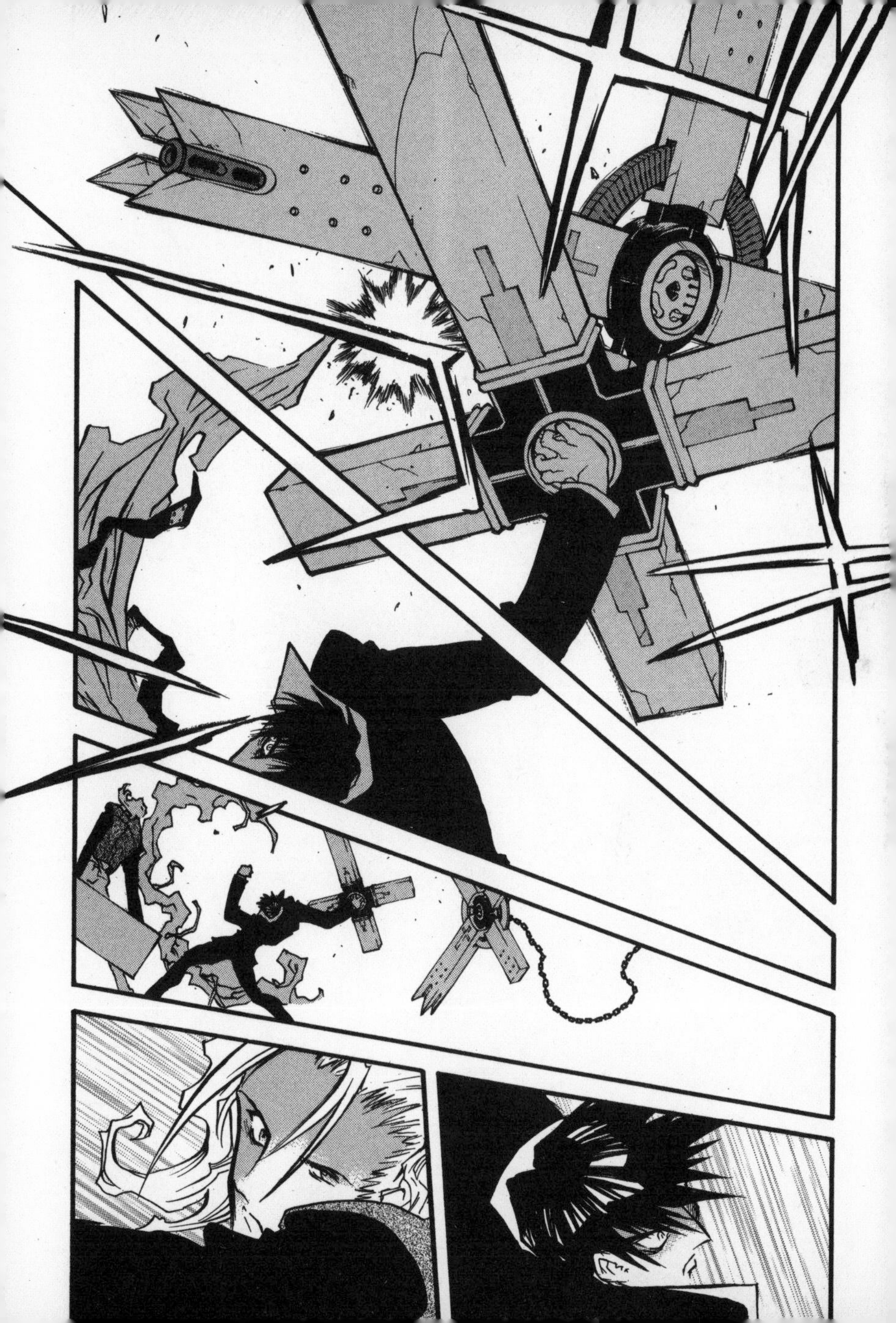

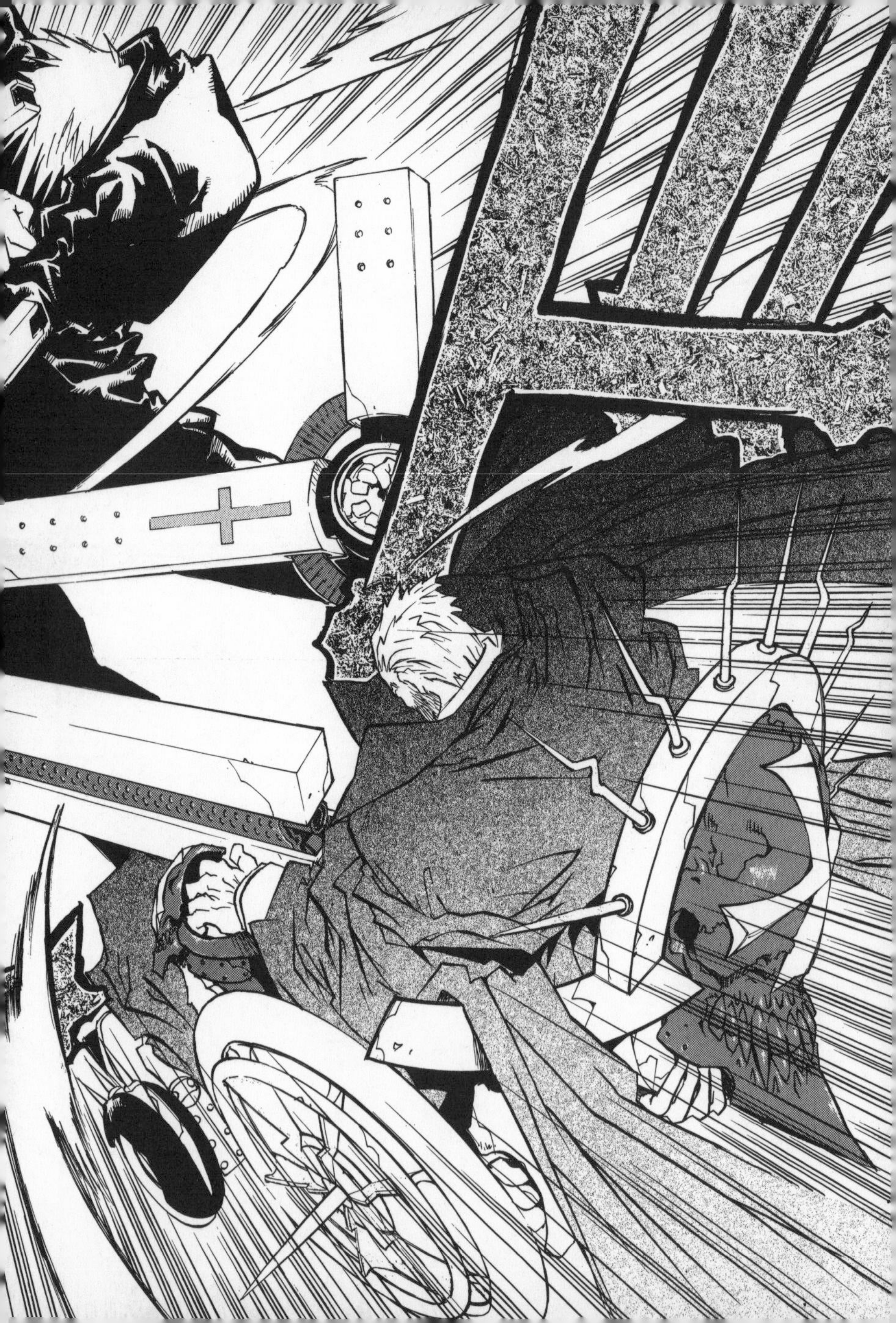

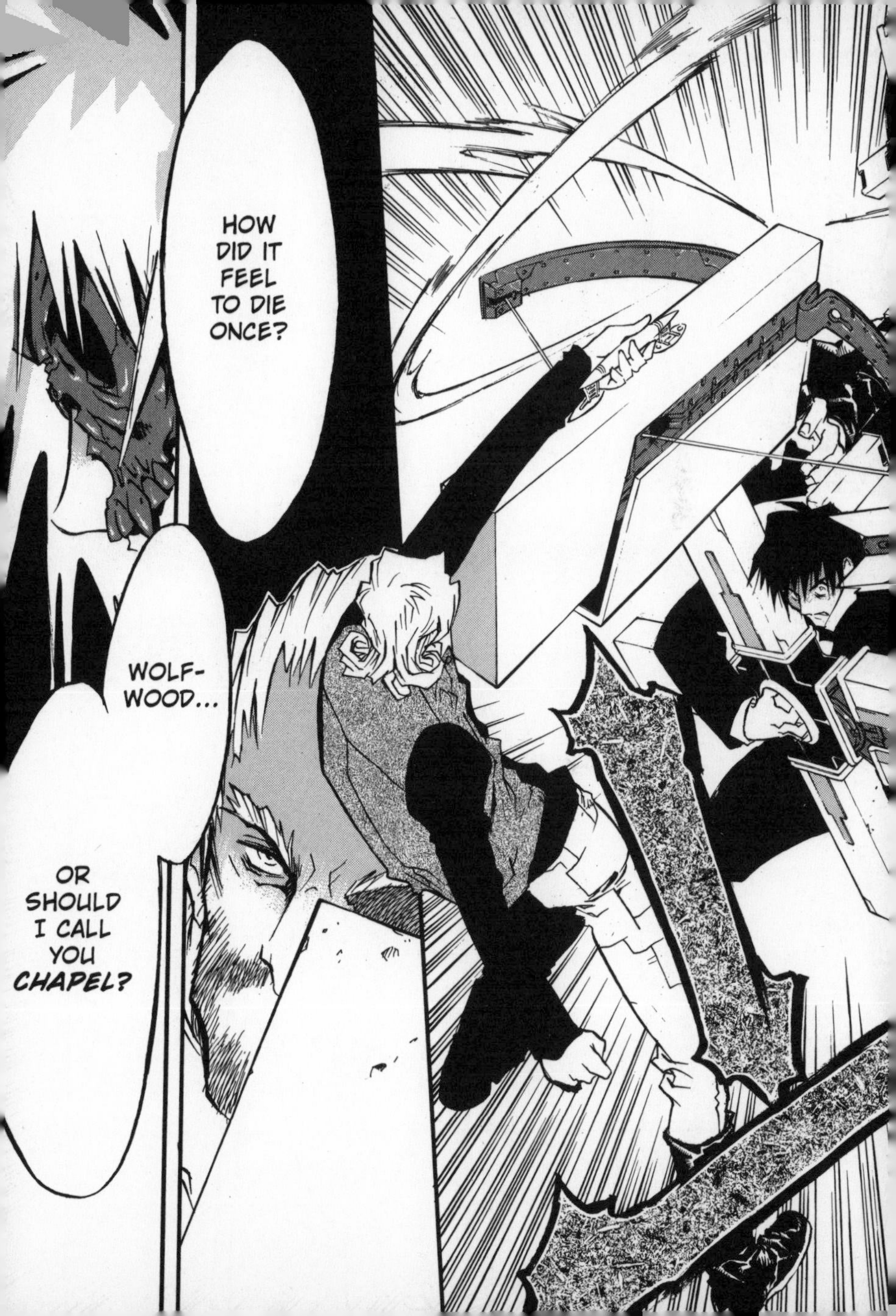
HOW DID IT FEEL TO DIE ONCE?
WOLF-WOOD...
OR SHOULD I CALL YOU CHAPEL?

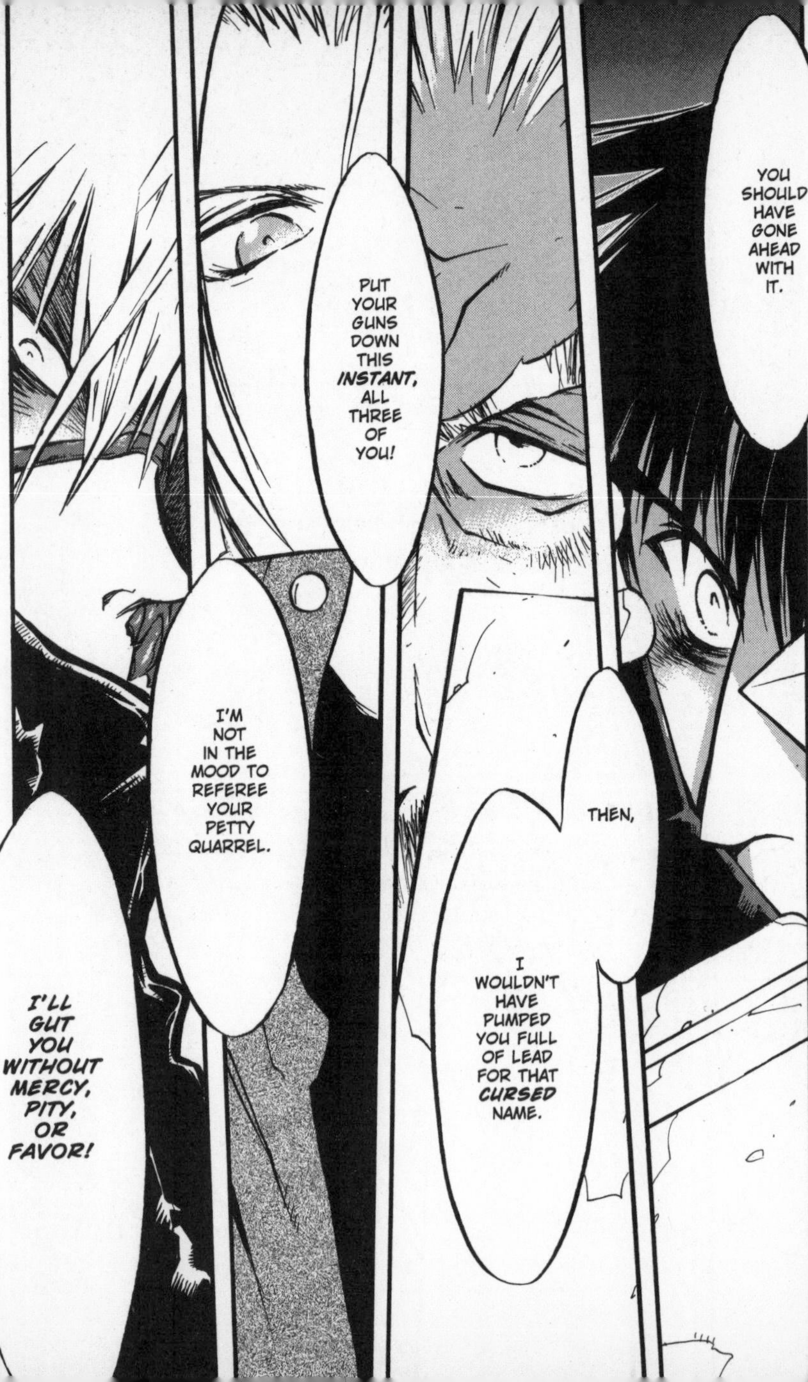
YOU SHOULD HAVE GONE AHEAD WITH IT.
THEN,
I WOULDN'T HAVE PUMPED YOU FULL OF LEAD FOR THAT CURSED NAME.
PUT YOUR GUNS DOWN THIS INSTANT, ALL THREE OF YOU!
I'M NOT IN THE MOOD TO REFEREE YOUR PETTY QUARREL.
I'LL GUT YOU WITHOUT MERCY, PITY, OR FAVOR!

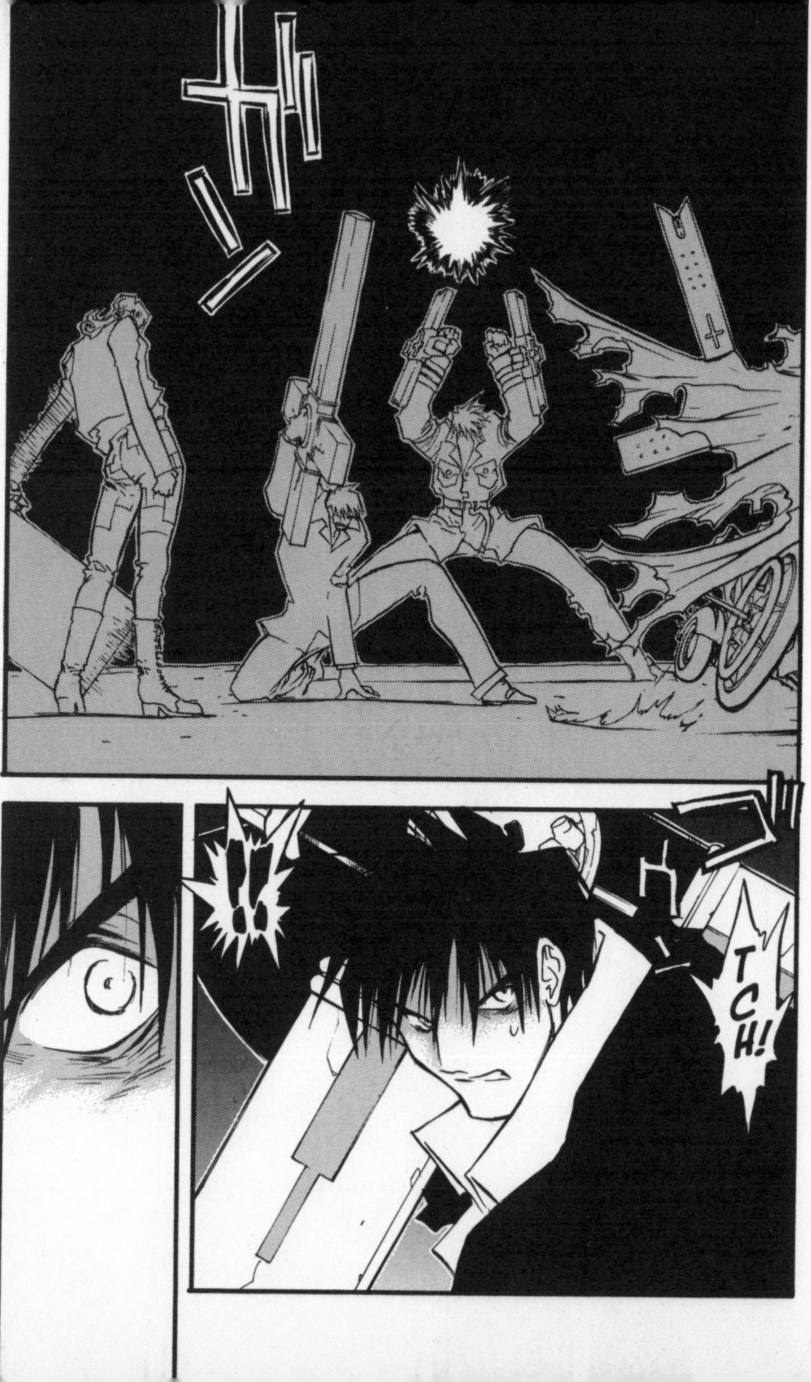
TCH!
!!

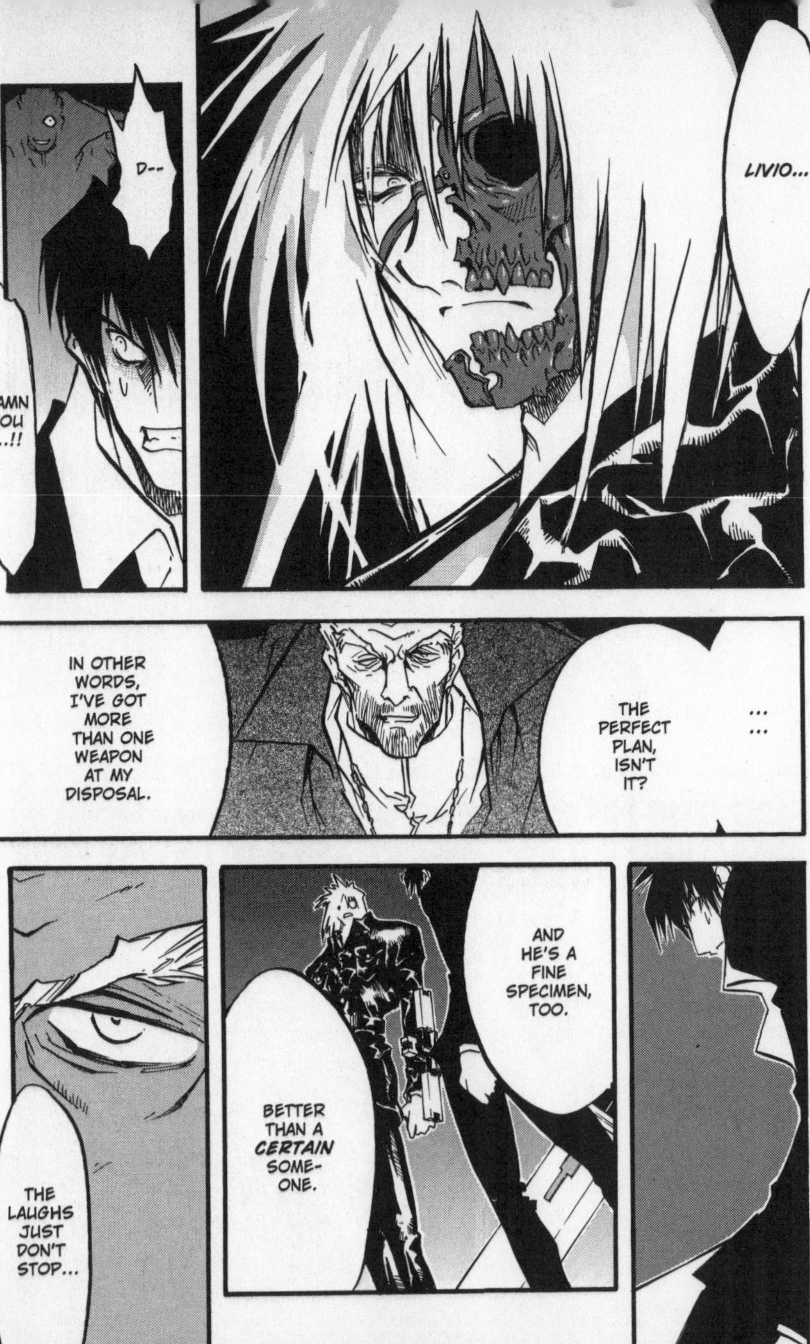
LIVIO...
D--
DAMN YOU ...!!
......
THE PERFECT PLAN, ISN'T IT?
IN OTHER WORDS, I'VE GOT MORE THAN ONE WEAPON AT MY DISPOSAL.
AND HE'S A FINE SPECIMEN, TOO.
BETTER THAN A *CERTAIN* SOME-ONE.
THE LAUGHS JUST DON'T STOP...

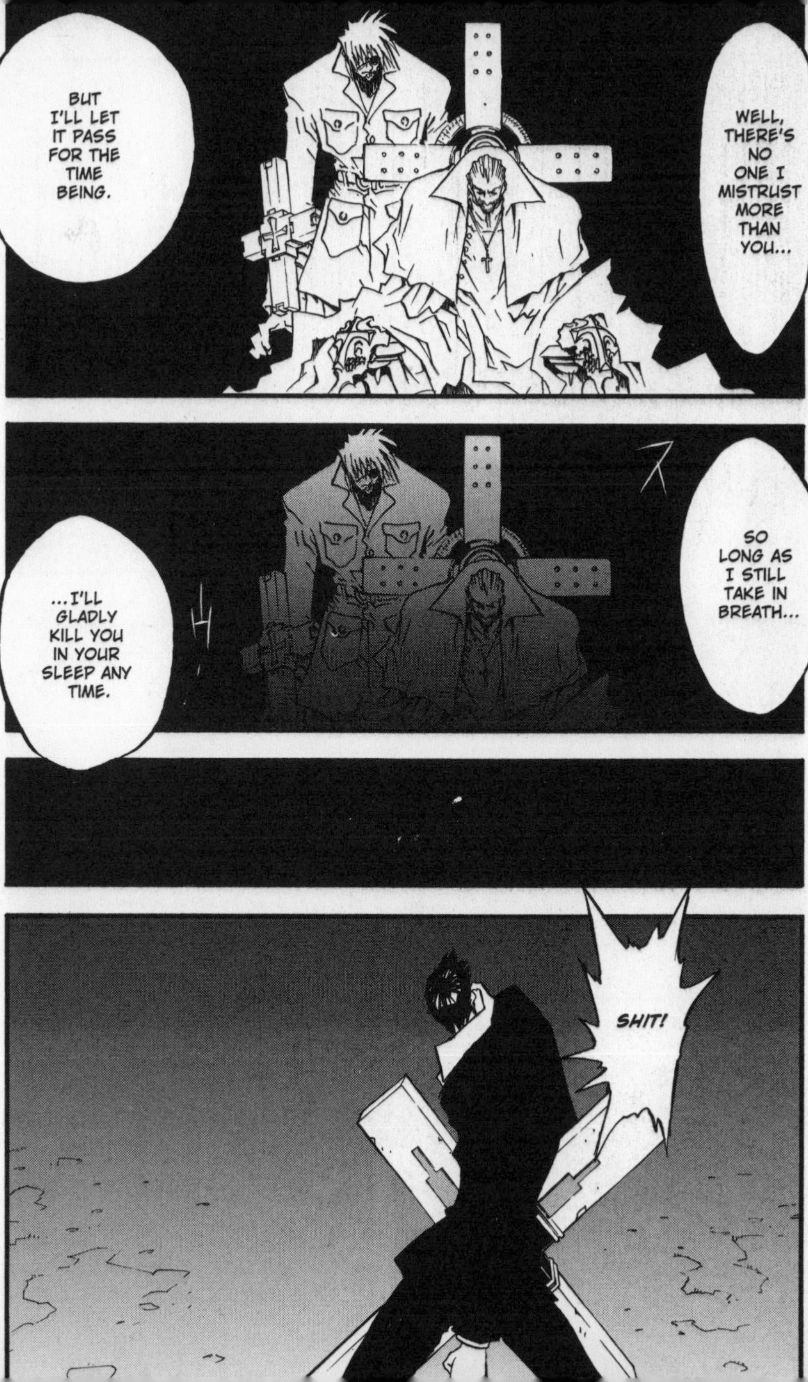
WELL, THERE'S NO ONE I MISTRUST MORE THAN YOU...
BUT I'LL LET IT PASS FOR THE TIME BEING.
SO LONG AS I STILL TAKE IN BREATH...
...I'LL GLADLY KILL YOU IN YOUR SLEEP ANY TIME.
SHIT!

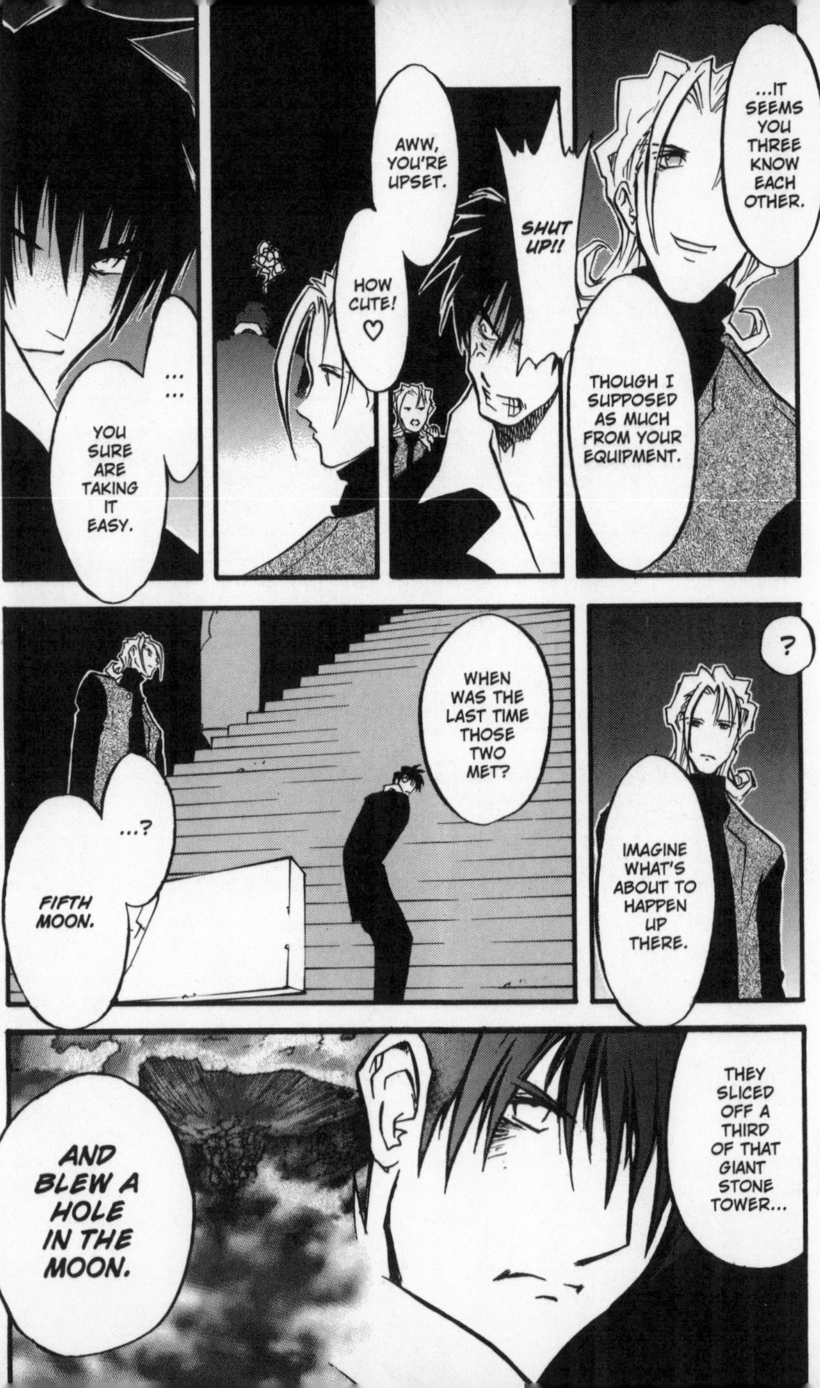

...IT SEEMS YOU THREE KNOW EACH OTHER.
THOUGH I SUPPOSED AS MUCH FROM YOUR EQUIPMENT.
AWW, YOU'RE UPSET.
HOW CUTE! ♡
SHUT UP!!
... ...
YOU SURE ARE TAKING IT EASY.
?
IMAGINE WHAT'S ABOUT TO HAPPEN UP THERE.
WHEN WAS THE LAST TIME THOSE TWO MET?
...?
FIFTH MOON.
THEY SLICED OFF A THIRD OF THAT GIANT STONE TOWER...
AND BLEW A HOLE IN THE MOON.

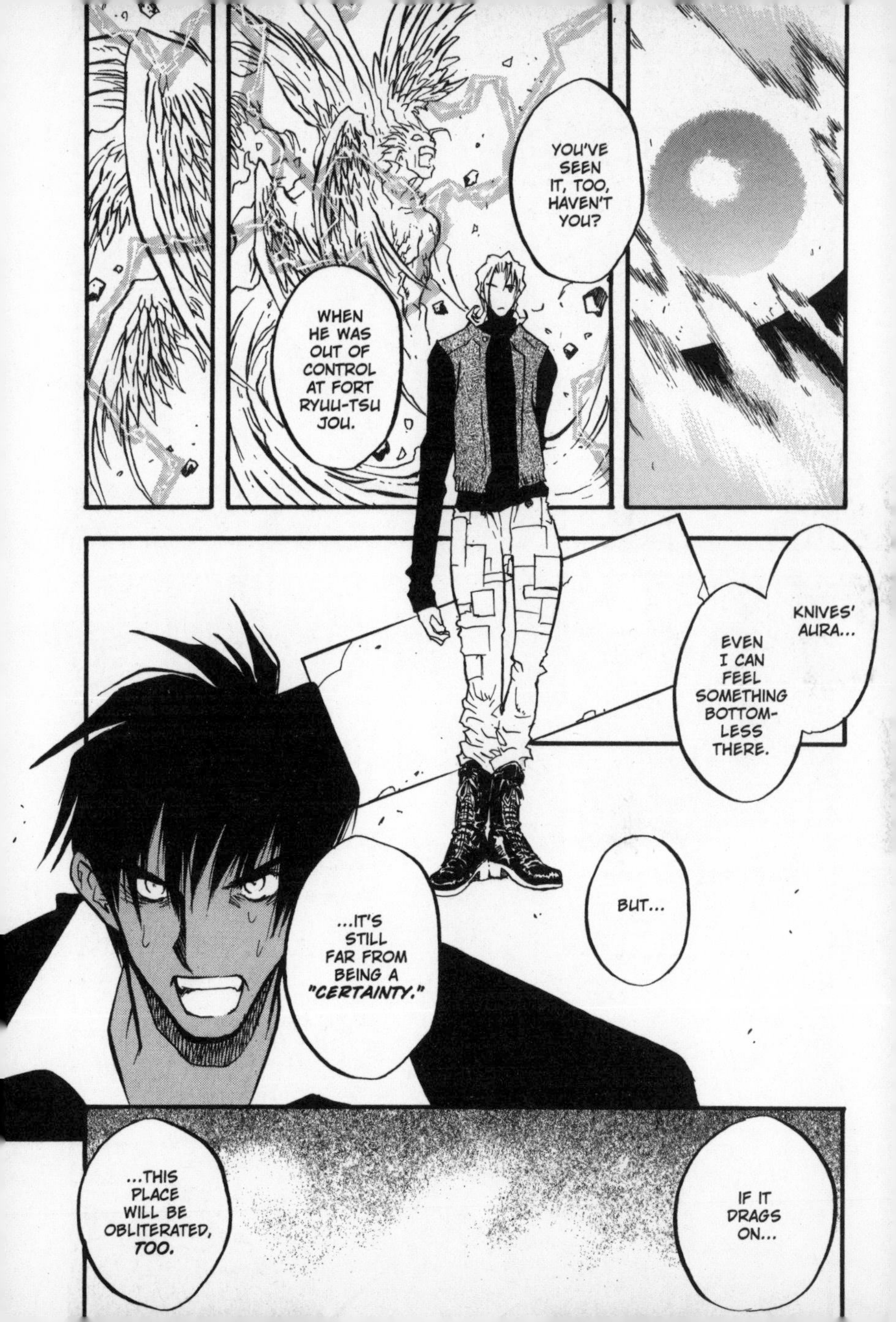
YOU'VE SEEN IT, TOO, HAVEN'T YOU?
WHEN HE WAS OUT OF CONTROL AT FORT RYUU-TSU JOU.
KNIVES' AURA...
EVEN I CAN FEEL SOMETHING BOTTOM-LESS THERE.
BUT...
...IT'S STILL FAR FROM BEING A **"CERTAINTY."**
IF IT DRAGS ON...
...THIS PLACE WILL BE OBLITERATED, **TOO.**

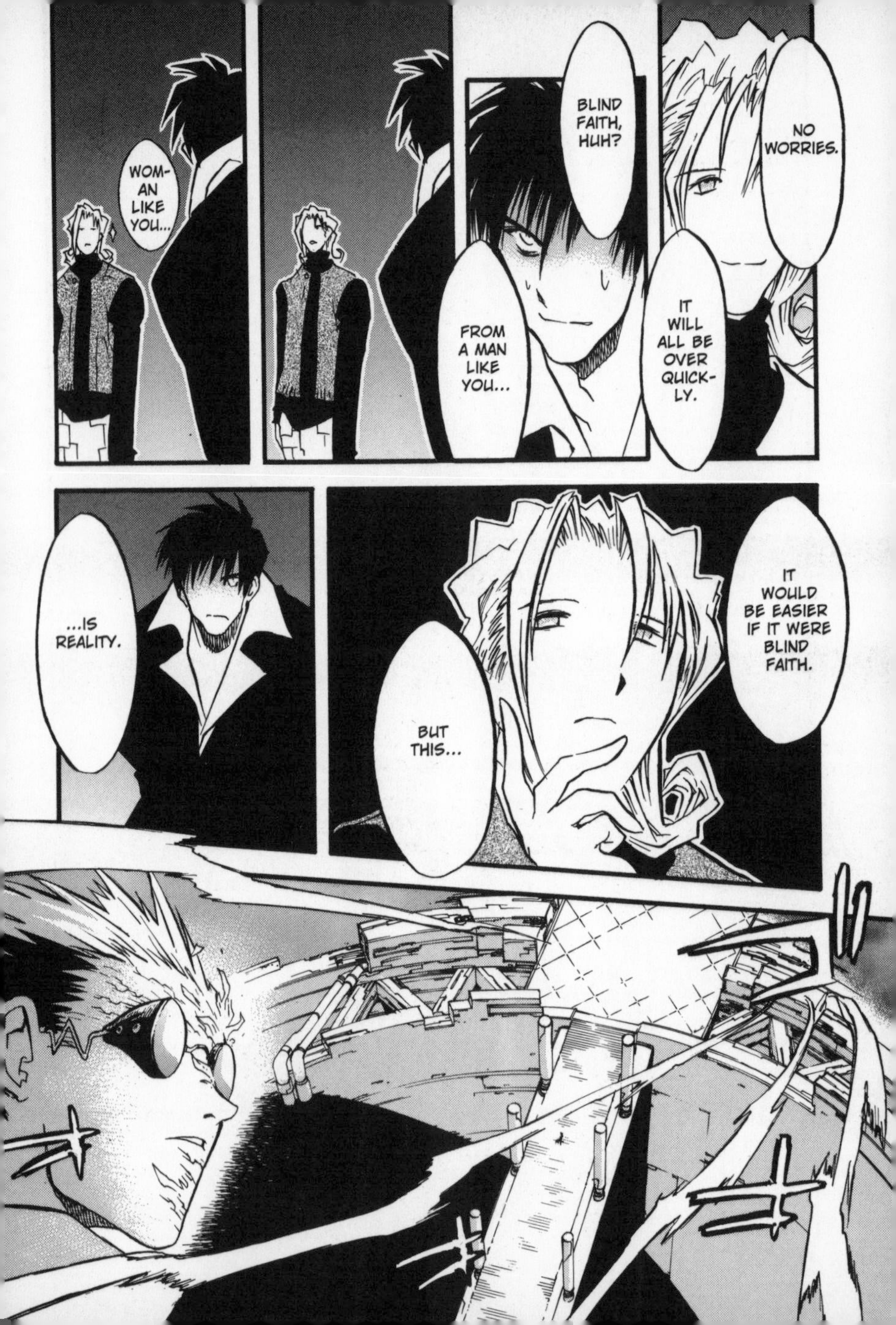
NO WORRIES.
IT WILL ALL BE OVER QUICK-LY.
BLIND FAITH, HUH?
FROM A MAN LIKE YOU...
WOM-AN LIKE YOU...
IT WOULD BE EASIER IF IT WERE BLIND FAITH.
BUT THIS...
...IS REALITY.

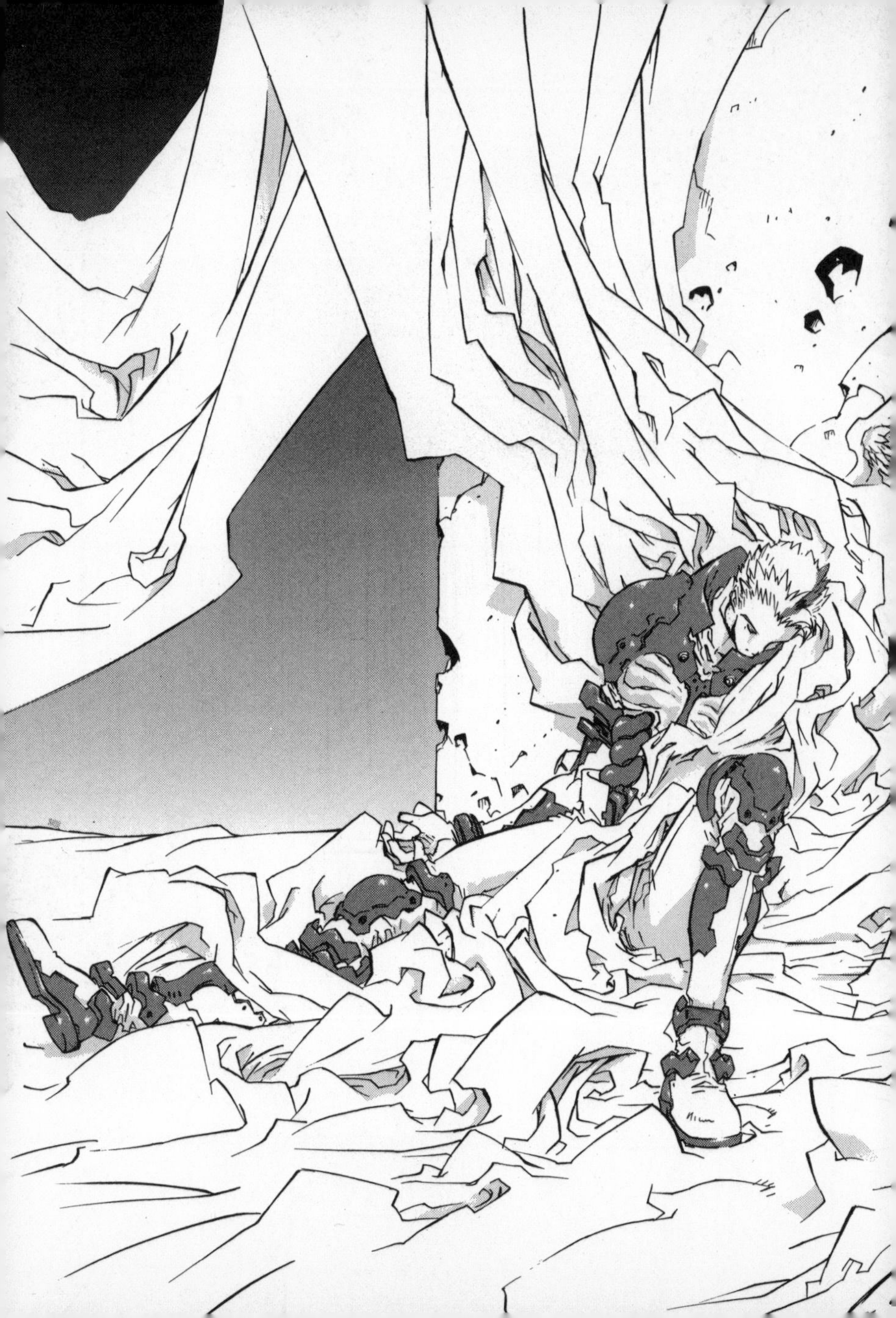

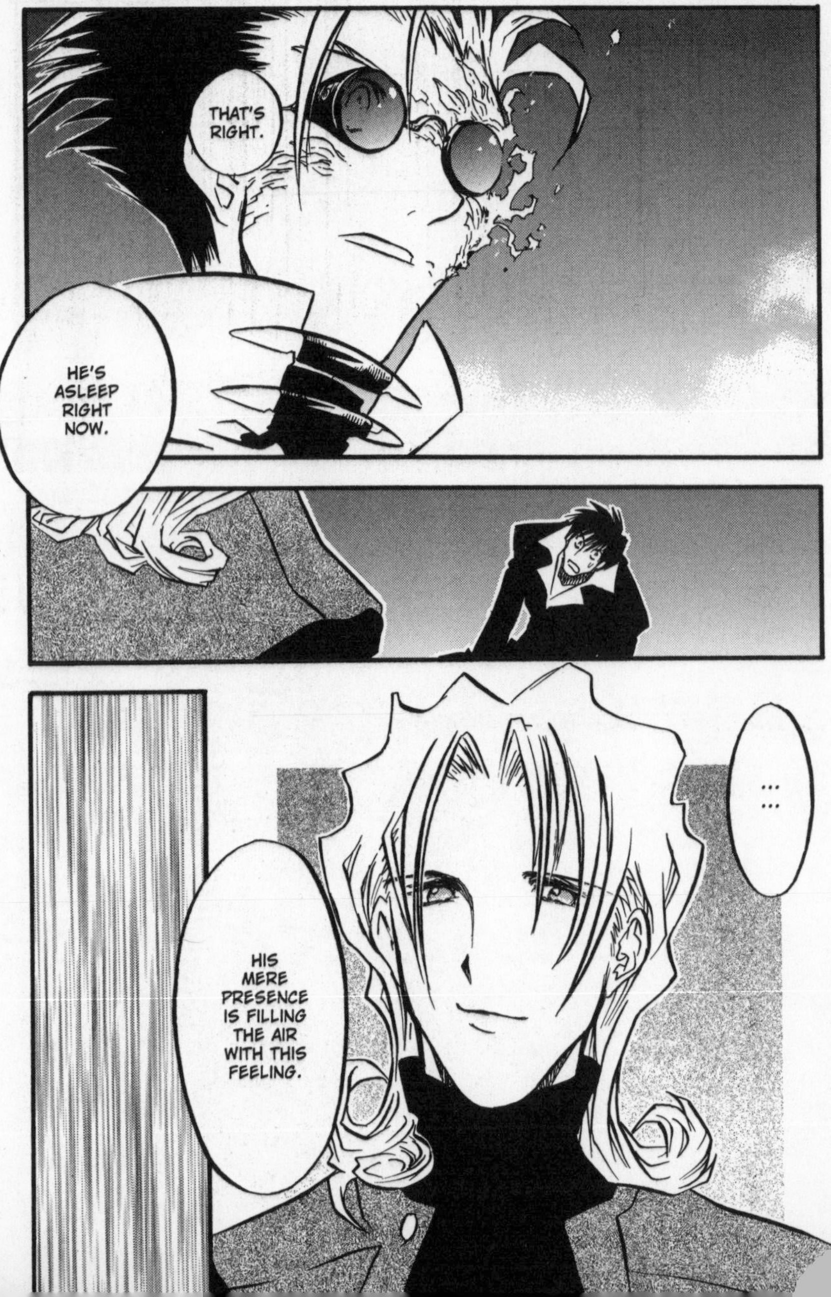
THAT'S RIGHT.
HE'S ASLEEP RIGHT NOW.
...
...
HIS MERE PRESENCE IS FILLING THE AIR WITH THIS FEELING.

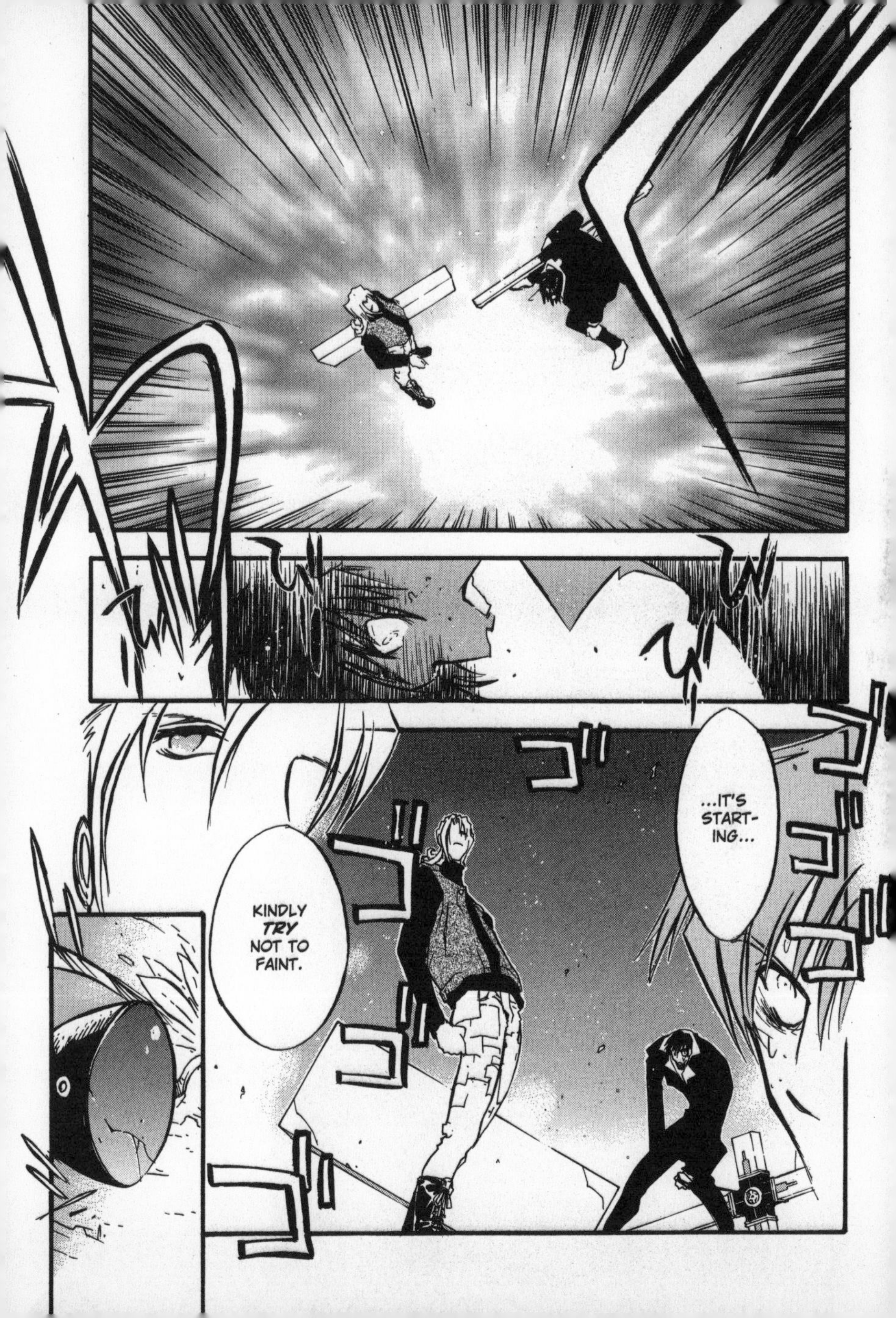
...IT'S STARTING...
KINDLY *TRY* NOT TO FAINT.

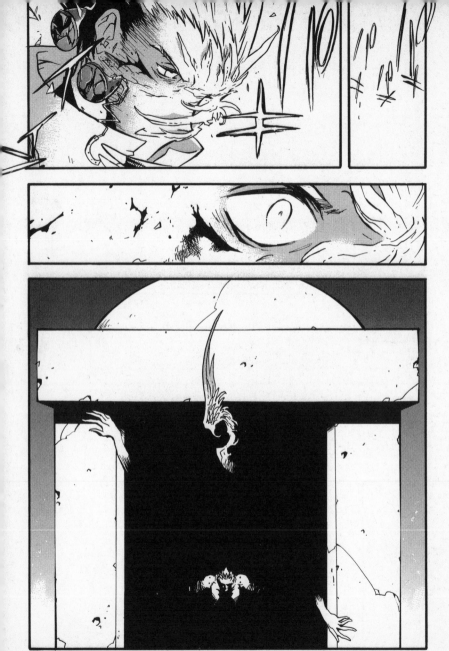

#5. WHEN THEY ARRIVED, IT WAS ALREADY
THE BEGINNING OF THE END/END

TRIGUN MAXIMUM

YASUHIRO NIGHTOW

DEEP SPACE PLANET FUTURE GUN ACTION!!

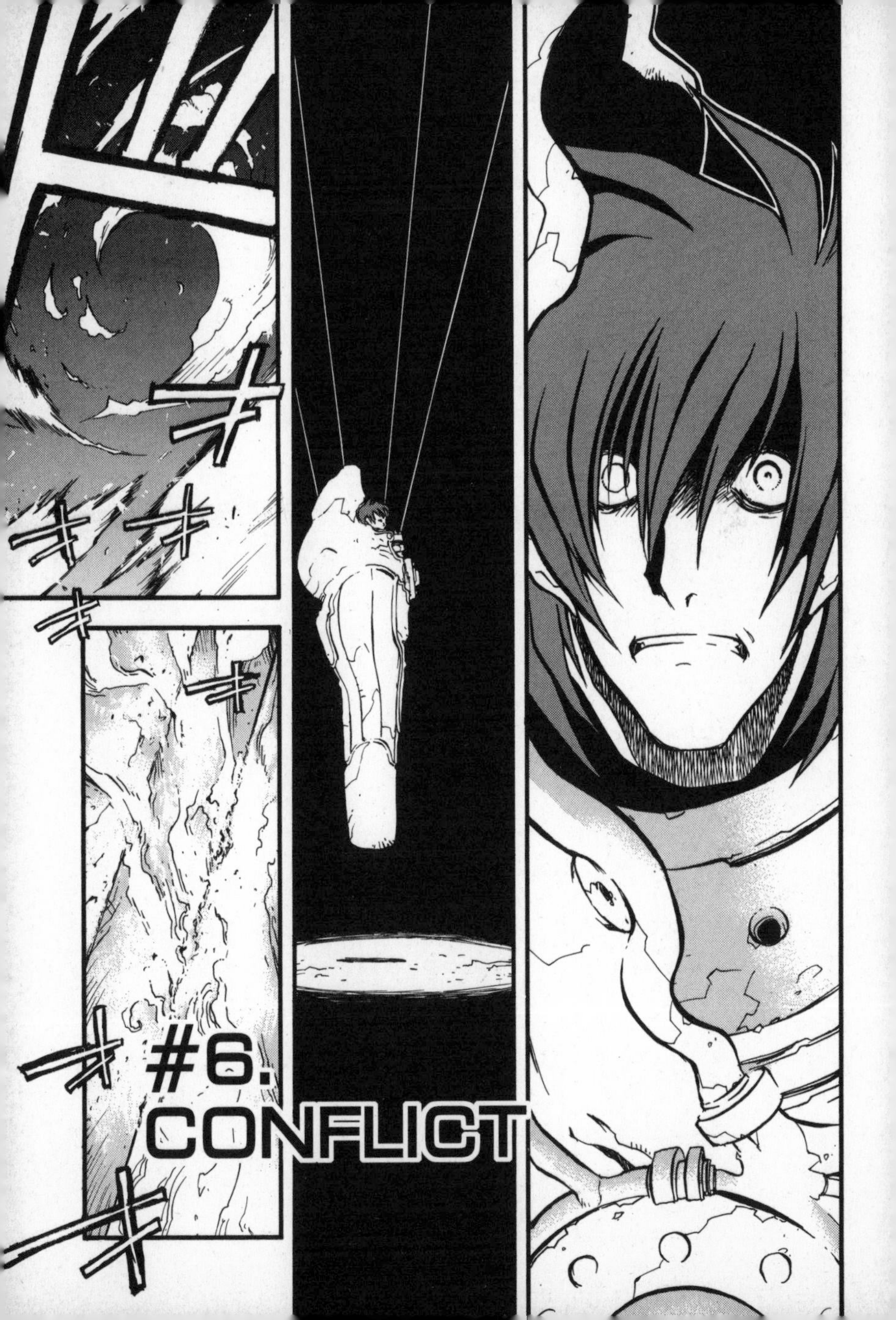

#6.
CONFLICT

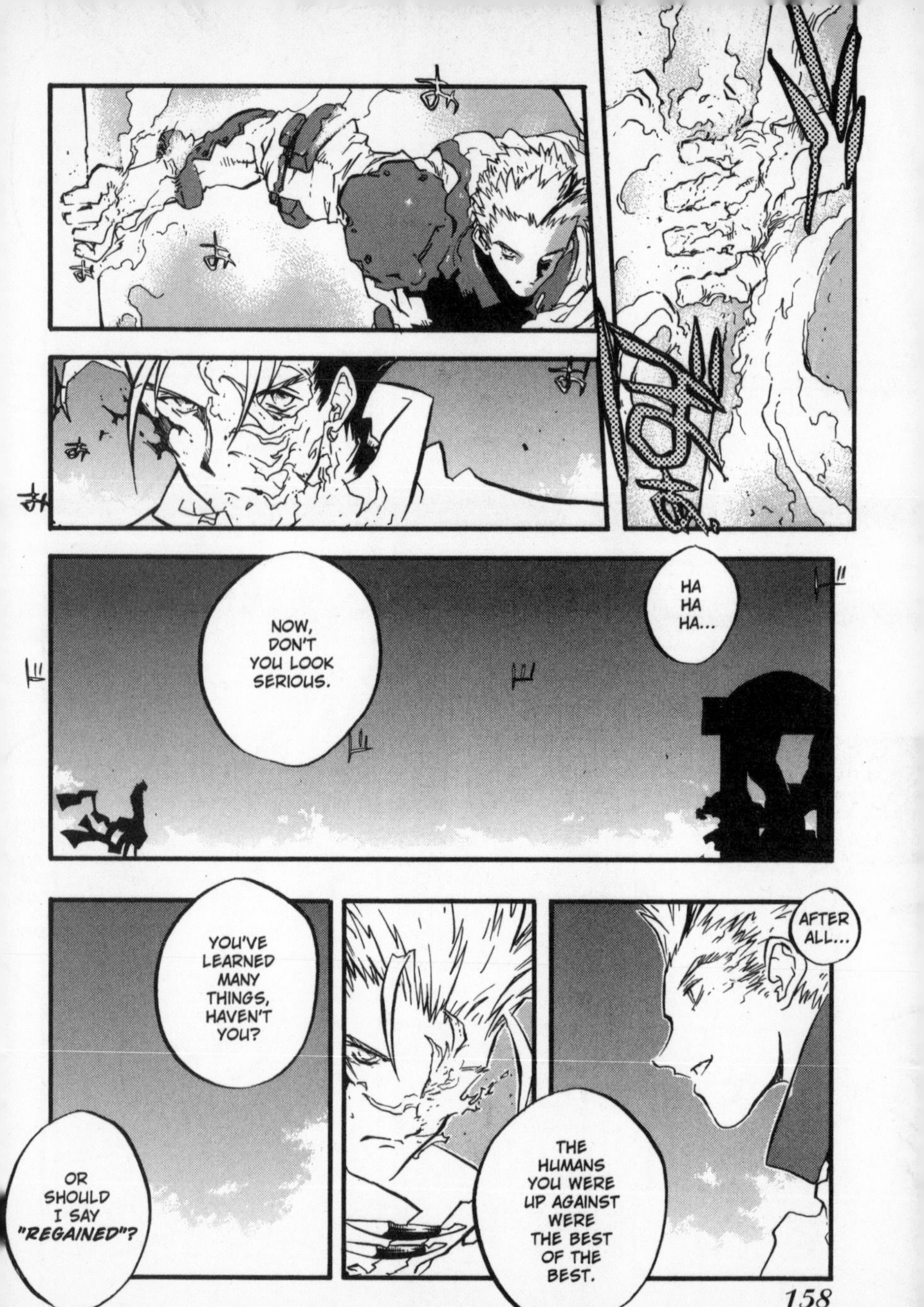
HA HA HA...
NOW, DON'T YOU LOOK SERIOUS.
AFTER ALL...
THE HUMANS YOU WERE UP AGAINST WERE THE BEST OF THE BEST.
YOU'VE LEARNED MANY THINGS, HAVEN'T YOU?
OR SHOULD I SAY "REGAINED"?

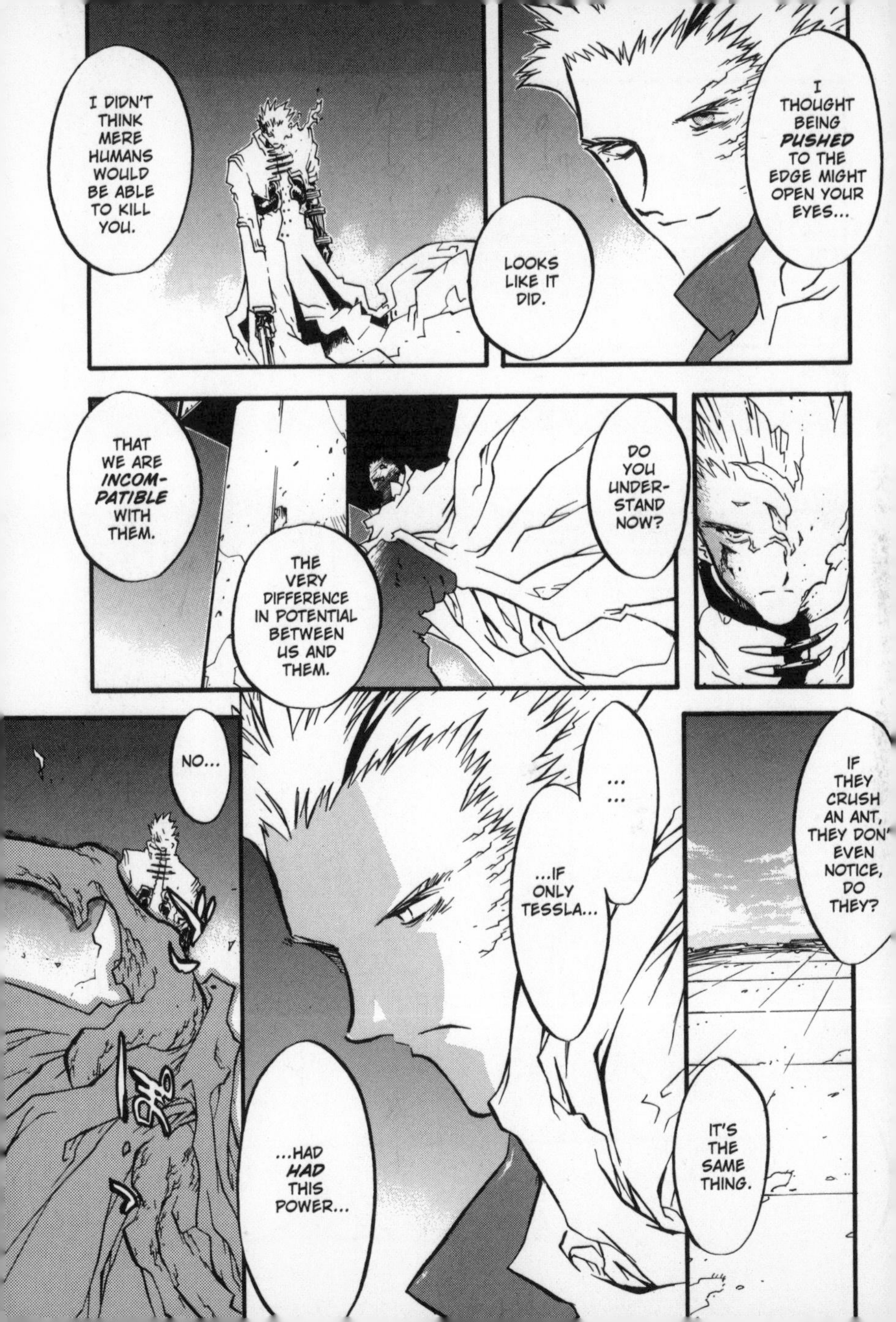
I THOUGHT BEING *PUSHED* TO THE EDGE MIGHT OPEN YOUR EYES...
LOOKS LIKE IT DID.
I DIDN'T THINK MERE HUMANS WOULD BE ABLE TO KILL YOU.
DO YOU UNDERSTAND NOW?
THE VERY DIFFERENCE IN POTENTIAL BETWEEN US AND THEM.
THAT WE ARE *INCOMPATIBLE* WITH THEM.
IF THEY CRUSH AN ANT, THEY DON' EVEN NOTICE, DO THEY?
IT'S THE SAME THING.
......
...IF ONLY TESSLA...
NO...
...HAD *HAD* THIS POWER...

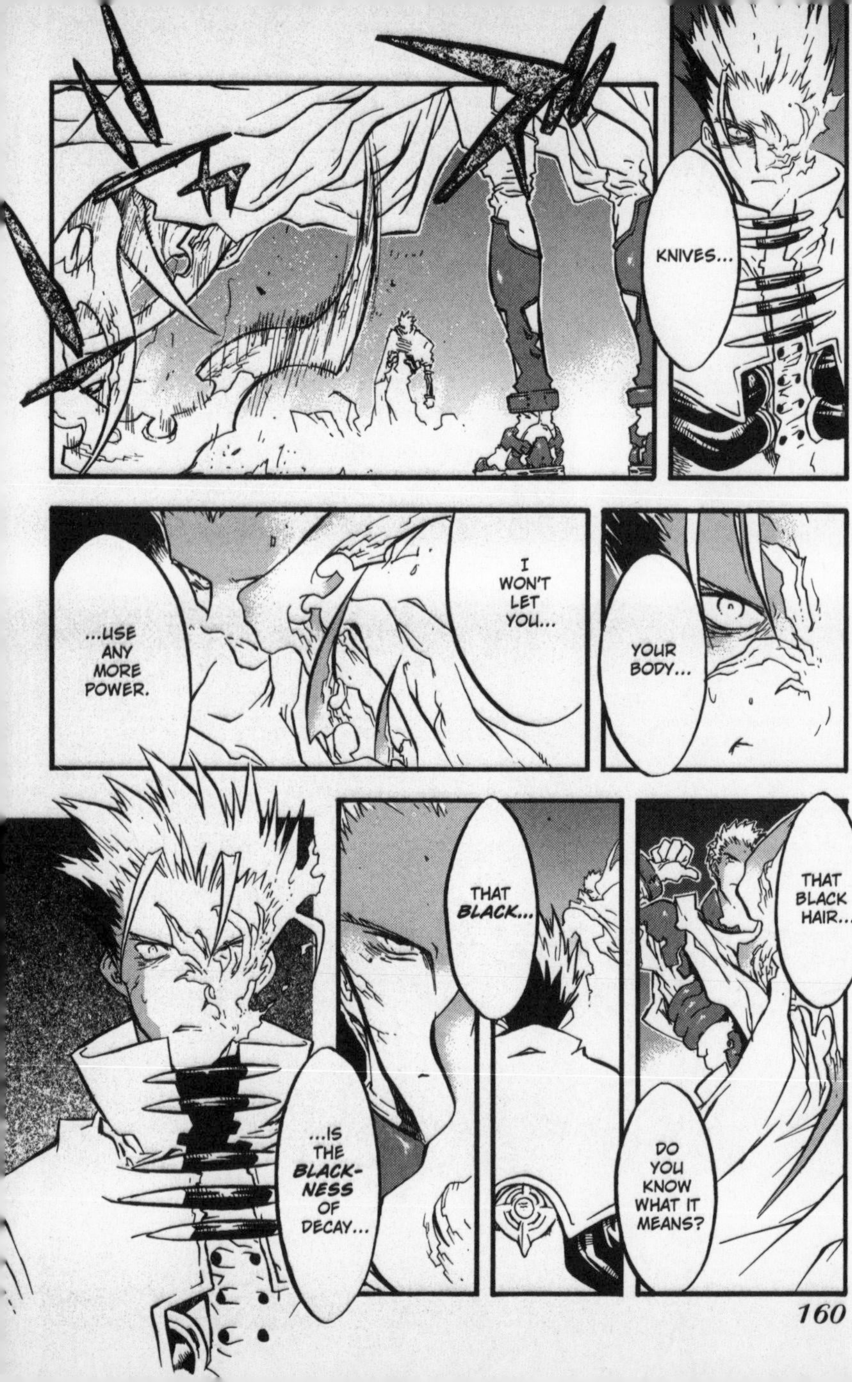
KNIVES...
YOUR BODY...
I WON'T LET YOU...
...USE ANY MORE POWER.
THAT BLACK HAIR...
DO YOU KNOW WHAT IT MEANS?
THAT BLACK...
...IS THE BLACKNESS OF DECAY...

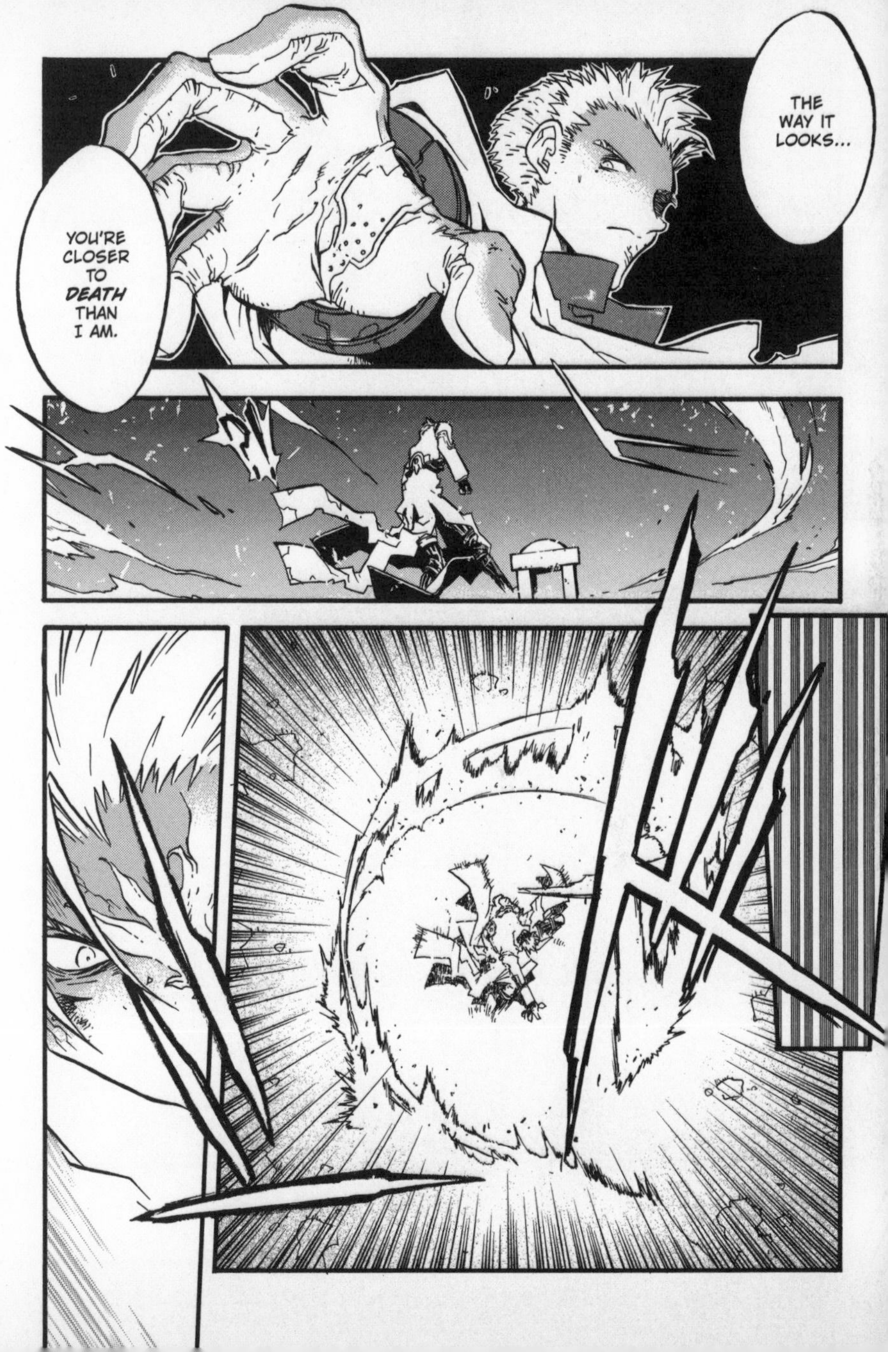
THE WAY IT LOOKS...
YOU'RE CLOSER TO *DEATH* THAN I AM.

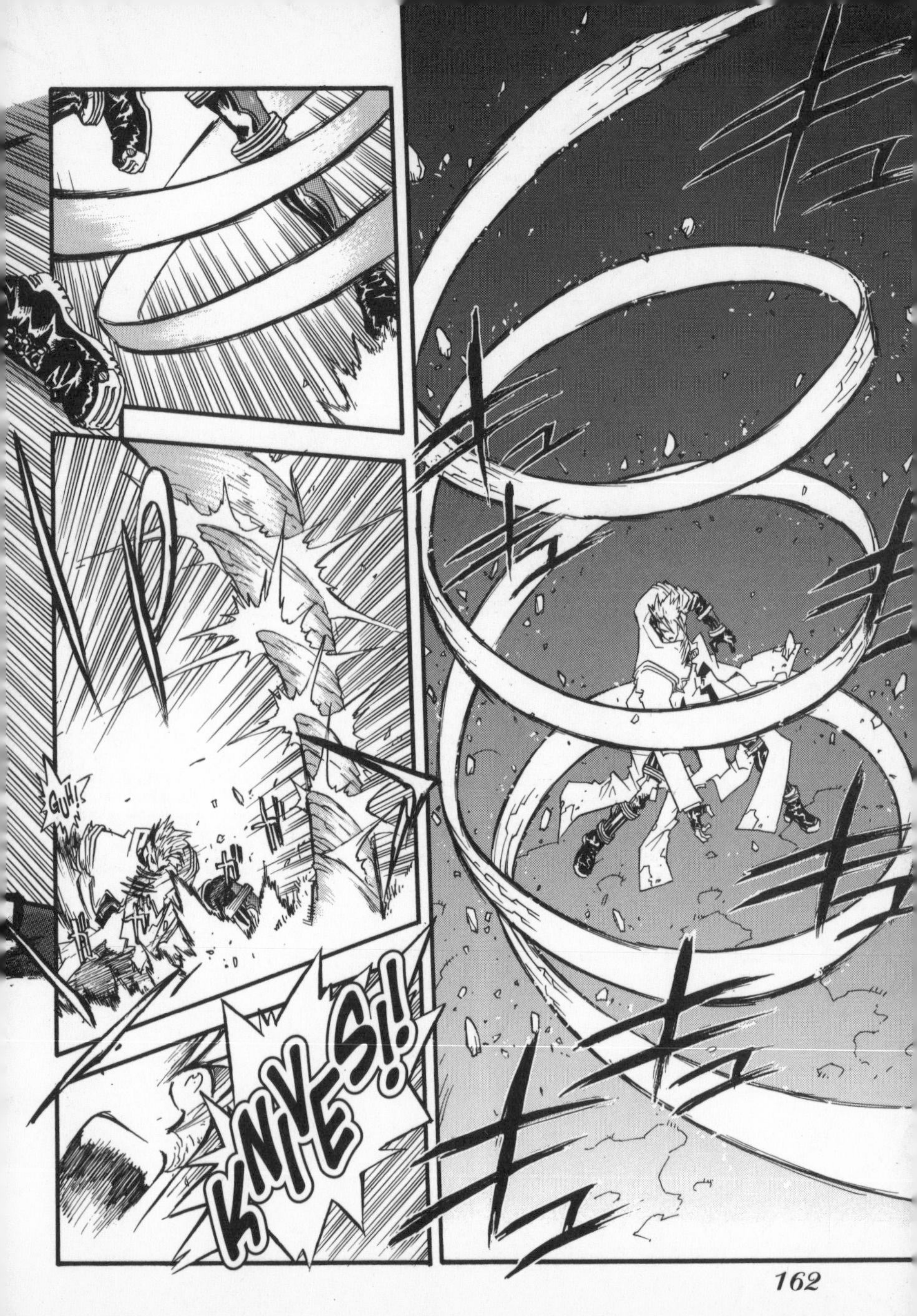
GUH!
KNIVES!!

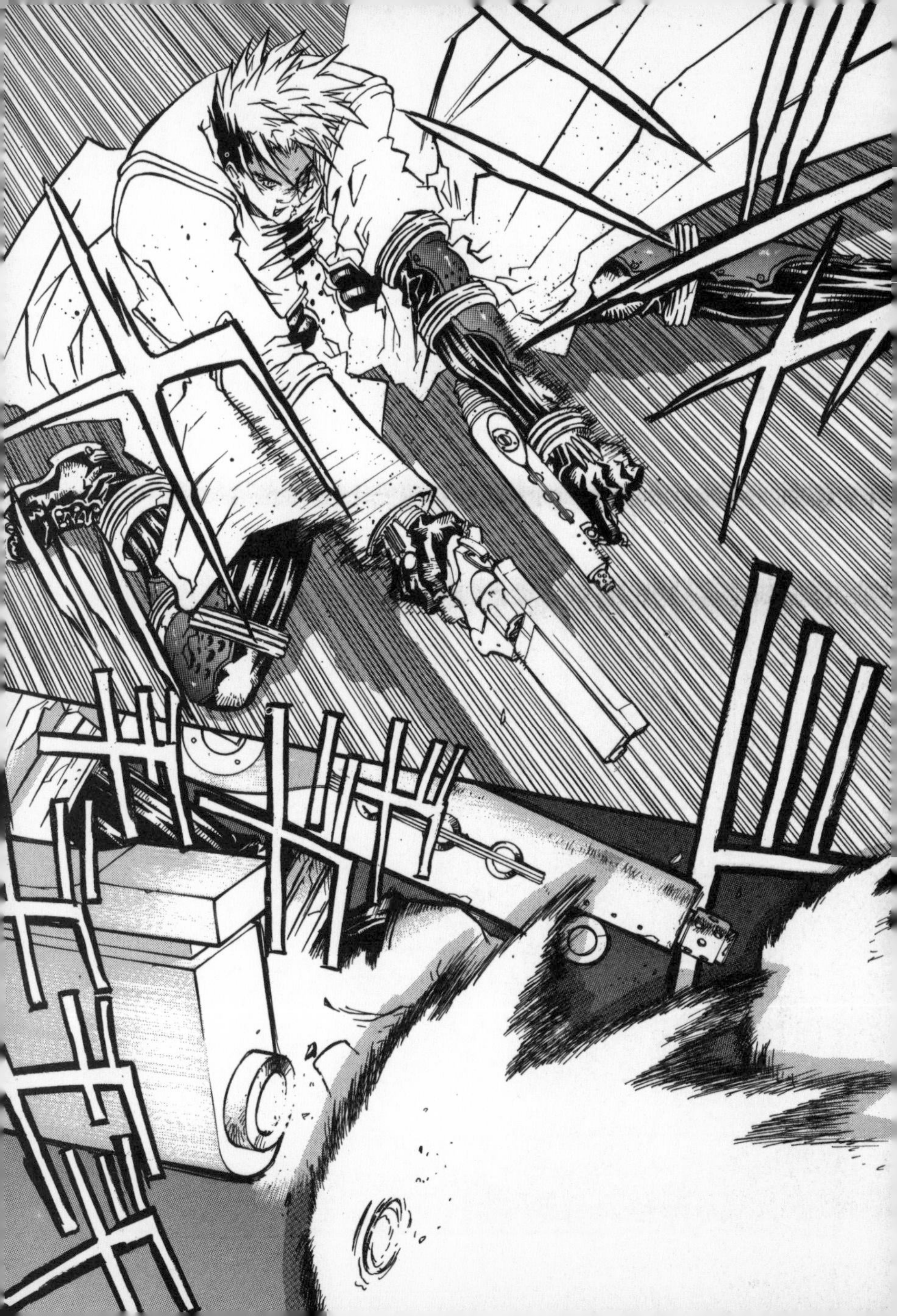

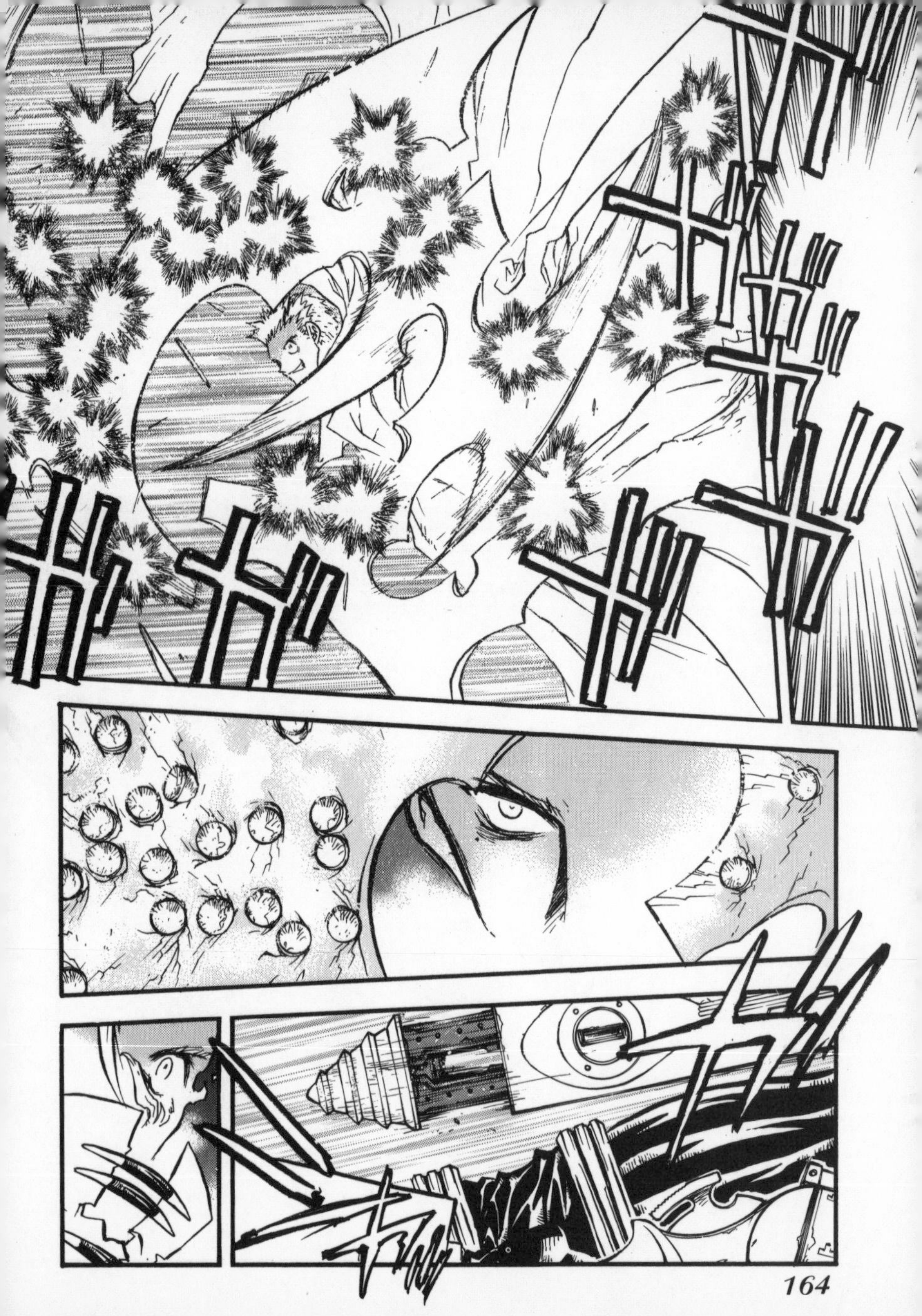

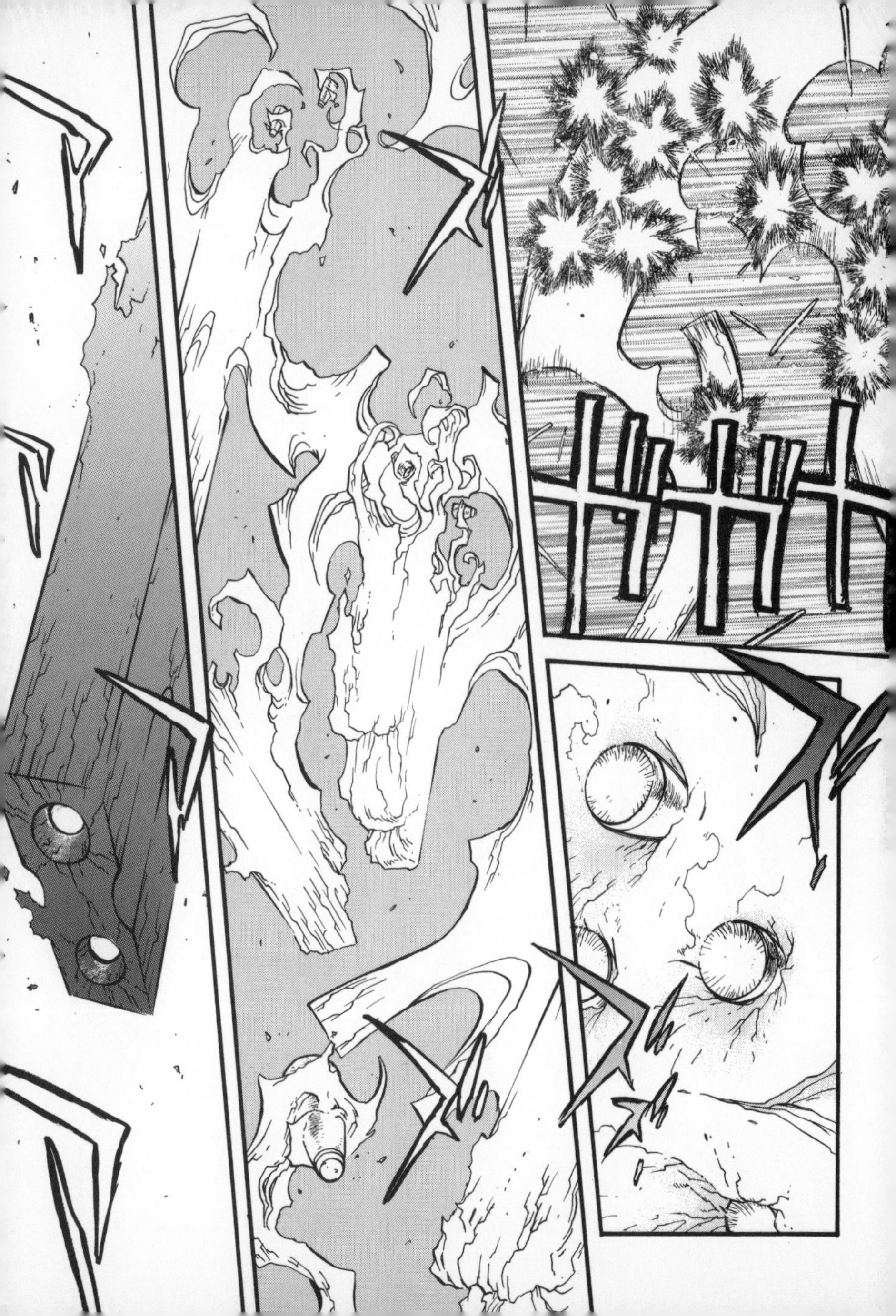

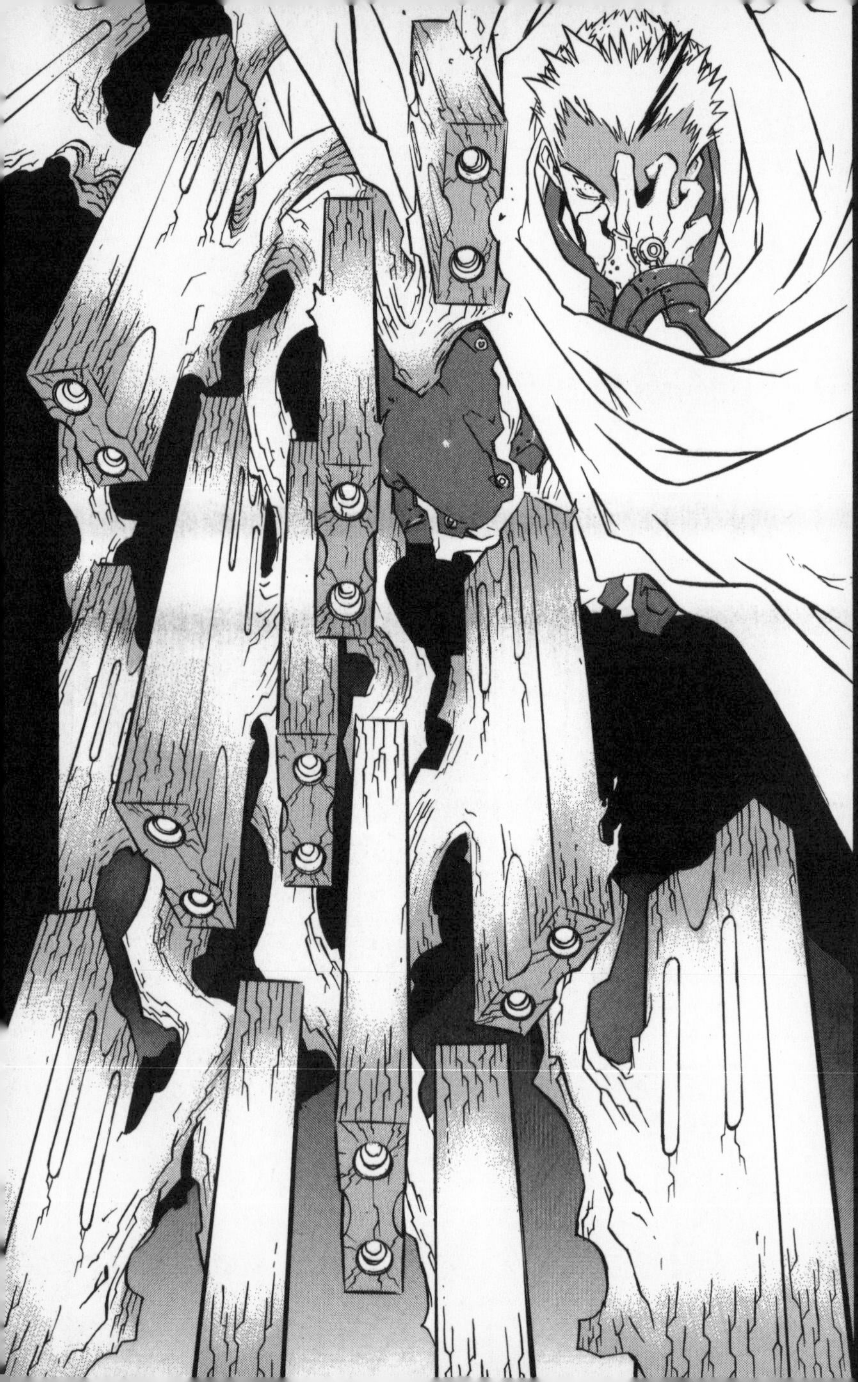

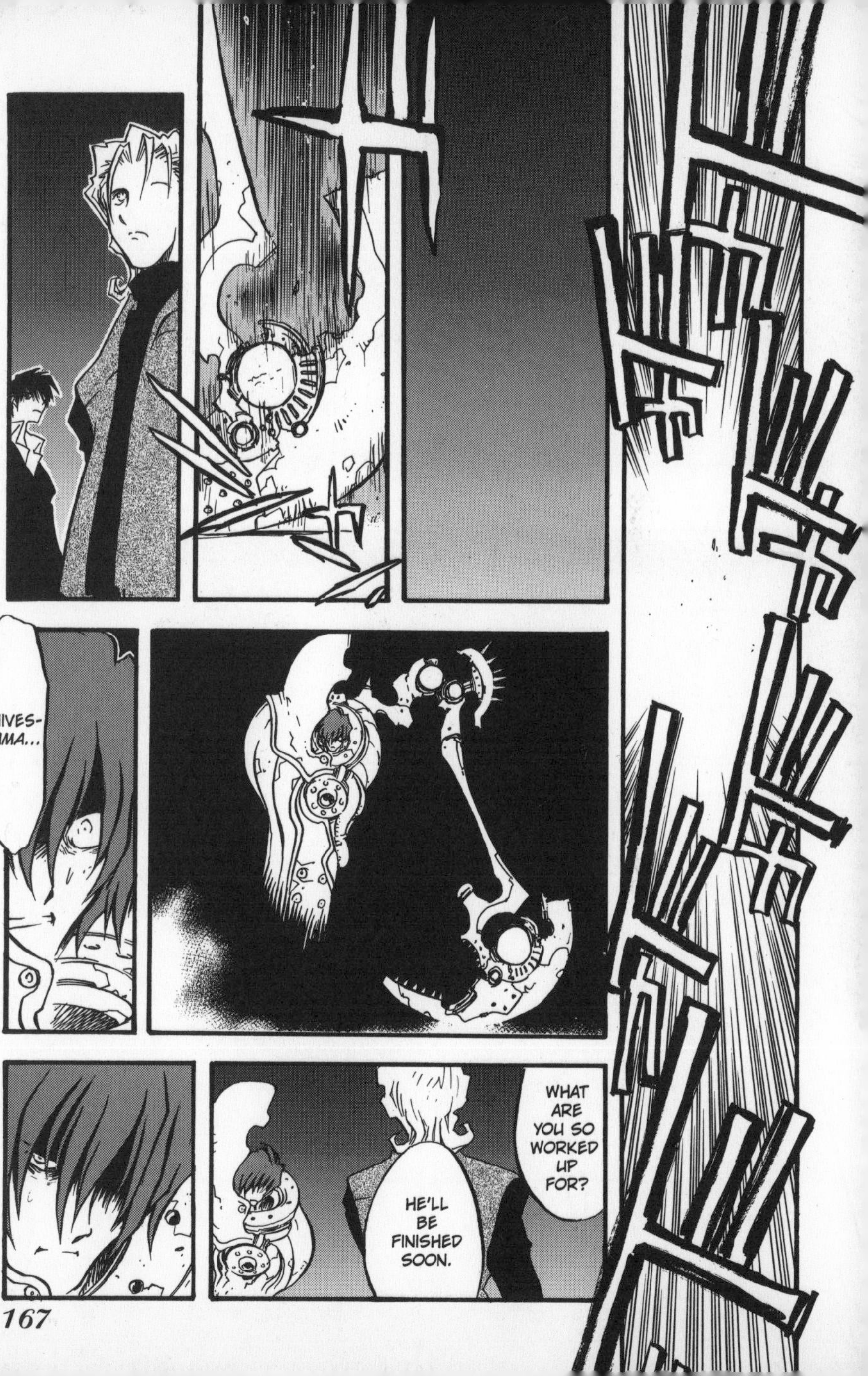
KNIVES-SAMA...
WHAT ARE YOU SO WORKED UP FOR?
HE'LL BE FINISHED SOON.

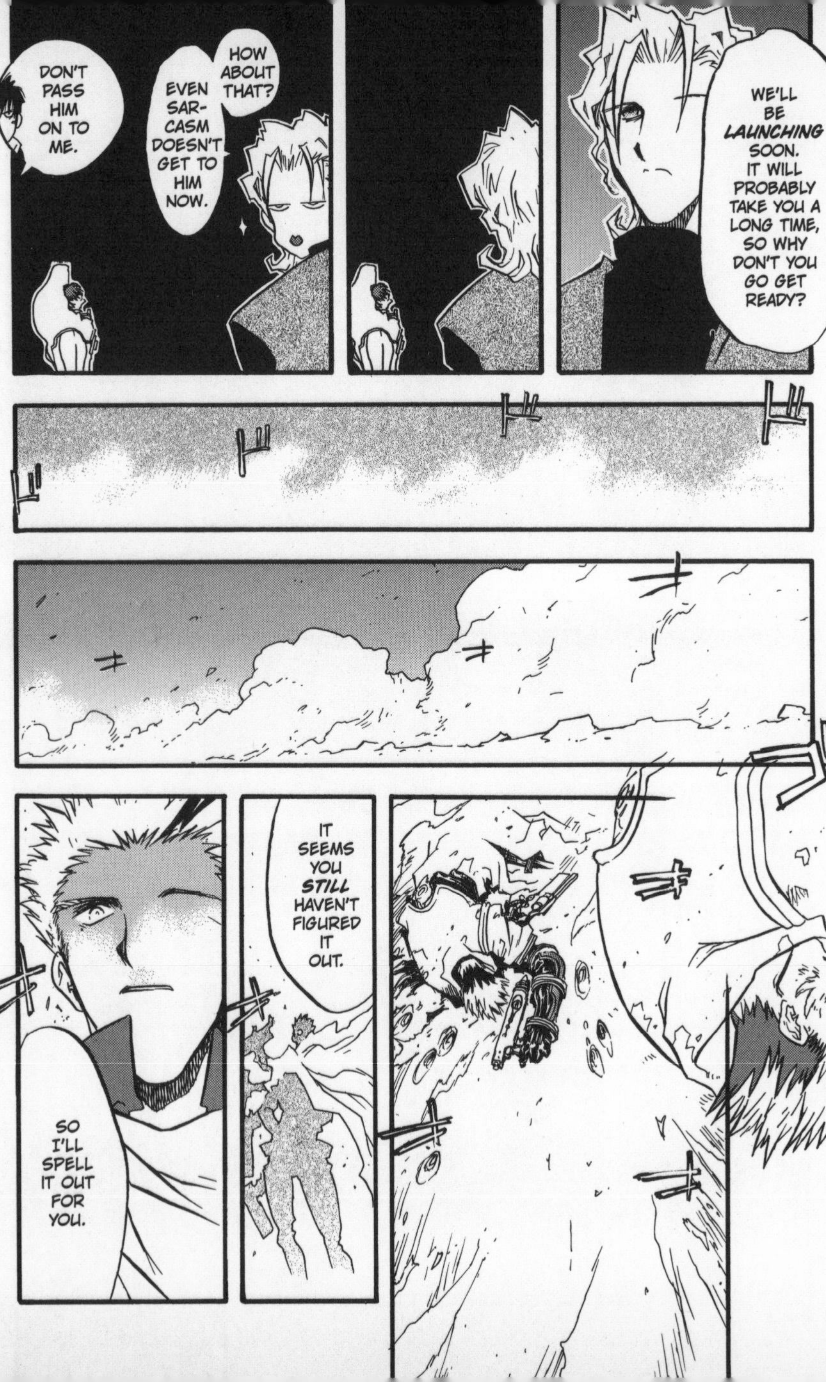
WE'LL BE LAUNCHING SOON. IT WILL PROBABLY TAKE YOU A LONG TIME, SO WHY DON'T YOU GO GET READY?
HOW ABOUT THAT?
EVEN SARCASM DOESN'T GET TO HIM NOW.
DON'T PASS HIM ON TO ME.
IT SEEMS YOU STILL HAVEN'T FIGURED IT OUT.
SO I'LL SPELL IT OUT FOR YOU.

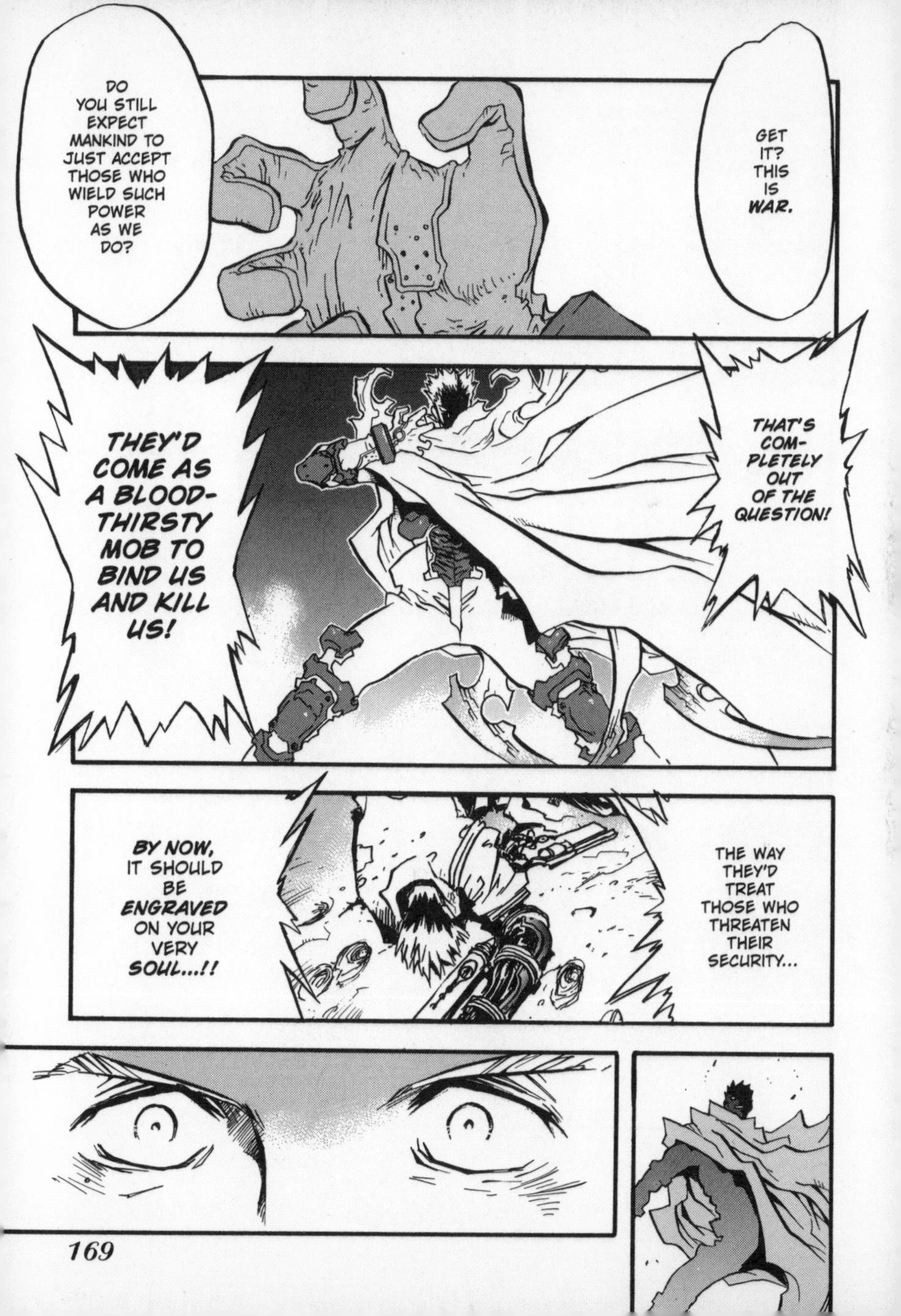
GET IT? THIS IS WAR.
DO YOU STILL EXPECT MANKIND TO JUST ACCEPT THOSE WHO WIELD SUCH POWER AS WE DO?
THAT'S COMPLETELY OUT OF THE QUESTION!
THEY'D COME AS A BLOOD-THIRSTY MOB TO BIND US AND KILL US!
THE WAY THEY'D TREAT THOSE WHO THREATEN THEIR SECURITY...
BY NOW, IT SHOULD BE ENGRAVED ON YOUR VERY SOUL...!!

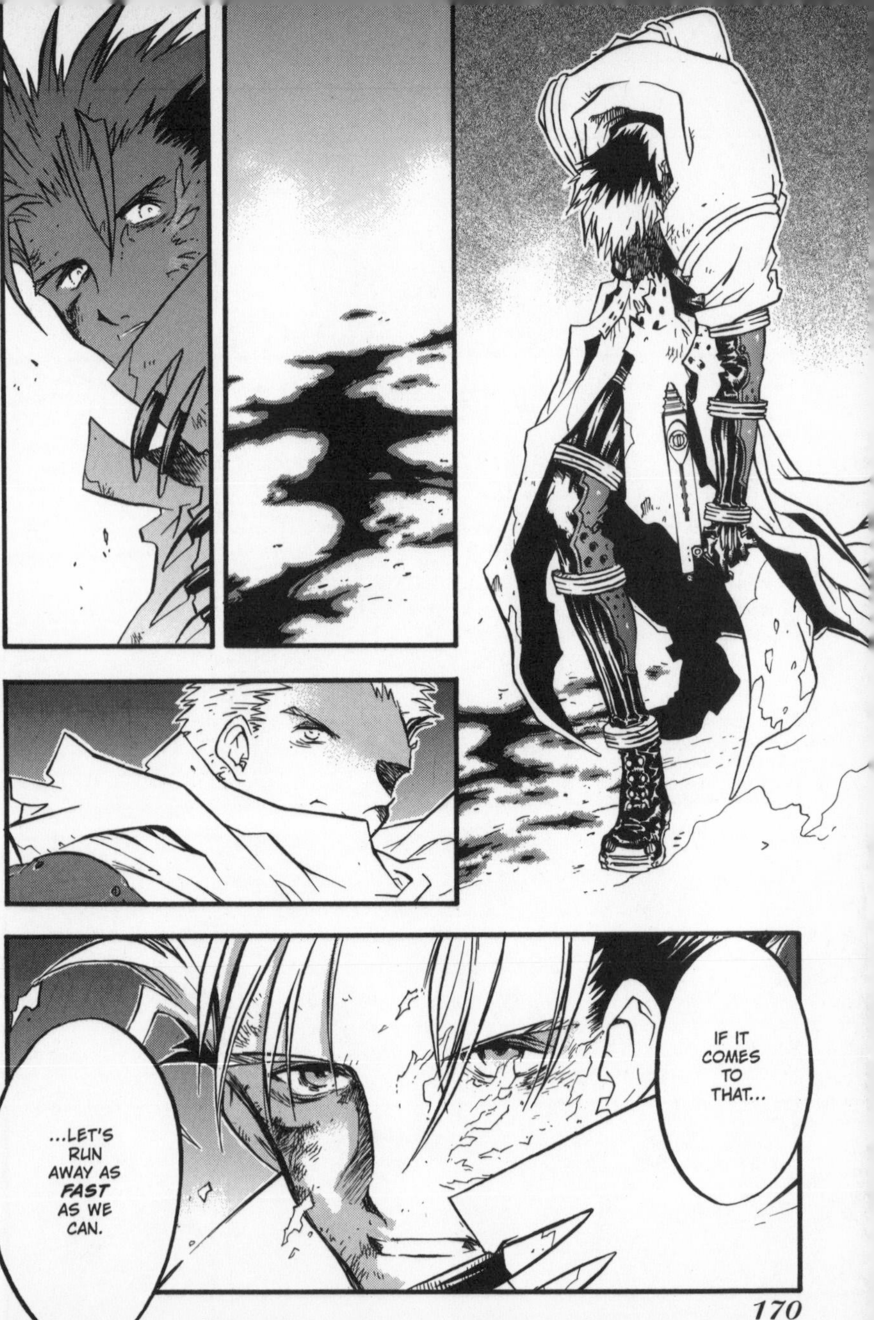
IF IT COMES TO THAT...
...LET'S RUN AWAY AS FAST AS WE CAN.

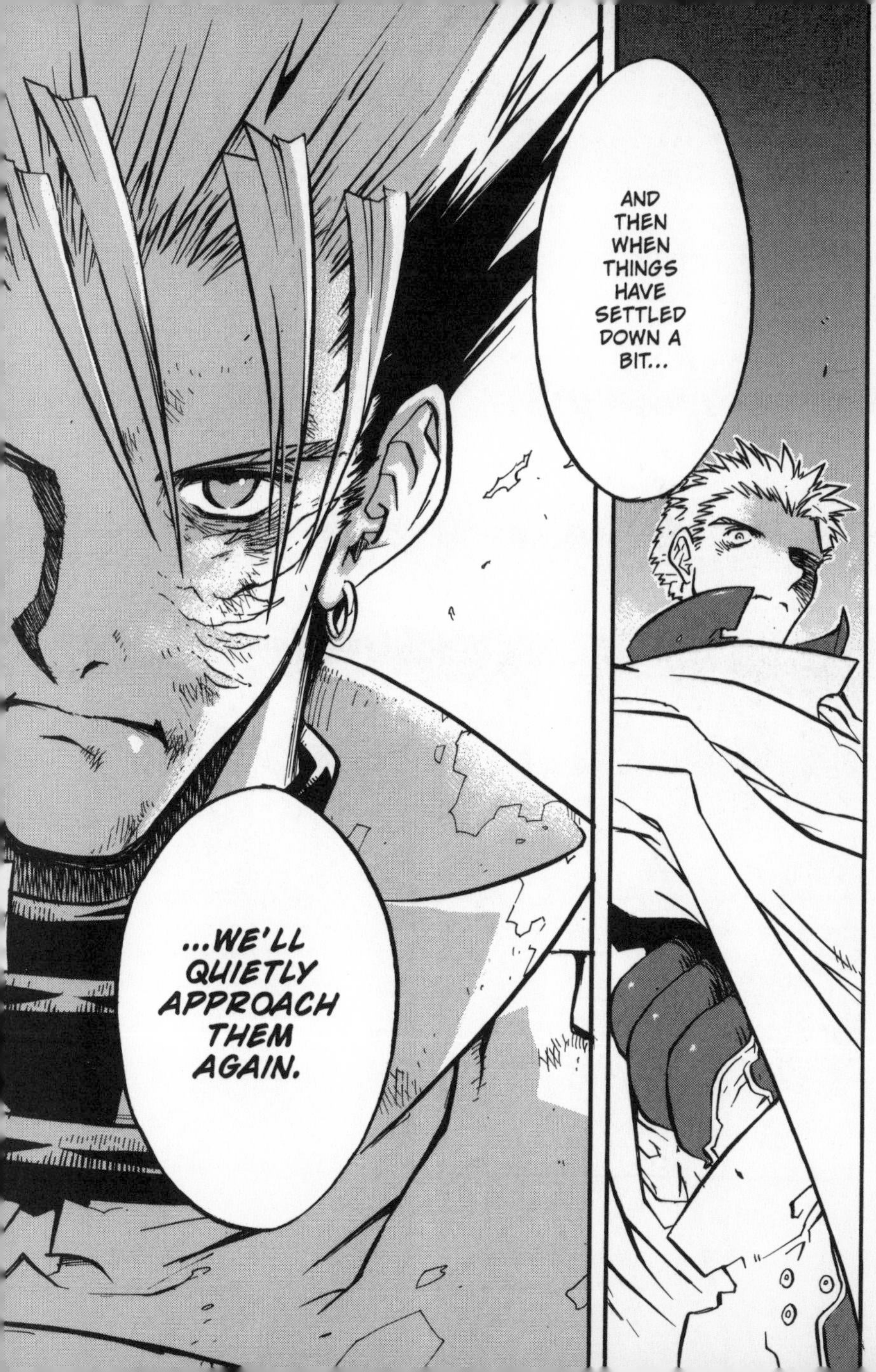
AND THEN WHEN THINGS HAVE SETTLED DOWN A BIT...
...WE'LL QUIETLY APPROACH THEM AGAIN.

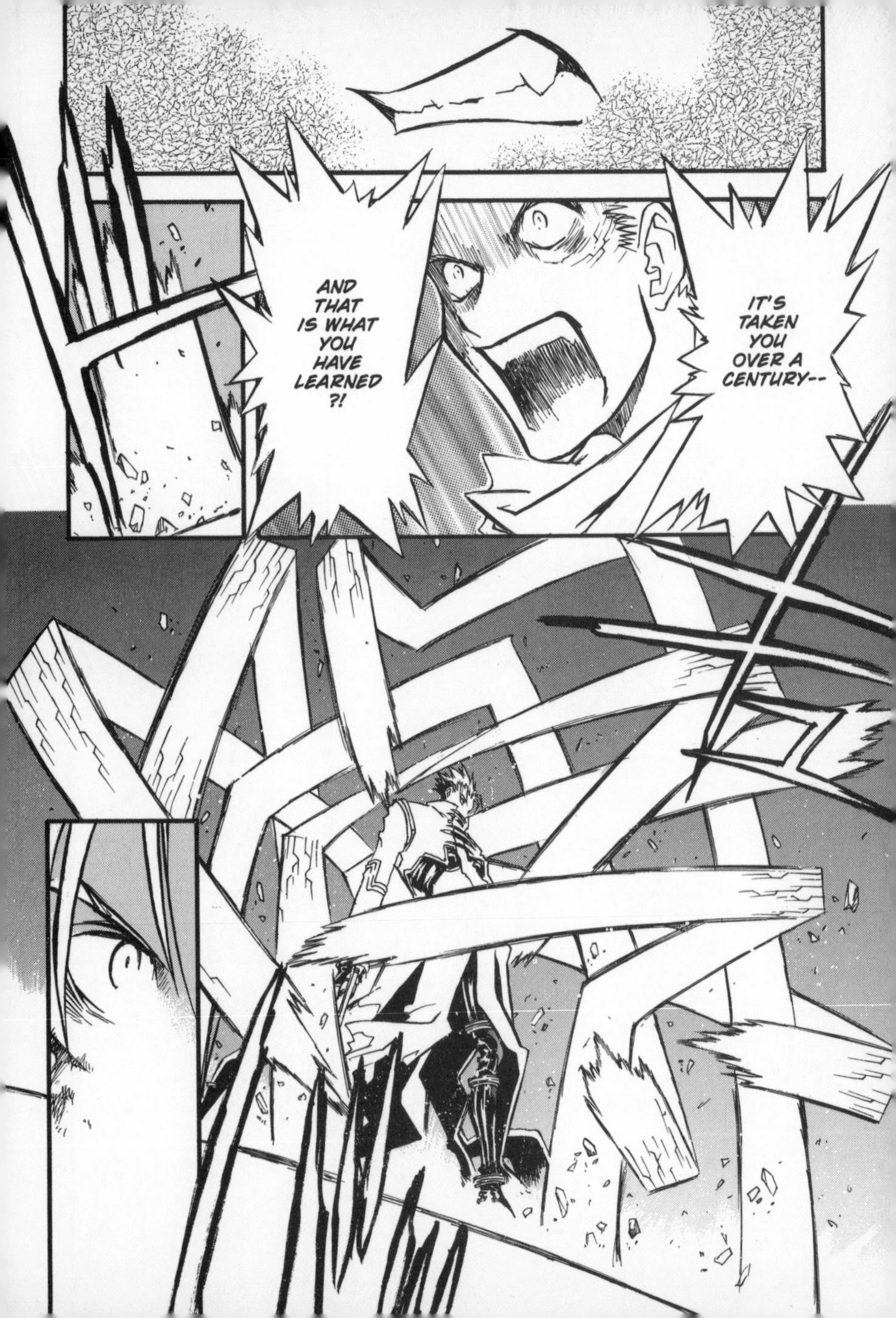
IT'S TAKEN YOU OVER A CENTURY--
AND THAT IS WHAT YOU HAVE LEARNED ?!

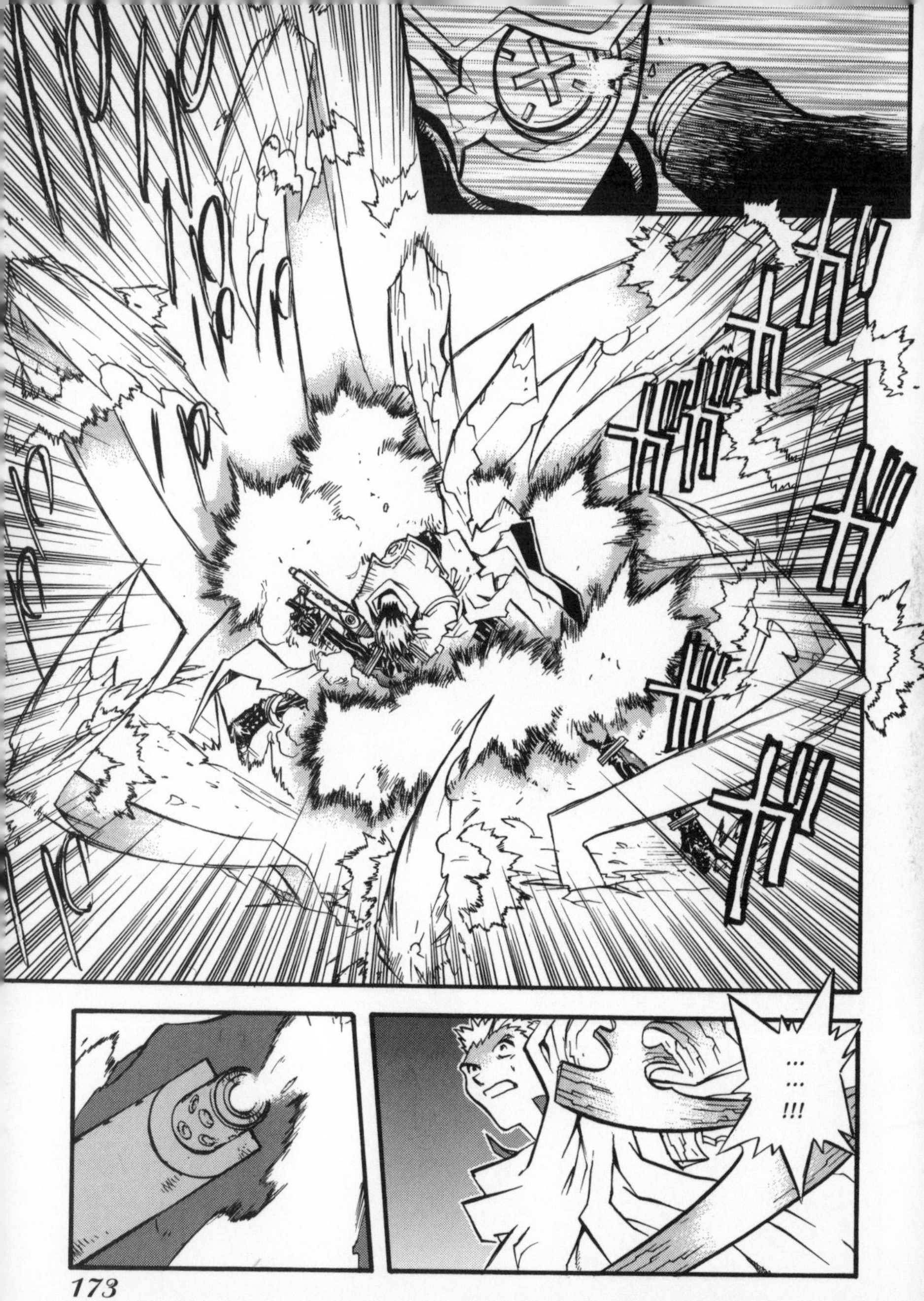
...
...
!!!

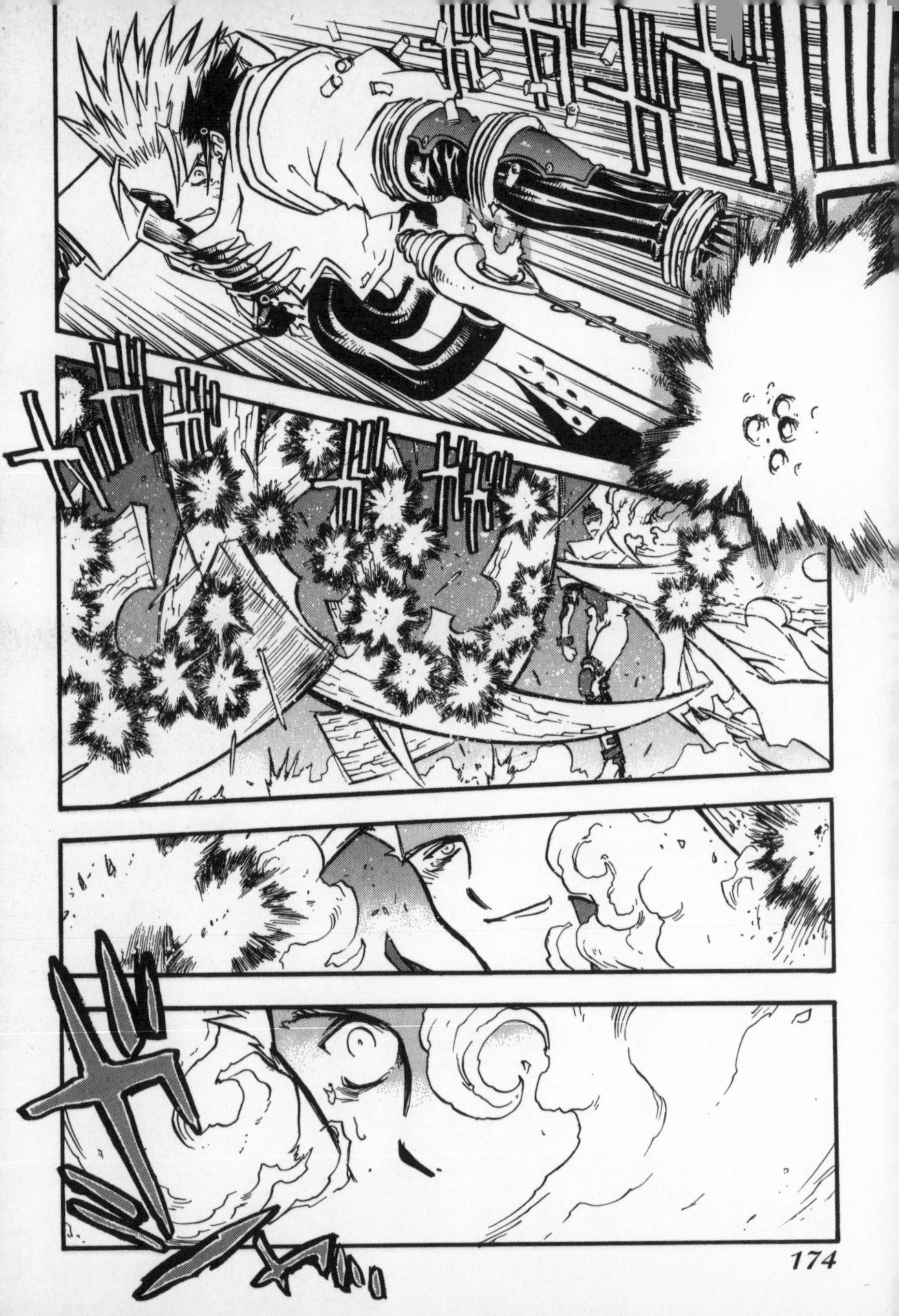

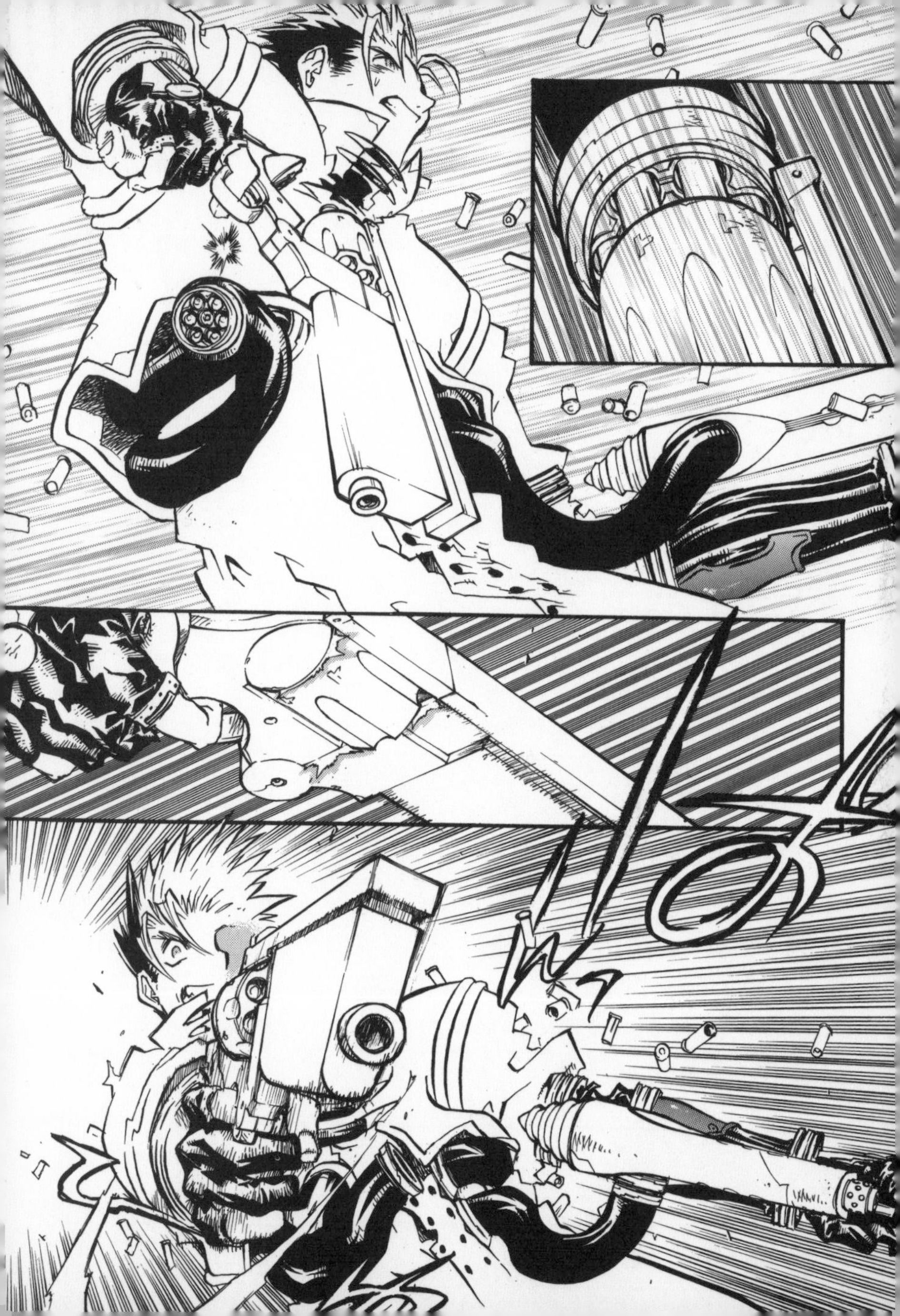

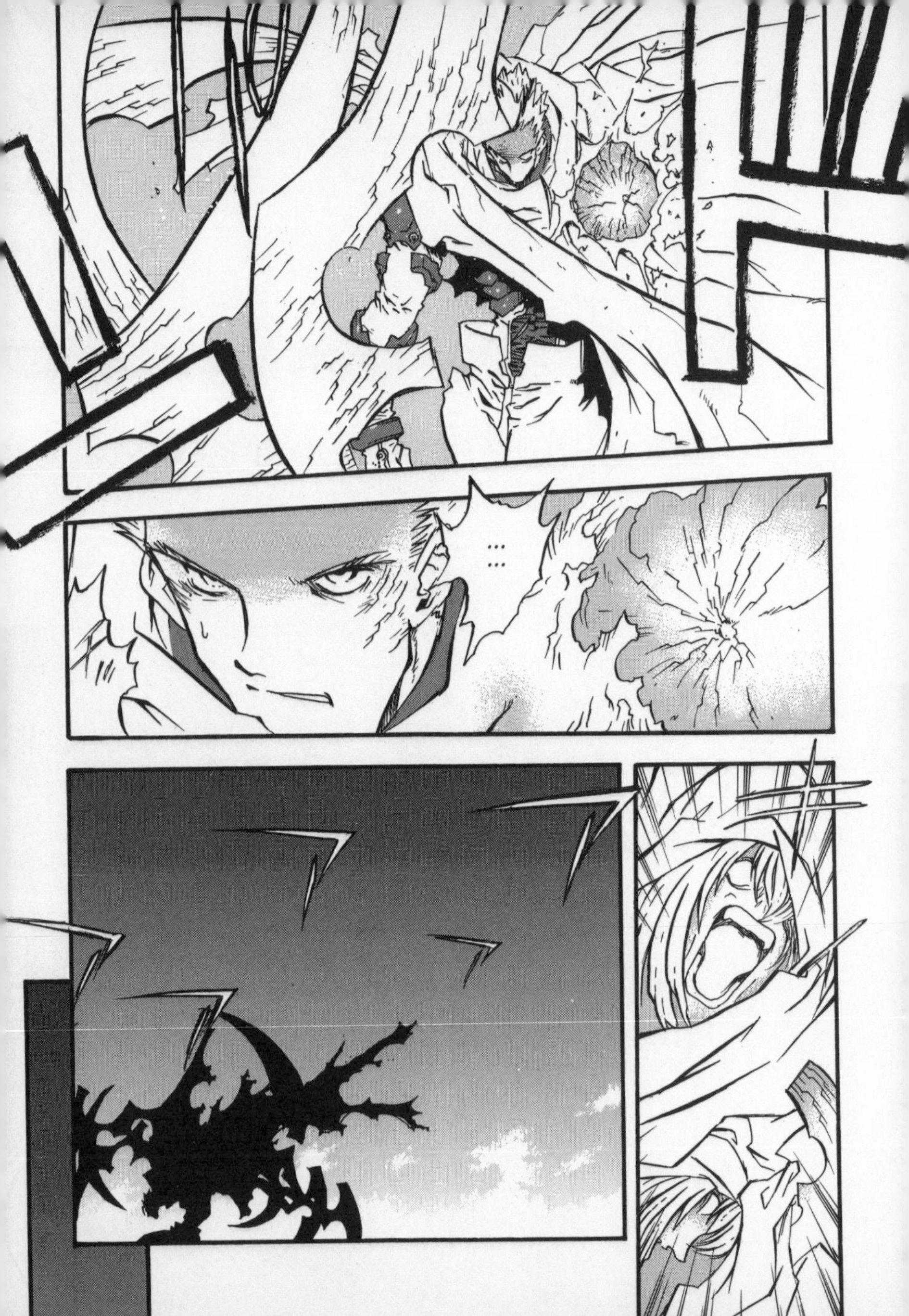
...

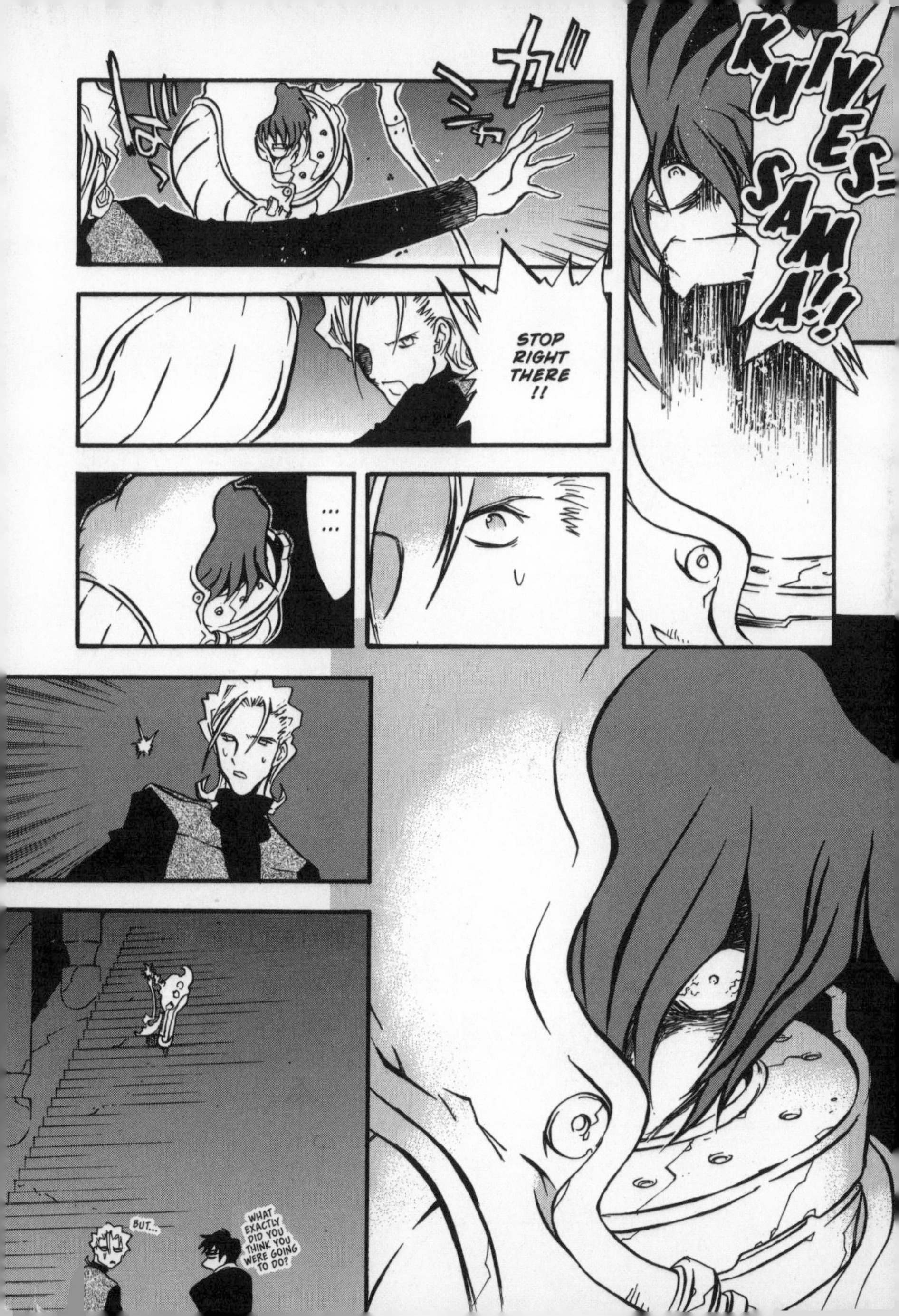
KNIVES-SAMA!!
STOP RIGHT THERE!!
......
WHAT EXACTLY DID YOU THINK YOU WERE GOING TO DO?
BUT...

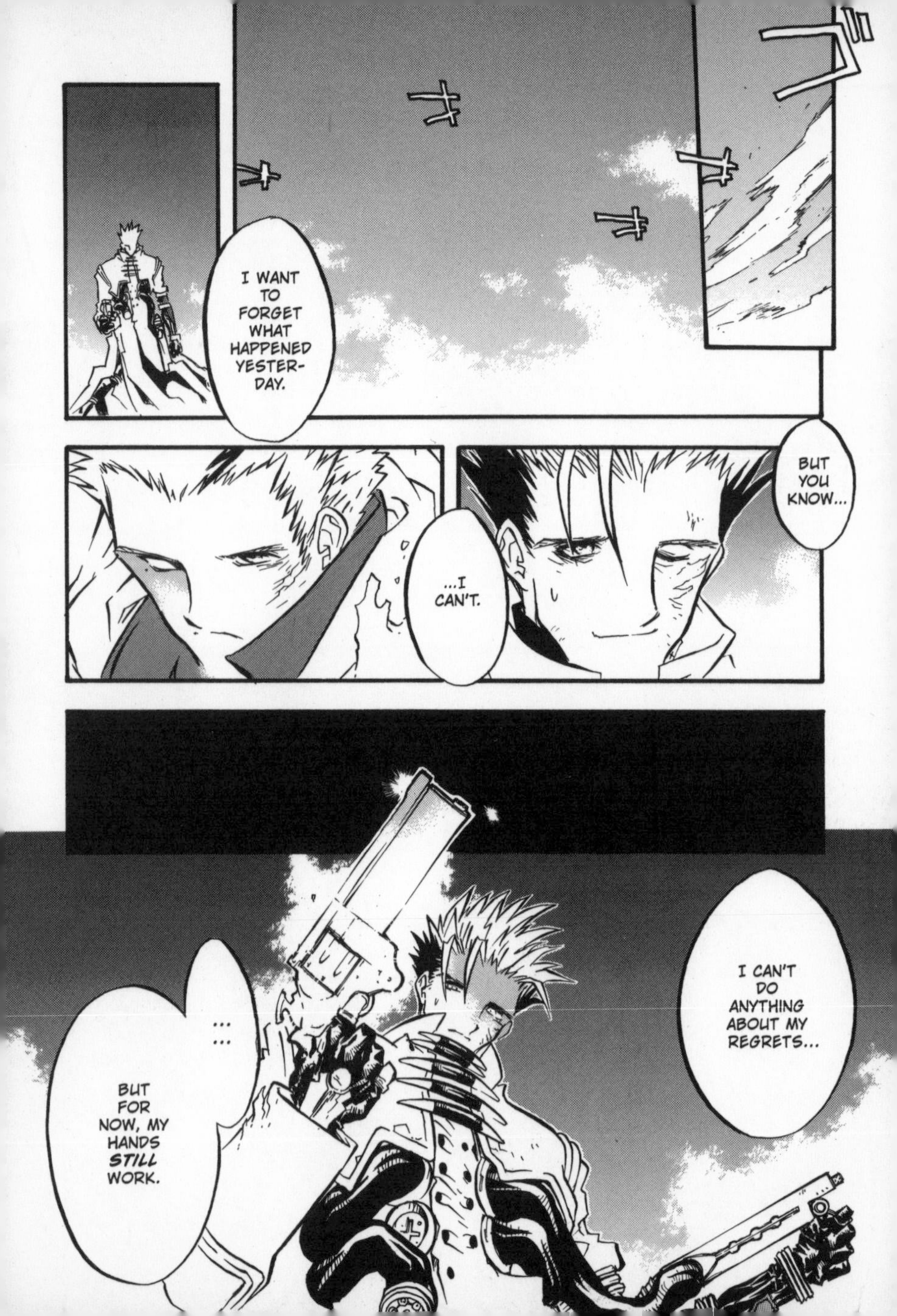
ゴ
オ
オ
オ
オ
I WANT TO FORGET WHAT HAPPENED YESTER-DAY.
BUT YOU KNOW...
...I CAN'T.
I CAN'T DO ANYTHING ABOUT MY REGRETS...
... ... BUT FOR NOW, MY HANDS *STILL* WORK.

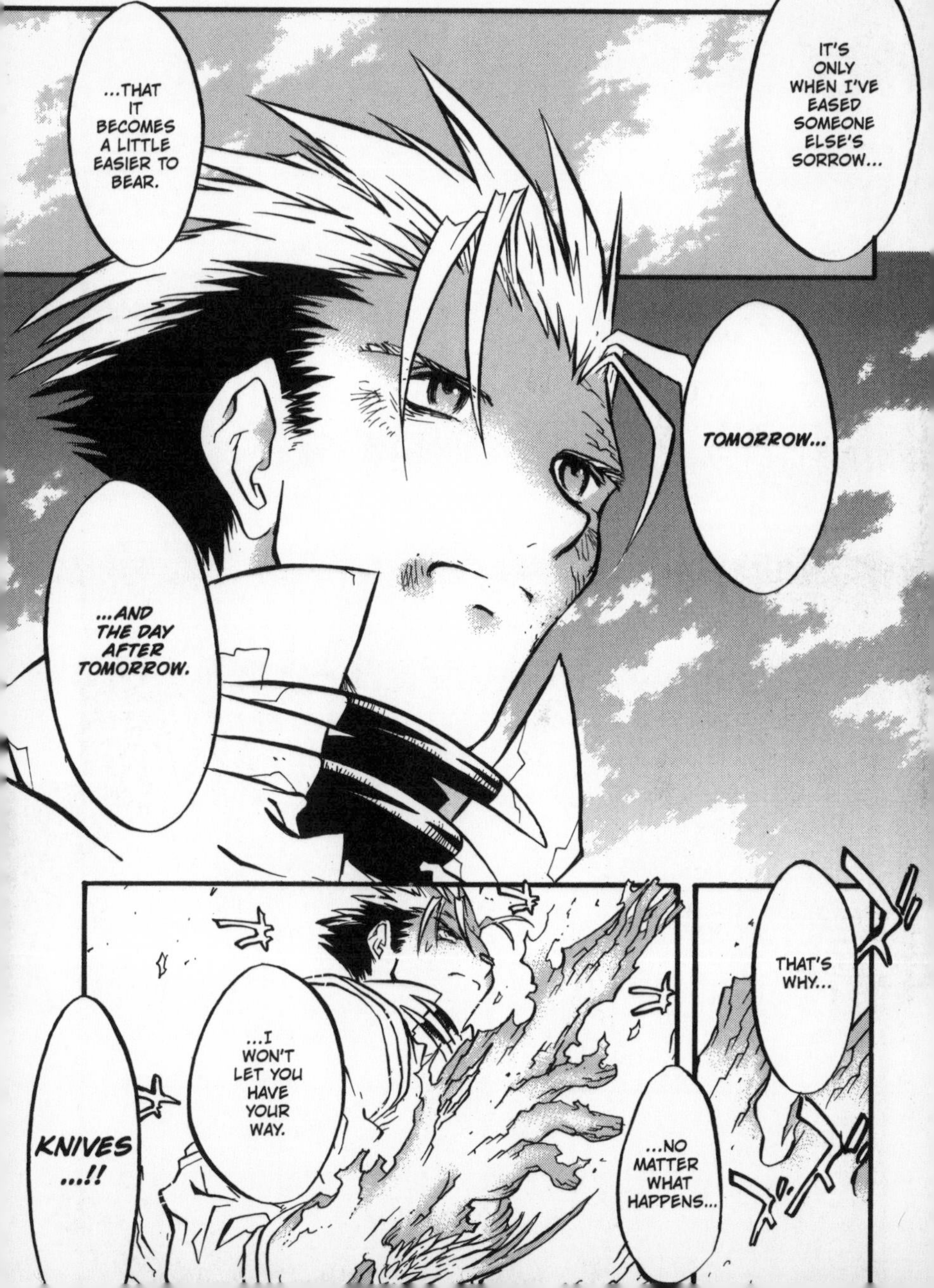
IT'S ONLY WHEN I'VE EASED SOMEONE ELSE'S SORROW...
...THAT IT BECOMES A LITTLE EASIER TO BEAR.
TOMORROW...
...AND THE DAY AFTER TOMORROW.
THAT'S WHY...
...NO MATTER WHAT HAPPENS...
...I WON'T LET YOU HAVE YOUR WAY.
KNIVES ...!!

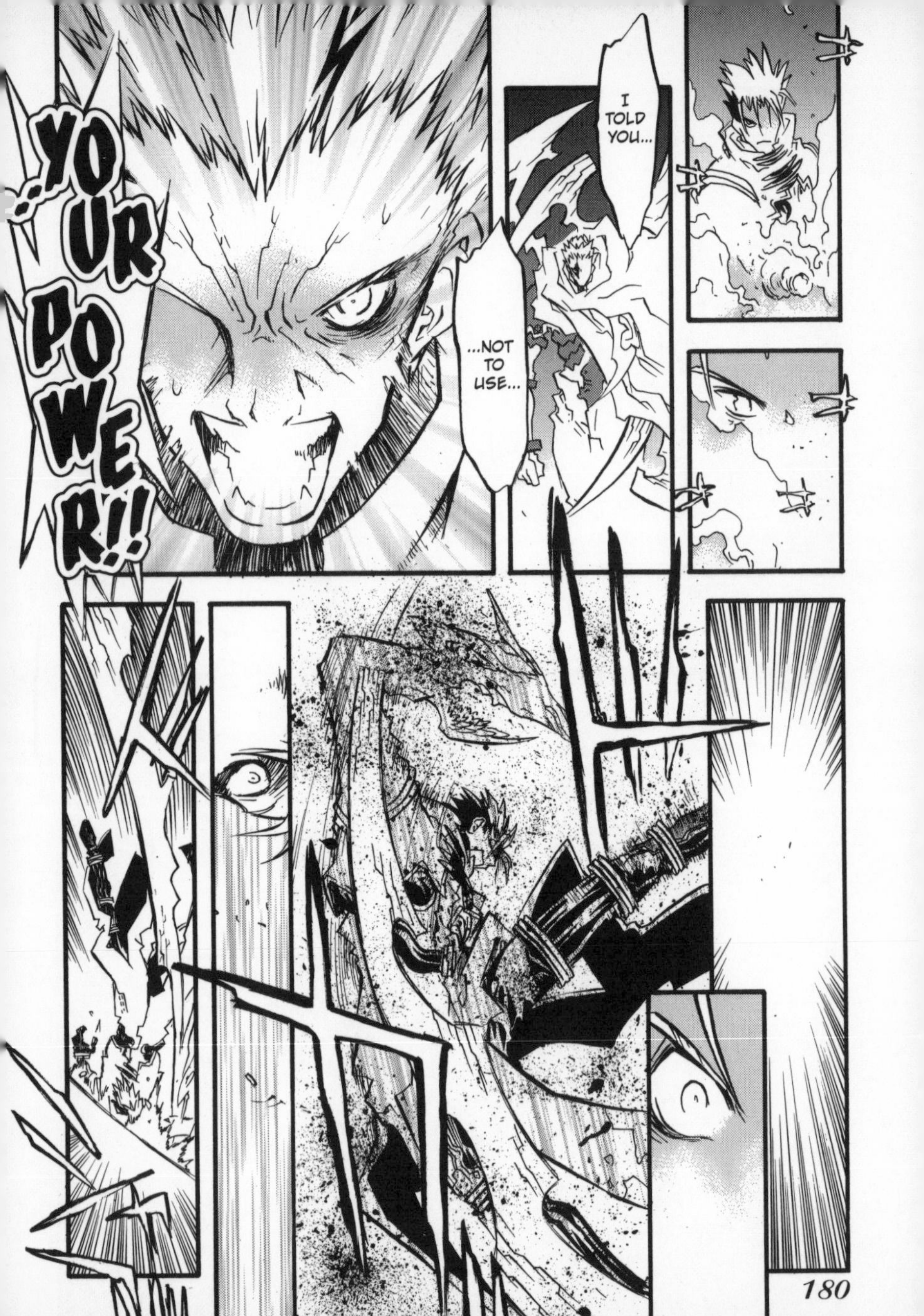
I TOLD YOU...
...NOT TO USE...
...YOUR POWER!!

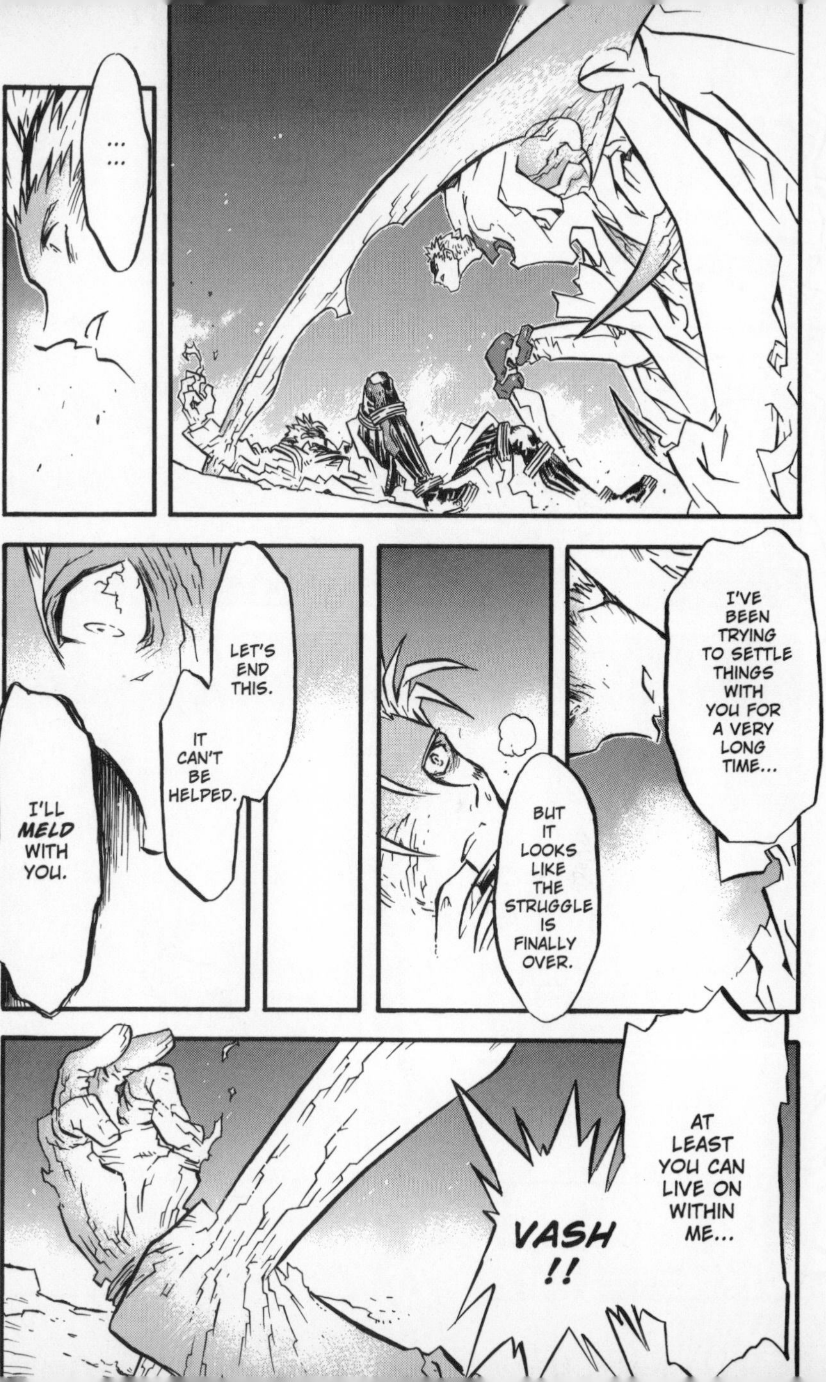
……
I'VE BEEN TRYING TO SETTLE THINGS WITH YOU FOR A VERY LONG TIME...
BUT IT LOOKS LIKE THE STRUGGLE IS FINALLY OVER.
LET'S END THIS.
IT CAN'T BE HELPED.
I'LL MELD WITH YOU.
AT LEAST YOU CAN LIVE ON WITHIN ME...
VASH!!

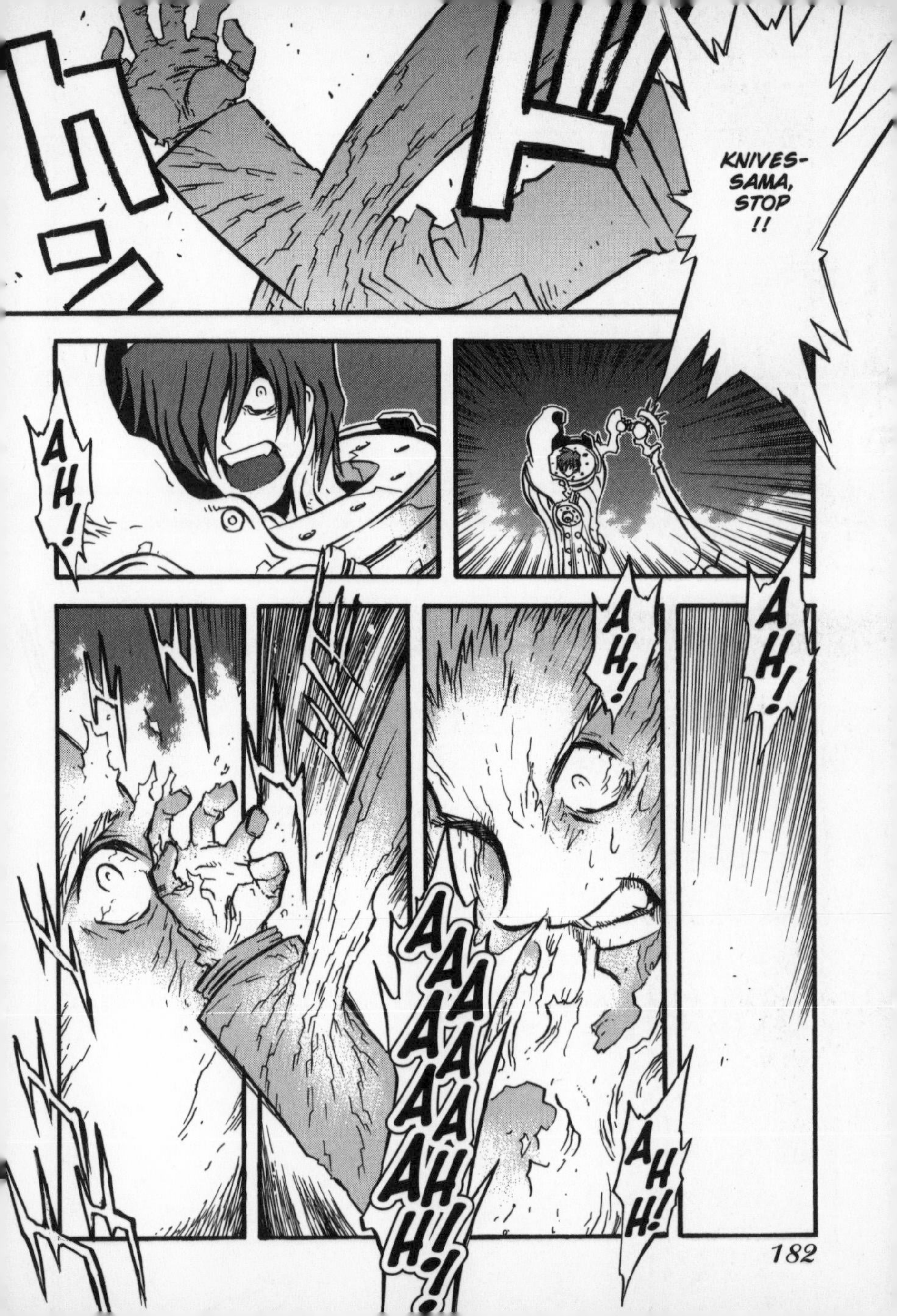
KNIVES-SAMA, STOP!!
AH!
AH!
AH!
AAAAAAAAAHHH!!
AHH!

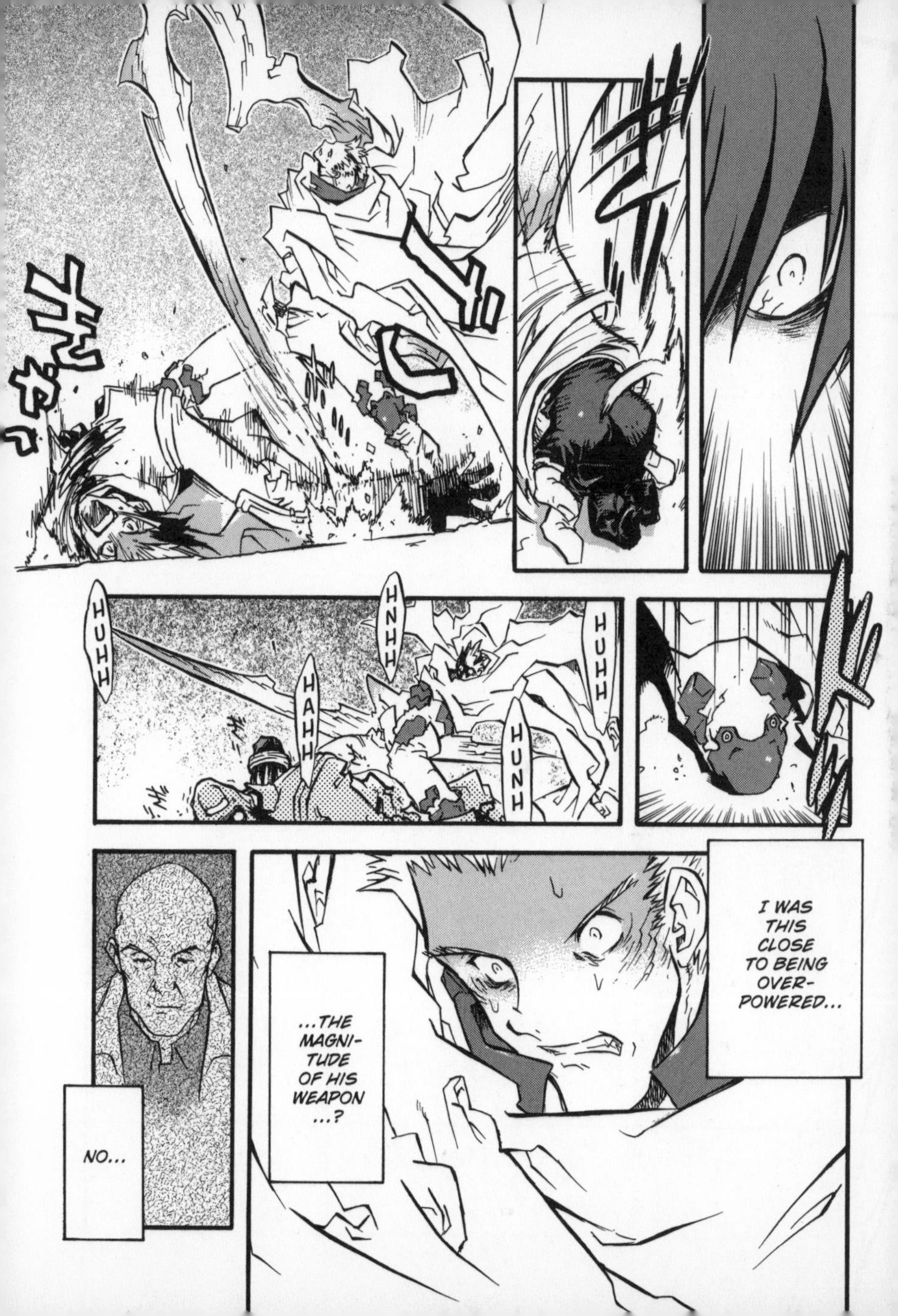
HUHH
HUNH
HNHH
HAHH
HUHH
I WAS THIS CLOSE TO BEING OVER-POWERED...
...THE MAGNI-TUDE OF HIS WEAPON ...?
NO...

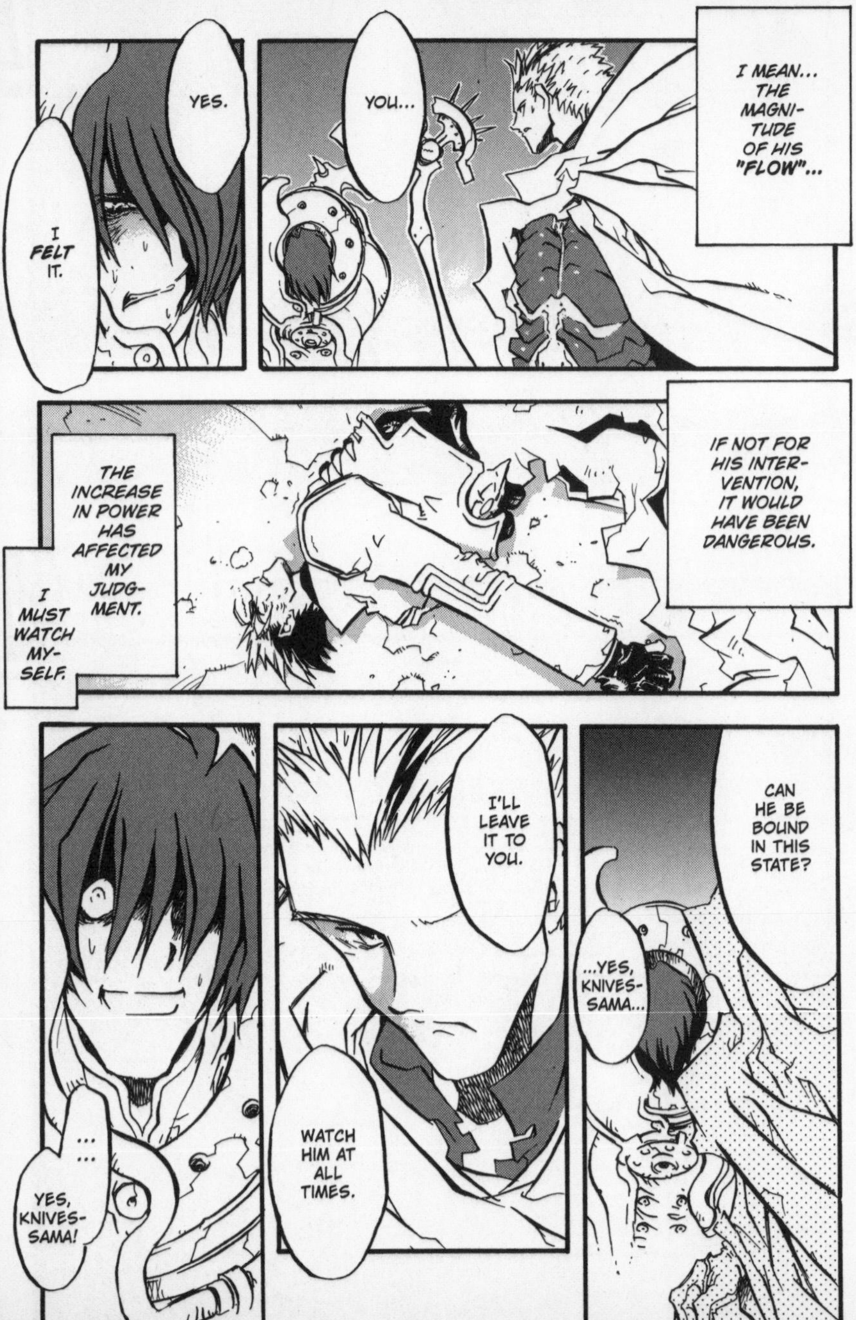
I MEAN... THE MAGNITUDE OF HIS "FLOW"...
YOU...
YES.
I FELT IT.
IF NOT FOR HIS INTERVENTION, IT WOULD HAVE BEEN DANGEROUS.
THE INCREASE IN POWER HAS AFFECTED MY JUDGMENT.
I MUST WATCH MYSELF.
CAN HE BE BOUND IN THIS STATE?
...YES, KNIVES-SAMA...
I'LL LEAVE IT TO YOU.
WATCH HIM AT ALL TIMES.
... ...
YES, KNIVES-SAMA!

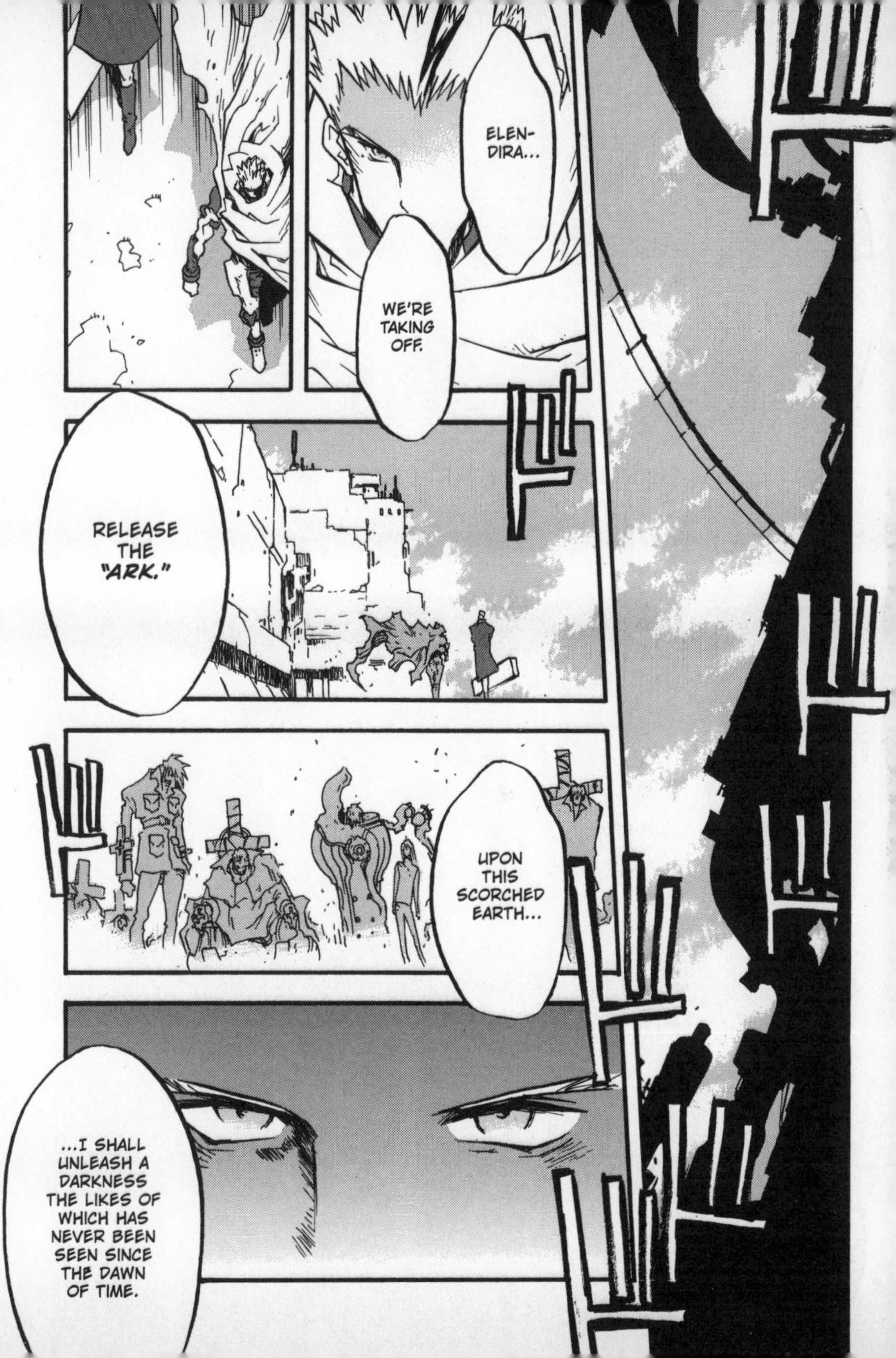
ELEN-
DIRA...
WE'RE TAKING OFF.
RELEASE THE "ARK."
UPON THIS SCORCHED EARTH...
...I SHALL UNLEASH A DARKNESS THE LIKES OF WHICH HAS NEVER BEEN SEEN SINCE THE DAWN OF TIME.

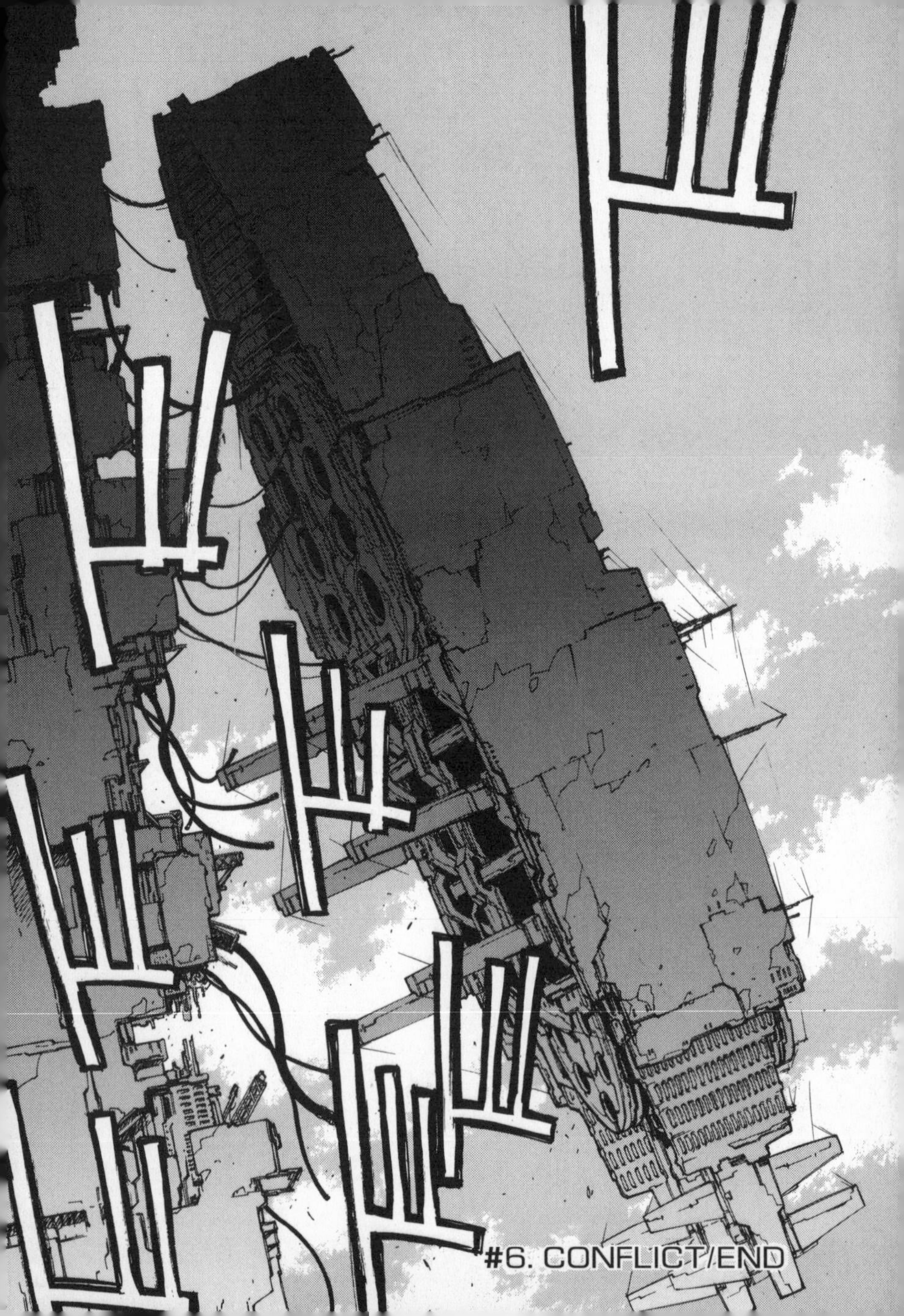

#6. CONFLICT/END

TURN TO THE NEXT

TRIGUN MAXIMUM
YASUHIRO NIGHTOW

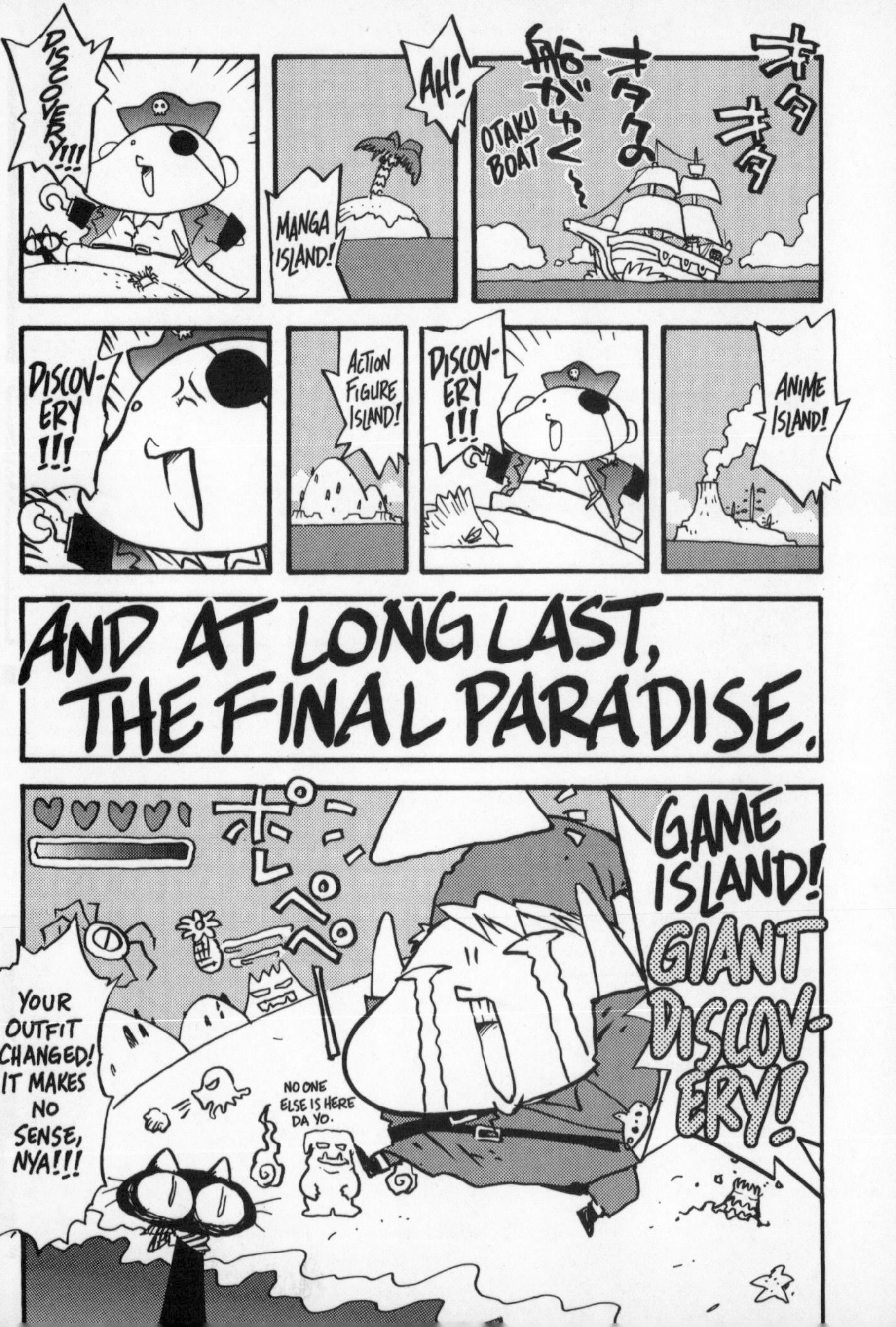
オタオタ
オタク船がゆく～～
OTAKU BOAT
AH!
MANGA ISLAND!
DISCOVERY!!!
ANIME ISLAND!
DISCOV-ERY!!!
ACTION FIGURE ISLAND!
DISCOV-ERY!!!
AND AT LONG LAST, THE FINAL PARADISE.
GAME ISLAND!
GIANT DISCOV-ERY!
NO ONE ELSE IS HERE DA YO.
YOUR OUTFIT CHANGED! IT MAKES NO SENSE, NYA!!!

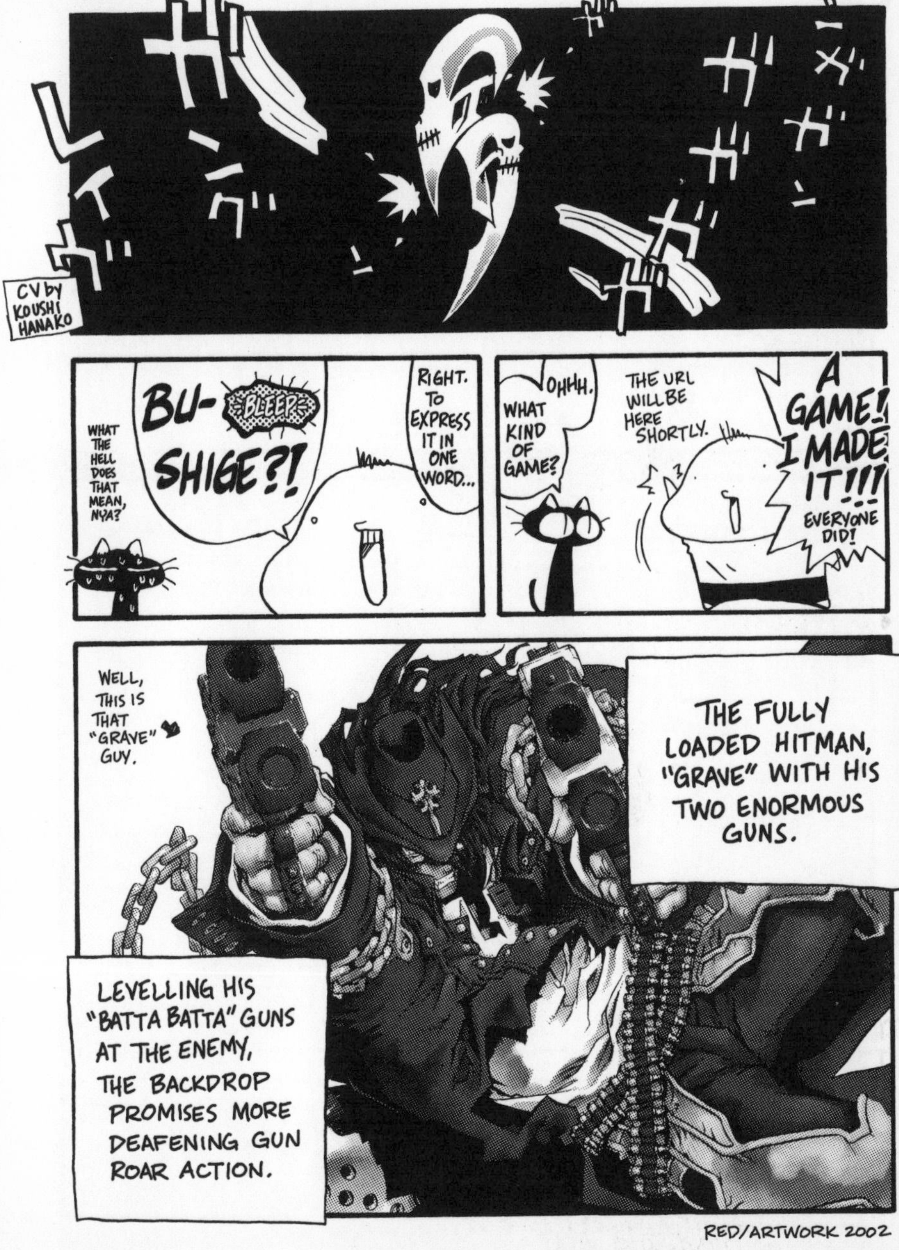
CV by KOUSHI HANAKO
A GAME! I MADE IT!!!
EVERYONE DID!
THE URL WILL BE HERE SHORTLY.
OHHH.
WHAT KIND OF GAME?
RIGHT. TO EXPRESS IT IN ONE WORD...
BU- BLEEP SHIGE?!
WHAT THE HELL DOES THAT MEAN, NYA?
THE FULLY LOADED HITMAN, "GRAVE" WITH HIS TWO ENORMOUS GUNS.
WELL, THIS IS THAT "GRAVE" GUY.
LEVELLING HIS "BATTA BATTA" GUNS AT THE ENEMY, THE BACKDROP PROMISES MORE DEAFENING GUN ROAR ACTION.

RED/ARTWORK 2002

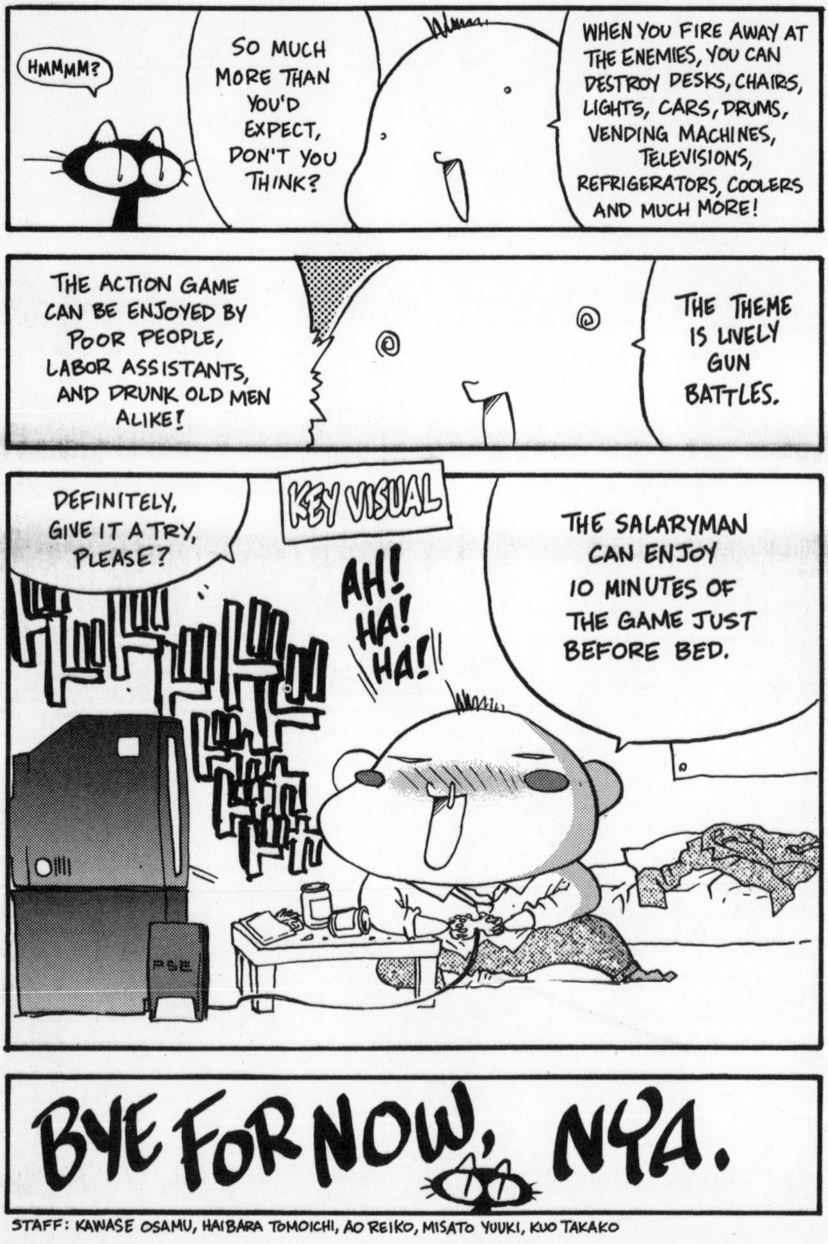
WHEN YOU FIRE AWAY AT THE ENEMIES, YOU CAN DESTROY DESKS, CHAIRS, LIGHTS, CARS, DRUMS, VENDING MACHINES, TELEVISIONS, REFRIGERATORS, COOLERS AND MUCH MORE!
SO MUCH MORE THAN YOU'D EXPECT, DON'T YOU THINK?
HMMMM?
THE THEME IS LIVELY GUN BATTLES.
THE ACTION GAME CAN BE ENJOYED BY POOR PEOPLE, LABOR ASSISTANTS, AND DRUNK OLD MEN ALIKE!
THE SALARYMAN CAN ENJOY 10 MINUTES OF THE GAME JUST BEFORE BED.
AH! HA! HA!
KEY VISUAL
DEFINITELY, GIVE IT A TRY, PLEASE?
BYE FOR NOW, NYA.

STAFF: KAWASE OSAMU, HAIBARA TOMOICHI, AO REIKO, MISATO YUUKI, KUO TAKAKO